Chicana Leadership

D0924069

Chicana Leadership
The *Frontiers* Reader

EDITED BY
YOLANDA FLORES NIEMANN
WITH SUSAN H. ARMITAGE,
PATRICIA HART, AND
KAREN WEATHERMON

UCD WOMEN'S CENTER

University of Nebraska Press, Lincoln and London

© 2002 by the Frontiers
Publishing, Inc.
All rights reserved
Manufactured in the United
States of America

♾

Cataloging-in-Publication
data available
Library of Congress Control
Number: 2002018112

ISBN: 0-8032-8382-2

Contents

Introduction

Chicanas: Dispelling Stereotypes while Challenging Racism, Sexism, Classism, and Homophobia

Who are Chicanas? From where and whom do we learn about Chicanas? Until the relatively recent advent of Chicana scholars and scholarship, social science writings about the Chicana repeated the still-current stereotype of her as a willing participant in or passive victim of her oppressive circumstances. Scholarship on the role of Chicanas in shaping their own lives and their communities has been relatively scarce, resulting in a dearth of nonstereotypical knowledge about these women. This collection brings together writings by Chicanas that begin to address this void.

CHICANAS: FROM STEREOTYPES TO CONTEXTUAL REALITIES

Chicanas assume positions of leadership in virtually every area of their lives and their communities, but instead of receiving recognition, they are persistently represented as submissive, docile, and passive.[1] Indeed, when Chicanas/os are asked to list the traits they believe characterize Chicanas, they, too, include "passive" and "submissive."[2] Countless examples of Chicanas' activism are never included in textbooks or in the media, which means their activism is often not validated, even within their own communities. Known examples of Chicana activism begin with the women who fought alongside men in the Mexican Revolution, women who led organizations such as the United Farm Workers and Communities Organized for Public Service (COPS), and those organizing boycotts against major corporations such as Levi's. Other examples include Hispanic women who worked as labor activists in the cannery, agricultural, packing, garment, clothing, and high-tech industries.[3] Hispanic women today run the Southwest Organizing Project (SWOP), a social justice organization that fights for environmental and economic justice in communities of color and serves as a voter registry.[4] Another example of grassroots community activism is the group Mothers of East Los Angeles, which has formed family- and culture-based networks to increase the quality of urban life. The group's activism includes fighting the placement of incinerators in neighborhoods of color.[5] However, Hispanic women's activism is often unchampioned and ignored, and the stereotype of the passive Hispanic woman persists. For twelve years I have taught courses that either focus on Chicanas in U.S. society or include Chicanas/os as a focus along with other groups studied. My students – including a high percentage of Chicana/os – are continually surprised that Chicanas have engaged in so much leadership affecting their own communities and the larger society.

Why don't people have a more accurate perception of who Chicanas are? There are several reasons why stereotypes persist. First is that, even today, little information has been disseminated to contradict the stereotypes. History texts present race and ethnicity in a manner that justifies stereotypes.[6] Media representations, when they exist, are generally stereotype-consistent. Second, stereotypes are often generated and perpetuated by dominant forces that seek to justify the treatment and lower social status of a given group.[7] Third, Chicanas/os suffer from factors beyond their control, such as discrimination and poverty; as a result, their oppression appears to be a function of inherent traits rather than the result of institutional and individual racism.[8] Fourth, regardless of how and why stereotypes are formed and maintained, they are very difficult to change.[9]

CHICANAS' CONTEXTUAL REALITIES

The articles in this collection all contribute significantly to a contextual, nonstereotypical understanding of Chicanas' experience. This approach includes understanding that (1) Chicanas are women who function in a patriarchal society, (2) Chicanas are overrepresented in the lower socioeconomic and poverty categories in a capitalistic system, (3) Chicanas are racial minorities who lack representative and economic power within the United States, and (4) Some Chicanas are lesbians in a predominately heterosexual society. As a result of their triple or quadruple minority status, Chicanas and their experiences can be understood only in the context of societal sexism, classism, racism, and homophobia. Following are some brief examples of these contextual factors.

Racism

Chicanas observe and experience the effects of racism on the men and children of their community along with the effects of that racism in their own lives.[10] Racism sets up a social structure that situates groups according to a social hierarchy that affords each ethnic/racial group relative status compared to other groups. Whites are undeniably at the top of this hierarchy, as evidenced by their positions of power, their wealth, and their land and corporate ownership relative to that of other groups.[11] One need only look at the racial makeup of the U.S. Senate and the U.S. Supreme Court for evidence of a hierarchy. The privileges that come with this power and status include having representative voices in government, industry, education, financing, and health systems, and in all policies and processes that affect people's everyday lives. These privileges have been historically denied to members of colonized groups, including Chicanas/os.

Chicanas continue to experience colonization that compounds their marginality and often results in alienation, victimization, self-denial, assimilation, and ambivalence. In a context of colonization, minority women, and Chicanas in particular, live in borderlands caught between worlds.[12] Chicanas fit neither entirely in with the mainstream white culture nor in their mother culture. One consequence of this colonization is alienation. Chicanas attempt to bridge their world and the mainstream Anglo/white world, creating a hybrid, mestizo reality, the psychological impact of which is only beginning to be documented.[13]

Chicanas have also experienced racism as part of what is known as the women's movement. Historically, the women's movement has been so centered on white middle-class women that women of color have wondered, Rights for which women?[14] Women of color have not felt that the gains of the women's movement were their gains. Today the white women's movement places more emphasis on the plight of women in Third World countries than on the Third World conditions within U.S. borders under which some Chicanas and other women of color reside and work. Chicanas believe that, to this day, white women seem unwilling to acknowledge that as long as men of color are subordinate to white men, women of color are not free to focus on ending gender oppression.[15]

Nevertheless, Chicanas have persevered in recognizing that the nature of social inequality for women of color is multidimensional and that the understanding of their realities must emphasize interactions of race, class, and gender.[16] Chicanas' struggles with racism in the women's movement is related to their struggles with sexism within their own communities. Although they played major historical roles in the Chicano nationalist movement of resistance alongside men, they also had to end sexist oppression within this broader nationalist struggle to end racist oppression.[17] For their efforts, Chicanas were criticized for threatening solidarity with Chicanos.

Chicana loyalists saw the Chicana feminist movement as an antifamily, anticultural, and antiman, and therefore anti-Chicano, movement.[18]

Sexism

Chicanas live in a patriarchal U.S. society in which women are second-class citizens. Patriarchy is also embedded in their own Chicano communities. Manifestations of this sexism are extensive. Chicanas are likely to be paid less than men of any ethnic/racial group, and less than white women.[19] When they have college degrees, they gain fewer returns from their education than do men and white women.[20] Their lack of economic power is related to poor health care, higher exposure to crime, and unsafe housing, including exposure to environmental hazards.[21]

For Chicanas, racism also intersects with sexism because they are portrayed as "hot," eager for sexual favors, and, as a result, are subjected to sexual-racial objectification. Chicanas are thus stripped of their humanity, denied their individuality, and devalued.[22]

Chicanas are also subject to oppression from the men in their families.[23] Some Chicanos' reaction to societal racism, which denies them the full expressions of manhood accorded to white men, is to assert their domination and masculinity in the realm of personal relationships. Therefore, for Chicanas, issues surrounding sexism cannot be separated from racism. Because racism puts their men at such risk, Chicanas are hesitant to hand over their men to that societal structure, even to protect themselves and their children from domestic violence, incest, and sexual abuse.[24] Turning over their men to authorities may lead to temporary relief from the violence and oppression the men are causing. However, in the long run, the unfair treatment of their men leads to further oppression of the larger community, which eventually has a negative impact on the lives of Chicanas and their children. This gender oppression combines with what Maria Root describes as "insidious trauma."[25]

Homophobia

Chicana lesbians live at the margins of communities that are already marginalized. They suffer from both legal and illegal discrimination. In almost all parts of the United States, lesbians are denied the right to marriage and the protection that comes from that institution, including health and social security benefits. In many parts of the United States, lesbians can be denied the right to work or they can be fired solely because they are not hetero-sexual. Within their own communities, they are often seen and treated as traitors to cultural values, especially to those values related to women's roles as mothers and wives. This treatment comes from men and women within their own communities. Chicana lesbians may therefore find it difficult to live in a place where they might otherwise seek safe haven.

Classism

Economic power has an overarching effect on Chicanas. This power, or lack of it, determines where they live, which in turn has an impact on the quality of their own and their children's schools and the safety of their neighbor-hoods. Economic power determines whether or not they can afford health care. In addition class intersects with racism, sexism, and homophobia. For instance, women who are experiencing violence within their families are not free to leave because they don't have the economic resources to support themselves and their children. Chicana lesbians without financial power are not likely to hire an attorney to assist them when they have suffered illegal discrimination. Almost any example of oppression is mediated by eco-nomic power.

WHAT IS A CHICANA: A NOTE ON LABELS

The articles in this collection describe Chicanas using various labels, which deserve explanation. The label "Hispanic" came into popular use during the Reagan era after members of the administration decided on that label with-out consulting populations of Spanish-speaking descent. In some parts of the country Hispanic is considered to be a conservative term that empha-sizes the Spanish, white, European side of a people to the detriment of the Indian and brown sides. Since the Spanish migrated to North and South America and exploited the indigenous brown Indian, many people believe that to use the term "Hispanic" is to portray oneself as a "wannabe" white and to identify with the colonizers. For these reasons, many scholars and laypeople reject this label. This rejection of the term "Hispanic," however, does not prevail in Texas or in other states, where the term is widely used among laypeople. The term is also popular in New Mexico, Arizona, and other areas of heavy Spanish-speaking-descent populations in the United States – places where the term has not received the widespread negative reaction that it has received in other states, such as California.

Since the early 1970s many scholars and laypeople have adopted the label "Chicana/o." This label refers to U.S. citizens or residents of Mexican descent. The term "Chicano" became popular among activists during the civil rights movement. Feminists later added the label "Chicana" in an effort toward gender inclusivity and recognition of women's experiences. Some scholars now use Chicana/o to refer to women and men of Mexican descent. The term "Chicano" is the most militant label ever used by Mexican Americans. It is more widely accepted in California than in other states, as indicated by the number of academic centers that include the term in their names. None of the academic centers established in Texas, for example, has ever incorporated the term "Chicano."

Like the term "Hispanic," the label "Latina/o" is inclusive of all persons of Spanish-speaking descent. That is, no distinctions are made among and between the heterogeneous Spanish-speaking-descent populations of the world and of the United States. The label includes Puerto Ricans, Cubans, Mexican Americans, and South Americans, all of whom have very different current and historical experiences in the United States and in their countries of origin. While the label's inclusiveness has advantages, the disadvantage is that the label "Latina/o" obscures the current and historical distinctions between groups. In addition, the use of Latina/o, which refers to men and to women, can be cumbersome to use.

With all this said, it is critically important for readers to keep in mind that a label does not define a woman or her ideology and that labels are fluid and, for many women, interchangeable.

FRONTIERS HELPS CHICANAS CHALLENGE STEREOTYPES AND FACILITATE CONTEXTUAL AWARENESS

Frontiers: A Journal of Women Studies has been at the forefront of challenging stereotypes about Chicanas and facilitating awareness of the Chicana experience. *Frontiers* has disseminated information about stereotypes to Chicanas in independent articles throughout the past several decades and in four special issues, published in 1980, 1990, 1994, and 1999, dedicated to Chicanas. The collection in this volume is drawn from these special issues and represents articles that remain timeless and that inform us about Chicanas' experiences across various domains. These articles also remind us that there is no "prototypical" Chicana. Rather, Chicanas are members of a very diverse group. This diversity is largely derived from their social locations within the United States, which in turn are derived from their experiences of racism, classism, sexism, and homophobia. These articles not only inform non-Chicanas, they also inform Chicanas and their community members, thus raising critical consciousness and facilitating their personal and collective empowerment.

In this collection Cordelia Candelaria provides a critical understanding of Doña Marina, a young woman known as La Malinche, a whore and a traitor of indigenous people who were conquered by the Spaniards. An understanding of the origins and social construction of the label "Malinche" is critical, as Doña Marina's experience and reputation continue to have an impact on Chicanas today. Maxine Baca Zinn writes of the intersections of gender and ethnic identity. Her words remind us of the heterogeneity of the Chicana/o community and are particularly important today, given the battles over identity politics on many college campuses.

Roberta Fernández contributes to knowledge of Chicana identity as it emerged in the poetry and short stories of women writing for a Chicano journal between 1968 and 1974. She challenges the male-centered writing of that time that perpetuated the stereotype of the Chicana as passive. Her work also speaks to the importance of poetry in the Chicana community. Yolanda Broyles-González discusses the role of Chicana performers in one of the most constant artistic forces facilitating Chicanas' critical awareness and activism – the *Teatro Campesino*. She discusses the sexism that women had to endure from within their own communities, including placement in stereotype-consistent roles while also fighting racism from the wider society. Chicanas still experience this sexism and racism in various media today, including plays, cinema, and television. Margarita Cota-Cárdenas's discussion of literary activism reminds us of Chicanas' brilliance in their use of irony. Her contributions also speak to the triple or quadruple colonization of Chicanas and to the breaking of myths, especially those surrounding La Malinche and La Llorona.

Patricia Zavella also contributes to breaking stereotypes by discussing the vast diversity among Chicanas. She also emphasizes intersections of race, class, gender, and sexual orientation. In her interview with AnnLouise Keating, Gloria Anzaldúa, one of the most renowned Chicana scholars, directly addresses issues of lesbian identity. She tackles the still-current debate about whether lesbians are born with or socialized into their sexual orientation, as well as issues of spirituality and political involvement. Anzaldúa's thoughts contribute to the increase in Chicanas' critical consciousness that she facilitated in her pathbreaking books *This Bridge Called My Back: Writings by Radical Women of Color* and *Making Face/Making Soul*.

Antonia Castañeda provides a historiography of Chicanas' role in developing the California frontier. Although she focuses on one region, the work represents some of the many ways Chicanas' contributions and leadership have shaped other regions of the United States. Sarah Deutsch brings together labor history and autobiography to examine the construction of identity that includes social class and sexual orientation. She reminds us that identity is continually constructed and affected by social ecological contexts.

Margaret Rose examines the historic struggles for the unionization of California farmworkers that began in the early 1960s. Her discussion informs us of how Chicanas maintained traditional female patterns in their roles as wives and mothers. She shows how their activist roles developed within the context of their traditional roles. Similarly, Mary Pardo's discussion of Chicana activism in East Los Angeles is rooted in Chicanas' roles as mothers. These discussions remind us that because Chicana activism and traditional cultural values go hand in hand, we should not be surprised at the extent of Chicana activism.

Josephine Méndez-Negrete describes overt and subtle leadership exhibited through women's everyday resistance and activism. In particular, the Milagro County women created alliances with immigrants to advocate for the betterment of their lives in areas ranging from bilingualism to grassroots organizing. This article is of particular importance today, as the number of immigrants exceeds the number of U.S.-born Chicanas in many areas of the United States. As these women come into contact with each other, the quality of their interactions may depend on the extent to which immigrants see Chicanas as allies.

Angela Valenzuela's work on the role of relationships and social capital in education confirms that, for Chicanas, relationships are among the most important of all resources. Additionally her work emphasizes that the success of Chicanos is often highly dependent of the support of Chicanas. Maribel Sosa's journey from the fields to the university and then back to her community is an example of how Chicanas, through their formal education, often return home and benefit their communities. Her story also speaks to identity issues raised when Chicanas become one of the less than 10 percent of those in their communities who hold a college degree.

My own article is a reminder that even when Chicanas earn the highest degree awarded – the Ph.D. – they do not escape the discrimination that comes with their gender, ethnicity, and class background. Much too often Chicanas in academia experience this struggle and isolation without understanding what they are going through. At the same time, however, my story can serve to inspire other Chicanas in this situation to persevere and to go on to make contributions to scholarship and to their communities.

ISSUES NOT INCLUDED

The articles in this collection cover many areas of the Chicana experience. However, many issues are not adequately covered or are not covered at all. These should be addressed in future *Frontiers* issues and in other journals. These topics include but are not limited to the following: religion (especially the importance of the Virgen de Guadalupe), health, domestic violence, drugs and alcohol, identity politics, the role of Chicana/o centers in universities, the changing definition of manhood, biculturalism, ethnic identity, relationships with other women of color, third- and fourth-generation Chicanas, and middle- and upper-class Chicanas in the workplace.

Yolanda Flores Niemann

NOTES

1. N. D. Humphrey, "The Stereotypes and the Social Types of Mexican American Youths," *Journal of Social Psychology* 22 (1945): 69–78; E. S. Richards, "Attitudes of College Students in the Southwest Toward Ethnic Groups in the United States," *Sociology and Social Research* 35 (1950): 22–30; A. G. Dworkin, "Stereotypes and Self-Images Held by Native-Born and Foreign-Born Mexican Americans," *Sociology and Social Research* 49 (1965): 214–24; S. J. Andrade, "Social Science Stereotypes of the Mexican American Woman: Policy Implications for Research," *Hispanic Journal of Behavioral Sciences* 4 (1982): 223–44; J. M. Casas, J. G. Ponterotto, and M. Sweeney, "Stereotyping the Stereotyper: A Mexican American Perspective," *Journal of Cross-Cultural Psychology* 18 (1987): 45–57; and E. L. Carranza, "Stereotypes about Chicanas/os," *San Jose Studies* 19 (1993): 34–43.

2. Yolanda Flores Niemann et al., "Use of Free Response and Cluster Analysis to Determine Stereotypes of Eight Groups," *Personality and Social Psychology Bulletin* 20:4 (1994): 379–90; T. Mindiola, Yolanda Flores Niemann, and N. Rodriguez, *Black–Brown Relations and Stereotypes in Urban American* (Austin: University of Texas Press, forthcoming); and Yolanda Flores Niemann, "Stereotypes about Chicanas and Chicanos: Implications for Counseling," *The Counseling Psychologist* 29:1 (2001): 55–90.

3. T. Cordova, "Grassroots Mobilization by Chicanas in the Environmental and

Economic Justice Movement," *Voces: A Journal of Chicana/Latina Studies* 1:1 (1997): 32–56; and Mary Pardo, "Mexican American Women Grassroots Community Activists: 'Mothers of East Los Angeles,'" *Frontiers: A Journal of Women Studies* 21:1 (1990): 1–7.

4. Cordova, "Grassroots Mobilization by Chicanas."

5. Pardo, "Mexican American Women Grassroots Community Activists."

6. Joe R. Feagin, *Racist America: Roots, Current Realities, and Future Reparations* (New York: Routledge, 2000).

7. A. Aguirre Jr. and D. V. Baker, *Structured Inequality in the United States* (Upper Saddle River, N.J.: Prentice Hall, 2000); C. E. Thompson and H. A. Neville, "Racism, Mental Health, and Mental Health Practice," *The Counseling Psychologist* 27 (1999): 155–223.

8. D. W. Sue and D. Sue, *Counseling the Culturally Different*, 3rd ed. (New York: John Wiley & Sons, 1999). A more thorough discussion of the relationship between social contexts and stereotypes about Chicanas is found in Niemann, "Stereotypes about Chicanas and Chicanos" and in Yolanda Flores Niemann and P. Secord, "The Social Ecology of Stereotyping," *Journal for the Theory of Social Behavior* 25:1 (1995): 1–14.

9. S. T. Fiske and S. E. Taylor, *Social Cognition* (New York: McGraw-Hill, 1991); and Z. Kunda, *Social Cognition: Making Sense of People* (Cambridge: The MIT Press, 2000).

10. O. M. Espn, "Feminist Approaches," in *Women of Color: Integrating Ethnic and Gender Identities in Psychotherapy*, ed. L. Comas-Díaz and B. Greene (New York: Guilford Press, 1994), 265–86; and C. T. Gilkes, "'If It Wasn't for the Women . . .': African American Women, Community Work, and Social Change," in *Women of Color in U.S. Society*, ed. M. Baca Zinn and B. Thornton Dill (Philadelphia: Temple University Press, 1994), 229–46.

11. L. Comas-Díaz, "An Integrative Approach," in Comas-Díaz and Greene, *Women of Color*, 287–318.

12. Gloria Anzaldúa, *Borderlands/la Frontera: The New Mestiza* (San Francisco: Spinster/Aunt Lute, 1987).

13. Y. G. Flores-Ortiz, "Psychotherapy with Chicanas at Midlife: Cultural/Clinical Considerations," in *Racism in the Lives of Women*, ed. J. Adleman and G. Enguídanos (New York: Harrington Park Press, 1995), 251–60.

14. Y. G. Flores-Ortiz, "The Broken Covenant: Incest in the Latino Family," *Voces: A Journal of Chicana/Latina Studies* 1:2 (1997): 48–70.

15. M. Cotera, "Feminism: The Chicano and Anglo Versions: A Historical Analysis," in *Chicana Feminist Thought*, ed. A. M. García (New York: Routledge, 1997), 223–31.

16. B. M. Pesquera and D. M. Segura, "There Is No Going Back: Chicanas and Feminism," in *Mujeres Activas en Letras y Cambio Social* (MALCS), *Chicana Critical Issues,* ed. MALCS (Berkeley, Calif.: Third Woman Press, 1993), 95–116.

17. B. T. Dill, "Race, Class, and Gender: Prospects for an All-Inclusive Sisterhood," *Feminist Studies* 9 (1983): 131–50.

18. A. M. Garcia, "The Development of Chicana Feminist Discourse, 1970–1980," *Gender & Society* 3:2 (1989): 217–38.

19. M. E. Thomas, C. Herring, and H. D. Horton, "Racial and Gender Differences in Returns from Educations," in *Race and Ethnicity in America,* ed. Gail E. Thomas (Washington, D.C.: Taylor & Francis, 1995), 239–54.

20. Thomas, Herring, and Horton, "Racial and Gender Differences."

21. R. Davis, "Racial Differences in Mortality: Current Trends and Perspectives," in Thomas, *Race and Ethnicity in America,* 115–28; G. L. Rolison and V. M. Keith, "Drugs, Crime, Murder, and the Underclass: An Analysis of Aggregate Data from the Largest Metropolitan Areas," in Thomas, *Race and Ethnicity in America,* 129–44; G. O. Rogers, "Environmental Racism or Inequity: Comparative Study of Four Ethnic Groups," in Thomas, *Race and Ethnicity in America,* 187–204.

22. Comas-Díaz, "An Integrative Approach," 289.

23. Espín, "Feminist Approaches"; and M. P. P. Root, "The Impact of Trauma on Personality: The Second Reconstruction," in *Personality and Psychopathology: Feminist Reappraisals,* ed. L. S. Brown and M. Ballou (New York: Guilford Press, 1992), 229–65.

24. Y. G. Flores-Ortiz, "La Mujer y la Violencia: A Culturally Based Model for Understanding and Treatment," in *Mujeres Activas en Letras y Cambio Social,* 169–82; Flores-Ortiz, "The Broken Covenant"; M. R. Rodriguez, "(En)Countering Domestic Violence: Complicity and Definitions of Chicana Womanhood," *Voces: A Journal of Chicana/Latina Studies* 1:2 (1997): 104–41; and G. Romero and G. Wyatt, "The Prevalence and Circumstances of Child Sexual Abuse among Latina Women," *Hispanic Journal of Behavioral Sciences* 21:3 (1999), 351–65.

25. Root, "The Impact of Trauma on Personality."

Chicana Leadership

La Malinche, Feminist Prototype

CORDELIA CANDELARIA

"If there is one villainess in Mexican history, she is Malintzin. She was to become the ethnic traitress supreme."[1] Such is one version of the popular view of Malintzin or Doña Marina, as she was christened by Cortés's *padres*, or La Malinche, as she came to be known among the Aztecs. Indeed, in the current reevaluation of pre-Columbian culture among many Chicanos, La Malinche remains one of the few indigenous figures in the Conquest of Mexico to be viewed with contempt.

[La Malinche] was to become infamous in the history of Mexico. Not only did she turn her back on her own people, she joined the white men and became assimilated, serving as their guide and interpreter and generally assisting in the conquest. She was the first Mexican-American.[2]

Fortunately, Chicana writers and scholars have begun to correct such distortions. Nevertheless, even Moctezuma – the Aztec ruler most directly responsible for the ease of Spanish takeover – receives generally sympathetic understanding from American historians, past and present,[3] although he capitulated to the Spaniards prematurely.[4]

Over the years La Malinche has been the subject of biographical, fictional, and symbolic interpretation written in many different languages. Biographical accounts include Mariano Somonte's *Doña Marina, "La Malinche,"* and Adelaida R. del Castillo's "Malintzin Tenépal: A Preliminary Look into a New Perspective." Fictional treatments include Margaret Shedd's *Malinche and Cortés*. Octavio Paz's chapter, "The Sons of La Malinche" in *Labyrinth of Solitude* exemplifies the symbolic approach. To some extent each interpretation, though emphasizing one approach, has blurred its particular treatment by incorporating elements of the others, sometimes in random fashion. Paz's discussion, for example, depends on certain important aspects of her historical background, while Díaz's investigation attempts to flesh out an incomplete biographical record with hypotheses and speculations derived from modern psychology and pre-Columbian mysticism. These treatments provide fascinating reading and insight into La Malinche, the Conquest, and the concept of New World multiculturalism called *mestizaje*. Nevertheless, such commingling of approaches, of fact and speculation, sometimes limits the clearest understanding of the subject.

To learn as much as possible about the real La Malinche, the historical figure involved in the Conquest, requires careful development through two distinct investigative phases: (1) biographical reconstruction according to relevant primary sources, and (2) reconstruction of place, time, and ambience from relevant primary sources and sound secondary observations. Moreover, to comprehend La Malinche's impact on, and continuing significance to her culture and cultural descendants, a third phase is suggested: the analysis and interpretation of La Malinche as a cultural symbol. This third stage requires developing a symbolic synthesis from relevant literary and philosophical studies of this astonishingly important woman. This latter stage should clearly derive from incontrovertible evidence gathered in the first two stages to demonstrate that the symbol arises inevitably, not artificially, from the historical personage.

In accordance with this three-part model, the first two sections of this study provide fresh review of La Malinche's life, her service to Hernán Cortés, and her role in the Conquest of Mexico. In addition, the third part of this investigation will seek to describe the nature of La Malinche, the symbol that has emerged as a palpable reality within Mexican (and, to some extent, within Chicano) consciousness.

It is useful to examine *la conquista* with as much detachment as possible. In essence, it was a series of events whose overall effect contributed to what is now a permanent reality. The actual Conquest was an extraordinary military feat with the typical results of such "victories." There was the destruction of a way of life, in this case the destruction of a pre-Columbian civilization of apparently considerable achievement; the slaughter of hundreds of thousands of Native peoples; and the subjugation and enslavement of the survivors.

On the other hand, the dictatorial regime of Moctezuma that ruled Anáhuac (that is, the area surrounding what is now Mexico City) was plagued with severe internal problems. At the time of the Spanish invasion, discontent was pervasive among the various Native tribes because of the extensive Aztec taxation on goods and services, including human lives for religious sacrifice. The increase in human sacrifices under Moctezuma's tyranny made him and the Aztecs feared and hated in Anáhuac, particularly in remoter regions whose tenuous link to Tenochtitlan (present day Mexico City) was only tax-related.[5] In all fairness, it should be stated that the excesses of Moctezuma's regime simply culminated the tyrannical direction that the empire had taken under the influence of Tlacaellel, a previous leader. Thus Moctezuma invited rebellion by continuing policies which had led to disharmony and disunity among the Native tribes. Further, his extreme vacillation, stemming from his mysticism, made him ineffective as a leader. His indecisiveness in dealing with Cortés gave the Spaniards many political and military advantages.[6] We must, therefore, conclude that the Mexican Empire under Moctezuma was extremely vulnerable to internal destruction and that this vulnerability greatly strengthened Cortés's external effort.

Born around 1502 in Coatzacoalcos, a pre-Columbian Mexican province, La Malinche is believed to have originally been named Malinal after "Malinalli," the day of her birth, as was the custom at that time.[7] As daughter of an Aztec *cacique*, or chief, she was a member of a privileged, educated class. This fact probably helps to explain her later ability to serve the first New World *conquistadores* so brilliantly.[8] After her father's death and her mother's remarriage, Malinal was given away by her mother who sought to gain control of her daughter's inheritance for a son by her second husband.[9] A feature of Malinal's banishment from the Aztecs was her mother's compulsion to hold a cenotaphic burial (that is, a mock funeral) to explain her daughter's disappearance.[10] This is noteworthy because it indicates that custom did not condone the banishment of children, even girls.

Malinal was given to itinerant traders who eventually sold her to the ruling *cacique* of Tabasco, a province situated on the Yucatán coast. She lived in Tabasco until Cortés arrived there in 1519.[11] Because of her background in these widely separated provinces, Malinal knew both Nahuátl, the language of the Aztecs, and the Mayan dialects of her adopted people, the natives of Tabasco. As history demonstrates, her polyglot abilities, later to include Castilian Spanish, became the immediate reason for her singular role as Cortés's companion.

After his takeover of Tabasco, and in keeping with age-old historic traditions, Cortés received from the *cacique* a gift of twenty maidens to serve as domestic labor for the warrior-adventurers.[12] Malinal was part of the group. Probably because of its similarity to her Native name, she was christened "Marina" by the Spaniards and soon distinguished herself enough "to earn" from her captors the Spanish title of respect, *doña*. In fact, one Spanish historian asserts that her aristocratic bearing was such that within a month of the Spaniard's arrival, she was accorded the treatment that a *cacica* by birth might expect.[13] Similar homage was paid her by her compatriots who addressed her with the standard honorific title, *-tzin,* appended to their pronunciation of the European name, thus, Malintzin. The emergence of "Malinche" from Malintzin appears to be a solely linguistic phenomenon.

To fully appreciate La Malinche's role in the Conquest of Mexico it is appropriate to consider at this point the indigenous life patterns and customs in Mexico prior to European entry. What is known of the Native people and their culture comes primarily from the work of dedicated Franciscan scholars like Olmos, Motolínia, and particularly Sahagun, who is responsible for the *Florentine Codex* upon which most pre-Columbian scholarship rests. Each of these historians (or early anthropologists) gained access to reliable, firsthand information about pre-Columbian life, which they described meticulously in several works. With regard to the subject at hand, three areas of that life hold particular relevance: the basis of the social order, the role of religion in it, and the place of women in society.

The Aztec social order was built upon a class system that became increasingly defined and rigid as the tribe gained mastery over other tribes in the region. Originally organized according to clans (*calpulli*) with somewhat democratic internal lines of responsibility and power, the emergence of a central ruling class soon led to new divisions. The nobility (*pipiltin*) became the wealthiest and most powerful while the commoners (*macehualtin*) performed the labors needed to sustain the new order. Eventually the *pipiltin* developed its own class strata with the highest and smallest level providing the emperors. Conformity to this system was achieved by the populace's native obedience to custom and also by fear – human sacrifices were quite numerous.

Such a social order, especially in a preliterate society, historically parallels a strictly followed religious system. That was true for the Aztecs, who perceived sovereignty and religion as one.[14] "Habits of obedience, discipline, and conformity were manifest and constituted an unwritten code of morals and justice," and these habits were reinforced by "a code powerfully sanctioned by [religious] faith and by fear of punishment."[15]

In keeping with traditional biological determinism, women in Aztec society were barred from most occupations and activities guaranteed their male counterparts, and even in the smallest daily activity women were under strict discipline throughout their lives. On the other hand, daughters of the nobility received educations. Property rights were maintained through the mother's side.[16] Nevertheless, Aztec society was decidedly androcentric. At birth, for example, boys were presented with a spear and a shield, while girls were immediately provided with brooms and spinning wheels.[17] Women and girls were sexually exploited, especially among the *pipiltin*,[18] a phenomenon not unique to this culture. In addition, among the tribes of that time war was a solely masculine occupation. Not surprisingly most Native languages employed a single word for "male" and for "warrior."[19]

Clearly outside this cultural mold, La Malinche later often accompanied Cortés to the center of battle, and several surviving codices depict her carrying a shield. Furthermore, although women in pre-Columbian Mexico were not public figures, La Malinche's services to the Spaniards brought her conspicuously to the heart of the most pressing political issue facing Moctezuma's commonweal: how to handle the "supermen" – Cortés and his party. Accordingly, the Emperor's Nahuátl title, *Uei Tlatoani*, signifying "He Who May Speak," indicates that he alone was the supreme mouthpiece of and for his people and their deities. In this context, La Malinche's full significance as "*la lengua de los dioses*" (the tongue of the gods, that is, the Spaniards), as her compatriots called her, is magnified considerably. Despite this significance, however, La Malinche was a product of the indigenous culture with its strengths as well as its classist and religiously intense constraints. That she performed as extraordinarily well as she did attests both to her commanding character and to the compelling needs the Spaniards had of her services.

La Malinche's facile learning of Castilian Spanish, her familiarity with the country, and her insight into the Native customs and habits quickly made her indispensable to Cortés, whom she attended, even in battle, throughout his incursion into the heartland of Mexico. Her service to the Spaniards began as interpreter but rapidly became much more involved and substantively challenging. Even after the siege and capture of Tenochtitlan (the capital of Moctezuma's empire) and after Cortés's Spanish wife joined him, La Malinche remained his translator and advisor. As Somonte observes following one of his lengthy citations of Díaz's praises, "This demonstrates that Doña Marina's work, from the first, was not limited to relaying messages to Cortés, since the *mot juste* required seizing every initiative to persuade and capture the will of the Indians."[20]

Although sources vary regarding the number and gender of Cortés's heirs, La Malinche bore him his first son, Martin.[21] Their relationship has also been said to have spawned a new race, both literally and symbolically. The victorious Cortés's departure from New Spain in 1527 signals the end of La Malinche's public history. Except for brief mention regarding land assigned to her by the Conqueror, her subsequent life and her circumstances at death are open to conjecture. Suffice it to say here that archival documents containing the sworn testimony of her contemporaries indicate that La Malinche died in 1527 or 1528 at the probable age of twenty-five.[22] The likely cause of death was smallpox, which struck Mexico in epidemic proportions during that period.

This brief summary of what little we know of La Malinche was compiled from accounts written by firsthand participants in the events and from later sources relying on the earlier documents. Of these we get a varying assessment of her role. Considered together they support the conclusion that her paramount value to the Spaniards was not merely linguistic, for her interpreting went beyond translating from idiom to idiom, though that was difficult enough given the foreignness of the respective tongues. She was an interpreter/liaison who served as a guide to the region, as an advisor on Native customs and beliefs, and as a competent strategist. It appears that her least significant role to Cortés was that most often expected of women: her function as his mistress.

Although space limitations preclude a full account of firsthand descriptions of the Conquest – all demonstrating La Malinche's crucial role in it – a brief summary will illustrate the nature and extent of her contributions. Moreover, to appreciate the challenges she faced, Cortés's own accomplishments will first be reviewed.

He and his men landed on the coast of Yucatán in the spring, probably March, of 1519. The capture of Tenochtitlan was completed by August of 1520. In less than one and one-half years, Cortés had managed to journey to the Aztec capital across unfamiliar and extremely rugged terrain replete with hostile Native tribes. In that time he also managed to ally his small army with several tribes, notably in Texcoco, Tlaxcala, and Cempoala. Their help was indispensable in the defeat of Moctezuma and, eventually, Cuauhtemotzin. These encounters signaled the ultimate Aztec downfall.

Through La Malinche, "*la lengua*," Cortés was able to communicate two essential messages to the Natives they encountered during their inland trek. The *indios* were persuaded first that the Europeans could release them from their subjection to the Aztecs, and, second, that the appearance of the white men was divinely fated and foreshadowed the inevitable conquest of Mexico. "Doña Marina did not limit herself to being an interpreter only, but rather a collaborator involved in speaking to and discussing with the *caciques;* and with her brilliant mind, persuasion and dialogue were facilitated [for the Spaniards]."[23]

Through La Malinche, the liaison to the Natives, Cortés and his men and allies were saved from total destruction as they traveled. Upon their arrival in Tlaxcala, for example, her astute observations led her to uncover an indigenous conspiracy against Cortés. Through her he was able to use that discovery as a means of intimidating the people of Tlaxcala into an alliance.[24] Similarly, nearing Cholula, the imposing capital of an important province, La Malinche's friendship with an old woman allowed her to learn of the well-planned, well-prepared attack Moctezuma was about the launch there against the invaders. Armed with this information Cortés decided to change his plans and to circumvent Cholula before proceeding directly to Tenochtitlan. The change astonished the Natives and further persuaded them of the Spaniards' mystical powers.[25] On these and other occasions, La Malinche's presence made the decisive difference between life or death.

Because of La Malinche, the advisor, Cortés survived the tragedy of the famous *"Noche Triste,"* when he and his men were forced out of the Aztec capital. Injured and ill, the Conqueror was saved by La Malinche's ministrations. More than that, while he was febrile she was forced to join his assistants in making decisions regarding their subsequent plans. As Somonte puts it, "Doña Marina was involved in all these negotiations and her activities did not cease until the conquest of the great Tenochtitlan was realized."[26] Accordingly, her eloquent discretion in addressing the Aztec Emperor on behalf of Cortés had been viewed as contributing to the latter's successes in a way that prevented the loss of even greater numbers of lives.[27] Each of these instances, and many others, depended on La Malinche's understanding of the *indios* coupled with her insight into the minds and will of the conquerors.

Three of the important early accounts of the Conquest merit closer scrutiny here. Composed by Cortés himself, by one of his soldiers, and by a descendant of one of the Conqueror's Native allies, these three chronicles offer probing insight into the minds and motivations of these particular writers. They also allow today's student access into their eras and respective cultures. Of prime importance to the present study is their interpretation of La Malinche and her role in the Conquest.

In the first, Cortés's *Cartas de Relación (Five Letters of Relation to the*

Emperor Charles V), she is mentioned briefly twice.[28] In the Second *Carta* Cortés alludes to her in passing as "the interpreter whom I have, an Indian woman of this country."[29] In the Fifth *Carta* he writes:

I answered him [a native *cacique*] that I was the captain of whom the people had spoken as having fought with them in their country, of which he might assure himself from the interpreter with whom he was speaking, who is Marina whom I have always had with me since she was presented to me with twenty other women. She explained everything to him and how I had conquered Mexico, and told him of all the countries I had subjected and placed under the Empire of Your Majesty.[30]

In his lengthy epistolary report from the field, these are the sole written references to her during all the time he spent in Mexico. What we must bear in mind, however, is that these letters to the King were written in hopes of securing their author royal favor, prestige, wealth, and, eventually, a royal appointment as governor of New Spain. Thus Cortés's *Cartas* are understandably self-serving and one-sided, factors that account for his relegation of La Malinche's valuable service to these passing references. What is more, propriety argued against the married adventurer's presenting a fuller, forthright account of his high regard for his comely interpreter/mistress.[31]

Of prime importance, moreover, are the recorded examples of Cortés's esteem for La Malinche apart from the understandable, if lamentably chauvinistic, failure to acknowledge a "heathen consort" in letters to the Sovereign. First, Cortés named their illegitimate son after his own father, Don Martin, an act of considerable magnitude among the custom-oriented Europeans of that time.[32] Second, he assigned several partitions of land to her during his administration of Mexico.[33] That, too, was an important deed because she was not a member of the Spanish ruling class, which was automatically entitled to property ownership in post-Conquest New Spain. Finally, before returning to Spain, Cortés arranged a proper marriage for her with one of his soldiers, Don Juan Jaramillo, a Spanish nobleman:[34]

Her marriage to Jaramillo is the explanation and truth of that [cultural] marriage; it tells of a merging path, social and religious, to the Spanish [way of life], and this undoubtedly was the honor and highest esteem which a Spaniard like Cortés could have offered. The conquest and colonization of America by Spain pointed the way to the merging of the New World to the Christian culture of Europe; Marina's wedding to a Spanish gentleman had exactly the same import.[35]

Thus, although his *Cartas* minimize her presence and value to him during the momentous Conquest, Cortés evidenced his high regard for her through documented deeds of weighty, lasting significance.

A second important early account of the Conquest, *Obras Historicas* (historical writings), was written by Don Fernando de Alva Ixtlilxochitl, the descendant of Cortés's most important ally, the *cacique* of Texcoco, Ixtlilxochitl the Elder. Alva, as he is called by historians, wrote his chronicle from a substantial body of Native documents. Strangely, in the *Obra* dealing with the "coming of the Spaniards and the beginning of evangelical law" – Account 13, as it has come to be called – Alva scarcely mentions La Malinche at all. Since he purports to present the Native allies' version, his reduction of the interpreter's role is unusual. She was clearly a Native ally and the codices he was using show her prominently at the Conqueror's side.[36] Alva does stress, however, her influence in converting the Natives to Catholicism.

Marina, the tongue, was charged with establishing the Christian faith [among the *indios*], speaking at the same time of the King of Spain. In a very few days she learned Castilian, which excused Cortés from a good deal of work and which seemed almost like a miracle and was very important in the conversion of the natives and the promulgation of our blessed Catholic faith.[37]

In battle and in negotiations with Moctezuma, as well as with other indigenous officials, La Malinche appears actively engaged in the landmark events of her time, yet Alva largely overlooks her presence. With remarkable efficacy, then, this native-born, post-Columbian scholar minimizes one of the key figures of the Conquest. Alva's careful delimiting of La Malinche's important role leads to a threefold conclusion. He was, first, primarily concerned with establishing a record of the value of his namesake: Ixtlilxochitl the Elder, and the people of Texcoco in assisting the Spaniards. Neither Cortes's *Cartas,* nor Gómara's loyally slanted, pro-Cortés *Historia,* nor later Spanish versions gave proper acknowledgment of the indigenous help Cortés received and without which his efforts would have failed.[38] Alva simply wanted to correct the annals written by the conquerors.[39] Second, he was intent on documenting the extent of his countrymen's suffering at the hands of the Spaniards through a history presenting the Mexican view of the Conquest. His damaging description and assessment of what occurred account for the fact that his *Obras* were not published until the eighteenth century,[40] though they were written two centuries earlier.

It appears to me, finally, that Alva was perhaps unwilling or incapable of adjusting to the anomaly of a female's crucial role in molding the otherwise male-shaped events. In the pre-Columbian Mesoamerican culture, as in the European, men and women rigidly adhered to sex roles and class types. As discussed earlier, La Malinche's central role in the history of the region was exceptional for women of that period. Perhaps Alva, in writing of his people's role in *la conquista*, was simply reacting against the Spaniards' ultimate blasphemy: allowing a woman into a male-dominated public sphere.

The firsthand account that is generally regarded as the most extensive and accurate of the early Spanish histories is Bernal Díaz del Castillo's narrative, *Historia verdadera de la conquista de la Nueva España*. Though written long after his New World service to Cortés, his work is generally conceded to have few factual errors of any consequence. Díaz wrote his *Historia verdadera* to correct the distortions in the chronicle written by Gómara, who wrote about events in which he had not participated. Gómara's information source was largely his *compadre*, Cortés, whose self-serving narratives have been discussed above.

It was Díaz who introduced La Malinche's greatness to the world.

Before telling about the great Moctezuma and his famous City of Mexico and the Mexicans, I wish to give some account of Doña Marina, who from her childhood had been the mistress and *Cacica* of towns and vassals.[41]

Díaz unequivocally credits La Malinche's knowledge of the languages, of the Native customs, of the country, as well as her loyalty, bravery, and intelligence as being inestimably valuable to the *conquistadores*.

As Doña Marina proved herself such an excellent woman and good interpreter throughout the wars in New Spain, Tlaxcala and Mexico (as I shall show later on) Cortés always took her with him. . . . Doña Marina was a person of the greatest importance and was obeyed without question by the Indians throughout New Spain. . . . This was the great beginning of our conquests and thus, thanks be to God, things prospered with us. I have made a point of explaining this matter, because without the help of Doña Marina we could not have understood the language of New Spain.[42]

As William Prescott persuasively demonstrates, Cortés's ability to communicate fully with the Natives enabled him to acquire allies, a "weapon" earlier prospective conquerors had sorely lacked.[43]

After reviewing the Conquest and La Malinche's role in it, and in view of the negative comments about her cited at the beginning of this study, the question of her loyalties requires consideration. Was she a traitor to her people? Was she a treasonous puppet of the Spaniards? Should she be praised or condemned?

To attempt an objective response to these questions requires a reexamination of her situation at the time of the Spaniards' arrival in Mexico.

She became interpreter to Cortés when she was quite young, probably under seventeen. At thirty-five Cortés was already an established success in the West Indies where he held a modest office and estate.[44] Additionally, Cortés has been acclaimed as a man of great intelligence, military acumen, and intense tenacity; some compare his incursion into Mexico with the feats of Alexander and Caesar.[45] To suggest that a young woman could have thwarted the singleminded fervor of such a leader's intentions seems grossly naive. Even to hint that La Malinche could have misled the Spaniards and secretly aided the Aztecs indicates incredible ingenuousness, for, as discussed above, most tribes and their *caciques* loathed Moctezuma's dictatorship. This view also overlooks the inevitability of European conquest – they had the muskets and horses – once gold had been discovered in the New World.

In addition, as a product of the culture, La Malinche was subject to the same mysticism that enveloped Moctezuma. If the great Emperor himself was uncertain about the (im)mortality of the white men, surely La Malinche experienced the same uncertainty. She may have seen herself as a divinely selected participant in a most fateful destiny. Moreover, born female in a rigidly role-conscious society, La Malinche was bred to serve and to obey. She would have brought shame to the *cacique* of Tabasco and to her adopted people had she not obeyed and served as best she could. And finally, the fact that La Malinche had been betrayed by her mother and sold into slavery cannot be overlooked as a factor in a more complete interpretation and understanding of this remarkable woman. In this context, Valdéz's interpretation quoted earlier that "she turn[ed] her back on her own people, she joined the white men and become assimilated," becomes little more than weak slander.[46] What else could this outcast from the Aztecs, "her own people," have done?

The harsh view of La Malinche also ignores the apparent widespread respect accorded her by the Natives. That she was called "Malin*tzin*," a term of honor, may be attributed to her service to the awe-inspiring *conquistadores*. Nevertheless, her own personal qualities must have been impressive for she is prominently drawn in the Native codices where she appears expressive, strong, and forceful. The Mexicans even named a volcano and several other geographical sites after her. As one writer puts it, "She was adored by the Aztecs."[47]

To summarize, La Malinche played a major role in Cortés's conquest. Without her as interpreter/guide/advisor he might not have been *the* Conqueror of the Aztecs: her discovery of the Cholula conspiracy against the

Spaniards saved them from defeat and massacre, for instance.[48] Nevertheless, she does *not* deserve blame for the destruction of the Aztec Empire. This distinction needs stressing. Internally, the Empire's destruction had already begun during Moctezuma's reign and even earlier, and externally, destruction was assured when the first bar of gold crossed the Atlantic in Columbus's ship.

The fascinating story of this remarkable sixteenth-century woman might be read as an account of the prototypical Chicana feminist. La Malinche embodies those personal characteristics – such as intelligence, initiative, adaptability, and leadership – which are most often associated with Mexican American women unfettered by traditional restraints against activist public achievement. By adapting to the historical circumstances thrust upon her, she defied traditional social expectations of a woman's role. Accordingly, the exigent demands placed on her allowed La Malinche's astonishing native abilities to surface. While her twentieth-century cultural heirs might wish that *she* had become the liberator and led the fight against the European invaders, the abuse of her people by the Aztec rulers would have required that she also lead a rebellion against Moctezuma's regime. Such fantasies and speculations should not be allowed to obscure La Malinche's singular place in history.

NOTES

A very abbreviated version of this article appeared in *Agenda* 8:1 (1977): 21–22. The original, full-length version is included in *A History of the Mexican-American People,* ed. Julian Samora with Cordilla Chavez and Alberto L. Pulido, rev. ed. (Notre Dame, Ind.: University of Notre Dame Press, 1993).

1. T. R. Fehrenbach, *Fire and Blood: A History of Mexico* (New York: Macmillan, 1973), 131.

2. Luis Valdéz, "La Conquista de Méjico," *Actos y el Teatro Campesino* (Fresno, Calif.: Cucaracha, 1971), 58.

3. William H. Prescott, *Mexico and the Life of the Conqueror Fernando Cortés* (New York: Peter F. Collier, 1842), vol. 1, 431–36; Hernan (Fernando) Cortés, *Cartas de relación de la conquista de Méjico (His Five Letters of Relation to the Emperor Charles V),* trans. and ed. Francis A. MacNutt (Cleveland, Ohio: A. H. Clark, 1908), 187n; Fehrenbach, *Fire and Blood,* 93–101.

4. R. C. Padden, *The Hummingbird and the Hawk: Conquest and Sovereignty in the Valley of Mexico, 1503–1541* (New York: Harper Colophon, 1967), 124–26.

5. Fehrenbach, *Fire and Blood,* 90–101.

6. Prescott, *Mexico*, vol. 1, 221.

7. Mariano G. Somonte, *Doña Marina, "La Malinche"* (México: n.p., 1969), 55–57, 135; citations from Somonte's work were translated by Cordelia Candelaria. Another source states that her family name was Tenépal. See Gutierre Tibón, *Diccionario etimológico comparado de nombres proprios de persona* (México: Tallares de Editorial Fournier, 1956), 380.

8. Somonte, *Doña Marina*, 135; see also Padden, *Hummingbird and the Hawk*, 226, for a discussion of *cacicazgo*.

9. Bernal Díazz del Castillo, *Historia verdadera de la conquista de la Nueva España (The Discovery and Conquest of Mexico)*, trans. A. P. Maudsley, ed. Genaro Garcia (New York: Farrar, Straus, and Cudahy, 1956), 66–67.

10. Díaz, *Historia*, 66.

11. Díaz, *Historia*, 64.

12. Díaz, *Historia*, 66.

13. Salvador Madariaga, as quoted in Somonte, *Doña Marina*, 16–17.

14. Padden, *Hummingbird and the Hawk*, vii.

15. Justo Sierra, *The Political Evolution of the Mexican People*, trans. Charles Ramsdell (Austin: University of Texas Press, 1976), 36.

16. Padden, *Hummingbird and the Hawk*, 20–21.

17. Fehrenbach, *Fire and Blood*, 87–90.

18. Padden, *Hummingbird and the Hawk*, 16, 229, 250.

19. Fehrenbach, *Fire and Blood*, 8.

20. Somonte, *Doña Marina*, 23.

21. Somonte, *Doña Marina*, 169.

22. *Probanza*, cited in Somonte, *Doña Marina*, 137–44. Like Prescott, Gustavo Rodriquez, another historian of this subject, persists in giving a later date as La Malinche's time of death. Somonte's reassessment of the evidence strongly favors the view that she died from smallpox before 1530. See Gustavo A. Rodriquez, *Doña Marina* (México: Secretaria de Relaciones Exteriores, 1935), 64–65.

23. Somonte, *Doña Marina*, 24.

24. Somonte, *Doña Marina*, 25–26.

25. Somonte, *Doña Marina*, 28–31.

26. Somonte, *Doña Marina*, 43.

27. Somonte, *Doña Marina*, 50–51.

28. Cortés, *Cartas*. In his fine study of La Malinche, Somonte errs in writing that Cortés "only mentioned his extraordinary collaborator once" (*Doña Marina*, viii).

29. Cortés, *Cartas*, I, 217.

30. Cortés, *Cartas*, II, 273.

31. Cortés, *Cartas*, v–vi. Fernando de Alva Ixtilxochitl, *Obras historical (Ally of*

Cortés, Account 13), trans. and ed. Douglass K. Ballentine (El Paso: Texas Western Press, 1969), 125.

32. Prescott, *Mexico*, vol. 2, 334.

33. Prescott, *Mexico*, vol. 2, 333.

34. Prescott, *Mexico*, vol. 2, 333.

35. Hilda Krüger, as quoted in Somonte, *Doña Marina*, 113.

36. See Alva, *Obras historicas*. See also Miguel León-Portilla, *The Broken Spears: The Aztec Account of the Conquest of Mexico* (Boston: Beacon, 1962).

37. Alva, as quoted in Somonte, *Doña Marina*, 181.

38. See Francisco López de Gómora, *Historia de la conquista de México*, ed. Joaquin Ramirez Cabanas (México: Editorial lPedro Robredo, 1943).

39. Alva, *Obras historicas*, xi, 124.

40. Prescott, *Mexico*, vol. 1, 40–41n.

41. Díaz, *Historia*, 66.

42. Díaz, *Historia*, 67–68.

43. Prescott, *Mexico*, vol. 1, 245 *passim*.

44. Cortés, *Cartas*, 8–24.

45. Cortés, *Cartas*, 30; Sierra, *Political Evolution*, 53–62.

46. In a conversation with me in 1976, at Idaho State University, playwright Luis Valdéz acknowledged that his characterization of Doña Marina was historically invalid.

47. Sierra, *Political Evolution*, 55.

48. Díaz, *Historia*, 176–77.

Frontiers 5:2 (1980): 1–60.

Gender and Ethnic Identity among Chicanos

MAXINE BACA ZINN

The study of ethnic background and gender reveals differences and similarities in the lives of women and men from group to group.[1] However, it is commonly thought that different ethnic groups vary in their conceptions of masculinity and femininity. A major assumption in the sociology of gender is that race or culture is a primary determinant of differences in gender role identity. The gender identity of both black men and women and Hispanic men and women is commonly explained in terms of their historical and cultural heritage. Black men and women are frequently described as less sex typed than white men and women, and Hispanics are more strongly sex typed. These descriptions are based on implicit assumptions about the ethnic and cultural differences in the development of gender. Because research on gender and ethnicity is in its infancy, the assumption that there are substantial ethnic differences in gender has not been tested with comparative data.[2] It is striking that in the burgeoning literature on both gender and ethnicity, little attention is devoted specifically to the acquisition of identity on the part of Chicanas and Chicanos. Nor, for that matter, is identity as a specific topic considered in the recently published full-length works on Chicanas.[3] Intuitively, it makes sense to say that what it means to be a woman would vary according to whether one is Chicana, black, or white. However, the assumptions underlying this commonsense notion have not been examined, nor has it been conceptually specified.

Expressions of Chicano ethnic identity have characterized the past decade of the Chicano experience, and many of these expressions have been articulated by the women of La Raza. We know a great deal about our ethnic heritage, about our ethnic presence in America, but we know very little either about how our ethnicity contributes to our conceptions of ourselves as women and men or about how our conceptions of women and men contribute to our ethnic identity.

An advanced society such as ours contains many crisscrossing and often conflicting interests, and what complicates the situation is that we as individuals have multiple memberships.[4] It is possible that one source of identity will dominate the others. Questions can be asked concerning a person's primary identification from among group memberships. What will he or she say in answer to the question, "Who are you?" man or woman, Chicano, Mexicano, Latino?

The purpose of this paper is to examine conceptual and empirical issues surrounding the social identity of Chicanas. The basic question being addressed is how ethnicity and gender are reflected in the social identity of Chicanas, and for comparative purposes, Chicanos. The intent is not to test, but to clarify both data and theory by examining major perspectives on gender and ethnic identity and their application to Chicanos, by indicating the limitations of prevailing approaches, and by suggesting alternative directions for research.

The term Chicano will be used in both a generic manner (referring to both women and men of Mexican heritage) and in reference specifically to men when contrasted to Chicanas.

CHICANO GENDER AND ETHNIC IDENTITY: CRITIQUE AND CLARIFICATION

The disregard by social science in the matter of Chicana identity is well captured by psychologist Isabelle Navar.

> I had met a friend of mine who is quite involved in community outreach activities, and I was telling her about some opportunities for graduate study I had heard about. She asked me what I was doing and I told her I was in the process of writing an article about Chicana identity. She hooted eloquently and said "what identity?"[5]

This comment is far more revealing of the literature on Chicana identity than on the psychosocial reality of the Chicana. To say that there is almost no work on the relationship between ethnicity and gender among Chicanas is not to say that they have no identity. The dearth of scholarly work on the relationship between ethnicity and gender among Chicanas has been accompanied by widespread acceptance of erroneous assumptions about their social identities. Therefore, an adequate understanding of Chicana identity requires conceptual clarification as well as some comprehension of recent trends in the literature on social identity.

The common social science presentation of the submissive Chicana tells us more about the social science view of women of color than it does about their identity. The notion of the submissive Chicana has its roots in two distinct traditions:

The first tradition treats women as constitutionally and socially inferior to men, and therefore less interesting than men. The second tradition treats people of color as inherently or culturally inferior to Anglo-white people. Both of these social and intellectual ideologies have produced cultural stereotypes. Chicanas are variously portrayed as exotic objects, manipulated by both Chicano and Anglo men; as long-suffering mothers subject to the brutality of insecure husbands, whose only function is to produce children; and as women who themselves are childlike, simple, and completely dependent on their fathers, brothers, and husbands. Regardless of the specific characterization, Chicanas have been depicted as ignorant, simple women whose subservience and dependence results in the inability to make the home a productive unit for their families. Social scientists correctly analyzed Chicano social organization in terms of patriarchal-authoritarian principles, but they have incorrectly assumed this to mean that women are insignificant, and that they exert power only by manipulation. This assumption has rendered Chicanas undeserving of serious scholarly investigation.[6]

In comparison to other women, Chicanas are thought to reflect greater dependency and compliance. It should be noted, however, that this portrayal is one based on sociocultural expectations. Because it is a normative projection, its application to social identity may be qualified. Furthermore, it is restricted to an analysis of gender roles within the family. The major weakness in the description of the submissive Chicana is that it is based on the acceptance of a simplistic and one-dimensional notion of womanhood. Chicanas are depicted in terms of a single social category: that of their sociocultural role. Marisa Zavaloni finds this to be a flaw in the literature of all ethnics, pointing out that much previous work on racial and ethnic identity has been too exclusively focused on ethnic terms, without letting people define their own identities, particularly the importance to them of ethnic identity in a broader framework of social identity.[7] Her critique is pertinent to a number of problems in the literature on Chicanas.

The problem with making assumptions about gender identity on the basis of sex roles is that sex roles are normative, but not necessarily internalized. Furthermore, actual behavior among Chicanos and Chicanas is not as rigid as the roles themselves. Behavioral expectations are one thing, but whether people internalize them completely or behave according to those expectations is another matter entirely.

Contrary to the prevalent approach, which conceptualizes roles in terms of cultural values alone, recent research indicates that behavior of Chicanos varies according to life conditions and situations. The gender roles of Chicanos are changing both as a result of alteration in the broader society and in response to internal changes. The labor force participation of Chicanas has been a primary source of the erosion of traditional gender roles. The resources that they acquire in the public sphere enable them to select from a wider range of behaviors, and as such their roles undergo change.

Social categories link the individual psychologically to social structures. They locate the individual in social space, "a space consisting of the myriad of statuses and roles which society provides to its members, and which are integrated into various social structures."[8] The human environment encompasses, for each individual, quite a large number of social categories that constitute identity groups; one's national and ethnic membership, religion, social class, age, family status, and political party affiliation are all categorical sources of social identity.

Gender and ethnicity are categorical designations conferred on an individual at birth, and they operate to put these individuals in their designated social place, as well as to confer their social identity. Cynthia Fuchs Epstein maintains that sex and race are "dominant" statuses, determining the other statuses one is likely to acquire. In her words, "They are visible, and immutable, and impose severe limitations on an individual's capacities to alter the dimensions of their world and the attitudes of others."[9] The structural and psychological significance of the ascribed categories of race and gender hardly needs elaboration. Few would disagree that they are central to the study of stratification or that they are central to the study of social identity. Very little, however, is known about how the combination of race and gender affect status, and almost nothing is known about how their interrelationship affects social identity. This lack of knowledge is, of course, not limited to Chicanos, but is characteristic of the social identity literature in general. Discussions of gender and ethnicity have tended to take place within the context of family roles. What knowledge we do have of gender among ethnics comes from research on families and from implicit comparisons of behavioral expectations, that is, expectations imposed upon women and men in different ethnic groups.

Approaches to the study of social identity have been derived from a number of different frameworks. An examination of the gender identity literature and the ethnic identity literature reveals the presence of psychoanalytic orientations in both bodies of literature. The sociocultural framework is dominant in studies of ethnic identity.[10] Literature relating to gender among Chicanos reflects the application of both the psychoanalytic orientation and the sociocultural orientation. The sociocultural orientation suggests again the assumption that gender may be understood in terms of cultural differences, and that culture is a major determinant of gender. The psychoanalytic orientation, while also viewing men and women as products of their distinct cultural and historical experiences, stresses evaluative dimensions of social identity. The widely held notion of "machismo" and its counterpart of female submissiveness are rooted in assumptions about the self-evaluation of Mexicans and Chicanos. The unquestioned acceptance of the masculinity cult has been severely critiqued in recent years,[11] but it has been a primary explanatory concept for gender identity and gender roles of Chicanos. Cecilia Suarez describes the typical characterization:

The male is labeled as the one who has a tendency of male superiority and dominance through multiple sexual contests and the Chicana is described as defenseless and submissive to the macho.[12]

The social science literature views machismo as a compensation for feelings of inadequacy and worthlessness. This interpretation is rooted in the application of psychoanalytic concepts to explain both Mexican and Chicano gender roles. The widely accepted interpretation is that machismo is the male attempt to compensate for internalized inferiority by exaggerated masculinity. "At the same time that machismo is an expression of power, its origin is ironically linked to powerlessness and subordination."[13] The common origins of inferiority and machismo are said to lie in the historical "conquest of Mexico by Spain involving the exploitation of Indian women by Spanish men thus producing the hybrid Mexican people having an inferiority complex based on the mentality of a conquered people."[14] The view that inferiority is a universal response to conditions of domination was originally set forth by Alfred Adler, and came to be widely accepted by those who studied the Mexican national character. For example, Samuel Ramos and Octavio Paz[15] explained national character in terms of a "psychology of the oppressed," a psychology based on the premise that dominated people come to accept their inferiority. Exemplifying this reasoning, Albert Memmi contends that "in every dominated man, there is a certain degree of self rejection, born mostly of his downcast condition and exclusion."[16]

The idea that exaggerated masculinity is a compensation for the psychological inferiority created by domination is not made explicit in studies of Chicanos; however, acceptance of its underlying assumptions is present in the literature. For example, Leo Grebler proposes that patriarchal values became cultural ideals in Chicano families at least in part because of the weaknesses in the male role.[17] While interpretations of machismo among Chicanos do not follow strict psychoanalytic interpretations, they are consistently pejorative, associated with irresponsibility, inferiority, and ineptitude.

The consequences of machismo for women are more implicit. Females are said to be submissive, but there is an underlying theme of conflict between the sexes, and of suffering wives who become manipulative mothers creating dependency and maternal fixation in their sons. The frequent references to the "real power in the Chicano household" combined with the notion that mothers get their way by means of manipulating their powerless husbands and sons reflect this theme.

The idea that membership in minority groups operates to depress self-concept has been accepted in much theorizing about minority groups. First introduced by Kurt Lewin, the notion of self-hatred refers to negative evaluations that minority group members sometimes hold concerning their own groups, and the "damaged self-identity" those evaluations produce.[18] These are evaluative dimensions of social identity, and they have to do with the content of people's conception about themselves. While evaluative and substantive dimensions of social identity are distinct, both are related to the societal placement and evaluation of peoples. Interestingly for Chicanos, evaluative dimensions of their social identity (that is their supposed negative self-concept) are thought to be responsible for the rigid and unproductive gender role dichotomy and hence the gender category of their social identity. It is through their "collective inferiority" that gender roles are thought to take on their distinctive character.

The notion that Chicanos (both men and women) have negative self-concepts because of oppression remains unsubstantiated, and there are some theoretical arguments against it. Zavaloni argues that this is only one among a number of possible responses to a minority situation and probably not the most common one. Her comments on the interpretation of black self-concept are pertinent to Chicano self-concept:

White social scientists have traditionally interpreted the situation of blacks as an identity group in terms of a projection they would feel if they with their white identity were suddenly to become black. In other words, the perspective within which a given group identity is analyzed may be influenced by the fact that the analyst borrows the parameters with which he builds alter identity representation from his own identity, in this case, his whiteness.[19]

The damaged self-concept interpretation further ignores the possibility that alternative sources may contribute to the positive self-concept of Chicano men and women: that within their ethnic communities, within their families and kin groups, there are processes that contribute to their positive self-worth and positive identity.

Overreliance on the evaluative aspects of Chicano and Chicana gender identity have tended to obscure categorical components of social identity. This has produced a one-dimensional portrayal of Chicanas. The typical description of dependent and compliant women can hardly be applicable to an entire social category of women whose lives span a variety of conditions and social situations. With regard to the categorical components of their identity Chicanas belong simultaneously to many social categories. They are of Mexican heritage, they are women, they are young, they are old, they are workers, they are professionals, they are mothers, and so forth. The simple cultural description ignores the multiple sources of identity.

The recent proliferation of Chicana literature (by that I mean work on Chicanas by Chicanas) recognizes the existence of multiple identity categories and suggests that Chicana identity comes from the interaction of those categories. The impressionistic evidence that they provide is significant. The early calls for women to take pride in their cultural heritage and to reject the women's liberation movement produced exhortations for women to be "Chicana Primero."[20] This gave way to the image of "La Nueva Chicana" – women seeking to redefine the cultural stereotypes imposed upon them.[21] In those attempts women called for a combination of the strengths of their womanhood with the strengths of their cultural heritage. Evey Chapa encouraged women to "affirm their identity as a Mexican American and a woman," and to define their roles within this context.[22] Juliette Ruiz, too, wrote of the dual identity of Chicanas and the increasing self-awareness among Chicanas.[23] This Chicana literature contains an important message: that is, if we are to comprehend the nature of Chicana identity, we had best attempt to understand the dynamic relationship between gender and ethnicity.

These discussions of Chicana identity have been generated in the context of a larger struggle for racial equality. They point to the dynamic nature of the self-identity process. As Chicanos challenged the larger societal processes that led to their subordination as ethnics, they began to articulate the new conceptions of ethnic identity. In this process of redefining ethnic identity, Chicanas challenged processes that led to their subordination as women and also articulated new conceptions of their identities as ethnic women.

EMPIRICAL FINDINGS RELATED TO THE SOCIAL IDENTITIES OF CHICANOS

Studies of the social identity of Chicanas and Chicanos are "scattered over a variety of topics with findings which at times appear contradictory."[24] The lack of empirical research on the relationship of gender to ethnicity, and the conceptual confusion of identity and role make it difficult to compose either a clear or consistent summary of the social identities of Chicanas. Despite its fragmented nature, the existing information can shed light and generate further questions on the relationships between gender ethnicity and Chicano identity.

Existing literature tends to be at least implicitly comparative, pointing to similarities and differences between Chicanos and Anglos on the one hand, and between Chicanos, male and female, on the other hand. Viktor Gecas reports that the research on the social identity of Chicanos "has stressed the evaluative dimension with inconclusive results."

Coleman (1966) and Hishiki (1969) found the self evaluation of Mexican American children to be lower than those of Anglo children, while De Blassie (1979), and Healy (1970), and Carter (1968) found no significant differences between the two groups.[25]

Maria Nieto Senour reviewed the evaluative research with an eye to the differences between Chicanos and Chicanas and concluded that Chicanas are "suffering more from oppression."

With respect to personality characteristics, Chicanas show (a) lower self esteem, (b) more field dependence, (c) greater identity with families and homes that tend to give males greater status, (d) more concern about their physical selves, (e) less well defined psychic selves, (f) more death dreams, and (g) more depression. With respect to social dimensions, Chicanas appear not to reject dark skin as much as Chicanos, yet chose Mexican Americans less frequently than do boys. Chicanas also appear to be more prosocial and less competitive than Chicano males.

In school, girls show less achievement and a more generalized negative reaction than do boys.[26]

Differences between Chicanos and Chicanas have also been found in studies of categorical dimensions of social identity. The existing research reveals differences in the importance of identity components for men and women. R. L. Derbyshire found that adolescent girls experience less conflict over their own identities and social roles, that they select family related components and social roles, while boys identify more closely with machismo and the husband roles of the traditional Mexican culture.[27] Gecas also found differences in the identity characteristics of parents: "Mothers mention family identities somewhat more frequently while fathers were more likely to refer to their work or occupational roles."[28] Furthermore, Gecas found, as have others, that for children the most frequent identity category was gender; like adults the identity characteristics of children differed – girls being more likely to think of themselves in terms of family and boys in athletic terms. This finding is consistent with the general identity research that identifies differences for men and women. According to Clarice Stasz Stoll, the most frequently mentioned roles for both sexes are those that are gender specific marital identification, and other family roles.[29] Women use familial referents much more than men. Similarly, most occupational identities are gender specific because jobs in America are sex segregated. Gecas explains that the father is held responsible for providing for the family, while the mother's activity revolves around her family and home, and this constitutes a major arena for her self-definition.[30] An important issue here is the salience of gender versus ethnicity in the identity of Chicanas and Chicanos. While findings are inconclusive, they do suggest differences for women and men. Senour reports:

According to Derbyshire, (1968) Mexican American adolescent girls experience less conflict over their own identities and social roles than boys. He found girls identifying more closely with Anglo females and their maternal roles, while boys identified more closely with machismo and the husband roles of the traditional Mexican culture. In a comparison of Anglo and Chicano responses to sex-role related verbal stimuli, Martinez, Martinez, Olmedo, and Goldman (1976) found that Chicana responses resembled those of Anglos while Chicano males differed from other groups.[31]

On the basis of these findings, it is tempting to suggest that Chicana gender identity is more similar to that of Anglos in their common choice of family categories, while Chicano gender incorporates cultural differences in their total identity configurations. However, it would be incautious to conclude that ethnicity contributes more to the identity of Chicanos than Chicanas without further research.

Recent research challenges the common assumption that gender identity differs according to sociocultural expectations. Gecas compared Latin American and Anglo adolescents with regard to the relative salience of four identity sources, those of gender, religion, family, and peer group. He found that for both males and females in Latin and Anglo cultures, gender emerged as the most prominent identity.[32] This finding was striking especially in view of the expectation that: "Gender identities should predominate in those societies which accentuate sex-role differences over those in which it is less pronounced. Latin cultures have been associated with sharper distinctions between masculine and feminine. . . ."

The assumption that Chicanas and Chicanos are more strongly sex-typed in terms of masculinity and femininity is contradicted by other recent evidence. Maria Nieto Senour and Lynda Warren conducted a study to question whether ethnic identity is related to masculine and feminine sex role orientation. They sampled 554 men and women students from black, Anglo, and Chicano populations; significant sex differences were found in all four analyses. Males scored higher on masculinity and lower on femininity, whereas females scored higher on social desirability than males across the ethnic groups. While the results of this study cannot be considered conclusive with regard to the relationship between ethnicity and gender orientation, Senour and Warren's findings provide a challenge to the prevailing ethnic stereotypes. They state:

Mexican American males did not emerge as super masculine in comparison to Black and Anglo males, and Mexican American females were found to be no more feminine than their Black and Anglo counterparts.[33]

These few studies suggest that the relationship between ethnicity and gender identity is far from clear where social identity is concerned. They do, however, suggest concerns which should be addressed in future research.

ISSUES IN THE SOCIAL IDENTITY RESEARCH OF CHICANOS

The recent attention currently being devoted to the study of both ethnicity and gender promises that the interaction of these categories will become an important area of scholarly inquiry. This will require careful consideration of a number of important issues.

Examination of existing literature reveals that the most immediate areas of concern are those of interpretation by social scientists and conceptualization and measurement of multiple identity categories. Zavaloni maintains that much of the irrelevance of social science to social identity issues is the result of blinders to the existence of a variety of perspectives due to different identity experiences. Many of the interpretations of ethnic identity, she argues, are formed on the basis of assumptions derived from the self-identity of those conducting the research.[34] What needs to be done, then, is to construct studies of Chicanas and Chicanos that are not representative of external or imposed categories. This means allowing the frame of reference of the subjects to be incorporated into the interpretative structure of the research.

The second issue, the conceptualization and measurement of multiple identity components, has been avoided by splitting the issues into subfields of research. We have studies of nationalism, of ethnic identity, of sex roles, or sex identity, but it is doubtful whether progress can be made in social identity research if the problem of the total dynamics of social representations is not tackled.[35] Zavaloni cautions that a study of the total dynamics of social identity representations may turn out to be a complicated task. It is easy to apprehend – but difficult to analyze – that a Chicana reacts or thinks simultaneously as a woman, a Chicana, a teacher, and so forth.

The issue of multiple identity sources raises the question of ethnic identity and gender identity for Chicanos and Chicanas. Generally, it has been assumed that one's ethnic identity is more important than one's gender identity. Helen Mayer Hacker maintains that minority group membership is more salient than dominant group membership, and that at the present time race consciousness would probably triumph over sex consciousness.[36] Whether this is true of Chicanos is a question for further research. Undoubtedly, that research will reveal differences in the salience of ethnic and gender identity for men and women in different social circumstances. Laurie Davidson and Laura Gordon also raise some important considerations which are pertinent. According to them, the social factors affecting the development of gender in ethnic groups include: (1) the position of the group in the stratification system, (2) the existence of an ethnic community, and (3) the degree of self-identification with the minority group.[37]

The question of whether gender is more important for men or women may be mediated by ethnicity, as well as by an individual's ranking on different dimensions of stratification. Stoll maintains that gender identity is a more profound personal concern for males in our society than it is for women because women can take it for granted that they are female.[38] This speculation may have implications for Chicanos as well. Perhaps it will be found that the ethnic differences in the salience of gender are not one of degree, but that their relative significance has different meanings. In other words, gender may not be a problematic identifier for women if they can take it for granted, though it may be *primary* because many still participate in society through their gender roles. Men, on the other hand, have had more roles open to them. That is, men in the dominant society have had more roles open to them. However, this has not been the case for Chicanos or other men of color. Perhaps manhood is important for those who do not have access to other sources of social identity. This suggests that an emphasis on masculinity is not due to some internalized collective inferiority on the part of Chicanos. To be *"hombre"* may be a reflection of both ethnic and gender components and take on greater significance when other sources of social identity are structurally blocked. Chicanos have been excluded from participation in the dominant society's political-economic system; therefore they have been denied access to authority that men in other social categories have. My point is that gender may take on a unique significance for men of color. This is not to justify traditional masculinity, but to point to the need for understanding societal conditions that might contribute to the meaning of gender among different social categories.

In the same way, the finding that Chicanas are similar to other women in their gender identification may reflect the common structural position of women, that is, their linkages with kinship systems and domestic sphere activities. But given the fact that all cultural groups are experiencing changes in assymetrical social placement of women and men, this too can be expected to exhibit variability even with ethnic groups.

Thus, we can speculate that occupation, residence, education, and all of the components of socioeconomic status will contribute to differences in total social identity configurations of Chicanos and Chicanas. This points to the need for research that compares the components of women and men in different structural positions. Perhaps we shall reach a point where we need not ask whether gender or ethnicity is more important, but where we can examine the interactive nature of those two ascribed categories, and how they contribute to emerging Chicano ways of life.

NOTES

This paper was presented at the Pacific Sociological Association, San Francisco, April 10, 1980.

1. Laurie Davidson and Laura Kramer Gordon, *The Sociology of Gender* (Chicago: Rand McNally College Publishing, 1979), 120.

2. Marjorie Randon Hershey, "Racial Differences in Sex Role Identities and Sex Stereotyping: Evidence against a Common Assumption," *Social Science Quarterly* 58:4 (1978): 583–96.

3. Alfredo Mirandé and Evangelina Enríquez, *La Chicana: The Mexican-American Woman* (Chicago: University of Chicago Press, 1979); Margarita Melville, ed., *Twice a Minority: Mexican American Women* (St. Louis, Mo.: C. V. Mosby, 1980).

4. Helen Mayer Hacker, "Class and Race Differences in Gender Roles," in *Gender and Sex in Society,* ed. Lucile Duberman (New York: Praeger, 1975), 169.

5. Isabelle Navar, "Como Chicana Mi Madre," *Encuentro Femenil* 1:2 (1974): 11.

6. Maxine Baca Zinn, "Chicanas: Power and Control in the Domestic Sphere," *De Colorers, Journal of Emerging Raza Philosophies* 2:3 (1975): 19–31.

7. Marisa Zavaloni, "Social Identity: Perspectives and Prospects," *Social Science Information* 13:3 (1973): 65–91.

8. Viktor Gecas, "Self Conceptions of Migrant and Settled Mexican Americans," *Social Science Quarterly* 54:3 (1973): 579–95.

9. Cynthia Fuchs Epstein, "Positive Effects of the Multiple Negative: Explaining the Success of Black Professional Women," in *Changing Women in a Changing Society,* ed. Joan Huber (Chicago: University of Chicago Press, 1973), 150–73.

10. Arnold Dashevsky, "Theoretical Frameworks in the Study of Ethnic Identity: Toward a Social Psychology of Ethnicity," *Ethnicity* 2 (1975): 10–18.

11. Miguel Montiel, "The Social Science Myth of the Mexican American Family," *El Grito* 3 (1970): 56–63; Alfredo Mirandé, "Machismo: Rucas, Chingasos, y Chingaderas," *De Colores,* forthcoming.

12. Cecilia C-R Suarez, "Sexual Stereotypes: Psychological and Cultural Survival," *Regeneración* 2:3 (1973): 17–21.

13. Mirandé, "Machismo," 2.

14. Fernando Peñalosa, "Mexican Family Roles," *Journal of Marriage and the Family* 30 (1968): 682–85.

15. Samuel Ramos, *Profile of Man and Culture in Mexico,* trans. Peter G. Earle (1934; rpt. Austin: University of Texas Press, 1962); Octavio Paz, *The Labyrinth of Solitude,* trans. Lysander Kemp (New York: Grove Press, 1961).

16. Albert Memmi, *Dominated Man* (Boston: Beacon Press, 1968), 86.

17. Leo Grebler, Joan W. Moore, and Ralph C. Guzman, *The Mexican American People: The Nation's Second Largest Minority* (New York: The Free Press, 1970), 360.

18. Kurt Lewin, *Resolving Social Conflicts* (New York: Harper & Row, 1948).

19. Zavaloni, "Social Identity."

20. Enriqueta Longauex y Vásquez, "Soy Chicana Primero," *El Cuaderno* 1:1 (1972). See also Enriqueta Longauex y Vásquez, "The Mexican-American Woman," in *Sisterhood is Powerful*, ed. Robin Morgan (New York: Vintage, 1970), 379–84.

21. Viola Correa, "La Nueva Chicana," in *La Mujer en Pie de Lucha*, ed. Dorinda Moreno (Mexico: Espina del Norte Publications, 1973).

22. Evey Chapa and Armando Gutíerrez, "Chicanas in Politics: An Overview and a Case Study," in *Perspectivas en Chicano Studies*, ed. Reynaldo Flores Macias (Los Angeles: National Association of Chicano Social Science, 1977), 137–55.

23. Juliette S. Ruiz, "Sociology of the Chicana: Course Proposal in New Directions," in *Education Estudios Femeniles de la Chicana* (San Francisco: Montal Educational Associates, 1974).

24. Maria Nieto Senour, "Psychology of the Chicana," in *Chicano Psychology*, ed. Joe L. Martínez Jr. (New York: Academic Press, 1977), 334.

25. Gecas, "Self Conceptions," 579. See also J. S. Coleman, *Equality of Educational Opportunity* (Washington, D.C.: U.S. Government Printing Office, 1966); Patricia C. Hishiki, "The Self Concepts of Sixth-Grade Girls of Mexican-American Descent," *California Journal of Educational Research* 20 (March 1969): 56–62; R. R. De Blassie and G. W. Healy, *Self Concept: A Comparison of Spanish American, Negro, and Anglo Adolescents across Ethnic, Sex, and Socio-Economic Variables* (Las Cruces, N.M.: ERIC-CHESS, 1970); and Thomas Carter, "Negative Self Concept of Mexican American Students," *School and Society* 95 (1968): 217–19.

26. Senour, "Psychology of the Chicana," 337.

27. R. L. Derbyshire, "Adolescent Identity Crisis in Urban Mexican-Americans in East Los Angeles," in *Minority Group Adolescents in the United States*, ed. E. B. Brody (Baltimore: The Williams and Wilkins Co., 1968). See also Gecas, "Self Conceptions"; J. L. Martinez Sr., J. L. Martinez Jr., E. L. Olmedo, and R. D. Goldman, "The Semantic Differential Technique: A Comparison of Chicano and Anglo High School Students," *Journal of Cross Cultural Psychology* 7 (1976): 325–33.

28. Gecas, "Self Conceptions," 586.

29. Clarice Stasz Stoll, *Male and Female: Socialization, Social Roles, and Social Structure* (Dubuque, Iowa: Wm. C. Brown Co., 1974), 105.

30. Gecas, "Self Conceptions," 586.

31. Senour, "Psychology of the Chicana," 333.

32. Viktor Gecas, Darwin L. Thomas, and Andrew J. Weigert, "Social Identities in Anglo and Latin Adolescents," *Social Forces* 51:4 (1973): 477–84.

33. Maria Nieto Senour and Lynda Warren, "Sex and Ethnic Differences in Masculinity, Femininity, and Androgyny," paper presented at the Western Psychological Association, Los Angeles, 1976.

34. Zavaloni, "Social Identity," 77.

35. Zavaloni, "Social Identity," 80.

36. Hacker, "Class and Race Differences," 170.

37. Davidson and Gordon, *Sociology of Genders*, 120.

38. Stoll, *Male and Female*, 105.

For further information and discussion, see the following references: Alfred Adler, *Individual Psychology* (Patterson, N.J.: Littlefield, Adams, and Co., 1959); Carl J. Couch, "Family Role Specialization and Self Attitudes in Children," *Sociological Quarterly* 3 (1962): 115–21; and Janet Shibley Hyde and B. G. Rosenberg, *Half the Human Experience: The Psychology of Women* (Lexington, Mass.: D. C. Heath and Co., 1976).

Frontiers 5:2 (1980): 18–24.

Abriendo caminos in the Brotherland

Chicana Writers Respond to the
Ideology of Literary Nationalism

The decade between 1965 and 1975 was a period of intense turmoil in many Mexican American communities throughout the Southwest and California as a heightened ethnic consciousness led to protests over the denial of full and equal civil rights. The struggle for civil rights that came to be known as the "Chicano movement" was characterized by demonstrations, boycotts, strikes, and sit-ins. A cultural component quickly emerged out of the confrontation with social institutions. Its emphasis was on the conceptualization of identity as nationality; full political rights and economic and social participation were its primary goals.[1]

In contrast to other civil rights efforts, the Mexican or Chicano movement emerged out of land and labor issues in the mid-1960s when, out of previous efforts to unionize agricultural workers, César Chávez founded the National Farm Workers of America in Delano, California.[2] The first public manifestation of the Chicano movement was a strike in Delano by grape pickers on September 16, 1965. Soon after, the cultural component of the movement was ignited by Luis Valdez, who founded the Teatro Campesino in the fields of Delano as a means of raising the political consciousness of the farmworkers; throughout the country, other Chicano theatrical groups quickly emerged, adapting the artistic and political goals of the Teatro Campesino to local issues. By the late 1960s, a heightened activism in Mexican American communities throughout the Southwest paralleled the efforts of Chávez's union; these included Reies López Tijerina's landownership claims in New Mexico, the rise of militant nationalism in Colorado, and the rise of La Raza Unida Party in Texas. Within the larger context of social rebellion brought about by the war in Vietnam, the war on poverty, the black power movement, and the women's movement, Chicano men and women were in the process of reinventing themselves, their images, and their communities.[3]

Definitions of nationalism vary according to the discourse of the moment. Hans Kohn defines nationalism as the political creed that underlies the cohesion of modern societies and legitimizes their claim to authority.[4] "Nationalism has also become a socially revolutionary movement," Kohn states, "demanding equal economic and educational opportunities for all members of the national group and the active promotion of the welfare of the socially underprivileged classes."[5]

Another view of nationalism focuses on the role that imagination and myth play in the development of the self-image that precedes nation-creation. Already, in the 1920s, the Peruvian socialist essayist José Carlos Mariátegui was stating that unlike the definitions of some of the pioneering theorists of nationalism who viewed the nation in terms of political creeds, "The nation . . . is an abstraction, an allegory, a myth that does not correspond to a reality that can be scientifically defined."[6]

In an important study on nation-building, Benedict Anderson defines "nation" as an "imagined community" because "the members of even the smallest nation will never know most of their fellow-members, meet them, or even hear them, yet in the minds of each lives the image of their communion."[7] Nation-building, Anderson asserts, is closely tied to print communities formed around newspapers and novels that nurture the preconceived notions that groups have of themselves as they wish to be, as they imagine themselves to be.[8] "Nations, then," reiterates Timothy Brennan, "are imaginary constructs that depend for their existence on an apparatus in which imaginative literature plays a decisive role."[9] With the intricate networks that they have built across the country, Chicanos and Chicanas have indeed a strong sense of their imagined communities in more ways than one. Often, however, the community imagined by the men and that imagined by the women are in essence different from and conflictive with each other. Between 1965 and 1975, the opposing relationships that Chicanas/os held regarding gender issues resulted in different assumptions about what constituted oppression. This often led to the formulation of conflicting solutions for the same situation. Generally, Chicano cultural nationalists adhered to the traditional perception of women's roles espoused by modern nationalist movements in general, which are characterized by a defensive cultural conservatism and a tendency to view women's liberation as a threat to the traditional institution of the family and to the ingrained female subordination found in patriarchal systems.

The document that gave birth to the Chicano nation, the "Plan Espiritual de Aztlán," offers a good example of a gender-based interpretation of oppression. "Aztlán" – the land of the north – was the mytho-historical place of origin from whence the Aztecs had set out in search of a new homeland. Their peregrination lasted two hundred years; and at the end of this journey they established themselves in the Valley of Mexico in the late twelveth century. The historical myth of Aztlán served as the political motif around which a sense of community was invented in the late 1960s. Serving as the basis for the reclamation of the original homeland, Aztlán was indeed an imagined community.

Credited by critics of Chicano literature as the originator and main exponent of this Amerindian myth of Aztlán, the poet-theorist Alurista understood that national consciousness presupposed the existence of a nation, which in the classic sense had a common culture, a language of its own, a territory that had been held in common over many generations, an economy of its own, and a sociopolitical structure. Alurista was aware that he was inventing a sense of community for the movement, for he saw Aztlán as "an ancient Nahuatl myth which described the prehistoric motherland of the Indians in the American continent, [and] became a contemporary metaphor for a nation in the making."[10]

Alurista noted that the need for the self-redefinition of Chicano identity was tied to two common threads. First, self-definition was based on a cultural heritage that distinguished Chicano culture from that of the United States. He recognized that the uniqueness of Chicano culture could be used not only as a source of pride but also as a motivating catalyst and a dynamic force for resistance. Second, a self-redefinition was connected to a nationalist consciousness which differentiated Chicanos from other immigrants to the United States since it was, originally, the United States that came to Mexicans, occupying Mexican territory by the force of arms.[11] In Alurista's words, "Xicano culture became a force of resistance against the total assimilation and the consequent self-denigration of Xicanos in the U.S. Language was, and is, clearly the vehicle par excellence for this cultural resistance and, upon occasion, the cultural offensive against the cultural imperialism of the U.S."[12]

With this estimation, Alurista, like other Chicano cultural nationalist theorists of the late 1960s, understood the battle on the ideological front to be one against racism and capitalism. This perception can be found in the manifesto that framed the ideology of the Chicano movement, "El Plan Espiritual de Aztlán," formulated in 1969 at the Crusade for Justice's first National Chicano Youth Conference in Denver.

In keeping with the values of the movement, the "Plan Espiritual de Aztlán" was written in two versions, one in Spanish and one in English although the Spanish title was kept in the English version.[13]

EL PLAN ESPIRITUAL DE AZTLÁN

In the spirit of a new people that is conscious not only of its proud historical heritage, but also of the brutal "gringo" invasion of our territories, we, the Chicano inhabitants and civilizers of the northern land of Aztlán, from whence came our forefathers, reclaiming the land of their birth and consecrating the determination of our people of the sun, declare that the call of our blood is our power, our responsibility, and our inevitable destiny.

We are free and sovereign to determine those tasks which are justly called for by our house, our land, the sweat of our brows and by our hearts. Aztlán belongs to those that plant the seeds, water the fields, and gather the crops, and not to the foreign Europeans. We do not recognize capricious frontiers on the bronze continent.

Brotherhood unites us, and love for our brothers makes us a people whose time has come and who struggles against the foreigner "gabacho" who exploits our riches and destroys our culture. With our heart in our hands and our hands in the soil, we declare the independence of our mestizo nation. We are a bronze people with a bronze culture. Before the world, before all of North America, before all our brothers in the bronze continent, we are a nation, we are a union of free pueblos, we are AZTLAN.

Denver Conference, March, 1969

EL PLAN ESPIRITUAL DE AZTLÁN

En el espíritu de una Raza que ha reconocido no solo su orgullosa herencia histórica, sino también la bruta invasión gringa de nuestros territorios, nosotros los Chicanos habitantes y civilizadores de la tierra norteña de AZTLÁN, de donde provinieron nuestros abuelos solo para regresar a sus raíses [*sic*] y consagrar la determinación de nuestro pueblo del sol, declaramos que *El Grito* de la sangre es nuestra fuerza, nuestra responsabilidad y nuestro inevitable destino. Somo libres y soberanos para señalar aquellas tareas por las cuales gritan justamente nuestra casa, nuestra tierra, el sudor de nuestra frente y nuestro corazón.

AZTLÁN pertenece a los que siembran la semilla, riegan los campos, y levantan la cosecha, y no al extranjero europeo. No reconocemos fronteras caprichosas en el Continente de Bronce.

El carnalismo nos une y el amor hacia nuestros hermanos nos hace un pueblo ascendiente que lucha contra el extranjero gabacho, que explota nuestras riquezas y destruye nuestra cultura. Con el corazón en la mano y con las manos en la tierra, declaramos el espíritu independiente de nuestra nación mestiza. Somos la Raza de Bronce con una cultura de bronce. Ante todo el mundo, ante Norte América, ante todos nuestros hermanos en el Continente de Bronce, somos una nación, somos una unión de pueblos libres, somos AZTLÁN.[14]

In this manifesto, we have a typical example of a political myth of origin and reclamation, that is, the reclamation of the land of ancestral origin based on blood ties: "We, the Chicano inhabitants and civilizers of the northern land of Aztlán, from whence came our forefathers, reclaiming the land of their birth and consecrating the determination of our people of the sun, declare that the call of our blood is our power, our responsibility, and our inevitable destiny."[15]

Reclamation is in the name of those whose hands nurture the land and gather its fruits: "Aztlán belongs to those that plant the seeds, water the fields, and gather the crops, and not to the foreign Europeans. We do not recognize capricious frontiers on the bronze continent."[16] The inheritors of the land are those whose time has come to give birth to themselves: the brothers who link hands with all the other brothers in the bronze continent.

Brotherhood unites us, and love for our brothers makes us a people whose time has come and who struggles against the foreigner "gabacho" who exploits our riches and destroys our culture. With our heart in our hands and our hands in the soil, we declare the independence of our mestizo nation. We are a bronze people with a bronze culture. Before the world, before all of North America, *before all our brothers* in the bronze continent, we are a nation, we are a union of free pueblos, we are AZTLÁN.[17] [emphasis mine]

Class and gender differences were articulated in the formulation of the "Plan," and the inheritors of the new Aztlán were to be the *campesinos* (the farmworkers) or those who worked the land, perhaps the working class, and clearly, those of a certain gender.

This final paragraph of the document needs to be read within the context of Richard Gilman's reference to sexism in language. "The nature of most languages," he reminds us, "tells more about the hierarchical structure of male-female relationships than all the physical horror stories that could be compiled. But that our language employs the words "man" and "mankind" [or in the case in point, "brother"] as terms for the whole human race [or an entire ethnic group] demonstrates that male dominance, the idea of masculine superiority, is perennial, institutional, and rooted at the deepest levels of our historical experience."[18] One can conclude, then, that conflict between Chicano cultural nationalism and Chicana feminism was already rooted in the very document that proclaimed Chicano self-determination.[19]

EXPRESSIONS OF CHICANA FEMINISM IN THE EARLY 1970S

Although Chicano nationalism was indeed grounded in a masculinist rhetoric, many women activists viewed the nationalist discourse as an emancipatory discourse for Chicanos as a people, and Chicanas played an active role in the efforts of the Chicano community to organize itself. Out of this participation came a growing consciousness of the Chicana's sexual as well as racial and ethnic oppression. Anna Nieto-Gómez's article "La Feminista" was an early attempt to describe this process and to give orientation to the numerous articles by women that began to emerge during the Chicano nationalist period.[20] In her many contributions to the discourse of Chicana feminism, Nieto-Gómez addressed her audience in a direct, commonsense style, insisting that the entire society must move forward together and that there needed to be a simultaneous struggle against racial and sexual oppression.

Raza power. Men, women and children. Everybody. When we say jobs, we mean jobs for all. But something I haven't mentioned is that a lot of the things that are going to change are those things that maybe we revere and sanction and call a part of our culture. If something in our culture that is advocating oppression is unable to be criticized, evaluated and changed, this is wrong.[21]

In general, the complaints of the emerging Chicana feminists of the early 1970s echoed those of women in other social and radical movements who found that even in the fight for social justice women remained second-class citizens. As Chicanas gained confidence in their dual struggle, they began to participate in Chicana caucuses and even in the international arena. In 1970, in Southern California, Francisca Flores founded the Comisión Femenil Mexicana, the first national Chicana organization. Two years later, at the Conferencia de Mujeres Por La Raza in Houston, Chicana issues were strongly debated and resolutions were passed regarding the position of the Chicana in the movement and in her community.[22] That same year, the

Chicana caucus at the first national convention of the La Raza Unida Party, held in San Jose, also passed a strong statement on the needs and concerns of Chicanas. Evey Chapa, elected as representative of the Texas State Commission of La Raza Unidad Party, claimed in an article on "Mujeres por La Raza Unida," that her party was the one political party to include in its Platform a section devoted to "la Mujer." Chapa noted that

Raza Unida Party declares the belief in the family structure as the basis of development, but also clearly states that it must be a total development of the family – men, women, and children. Raza Unida Party resolves in this section of the Platform, that equal rights includes mujeres [women], no matter what their status in life. In addition, Raza Unida Party resolves that the participation of women, to include the decision-making positions of Raza Unida Party, be actively continued through political education and recruitment of women.[23]

In 1973 Chicanas formed their own caucus at the convention of the National Women's Political Caucus (NWPC) in Houston and forced the NWPC to take a favorable stance on several Chicana issues. That same year Anna Nieto-Gómez founded *Encuentro Femenil* as a means of propagating Chicana feminist issues. (See "The Chicana Perspectives for Education.")[24] In 1975 Chicanas were active participants at the International Women's Year conference held in Mexico City.[25]

The efforts of these Chicana feminists of the early 1970s was received with mixed reactions by a community that was being reconstructed both by the Chicano cultural nationalists and the Chicana activists. As Chicana feminists, the women nonetheless adhered to the general goals of the Chicano movement even as they attempted to give greater equality to the women of their culture. Chicana feminist historian Cynthia Orozco identifies four sexist reactions that emerged out of the Chicano movement in regards to Chicana feminism: "1) 'El problema es el gabacho no el macho.' [The problem is white people, not the Chicano male.] 2) Feminism was Anglo, middle-class, and bourgeois. 3) Feminism was a diversion from the 'real' and 'basic' issues, that is, racism and class exploitation. 4) Feminism sought to destroy 'la familia,' supposedly the base of Mexican culture and the basis for resistance to domination."[26]

Orozco concludes that during the years of the Chicano movement, Chicana feminism was hampered because of a lack of ideological clarity on what gender meant. "At that time," she emphasizes, "Chicana activists did not recognize patriarchy as a system separate in origins and in everyday life and quite distinct from racism and capitalism. Chicanas struggled against the interconnectedness of this triple burden, but largely battled racism and capitalism on the ideological front."[27] Yet, Chicana feminists of the period – Anna Nieto-Gómez, Dorinda Moreno, Adelaida del Castillo, Sylvia Lizárraga, Rosaura Sánchez, Sylvia Gonzales, and Martha Cotera, among others – pointed out that, without their input, the Chicano movement would not attempt to end patriarchy, the system by which men dominate women.[28] They recognized that in order to transform human relations within Chicano culture, feminism was necessary as a theory, a method, and a practice.

For women writers, these conflicting ideologies posed a problem with regard to self-representation, for as long as a dichotomy existed within the Chicano movement with regard to the position of women in the culture, women writers would be called upon to make choices as to which images of women they would present in their work. Since few women writers were getting published in Chicano journals during that period, one must then pose a series of questions. Who were the writers whose work got into these journals? How did the traditional Mexican working-class, male perception of the family and of society in general affect the self-representation of these writers? In a period of social transformation, how did those writers present themselves as women and as Chicanas?

WOMEN WRITERS AND *EL GRITO*

To arrive at some answers to these questions, this study will now focus on the work of women writers as it was presented throughout the life span of *El Grito,* the first of the Chicano journals inspired by the Chicano movement. *El Grito* was published between 1968 and 1974 at the University of California, Berkeley. Its first issue carried an editorial statement that claimed that the review had been founded "to provide a forum for Mexican American self definition and expression on this and other issues of relevance to Mexican Americans in American society today." With its allusion to Miguel Hidalgo's *grito,* or battle cry, which proclaimed Mexico's War of Independence from Spain (1810), the title of the journal stressed contestation and renewal. The two main forces behind the review were its founder, Octavio Romano, a professor in the Department of Behavioral Science and the only ranking professor at Berkeley who self-identified as a Chicano, and its editor, Nick Vaca, a doctoral student in sociology at that same campus.[29]

In its initial years, *El Grito* was a multidisciplinary journal with a stronger interest in the social sciences and history than in literature. In 1971, however, Herminio Ríos, a doctoral student in the Department of Comparative Literature at Berkeley, joined the editorial board as literary editor. Two years later, in September 1973, at the beginning of its sixth year of publication, *El*

Grito devoted an entire issue to Chicana literature. This issue included the work of fifteen writers and was guest-edited by Estela Portillo, the best writer in that issue, and, of that cluster, the only one who can still be considered an active writer. Most of the other contributors were emerging student-writers whose poetry was identified as "excerpts from her writing." No doubt the majority of these contributors were students of Herminio Ríos.

Outside of that 1973 women's anthology, *El Grito* published the work of only five women writers: Clara Lefler, Diana Pérez, Diana de Anda, Leticia Rosales, and, again, Estela Portillo. During this period, a linguistic uniqueness became one of the distinguishing characteristics of Chicano literature. A literary piece might be written in English or in Spanish, or bilingually, with some smattering of *caló*, the unique language of the barrio.[30] When a work was situated in the present, often its theme was focused on a dichotomy: the warmth of life in the barrio contrasted with the alienating characteristics of Anglo society. Or thematically, a poem especially might remind readers of the grandeur of their Aztec past.

With the exception of Clara Lefler, a student in Alurista's Chicano poetry class at San Diego State University and the first woman writer to be published in *El Grito*, no other Chicano in the review aluded to Aztec civilization or made any reference to Aztlán.[31] A Mexican native, Lefler echoes Alurista's references to Aztec deities in well-structured bilingual poems.[32] She uses other themes of the literature of the "movimiento": the nobility of the farmworkers' relationship to the land and the closeness of the Chicano family.[33]

Of the women writers published in *El Grito*, Clara Lefler is the one who most reflects the ideology of Chicano literary nationalism both in its themes and style. One can conclude that although she was overly influenced by Alurista, his mentorship nonetheless gave her the distinction of being the first woman writer of the contemporary period to get her work published. The only woman writer in *El Grito* who addressed the issue of *campesino* life, one of the most important topics of the Chicano movement, was Isabel Flores. Compared to Lefler's image of the Chicano family, Flores's version is less romanticized. She describes the heat, dust, and hardship associated with the life of the farmworker and ends with a reminder that migrant work left little room for childhood daydreams. The reader is left with the impression that Lefler merely tapped into the thematic pool of Chicano cultural nationalism with its particular constructs for community-building. In contrast, Flores no doubt lived the life she portrays, and consequently refuses to romanticize poverty and hard labor.[34]

Lefler and Flores's poems emphasize nostalgic recollections on either a personal or a collective level. Lorenza Calvillo Schmidt, on the other hand, looks directly at the present. As an urban, university-educated, street-smart, and sensitive young woman, she is painfully aware of contemporary urban issues as she struggles against racism and sexism. Her poetry stands out for its vivid self-affirmation. In one poem, "califas," she presents herself as a *ruca,* the female equivalent of the "Pachuco." She is cool and free,

> *comiendo tacos de frijoles
> heading for the freeway
> california winds
> caressing teasing
> roadside trees,
>
> partially clad fruit trees
> like pregnant women
> full and about
> to burst into color
> presenting to the world
> the fruit of their many wombs.
>
> .   .   .   .
> califas music
>   los oldies but goodies
>   y yo waiting for a 7-up
>   yo y mi 7-up
>   heading for the freeway.[35]

*Lines in Spanish are translated in the notes.

In "Soy" ["I Am"], Calvillo Schmidt catalogues the various relationships that identify who she is. She lists the roles she plays and ends her poem with a syntactical subject/verb switch to emphasize self affirmation: "yo/I."

> soy hija de mis padres
> nieta de mis abuelos
> hermana de mis hermanos
> prima de mis primos
> amiga de mis amigos

> soy lorenza
>> lencha
>> lorraine
>> wa
>> panzas y
>> mija
>
> yo soy
> soy
> yo[36]

Calvillo Schmidt uses variations of her name in the second stanza to stress how the dimensions of her being are expanded and shifted according to the names by which others identify her. In short, she is who she is. She is herself.

In another poem, "Fellow Traveler," Calvillo Schmidt addresses her Chicana sisters. She connects with other women who painfully share the same enclosed space with her and, tapping into the liturgical rituals of communion and baptism, she takes the first step toward liberation. Even though she does not go beyond the first stage associated with consciousness-raising, she nonetheless acknowledges an oppression that is unique to women, an oppression based on gender identity. As opposed to the strong person who self-affirmed in the previous poem, in "Fellow Traveler" the poet feels small and vulnerable and, though she expresses solidarity with other women, at the end of this poem she emphasizes her lack of power by closing with an "i" in lower case.

> Fellow traveler
> Sister
>
> silent bodies in a room
> facing each other
> shrouded in a cloud of pain.
>
> Our pain
> permeating the room
> non-verbal articulation
> flowing from our eyes

Somewhere
>in the space between our two bodies
>our pain meets and merges
>a spiritual communion
>for we
>who are allowed nothing more.

Dear sister
>I was baptized today
>by the tears
>I shed for thee

>filled with your pain
>i cried
>at the recognition of my own.[37]

Calvillo Schmidt was one of two poets who, in *El Grito*, spoke with a gender-defined voice. The other poet, Adaljiza Sosa Riddell, who became one of the leading forces behind MALCS (Mujeres en Letras y Cambios Sociales/Women in Letters and Social Change) defined herself primarily in nationalistic terms rather than in feminist terms. Her three poems focus nostalgically on the past and on her loss of ethnic identity as a result of earlier choices she had made to assimilate into mainstream society. She contrasts her present life with that of a former lover who by selecting a different path from hers wound up in jail. Emphasizing the road-not-taken, she laments the loss of her possible other self as she attempts to reconnect to her culture. A sense of guilt for her gains – a common reaction evoked in many associated with the *movimiento* with its emphasis on solidarity with the oppressed – can be seen in her poems.

It is not surprising that in a period of social transition, a future Chicana feminist scholar should be more concerned with nationalistic issues treated from a personal angle than with feminist issues. Nor is this particular to the case of Chicano literature. Critic Edna Acosta-Belen has demonstrated how in the case of Puerto Rican writers a dichotomy also existed between feminist-oriented social changes and the defense of traditional patriarchal values associated with an agrarian world. In the case of Puerto Rican writers, Acosta-Belén notes, a sexist ideology considered women's liberation as something alien to the national cultural heritage.[38] This extreme dichotomy does not manifest itself in the poetry of Sosa Riddell; yet, her particular position demonstrates the conflict that existed in the early 1970s between a feminist position and a nationalist one. In fact, Sosa Riddell's poetry even more narrowly typifies a nationalist stage understood strictly in personal terms.

Como Duele

*Ese, *vato,* I saw you today
en Los y Sacra
en Santa Bárbara, Sanfra
and everywhere else.
You walked, Chicano chulo,
eagle on your jacket,
y "carnales y carnalas,"
y "Que Viva la Raza!"

But where were you when
I was looking for myself?
As I didn't know
Where the MAN and
**all his pendajadas
sent you,

> To Dartmouth, Los Angeles City College,
> Barber's School, La Pinta,
> Korea, Vietnam; too many of you
> returned wrapped como enchiladas
> in red, white, and blue.

A Chicano at Dartmouth?
I was at Berkeley, where,
there were too few of us
and even less of you.
I'm not even sure
that I really looked for you.
***I heard from many *rucos*
that you
would never make it.
You would hold me back;

From what we are today?
"Y QUE VIVA"
Finche, como duele ser Malinche.

*My name was changed, *por la ley.*
***Pobrecitos,* they believed in me,
That I was white enough
to stay forever,
that I would never find you again.

. . . .
***Finche, como duele ser Malinche.
Pero sabes, *ése,*
what keeps me from shattering
into a million fragments?
It's that sometimes,
you are muy gringo, too.[39]

In "Como Duele," a poem that betrays the ambiguous position of its author, Sosa Riddell moves from one theme to another in a rather confused fashion. In the first half of the poem, she utters the challenges that Chicanas had been voicing to each other throughout the *movimiento:* Why is my voice not a part of the discourse of Chicanismo? Where are we all going? And finally, what have we all become? Thus she blends in both her feminist concerns and her nationalist suspicion that exposure to the system of higher education produces cultural sellouts.

In the second part of the poem, beginning with "My name was changed por la ley," the poet shifts tone, theme, and voice to center on her personal relationship to the *movimiento* and, more specifically, on her own sense of a previous betrayal of her people when she left the barrio and a specific individual who followed a life course that was quite different from hers.

She ends the poem, not positively with a return to the feminist challenge, but rather negatively with an accusation that the Chicano brother at times is equally a sellout. More disturbing, the poet internalizes the negative point of view that the Mexican culture has traditionally held on "La Malinche": that she betrayed the Mexican race through her relationship to Hernán Cortés, the conqueror of the Aztecs. This view of Malinche has been persistently revised by Chicana writers and critics in the late 1970s and 1980s. Thus, by writing a poem in which the interpretation is dependent on seeing

Malinche-as-traitor, Sosa Riddell betrays her own ambiguity vis-à-vis the various conflicts between Chicano nationalism and Chicana feminism.

In fact, Sosa Riddell's other poems in *El Grito* also typify a nationalist position understood strictly in personal terms.

A UNO MÁS ANTES AHORA / TO SOMEONE FROM THE PAST

. . . . . .

Together we
should disappear
into the past,
where we belong.

. . . . . .

The Parting

. . . . . .

Today things are as they should be, but
You are now and forever lost to me.[40]

Like Sosa Riddell, most of the other women writers in *El Grito* did not convincingly foreshadow the work of Chicana writers of the mid- to late 1980s, such as Sandra Cisneros and Helena María Viramontes, who, in their fiction, question the position of women in their culture.[41] Yet, a few writers did go beyond expressions of nationalistic fervor. For example, Angélica Inda, one of the best poets published by *El Grito*, expresses solidarity with the Vietnamese people in a poem entitled "War Time." As did many other writers of color in the late 1960s and early 1970s, Inda identifies with the struggles of other Third World people and associates herself with a particular antiwar perspective.[42]

For the most part, however, the work of the young women writers published in *El Grito* did not demonstrate affiliation with any of the major struggles being waged on university campuses during the early 1970s: the anti-war demonstrations, the struggle to establish an Ethnic Studies Department or the emerging feminist movement, which in those years was rather problematic for women of color. Rather, the writers tended to accommodate to the male vision of women as passive both in public and private life. Diana López's poem, "La sociedad," reflects the dominant male ideology of the moment with regard to the role played by women in public life. In "La sociedad," there is a mild anti-war message as the men march off to participate in the public life of war. Yet, the poem gives the impression that the only role women play in public life is to be proud of their men, to mourn their loss, and eventually to go crazy with desperation.[43]

This passivity, resignation even, on the part of women is repeated over and over in the work written by students. Typical of the laments that issue forth in many of these poems is Leticia Rosales's anguish not only at having lost her lover but in recognition that he is now with someone else. Since she approaches her Nerudean poem in the guise of a poet, then acknowledges that she cannot write because of the mood she is in, Rosales gives in to her sense of loss and becomes overwhelmed in nonaction.[44]

One wonders at the self-representation of women as victims of a lover's desertion, and at the victim's inability to cope with her situation. Is this vision of women due to the youth of the poets, who obviously later disappeared from the literary scene? Did these young women write about loss and their reaction to it because young writers at an initial stage of their development sometimes write poetry when they feel sad or depressed? Or should we acknowledge that these young poets were actually opening paths for the literature of the late 1980s and early 1990s, when Chicana writers, having declared independence from the male themes of war, conquest, *carnalismo* (brotherhood) and other public rituals of domination, begin to explore the nature of relationships in their work?

I prefer to think that these young women neither acceded nor accommodated to the androcentric emphasis of Chicano cultural nationalism but instead attempted to voice their own personal contribution to Chicana/o emancipation. Following Carol Gilligan's evaluation of gendered psychological differences, I believe that these young women reflected their own psychological identity formation at a difficult period of personal formation. Their literary contributions to *El Grito* mirrored the tenuous position of Chicanas challenged by the class, gender, and ethnic issues of their day. Had they been able to survive as writers through one of the most tumultuous periods of contemporary history, in the 1990s they might even have been at the forefront of Chicana introspective poetry, such as that closely identified with Lucha Corpi, Barbara Brinson Curiel, and even with some aspects of Lorna Dee Cervantes's poetry.[45]

THE WORK OF ESTELA PORTILLO

The only woman writer associated with *El Grito* who continued as an active writer is Estela Portillo. Her early work clearly foreshadows the work of contemporary writers and is even a precursor of her own present work, for Portillo has rewritten almost all of her previously published work. In a telephone interview, she evaluated her own early work, and refreshingly admitted that, yes, twenty years ago, she was unique in the Chicano literary scene.

Portillo published five pieces in *El Grito* and, as has been noted, was the editor of the women's issue, which included two rather confusing works – an excerpt from a morality play and the only poem she ever wrote, "After Hierarchy," in which she synthesizes her six-hundred-page essay on Aldous Huxley's concept of utopia, the subject of her master's thesis.

"The Day of the Swallows" first appeared in a single issue of *El Grito,*[46] then was incorporated into the second edition (1972) of *El Espejo,* the first anthology of contemporary Chicano literature.[47] Two short stories that were later included in *Rain of Scorpions and Other Writings* (Berkeley: Tonatiuh-Quinto Sol, 1975) appeared in separate issues of the review: "The Apple Trees" (5:3 [spring 1972]) and "The Paris Gown" (6:4 [summer 1973]). As will be shown below, these two stories are out of sync with the thematics of Chicano literature of the early 1970s. But, I surmise that the later edition of *Rain of Scorpions* (Tempe: Bilingual Review Press/Editorial Bilingüe, 1993) has a most favorable reception, for her perspective of the moment is more in keeping with the feminist discourse found in women's literature in general and in the current work of Chicana writers, such as Ana Castillo and Sandra Cisneros or the poet Lorna Dee Cervantes.

Generally, though, Chicano critics have not been kind to Portillo. In his *Chicano Authors: Inquiry by Interview,* Juan Bruce-Novoa holds her up to ridicule.[48] And, as Luis Leal pointed out in his paper on "Hispanic/Chicano Literary Canon,"[49] Francisco Lomelí and Carl R. Shirley's *Dictionary of Literary Biography,* volume 82, dedicated to Chicano writers, has entries on fifty-one writers; of these, nine are women writers.[50] Estela Portillo is not among them though; at least for historical reasons, one could expect to find her in such a compilation of writers.

Interestingly, the 1993 edition of *Rain of Scorpions and Other Stories* includes seventy-four bibliographical entries of articles, theses, and dissertations that analyze Portillo's work; none, though, are substantial studies of any of her works. In addition to *Rain of Scorpions,* Portillo has published *The Day of the Swallows, Trini,* and *Sor Juana and Other Plays.* She completed a novel, *Mafiani,* and is working on a novelistic rewriting of "Sor Juana." Clearly, Estela Portillo is one of the most important writers of Chicano literature.

Of her work of twenty years ago, she says that it was the early attempts of a writer who had not yet mastered the art of writing. "I have learned," she told me, "that everything is in the rewrite. And when I first started to publish, I simply submitted my first draft to my publisher."[51] "The Apple Trees," her first story published in *El Grito*, was really the basis for a novel or at least a novelette, she feels. For this reason, she did not include it in *Rain of Scorpions*. "It had too many characters, the time span in the story was too long, and the psychological motivation for the main character's actions was too complex to be dealt with in a short story," she now understands.[52] "Paris Gown," however, ranks among her favorite stories, together with "The Burning," "Pay the Criers," and "If It Weren't for the Honeysuckle."

"Paris Gown" deals with a common theme in women's literature: a grandmother passing on to her granddaughter a lesson in living.[53] But, unlike that other classic example from Chicana literature – Lorna Dee Cervantes's portrayal of grandmother and granddaughter in the kitchen, watching the pudding thicken – the grandmother in "Paris Gown" is altogether out of the kitchen as she gives her granddaughter a lesson in sexual liberation. Theresa, the granddaughter, has gone to Paris to meet her expatriate grandmother, Clotilde, "sophisticated, chic and existentially fluent" (11). Clotilde explains to Theresa the reasons for her having left the home of her tyrannical father and tells the granddaughter, ". . . I know the instinct that respects all life, the instinct that understands equality, survives in all of us in spite of overwhelming, unfair tradition. Men know this instinct, too, although thousands of years of conditioning made them blind to the equality of all life. The violence of man against woman is a traditional blindness whose wall can be broken. . . . Men have attempted fairness since the beginning of time; it's just that sometimes they are overwhelmed . . . overwhelmed" (13).

About marriage in the traditional Mexican way, Clotilde says, "To marry meant to become the lonely mistress of a household where husbands took unfair freedoms, unfair only because the freedoms belonged to them and were unthinkable for women! Children were the recompense, but children should not be a recompense; they are human beings belonging to themselves, and we should not need recompense" (14). In order to prevent the marriage that Clotilde's tyrannical father (a foreshadowing of the father in Helena María Viramontes's "The Growing") intended for her and Don Ignacio, the wealthiest man in the area, Clotilde succeeds in her plot to liberate herself from becoming Don Ignacio's possession. But in doing so, she has to leave her people. Of this she says, ". . . of course there is a certain nostalgia . . . but no regrets. That's what I hope you will learn in your journeys . . . never to have regrets" (19). Her closing words of advice to Theresa are, "Yes, my child, I have known the depth of feeling in all its glorious aspects" (19).

How different this perspective was from the discourse of Chicano nationalism with regard to class and gender. Portillo writes about life in the Mexican American community but not necessarily about the working class (an aspect of canonization that Chicano critics have not yet fully addressed). No wonder that critics, upholding values of the nationalistic period, would have problems with Portillo's work.

Clotilde's advice to her granddaughter was something that the other young women of *El Grito* needed to hear. More than any other woman writer of this period, Estela Portillo expanded the perspective of Chicano literary nationalism. Her concern with themes dealing with sexuality, however, is still steeped in a moralistic mind-set. Juana, the lesbian protagonist of "The Day of the Swallows," commits suicide. Nina, the main character of "The Apple Trees," had been sold as a child by her grandmother to a group of four men who wound up gang raping her. The reader is led to understand that later, as an adult, Nina marries into the family of the brothers who committed the rape, and one by one she begins to eliminate them. But, she, too, cannot deal with the burden of revenge and winds up throwing herself down from a cliff near the apple orchards.

Portillo's feminism seems not to have been based on any theoretical framework. She seems to defy the theories on ideology of critics such as Terry Eagleton, who maintains that literary works are not mysteriously inspired or explicable simply in terms of their authors' psychology but are forms of perception; and as such they have a relation to the dominant way of seeing the world that is the social mentality or ideology of an age.[54] Rather, Portillo seems to fit more into Hélène Cixous's comparison, in "The Laugh of the Medusa," of women writers with birds and thieves. Cixous approvingly views the activities of all three as anarchistic: ". . . they fly the coop, take pleasure in jumbling the order of space, in disorienting it, in changing around the furniture, dislocating things and values, breaking them all up, emptying structures, and turning propriety upside down."[55]

In short, Estela Portillo's early work in *El Grito* was that of a groundbreaker. Of the nineteen writers published in this review, Portillo is the only one who can truly be identified as an *"abre-caminos,"* a pathfinder, although some of the other writers, particularly Lorenza Calvillo Schmidt, played a lesser role in paving the road for later writers. The new edition of

Rain of Scorpions and Other Stories will no doubt bring to Portillo her deserved credit as a writer. In the "Introduction" to the edition, Vernon Lattin and Patricia Hopkins note that the book presents to readers and literary critics "a gold mine of special material in that it revises five of the 1975 stories and therefore invites comparisons."[56]

With her play on Sor Juana Inés de la Cruz, *The Tenth Muse*, Portillo should receive the full credit she deserves as an American writer and for her historical role as an *abre-caminos* for Chicana writers. The only woman writer published in *El Grito* who survived the patriarchal challenges of Chicano literary nationalism, Estela Portillo expanded the self-image of Chicanos as a people. She opened the door for the more personalized fiction of the 1980s and early 1990s when Chicanas moved to the center of the text.

Portillo's works in *El Grito* demonstrate critic Marilyn Yalom's premise that women, in their writing as in their interpersonal relationships, are more likely than men to tap their emotions as they develop a feminist consciousness.[57] Portillo and other more recent Chicana writers have forged new images of female self-representation; by dealing with the intersection of class, gender, and race and/or ethnicity, Chicana writers have crossed the boundaries set by the cultural nationalists, thus broadening our understanding of the complexities of individual psychologies and their relationship to social structures. In the early 1970s, Estela Portillo's work in *El Grito* stood alone; today, she is joined by other Chicana writers such as Gloria Anzaldúa and Cherríe Moraga, whose feminist perspectives are informed by their own sharply defined Chicana indigenous feminism, one that has evolved out of their own circumstances.[58]

DIRECTIONS IN CHICANA LITERATURE

In 1981, with the publication of *This Bridge Called My Back: Writings by Radical Women of Color*,[59] Anzaldúa and Moraga opened up an alternative feminist discourse which, as Teresa de Lauretis notes, contributed to a "shift in feminist consciousness" in the United States.[60] "As editors," Moraga writes, "we sought out and believe we found, nonrhetorical, highly personal chronicles that present a political analysis in everyday terms."[61] The editors' goal was to have each contributor draw her feminism from the culture in which she grew, thereby eliminating the possibility of starting out with a theory, then providing examples to support the initiating theoretical position.

Anzaldúa, in what has become the most important contribution found in the book, advises women writers not to hesitate to erase the formulas taught by the university about what constitutes "good" and "universal" literature. She warns her sisters that "They convince us that we must cultivate art for art's sake. Bow down to the sacred bull, form. Put frames and metaframes around the writing. Achieve distance in order to win the coveted title 'literary writer' or 'professional writer.' Above all do not be simple, direct, nor immediate."[62]

Instead, Anzaldúa tells her audience that they must write about their personal experiences, and their personal vision.

The danger in writing is not fusing our personal experience and world view with the social reality we live, with our inner life, our history, our economics, and our vision. What validates us as human beings validates us as writers. What matters to us is the relationships that are important to us whether with our self or others. We must use what is important to us to get to the writing. *No topic is too trivial.* The danger is in being too universal and humanitarian and invoking the eternal to the sacrifice of the particular and the feminine and the specific historical moment.[63]

In a recent article on *This Bridge Called My Back,* Norma Alarcón reminds us that one of the contestations expressed by the editors of that book was expressly with hegemonic linguistic conventions. "If prevailing conventions of speaking/writing had been observed many a contributor would have been censored or silenced. . . . *Bridge* leads us to understand that the silence and silencing of people begins with the dominating enforcement of linguistic conventions, the resistance to relational dialogues as well as the disenablement of peoples by outlawing their forms of speech."[64]

The first journal of the Chicano movement, *El Grito,* had set out to create a space for Chicano writers by breaking the codes that had silenced them for so long. Once these codes were broken, Chicana/o writers as a group moved at a fast pace in their creative production. In the early 1970s Estela Portillo Trambley and, to a lesser extent, Lorenza Calvillo Schmidt and Adaljisa Sosa Riddell were some of the *abre-caminos* for Chicana writers. Portillo in particular added a new perspective on Chicano reality to the literature associated with the Chicano movement.

In the period between the late 1960s and the early 1980s, Chicana writers moved from a position of passivity and marginality to a politics of identity that directly confronted issues of race, class, ethnicity, and gender. Boistered in self-definition and self-affirmation by the sociopolitical goals of the Chicano movement, Chicana writers have also learned from the theoretical position of the feminist movement, and made their own contributions to the ever-evolving discourse on feminisms. As a consequence, their literature depicts a recognition of one's personal and cultural worth and provides new images in self-representation, nurtured by the preconceived roles that they have imagined for themselves and their communities. Clearly, the print community associated with *El Grito* initiated the pathway to the more recent relocation of the feminist self at the center of the text, a subject worthy of a separate study.

ACKNOWLEDGEMENTS

The following poems or excerpts are reprinted with permission of the copyright holders.

"Como Duele," "A Uno Más Antes Ahora," and "The Parting," by Adaljiza Sosa Riddell, from *El Grito* 7:1 (September 1973). "Como Duele" is included here as it appears in *Infinite Divisions,* ed. by Tey Diana Rebolledo and Eliana Rivero (Tucson: University of Arizona Press, 1993).

"Califas," "Soy," and "Fellow Traveller," by Lorenza Cavillo Schmidt, from *El Grito* 7:1 (September 1973).

Neither the publisher of *El Grito* nor the author of this article was able to locate Clara Lefler, Isabel Flores, Angelica Inda, and Diana López. Without their permission to quote from their poems, it has not been possible to include examples from their work.

NOTES

1. Juan Gómez Quiñones, *Chicano Politics: Reality and Promise, 1940–1990* (Albuquerque: University of New Mexico Press, 1990), 105.

2. Gómez Quiñones defines the term "Chicano" as follows: "To voice and express hopes and affirmations, and certainly the praxis of an overt identity, there came into use among the youth the term *Chicano,* a word used as a group referent since at least the turn of the twentieth century. Chicano denoted the person and group, while "Chicanismo" referred to a set of beliefs; in particular, a political practice. The emphasis of "Chicanismo" upon dignity, self-worth, pride, uniqueness, and a feeling of cultural rebirth made it attractive to many Mexicans in a way that cut across class, regional, and generational lines. In some way or other, most Mexicans had experienced, directly or indirectly, economic or social discrimination. These negative experiences increased the appeal of "Chicanismo"; it emphasized Mexican

cultural consciousness and heritage as well as pride in speaking [the] Spanish language and economic opportunity" (Gómez Quiñones, 104).

3. Ignacio M. Garca, *United We Win: The Rise and Fall of La Raza Unida Party* (Tucson: The University of Arizona, 1989), xiii.

4. Hans Kohn, "Nationalism," in the *International Encyclopedia of the Social Sciences* 11 (1968), 63.

5. Kohn, "Nationalism," 64.

6. José Carlos Mariátegui, *Seven Interpretative Essays on Peruvian Reality* (Austin: University of Texas Press, 1971), 183. For further elaboration, see Roberta Fernández, "Toward a Contextualization of José Carlos Mariátegui's Concept of Literary and Cultural Nationalism" (Ph.D. diss., University of California, Berkeley, 1990).

7. Benedict Anderson, *Imagined Communities: Reflections on the Origin and Spread of Nationalism* (London: Verso, 1983), 112.

8. Anderson, *Imagined Communities*, 30.

9. Timothy Brennan, "The National Longing for Form," in Homi K. Bhabha, *Nation and Narration* (London: Routledge, 1991), 49. For other studies of the role that the imagination plays in nation building, see Eric Hobsbawn, *The Invention of Tradition* (Cambridge: Cambridge University Press, 1983); and Doris Sommer, *Foundational Fictions: The National Romances of Latin America* (Berkeley: University of California Press, 1991).

10. Alurista, "Cultural Nationalism and Xicano Literature during the Decade of 1965–1975," in MELUS 8:2 (summer 1981): 25.

11. Alurista, "Cultural Nationalism," 23.

12. Alurista, "Cultural Nationalism," 24.

13. As one reads this declaration of cultural independence, Henry Tudor's definition of a political myth comes to mind: "A myth is an interpretation of what the myth-maker (rightly or wrongly) takes to be hard fact. It is a device men adopt in order to come to grips with reality; and we can tell that a given account is a myth, not by the amount of truth it contains, but by the fact that it is *believed* to be true, and above all, by the dramatic form into which it is cast. . . . What marks a myth as being political is its subject matter. . . . [P]olitical myths deal with politics. . . . A political myth is always the myth of a particular group. It has as its hero or protagonist, not an individual, but a tribe, a nation, a race, a class. . . . In the last analysis, it is always the group which acts as the protagonist in a political myth" (Henry Tudor, *Political Myth* [London: Macmillan, 1972]).

14. "El Plan Espiritual de Aztlán," in *Aztlán: Chicano Journal of the Social Sciences and the Arts*, Mexican American Cultural Center, UCLA, 1:1 (Spring 1970): iv–v. Alurista is identified as the author of "El Plan Espiritual de Aztlán" in *Aztlán: Essays*

on *the Chicano Homeland*, Rudolfo Anaya and Francisco Lomelí, eds. (Albuquerque: Academia/El Norte Publications, 1989), 11 and 247.

15. "El Plan Espiritual de Aztlán," iv–v.

16. "El Plan Espiritual de Aztlán," iv–v.

17. "El Plan Espiritual de Aztlán," iv–v.

18. Quoted in Alleen Pace Nilsen, "Linguistic Sexism as a Social Issue," in *Sexism and Language*, ed. Alleen Pace Nilsen et al. (Urbana: National Council of Teachers of English, 1977), 5.

19. This manifesto of Chicano cultural nationalism was not alone in expounding its particular point of view. Sociologist Mary Pardo's critique "A Selective Evaluation of El Plan de Santa Bárbara" (the manifesto that lay the theoretical framework for Chicano Studies programs in higher education) shows that in similar fashion to "El Plan Espiritual de Aztlán," this second document also did not make any reference to women or their issues. Pardo concluded that "El Plan de Santa Bárbara" was indeed a "man"-ifesto. See Mary Pardo, "A Selective Evaluation of El Plan de Santa Bárbara," *La Gente* (March/April 1984): 14–15.

20. Anna Nieto-Gómez, "La Femenista," in *Encuentro Femenil* 1:2 (1974), 34–47.

21. Anna Nieto-Gómez, "Chicana Feminism, Plática de Anna Nieto-Gómez," *Caracol* (January 1976): 5.

22. Judith Sweeney, "Chicana History: A Review of the Literature," in *Essays on la mujer*, Rosaura Sánchez and Rosa Martínez Cruz, eds. (Los Angeles: UCLA Chicano Studies Center Publications, 1977), 108.

23. Evey Chapa, "Mujeres por La Raza Unida," *Caracol* 1 (September 1974): 3. Because of its close ideological links with La Raza Unida Party, the San Antonio review *Caracol* included articles dealing with women's issues throughout its life span, 1974–1979. This is the subject of another article, included in the "Proceedings of the Regional Meeting of the American Literature Association," held in San Antonio in September 1993.

24. Anna Nieto-Gómez, "The Chicana Perspectives for Education," in *Encuentro Femenil* 1:1 (spring 1973): 34–61.

25. See Lupe Anguiano, "World Women's Challenge – A New Society Based on Justice and Peace," in *De Colores* 2:3: 32–40; and Amparo Aguilar, "Conferencia Internacional de Mujers, México, 1975," in *Caracol* (September 1975): 11, 16.

26. Cynthia Orozco, "Sexism in Chicano Studies and the Community," in *Chicana Voices: Intersection of Class, Race and Gender* (Austin: Center for Mexican American Studies, University of Texas, 1990), 12.

27. Orozco, "Sexism in Chicano Studies," 11.

28. See in chronological order: Anna Nieto-Gómez *Encuentro Femenil* 1:1 (1973)

and 1:2 (1974); Dorinda Moreno, *La mujer al pie de lucha* (Mexico: Espina del Norte Publications, 1973); Sylvia Gonzales, *The Chicana Perspective: A Design for Self-Awareness* (San Jose: Mexican American Graduate Studies, San Jose State University, 1974); Martha P. Cotera, *Diosa y Hembra: The History and Heritage of Chicanas in the U.S.* (Austin: Informations Systems Development, 1976); Rosaura Sánchez, *Essays on La Mujer* (Los Angeles: Chicano Studies Center Publications, University of California, 1978); Magdalena Mora and Adelaida del Castillo, eds., *Mexican Women in the U.S.: Struggles Past and Present* (Los Angeles: Chicano Studies Research Center Publications, 1980); and Adelaida del Castillo, *Between Borders: Essays on Mexicana/Chicana History* (Encino, Calif.: Floricanto Press, 1990).

29. As a publisher, Octavo Romano kept an active profile. In 1967, he published *El Espejo,* the first anthology of contemporary Chicano literature. *El Grito* (1968–1974) promoted the ideology of the Chicano Movement from an academic position. Then between 1975 and 1980, Romano published what he perceived to be an entirely new journal, *El Grito del Sol,* which appeared quarterly. Due to printing costs, in the last two years *El Grito del Sol* was kept alive but limited to half of the number of pages it had previously published. Between 1984 and 1988, the format was changed to that of a newsletter, which appeared under the title *El Grito del Sol Collection.* Between 1989 and 1991, the newsletter has appeared quarterly as *TQS News.* In 1992, *TQS News* was published bi-monthly (unpublished telephone interview with Olga Romano, December 4, 1992).

30. Two examples of *caló (vato* and *ruco)* can be found in the poem "Como Duele." The poem is translated in note 39. *Vato* and *ruco* both refer to a buddy or someone with whom one is closely associated.

The origins of *caló* are still unknown although linguists have found similarities between *caló* and the Spanish gypsy language. The lexicon of *caló* is not to be confused with other Chicano linguistic characteristics, such as code switching from English to Spanish, or with anglicisms, such as "watchar" = to watch or "parquear" = to park. "Nuestra circunstancia linguística [Our Linguistic Circumstance]," an article by Rosaura Sánchez on Chicano linguistic expression, appeared in *El Grito* 6:1 (fall 1972).

31. In the poem "Como Duele," Adaljiza Sosa Riddell does make reference to Malinche, traditionally viewed as the mother of the Mexican people. Malinche was Hernán Cortés's young Indian lover and his translator. Following the conquest of Mexico, she bore Cortés a child, Martín Cortés, who was taken away from her and sent to Spain to be educated. The patriarchal system in Mexico has popularly used the term "Malinche" and "malinchista" to refer to a traitor to Mexican culture. It is interesting to note that while Chicanas have been actively reinterpreting and vindicating the role that Malinche played in the Conquest of Mexico (1521), Sosa

Riddell, in this poem, has internalized the negative connotations associated with the term "Malinche": *"Pinche, como duele ser Malinche /* Shit, how it hurts to be a Malinche." In this verse, she uses the word to refer to her own past assimilation into the Anglo society. Chicano cultural nationalists popularly referred to Chicanas who associated romantically with Anglos as "Malinches"; yet, the term was not used reciprocally for men in similar relationships with white women. For a revisionist reading on Malinche, see Norma Alarcón, "Chicana Feminist Literature: A Revision through Malintzín/or Malintzín: Putting Flesh Back on the Object" [*sic*], in *This Bridge Called My Back: Writings of Radical Women of Color*, Cherríe Moraga and Gloria Anzaldúa, eds. (Watertown, Mass.: Persephone Press, 1981), 182–90. Subsequent editions have been published by Kitchen Table Press in Lathan, New York. See also Rachel Phillips, "Marina/Malinche: Masks and Shadows," in *Women in Hispanic Literature: Icons and Fallen Idols*, ed. Beth Miller (Berkeley: University of California Press, 1983), 97–114.

32. Clara B. Lefler, "La comunión de mis abuelos," *El Grito* 2:4 (summer 1969): 48.

33. Lefler, "La comunión," 47.

34. Isabel Flores, "I Remember," *El Grito* 7:1 (summer 1973): 80.

35. *eating bean tacos
Lorenza Calvillo Schmidt, "califas" in *El Grito* 7:1 (September 1973): 63.

36. I AM

I am a daughter to my parents
a granddaughter to my grandparents
a sister to my brothers
a cousin to my cousins
a friend to my friends

I am lorenza
lencha
lorraine

wa
tummy
my child
I am
I am
me

Lorenza Calvillo Schmidt, "Soy" in *El Grito* 7:1 (September 1973): 62.

37. Lorenza Calvillo Schmidt, "Fellow Traveler," in *El Grito* 7:1 (September 1973): 64.

38. Edna Acosta-Belén, "Ideology and Images of Women in Contemporary Puerto Rican Literature," in *The Puerto Rican Woman: Perspectives on Culture, History and Society,* ed. Edna Acosta-Belén (New York: Praeger, 1986, 2nd edition), 120–46.

39. *Hey, dude, I say you today
   in Los Angeles and Sacramento
   in Santa Barbara and San Francisco
   and everywhere else.
   You walked, Chicano cool,
   eagle on your jacket,
   and "Brothers and Sisters,"
   and "Que Viva la Raza!"

. . . .

Where the MAN and
**all his stupidities
sent you.

. . . .

***I heard from many home boys

. . . .

"AND QUE VIVA"
How it hurts to be Malinche.
Adaljiza Sosa Riddell, "Como Duele," *El Grito* 7:1 (September 1973): 76–78.

Through a mispagination in *El Grito* the first part of this poem was attributed to Lorenza Calvillo Schmidt. In Tey Diana Rebolledo and Eliana Rivero, eds., *Infinite Divisions* (Tucson: University of Arizona Press, 1993), 915, the last lines of the poem have been changed to
   It's that sometimes,
   you are el hijo de la Malinche, too.
   *. . . according to the law
   **Poor things . . .
   ***Shit, how it hurts to be a Malinche

40. Sosa Riddell, "A Uno Más Antes Ahora" and "The Parting," *El Grito* 7:1 (September 1973): 77–78.

41. See Sandra Cisneros, *The House on Mango Street* (Houston: Arte Público Press, 1984). Arte Público Press published a second and third printing of this book in 1985 and 1986. The first Vintage Contemporaries edition was published in New York in 1991.

See also Helena María Viramontes, *The Moths and Other Stories* (Houston: Arte Público Press, 1985).

42. Angelica Inda, "War Time," *El Grito* 7:1 (September 1973): 58.

43. Diana López, "La sociedad," *El Grito* 2:2 (winter 1970): 40–41.

44. Leticia Rosales, "Hoy," *El Grito* 7:3 (March–May 1974): 68. Rosales's two poems are the only contributions by women included in a poetry issue dedicated to the work of twelve poets. Her other poem, "Bar," also deals with the loss of her lover.

45. Lorna Dee Cervantes, *Emplumada* (Pittsburgh: University of Pittsburgh Press, 1981). See also *From the Cables of Genocide: Poems on Love and Hunger* (Houston: Arte Público Press, 1991); and Lucha Corpi, *Palabras de mediodía/Noon Words* (Berkeley: El Fuego de Aztlán Publications, 1980). See also *Variaciones sobre una tempestad/Variations on a Storm* (Berkeley: Third Woman Press, 1990); and Barbara Brinson Curiel, *Speak to Me from Dreams* (Berkeley: Third Woman Press, 1989).

46. Estela Portillo, "The Day of the Swallows," *El Grito* 4:3 (spring 1971): 4–47.

47. Estela Portillo, "The Day of the Swallows," in *El Espejo/The Mirror: Selected Chicano Literature*, Octavio Romano and Herminio Ríos, eds. (Berkeley: Quinto Sol Publications, 1972): 149–93.

48. Juan Bruce Novoa, *Inquiry by Interview* (Austin: University of Texas Press, 1980).

49. Luis Leal, "Hispanic/Chicano Literary Canon," paper delivered on November 19, 1992, at "A Joint Conference: Recovering the U.S. Hispanic Literary Heritage and Two Decades of *The Americas Review*" held at the University of Houston, November 19–21, 1991.

50. Francisco A. Lomelí and Carl R. Shirley, eds., *Dictionary of Literary Biography*, vol. 82 (on Chicano writers), (Detroit: Gale Research Inc., 1989).

51. Unpublished telephone interview with Estela Portillo, November 16, 1992.

52. Interview with Estela Portillo.

53. Estela Portillo, "The Paris Gown," in *El Grito* 7:4 (summer 1973): 11. For further elaboration on the grandmother theme, see Tey Diana Rebolledo, "Abuelitas: Mythology and Integration in Chicana Literature," in *Woman of Her Word: Hispanic Women Write*, ed. Evangelina Vigil (Houston: Arte Publico Press, 1983). Special issue of *Revista Chicano Riqueña*, 11:34 (1983): 148–58.

54. Terry Eagleton, *Marxism and Literary Criticism* (Berkeley: University of California Press, 1976).

55. Hélène Cixous, "The Laugh of the Medusa," in *New French Feminisms*, ed. Elaine Marks and Isabelle de Courtivron (New York: Schoken Books, 1981), 258.

56. Vernon E. Lattin and Patricia Hopkins, "Crafting Other Visions: Estela Portillo Trambley's New *Rain of Scorpions*," in Estela Portillo Trambley, *Rain of Scorpions and Other Stories* (Tempe: Bilingual Press/Editorial Bilingüe, 1993), 1. So as not to interrupt the thrust of this study, I have opted not to compare the two versions of "Paris Gown," which are quite different in presentation. Portillo has eliminated

some of the preaching aspects found in the first version, but I am not convinced that the second version is actually a stronger rendition, especially with regard to the ending of the story.

57. Marilyn Yalom, "Book Review Article: *Social Science and the Self: Personal Essays on an Art Form* by Susan Krieger, and *Getting Personal: Feminist Occasions and Other Autobiographical Acts* by Nancy K. Miller," in *Signs* (winter 1993): 457. Yalom attributes this perspective to the two authors whose work she reviews.

58. See Norma Alarcón, "The Theoretical Subject(s) of *This Bridge Called My Back* and Anglo-American Feminism" in *Criticism in the Borderlands: Studies in Chicano Literature, Culture and Ideology,* ed. Héctor Calderón and José David Saldívar (Durham: Duke University Press, 1991), 28–39. See also María González, "Toward a Feminist Identity: Contemporary Mexican American Women Novelists," (Ph.D. diss., Ohio State University, 1991).

59. Cherríe Moraga and Gloria Anzaldúa, eds., *This Bridge Called My Back.* See note 31.

60. Teresa de Lauretis, *Technologies of Gender* (Bloomington: Indiana University Press, 1987), 10.

61. Cherríe Moraga, "Introduction," *This Bridge Called My Back,* xxiv.

62. Gloria Anzaldúa, "Speaking in Tongues: A Letter to 3rd World Women Writers," *This Bridge Called My Back,* 167.

63. Anzaldúa, "Speaking in Tongues," 170.

64. Norma Alarcón, "The Theoretical Subject(s) of *This Bridge Called My Back,*" 36.

Frontiers 14:2 (1994): 23–50.

The Living Legacy of Chicana Performers

Preserving History through Oral Testimony

YOLANDA BROYLES-GONZÁLEZ

Virtually nothing is known about the participation of Chicanas in the two-hundred-year history of theater in what is today the southwestern United States.[1] Secular and of course ritual performance forms – storytelling, song, theater, healing practices, prayer, hymns, and blessings – have existed for the past two centuries and much longer, but the role of women in these performances has become a lost legacy. As in other realms of history, women in performance have been erased. And the erasures and distortions born of gender discrimination are intensified in the case of Chicanas, where race and class discrimination have made their reality appear triply insignificant to mainstream keepers of the historical record, in this case theater historians. Chicana performance for the most part belongs to working-class women's history; Chicana performers have typically come from the working class and have rarely left it.

In researching and reconstructing Chicana performance history, therefore, I have found my richest and almost exclusive source of information to be women performers themselves. It is through oral histories – hours and hours of audiotape interviews – that I have begun to develop an understanding of the life, work, and struggles of Chicana performers. I began interviewing Chicanas almost ten years ago. None of these women had ever delivered an oral history before; despite the prominence of oral history in the 1970s and 1980s, it has not been fully exploited in research on Chicanos. The oral history collection I have assembled constitutes the most extensive testimonial archive on Chicana performers in the United States.[2] What I offer below – a segment from one oral history with performer Diane Rodríguez, a veteran of El Teatro Campesino – is a brief fragment demonstrating only some of the research directions that this collection supports. Yet it illustrates the treasure house of insight that is oral history, and its relevance to Chicana performance history.

Oral histories, for instance, allow us to begin to reconstruct the role of women in the popular tradition of itinerant tent shows in the Southwest. Chicanas were often the dominant forces or leaders in those acting ensembles. Only one of these women has been even briefly documented: La Chata Noloesca, who headed an international touring company and reached the big time of Spanish-speaking New York vaudeville. There is much yet to be uncovered about such women. In my interviews with the legendary Chicana singer Lydia Mendoza, for example, I began to reconstruct the performance history of her mother, Leonor Zamarripa Mendoza, who headed the Mendoza family touring variety show. Leonor Zamarripa Mendoza functioned as artistic director, arranged the musical numbers, helped improvise the comic sketches, and for many years sewed all the costumes – not to mention the fact that she taught Lydia Mendoza how to play the guitar.

One of the collection's principal emphases is the history of El Teatro Campesino, founded in 1965 as a vehicle of Chicano political activism. In its beginnings El Teatro Campesino performed mainly *actos* (highly improvisational skits) that gave bold, humorous expression to the labor problems of farmworkers. In addition to regular performances in support of the United Farm Workers Union – often on the backs of flatbed trucks – the group also played college campuses and repeatedly toured Europe.

In the course of the 1970s El Teatro Campesino changed from a farmworkers' group to a predominantly student group. As the group's thematics broadened to include a variety of Chicano issues – educational, cultural, spiritual – Teatro Campesino plays became longer and more intricate. Yet the vivacious performance style established in the early years remained a constant throughout El Teatro Campesino's development, even after its dissociation from the union in 1967. It was a style deeply rooted in the oral performance tradition of Mexican popular theater and indigenous (Aztec and Mayan) wisdom. Among the popular traditional genres adopted by El Teatro Campesino were the seasonal sacred pageants performed in Chicano/Mexican communities for hundreds of years, the dramatized *corrido* (traditional narrative ballad), and the *mito* (myth). Plays using combinations of these forms were also performed, all of them based in the Theater of the Sphere performance school developed by the company.[3]

A great deal has been said and written about El Teatro Campesino, and much of that commentary has of course relied to some extent directly on the company's performances. But it has relied equally – particularly in the years immediately following El Teatro's founding, and again later – on statements made by Luis Valdez. One voice has represented the company to the outside world; one vision has become the official one. When I began writing about the Teatro from a woman's perspective, a whole new history emerged. I cannot here enumerate the contributions of the individual women of El Teatro Campesino; let me say simply that they were in the forefront of the company's creative achievement, as I have shown elsewhere.

In addition to reconstructing women's role in traditional Chicano/Mexicano performance arts, oral history can also provide a minority perspective on the contemporary white mainstream performance arts and on the barriers that women of color encounter in commercial theater. The experiences of Chicana/Mexicana women who have successfully mainstreamed and of those who have not have never been studied and documented. Diane Rodríguez, in the following oral history, gives us insight into that experience as well as other dimensions of her life as a performer.

Diane Rodríguez came to El Teatro Campesino in 1970 at the age of eighteen and became a full-time member in 1973 after completing her B.A. at the University of California at Santa Barbara. The segments of oral history presented here are from the year 1983, when she was positioned between a desire to continue within a dissolving Teatro Campesino ensemble and concomitant efforts to find work within the world of commercial theater. This document speaks to a range of experiences anchored in the dailiness of a performer's work, but it also highlights the 1980s trend from artistic collectivity to individuality, a trend furthered both by the withdrawal of public funding for alternative organizations and projects under Reaganomics and by the decrease in political militancy as compared to earlier decades. In 1983, after the Teatro Campesino playhouse in San Juan Bautista "went dark," most former ensemble members moved away to work elsewhere. Diane Rodríguez is active in theatrical work, has acted in various feature films, and can currently be seen performing in the comedy act "Latins Anonymous" out of Los Angeles. She has also done costume design for various shows and teaches acting classes for youth at Plaza de la Raza in Los Angeles.

BROYLES-GONZALEZ: Could you describe what you have done outside your work with El Teatro Campesino? What is a Chicana up against in the world of "commercial theater," or theater that is not alternative, as the Teatro Campesino used to be? Do you regard your experiences as representative?

RODRIGUEZ: The last performance I did here in San Juan Bautista was in

January of 1982, and I didn't perform again until this fall. So it was over a year and a half, almost two years, that I didn't perform here. I think my experiences are pretty representative. That's on my mind a lot right now: how and why I've only reached a certain point . . . in commercial theater. One of the reasons is because I've been doing Teatro Campesino, and that's been my choice, my career.

Barely two years ago I decided to venture out to see how I fared. And then there were many realizations. . . . But one of the big things was that I went to San Diego to the Old Globe Theatre, and there I saw my old ex-roommate. . . . We first met in 1972, and I loved her, I loved her. I've never loved a woman like that. I mean I wanted to talk forever. I wanted to sit up until five in the morning, all night, just talking about whatever. It was usually she that would say, "We should go to bed, we have a class in the morning." . . . That was in college, when I was in Santa Barbara. And she was an inspiration. . . . She was an actress. And I was an actress. Of course, she's Irish so she looks very "American," very classic. She can pass for Irish or Greek or Jewish; she's got a wonderful "universal" look. And of course I look very Latin, very Indian, very dark.

In school I got cast in roles that were mostly comical and were definitely not me, and very far and few between. My friend Chris and I were at the same level. I didn't look up to her; it was a fair exchange, and I always felt good about that. Well, ten years have passed. . . . In the meantime I've done the Teatro Campesino, and I've been very proud of what I've done and the way that the group has gone. I saw Chris and we were reunited after all this time. Here she was in the commercial theater and doing leads. And I was called by the Old Globe Theatre in San Diego to do an educational tour in which there are four people that they hire, and they have to fill certain slots. I filled the "woman" slot and the "ethnic" slot. (Actors Equity – the actors' union – demands that the theater fill certain slots.) I was then offered a small role in their year subscription season. I did that and made a lot of money and was able to do Shakespeare, though for a children's tour, and was able to work with some good people in a small ensemble piece, although I had a small role. And here was Chris a year older than I was, and I felt of equal talent. . . . But I had certainly another look, and it's far easier for her to get roles. It is, and that's the reality. There are no roles for us, for me, for any of the women that have worked with El Teatro Campesino; there are so few roles. And in the film industry, there are certain slots that you do fill but they are so menial that money-wise it may be good, but image-wise it's senseless. I've also been trying to make a dent in regional theaters. I have been writing notes, sending resumes, calling people, because I want to work. I don't want to just be cast because of a slot. I know that the Actor's Union is trying to have theaters hire what they call "ethnics" – I hate that term, but that's what we're all under: "ethnics." But I want them to hire me because of what I can give you in a show, not just to fill that slot.

I wrote to the casting director at the Old Globe Theatre in San Diego and I said, "David, let me know if there's anything this season. But *please,* I don't want to do educational tours. I've paid those dues for you. Two shows, two tours. And it's hard performing for kids, high school, junior high, or grammar school. It's the bottom of your list, you know. That show is the bottom, that tour is on the bottom scale of your whole theater operation." And I don't want that. I'd rather not do it, not work, even though it pays. It paid well for me because I did double jobs, I had to work double hard. And that's the other thing: I have to work harder than anybody. . . .

B: What theater houses have you auditioned for?

R: I've auditioned for the Berkeley Repertory Theater. ACT is closed; they have their own company and they don't audition outside. I've auditioned for the Berkeley Rep, and the San Jose Repertory Theater came to see me in the *Pastorela*. . . . Those were the two biggest ones besides ACT in the Bay area. And then I've worked at the Old Globe, which is the other big regional theater. The other one in California is the Mark Taper Forum, and the South Coast Rep, which is in Irvine. I've auditioned for the majority of them. . . . In case something doesn't happen here in San Juan Bautista, I've got to make a living somewhere. . . .

B: So you're prepared to work somewhere else, in Denver, for a few months?

R: Usually the engagement lasts eight weeks, two months . . . not too bad. It's like a three-week rehearsal, or a two-week rehearsal, and a six-week or five-week run. All that involves is memorizing your lines and talking. I mean, it doesn't involve creating a new piece, like we've always done in the Teatro. It's much different from what we've done in San Juan Bautista. . . .

You know, recently I got a Christmas card from a friend that I met through Peter Brook. Her name is Helen Mirren. She's a very big actress in London. . . . I seem to have these friends that are very white and are doing very well. And I always wonder if I had been white, where I would be. You always wonder. . . . I do, at least, in this business. Of course, everyone could say, . . . "If I had had a different mouth, I wonder where I would be?"

B: But it happens to too many Chicanas. There's a pattern. I mean, look at Socorro Valdez, for example. She runs on pure talent, but she has none of the looks that sell.

R: Her looks are not marketable outside El Teatro Campesino. She'll always get the role of maid or campesina. I'm real negative, you know, about that. I don't think it's changed in the last ten or fifteen years. I think it's real hard in commercial acting. I think people are racist; there's still a lot of racism. People have kind of just shifted and hid it under the table a little bit, but I think it's just as strong as it has ever been. I really do. People would be much more comfortable if you never mentioned what ethnicity you are, if you never made yourself a little different. . . . If you're going to start saying, "You know, I'm a Chicana. And hey, there's a saying in Spanish . . ." Well, I've been teased constantly about that. And teased in a patronizing way. They don't know how to deal with you. And when you're an actor, and you work in those big theaters, you work with people from Ohio, not just Californians. Ohio or Missouri or any other place. The only Mexicans they knew – and they call you Mexican – are the farmworkers that pass through. So for you to be acting with them is very foreign to them. . . . The chances for Chicanas in their profession are very limited. And the profession is based on looks; 99 percent of the job is based on looks. Certainly if you're what the standard beauty is, it's easier. If you have a really gorgeous look to you, then you've got it easier.

B: What startled me was the realization that this was also happening in the Luis Valdez production *Corridos;* . . . casting decisions were based primarily on good looks and secondarily on talent.

R: You know, you're right; it's unfortunate because the show could have been better with performers that are more developed. . . . Socorro was a real knockout in terms of the women; and she stood out *so much* because the others didn't reach out. It really needs to be evened out, because otherwise it's going to be a little off balance. It's great for her, but in terms of the whole ensemble, it's not going to quite work.

Socorro Valdez has lived through the experience of El Teatro Campesino. The other *Corridos* cast members have not. With the Teatro Campesino women . . . you're performing to be an actor, you're performing because there is a reason, there's something you want to communicate, there's something you want to show; it's important and you want audiences to see it. . . . It's urgent. It's in your very being, that urgency to be on stage. There is a general energy or movement that . . . all have . . . developed . . . through osmosis in working with each other and watching each other. There's a style that we all have when we act. I've trained so that I can act in another style: more subtly, and more realistic, more naturalistic. I've had to train outside Teatro Campesino for that; and I'm confident when I do that kind of acting as well. But the Teatro Campesino style is not what a lot of people can do, either: the movement, the body . . . making that spine come alive . . . so that it's moving the body, so that the bones and everything are moving with you. Working with the *calavera* [skeleton costume], that's an amazing thing, because when you're not being *calavera* you're still aware of every movement. And the sense of comedy. Not that every piece was funny, but Teatro was humorous. We have a sense of comedy and of what is funny, what is joyful, what is play, and that's important, too. . . .

B: It seems that the plays since *Fin del mundo* [1980] are very different from the ones before in terms of the sense of "urgency" you referred to, as well as in terms of acting style. You don't have the old Teatro Campesino ensemble acting in the productions since *Fin del mundo*. The temporary hired actors do not possess the sense of urgency you mentioned. El Teatro Campesino is no longer an ensemble but rather a production company. Where is it headed?

R: I think we're really searching. . . . This year there's *Corridos.* . . . We're going to do the *Virgen del Tepeyac* next year . . . but anything else we're not sure of. We don't know what kind of material to do; we don't know at this point what we're doing. We're all committed to make it work, but we don't know how it's going to work yet. Are we all going to come back as we did before? That is a real possibility. I could see us making a complete turn. We [the ensemble members] have been dispersed, but perhaps a year down the line we'll all be together again . . . myself, Luis Oropeza, Joe, Andres, Socorro, Olivia, Smiley, Roberta. . . .

We have to figure out how we're going to do new plays so that we develop people to write our material. Not our material, but material that other people can do as well, other pieces that can be performed not just in California but all over the country. . . . There's so little material that we can perform like that. The black population, you know, surpasses the Hispanic population in this country, and they do have more of a body of theatrical work. There are more plays that can be performed by black performers. We don't even have that . . . and when you take most of Luis Valdez's plays, or . . . something like *Fin del mundo* and script it, it doesn't make sense. Because the piece that we performed in 1980 was a visual piece, and to explain that in a script and to have another theater company do it – well, they just couldn't. So the search is to find someone who can write a play that can be produced by other people, a play that doesn't take a Teatro Campesino to do it.

B: Everywhere I go, Chicanos are saying, "We have no theater pieces." Certainly we don't have a strong theater tradition of that kind. We have a tremendously strong popular theater, a theater tradition based on improvisation and nonverbal theatrics – like everything that the Teatro Campesino was doing. The Teatro Campesino did not invent that style, but rather reproduced it because the members of the Teatro had grown up in that tradition. Almost every character of the Teatro had already existed in some form in Mexican popular theater. . . . It's an oral tradition, not a print culture or "script" tradition. If some Chicanos have now surrendered the tradition of improvisational theatrical creation, then they naturally will find themselves floundering without plays, because ready-made plays are a phenomenon of print culture. Even within the Teatro Campesino it wasn't until 1980, as far as I can tell, that something was scripted before you started working on it.

R: Yeah, '79, I guess. . . . Scenes were created and then more scenes were added, all based on our improvisations. We've basically not written things down. . . . Is it now that we're going to change that? That . . . for these next hundred years, or fifty years, we're going to try to change or evolve that tradition so that we can then have play scripts that can be produced by others? . . . It's not change, but evolve.

B: I find that things usually change of their own accord as one's economic class changes. Certain types of cultural practices thrive within certain kinds of material conditions, and not in others. Print culture has traditionally been an artistic domain of the bourgeoisie. I think that wanting now to have scripts after having made *Zoot Suit* is not accidental. A different class consciousness began to emerge. It's like changing classes. Suddenly individual playwriting is the thing and the oral performance tradition is no longer valued; it appears deficient to some.

R: It's a class thing. Definitely. And I know that I want a better standard of life. In some ways I'm satisfied with this standard of life. We don't always get a paycheck every month, but we manage. We don't have a family. . . . If we did we'd have to do better than what we do now. And grassroots means not having much money. . . . That's what it meant all the years we were doing it. . . . I personally don't want to live that way any more.

As I said the other day, if it came to us having a project and a life and death situation with the Teatro Campesino, I'd work for very little to keep it going. But I have to be assured that down the line I'd get something; that I would be taken care of. I think Olivia and I both agreed: If next January we're going to come work for menial because it's going to help improve our entire situation here with this company, then I'd do it. . . . But I've got to know that there's a payoff. For example, I might rehearse for free but then tour and then draw a salary. . . .

B: I don't know, maybe the old troupe could get into show business, but it doesn't seem like show business is into that kind of group act.

R: We just have to get the right steps here; we have to develop material here and then take it out. . . . We still have to sit down and decide: who's going to do it? When are we going to do it? What are we going to write about? Those questions take planning and time and we have not actually answered them. We've sat down many a time to talk; but money has dictated other things. We really need to sit down and reorganize. . . . The present organizational chart of the company was developed for a grant that we got from the NEA, the institutional advancement grant. Then because federal funding was cut, we probably only got half of the grant, if even that. And here we're left with this huge overbuilt organizational chart, which does not function for us, and we're still working under that chart.

B: A chart which includes groupings such as the "Core Group" and "The Board of Directors," etc.?

R: Yes, all that stuff. It was created in an effort to make us bigger, to support a larger company. And it's not working. We haven't figured out our financial base yet. . . . Those kinds of things need really to be looked at this next year before we can even plan a show or plan artistically what we're doing. We certainly had things that we wanted to do this year, but just because of . . . our finances, that's just not possible. We're going to have to say no to certain projects. . . . The NEA budget was cut and money was not allotted any more.

I have no sense of how it would all change. It's very complicated. We're all sort of sticking it through and seeing where it's going to all go. It's just a struggle. We had a meeting the other night, you know. We have come to a point of asking: Where are we going now? It was a good meeting, and we all felt very committed to staying and seeing it out: making sure that we followed our course, whatever it's going to be, that we be here to do it, and I'm committed to that. It's important, and we can't let it go. . . . And all of us have got to take an active part. . . . We have to be more active than we have ever been.

B: How can you be active here with El Teatro Campesino when you are having to look for work elsewhere? How can a company be sustained when people come and go as the occasion arises?

R: Well, when I was gone I wasn't as active as I am now. You just take time off and trust that everyone else will keep it going while you're gone and then come back and plug in when there's work for you. Luis Oropeza, for example, has been gone a long time. He comes to all our meetings, but he hasn't been here in ages. And he is definitely willing to come back. But he's got to come back for a solid thing.

B: How have you gone about trying to establish yourself as an actress outside El Teatro Campesino? Have you had to retrain into another style of acting?

R: I think you have to think of yourself as a business, as a product . . . so as to be prepared. You always have to think basic things. You have to think . . . is my hairdo versatile? Is my hair too short and too spiked? . . . If your mouth is too big and if your teeth are too big, you're only going to play certain roles. Hardcore reality; face the facts. . . . This is what you want to do in the outside commercial world. Here in San Juan Bautista with El Teatro Campesino, I've been able to do more than that because I'm not as stereotyped as I am out there.

You have to really be in check and realistic. Are you a lead? a character actress? . . . And then you have to market yourself that way. If you're weak in certain aspects, you've got to be realistic. If you're not too good in the subtle acting of the naturalistic style, if you've done Chicano teatro for ten years and you're real good at the movement and the big characters and the comedy, but you can't fine tune it, you've got to go into training of a different kind. Luis Oropeza, because he was in San Francisco, was instrumental in getting me familiar with what was happening there and I went to a wonderful acting school called the Jean Shelton Acting School. . . . I studied there for two years off and on. . . . And then I would take dance wherever I was. . . . In San Diego, I found a dance school, which is my favorite, and I went and studied there for nine months. . . . And whenever I could I took voice, mostly singing. . . . You have to go out and compete, and there's so many kids in this country that are going to professional acting training schools. . . . There are training programs in many universities. Approximately seven of them are real good. So you have to be up to par.

B: The training in the Teatro Campesino, if I understand it correctly, is not quite transferable to the outside world. There is that division in styles.

R: There is the division in styles. But there's always something special about you as a Teatro person. . . . People say that there's a presence. You're always noticed in a show, always. You know, it's just a special energy that comes from being with the Teatro. And to me, that's worth it all. . . .

B: What you mentioned about the self having to become a business and having to package yourself in a certain way, does that then stereotype you in your own eyes?

R: No, . . . I know I'm very versatile. I know I can play youth; you know, I have a sense of youth and I have a sense of age and I can play a lot in between. I can play very feminine or very masculine. I can play very high drama or I can play low farce. . . . As far as being stereotyped: They're going to stereotype you in commercial theater; you don't have to do anything. And I'm not saying that commercial theater is what you should go after, either. That's why I want the Teatro Campesino to work out for us. I would rather really not have to deal with the business. If I get called and I go in for a reading and I get cast, that's fine. But I'm not gonna be down in Los Angeles waiting around. I'm just not the type. I've got to be doing something here. And that's why this is here. . . . We haven't quite figured out all the angles yet, but I'm confident we will. And we'll come back again with something different and new and exciting.

B: Why don't the former ensemble members all get together and do something? Does it have to go through the office? Sometimes I get the impression that the new Teatro Campesino organization – the top-heavy administrative body – effectively stifles creativity and creative initiative.

R: But I don't think we want to do that. We've already done that. . . . I like having organization and I like being paid. And I like having my standard of living higher, and I like being in a professional theater company versus what is known as an alternative theater company. I like that more now at age thirty-two. Alternative theater companies – like the Teatro Campesino until now – don't pay as well, or pay anything, or pay very little, and you live collectively. Teatro de la Esperanza, for example: They pay and they share responsibilities and the whole thing. I'm not there. I don't want to do that any more. . . . But I still have not left behind the cause of why I'm doing theater. I just want it to be different. . . . I want it to be on another level.

B: What is the piece you have enjoyed the most with the Teatro? Is there anything that stands out particularly in that spectrum of experiences?

R: Roles? Very few; there have been very few roles in Teatro Campesino that I have thoroughly enjoyed. Because of what they're saying and who they are. I've played María Rasquachi, the wife in *La gran carpa de la familia Rasquachi*. . . . She was strong, but she wasn't my favorite. I just wouldn't want to be in her situation . . . a victim of economics and machismo. . . . The two roles that I have enjoyed the most have been Satanás [Satan] and La Muerte [Death]. They've been basically androgynous roles. I haven't enjoyed the women roles at all. . . . I've played the mother, the girl friend . . . the standards – the role of Chata in *Fin del mundo* (1980), who I never liked and I never did well because I couldn't like her. I couldn't. It's too bad, because I didn't think I could do justice to the role – if there was any justice to that role. . . . What has been fun is the opportunity to play that male/female role like Satanás . . . oh, it's wonderful, it's freedom. Like Satanás or La Muerte in *La Carpa*. It was a wonderful, wonderful piece. And the roles of Satanás or Muerte are wonderful because you can do everything. . . . As far as the women and as far as the repertory goes, that has been a strong point. The women have also managed to play men or males very well. The men played women's roles in the early days, but I don't think the men played women with credibility; I think it was more like a joke. The female roles have been weak. The nonfemale roles I've played have not been weak. These nonfemale roles – well, they stand out.

B: What is your sense nowadays of school kids; when you perform in schools, when you talk with them?

R: I go into some of the schools and they vaguely know what a Chicano is but they really don't. Even in colleges, they just don't know. They don't know what the Teatro Campesino was or what the sixties or seventies meant and what we were striving for. They don't know. They're very individually oriented, just toward themselves. There's not a social sense to them.

You know, I can't have just the responsibility to myself; I feel a sense of responsibility to more. When I was in San Diego, I spoke to classes at the university. And whenever I'm asked, I say that my generation had to keep pushing to get through. I try to let everyone know that there's something still to be gained and we haven't gotten it yet. We still have to fight a little bit more.

B: One of the things I have observed is the sense of loyalty that Teatro Campesino members to some extent share. Where do you stand emotionally with the Teatro? And is it hard to share that emotion? How has that evolved?

R: We are in love with the Teatro Campesino. . . . It's difficult to talk about El Teatro Campesino to outside people because it's like a marriage. You know, you just don't really talk about what's going on inside. . . . I also see everyone having more . . . belief in themselves and what they can do. We used to have a general, collective sense of what we could all do, but we were almost faceless. We were in the Teatro Campesino . . . and who knew who

Olivia was? Who knew who Diane was? And now it's better for us now, at our age, that we are known as who we are as individuals and what we each have to contribute. . . . Most of us are thirty or plus now. . . . It's good for us to be able to express how the struggle has been for us. . . . It's a joyful struggle; you do it because there's hope and there's progress and it's joyful; but it is a struggle. And to be under someone's wing or many people's wings, to be in the shadows for many years and to believe that one day you'll come out, you must have a strong sense of yourself. That's what's happened to a lot of us. When Felix and Lilly came, they were a very strong force in the company, very strong, very, very influential. When they left, a light happened, a shadow had been lifted, and all of us started blossoming, growing. That was in 1976. It was wonderful. It was as if this darkness had been lifted from us, and that started off an evolution that continued into 1979. Luis was in New York with *Zoot Suit* and Joe [José Delgado] was here, and there was not enough money to pay for us, to pay our salaries . . . and Joe said, "I've got to lay everyone off." We had never been laid off. So in 1979 there was another point where we had to begin fending for ourselves and trying to make a living on our own, while still staying close. It's been a struggle, and all of us are here because we want to be here and because we believe in it. And that makes me feel good – to look around at everybody and know that they all want to be here. It's not that someone is dictating to us that we must be here and must believe what they are saying. Rather, we all have our own input and we all want to be here because we can contribute.

B: It's interesting that there was what you call this faceless bunch of people. Yet there was one person [Luis Valdez] that was not faceless. His name was made known; and in this society that means that he would be viewed as the one with the monopoly on talent. He would come to be regarded as the great individual.

R: Nobody knows how to deal with a group. America is not equipped for that. They don't know how to deal with a group. They deal with individuals. They understand individuals; the business understands individuals. Show business is set up on individual status, you know. . . . I've been able to work so many years and not have to get another job because I've had a group. Of all my actor friends, I think I've been the one who has been the most employed throughout most of these last ten to twelve years, because I belong to a group. . . . I wish more people had an opportunity to belong to a group. Because you can really do a lot more. You can really be more of a theater artist, and not just one specialized thing. You can do many things and develop them all equally. . . . You know my friend Chris, she's a wonderful actress, but I also can do costume design. There was a need in El Teatro Campesino, and I had to fill it. That came from doing group work. Costume design was my other focus. I'm continually working on that and can make a living on it. . . . Of course I need training, I'm not by any means fully trained for it. But I can definitely get it together and do a show. . . . Eventually, I'm sure it will blossom into designing for other theater companies, but I'm not really going after that at this point. I have a knack for it, and an interest, and a love for it. . . . I like fitting people, and I like putting them into a costume. Costuming is a work dimension that allows me to be more of a total artist in the theater. Or more spherical. I've thoroughly appreciated that opportunity. . . . I started doing it in '75. A long time ago. . . .

Another [thing] I developed is that *si se puede* attitude that I remember chanting forever when we were on marches. It sticks with me. Isn't that amazing? When those things are said, . . . generally . . . people don't take them individually to heart. But here it sunk in. . . . I thought, "O wow, I can do this." And acting – if you're not a natural, there's so much to learn. You can be talented and not be a natural. A natural is someone who just doesn't need training. They don't need voice training, for example; they can just do it. They've got all the instrument ready when they're young. But for someone like me: you have talent, but you just have to carve it out. It's all there, it's a diamond, but it's got to be polished. . . . In order to have been a part of this company, you have to have incredible strength. You also have to have your ego very much in check, because no one lets you get away with anything that you don't deserve to get away with. Do you know what I mean? You'll be teased if it's real phony. Almost like a family. They help mold you. Those of us who have survived all the changes have a strength.

B: Why do you do theater?

R: Just in terms of my own essence and spirit, I do theater because I'm crazy and need an outlet. . . . It helps me be crazy and live calmly. . . . For me personally, it's . . . the way I can live and expend my energy, because I have tons of it and don't know what to do with it normally. That's one reason. The other is because what we do here is important. I'm concerned about all my other Chicano brothers and sisters. I want to do material that relates to us. I want to do material that we can share, that's not just solely for a Chicano audience: material that can bring others in and can give a view of how we look, how we think, how we feel. And sometimes the pieces don't totally accomplish that. But they accomplish one part of it, and that's good. We have to strive to make it better in the next piece. To express values, new values, express ways of living here, express what it is to be an American of my color, in my color . . . that's why I like doing it. It's expressive.

NOTES

1. Among the pioneers in the reconstruction of Chicana performance history are Tomás Ybarra-Frausto, "La Chata Noloesca," and Yvonne Yarbro-Bejarano, "Teatro poesía by Chicanas in the Bay Area: Tongues of Fire," both published in *Mexican American Theatre: Then and Now,* ed. Nicolas Kanellos (*Revista Chicano-Riqueña* 11:1 [1983]). Also pertinent are other incisive essays by Yarbro-Bejarano, such as "The Role of Women in Chicano Theater-Organizations," *Revista Literaria de El Tecolote* 2:3 (1981): 4, and "The Image of the Chicana in Teatro," in *Gathering Ground: New Writing and Art by Northwest Women of Color,* ed. Jo Cochran, J. T. Stewart, and Mayumi Tsutakawa (Seattle, Wash.: Seal Press, 1984), 90–96. On Chicana performers of El Teatro Campesino, see Yolanda Broyles-González, "Women in El Teatro Campesino: '¿Apoco estaba molacha La Virgen de Guadalupe?'" in *Chicana Voices: Intersections of Class, Race, and Gender,* ed. Teresa Cordova et al. (Austin: Center for Mexican American Studies, University of Texas, 1986), 162–87, and "Toward a Re-Vision of Chicano Theatre History: The Women of El Teatro Campesino," in *Making a Spectacle: Feminist Essays on Contemporary Women's Theatre,* ed. Lynda Hart (Ann Arbor: University of Michigan Press, 1989), 209–38. On the construction of the female subject in Chicano theater, see Yvonne Yarbro-Bejarano, "The Female Subject in Chicano Theatre: Sexuality, 'Race,' and Class," *Theatre Journal* (December 1986): 389–407.

2. I have interviewed various women numerous times during the past ten years. All my interviews are an ongoing process. The ongoing interview allows documentation of different stages of development in a performer's life. Such interviews are more complete and accurate than something recollected from the distant past, and they go into much greater depth than one-shot interviews – not to mention that a person being interviewed takes a one-shot interview and interviewer far less seriously than an interviewer who has established a long-term relationship with the interviewee. The oral history segment presented here was collected December 28, 1983, in San Juan Bautista, California, at the home of Diane Rodríguez.

3. One chapter of my book *El Teatro Campesino: Theater in the Chicano Movement* (Austin: University of Texas Press, 1994) treats the Theater of the Sphere performance philosophy.

Frontiers 11:1 (1990): 46–52.

The Faith of Activists

Barrios, Cities, and the Chicana Feminist Response

MARGARITA COTA-CÁRDENAS

Several years ago, I published a paper entitled "The Chicana in the City as Seen in Her Literature."[1] There were two principal conclusions in that study that would be relevant in studying Chicana cultural identity: first, that the Chicana as seen in her literature appeared to perceive herself as a marginal figure in her world; and second, that even the briefest examination of literature about or by contemporary Chicanas in an urban setting revealed a growing self-awareness on the part of Chicanas. My earlier work focused especially on the Chicana's ironic perception of herself and her reality or space within the macho (male-dominated) Chicano culture. The present study seeks to confirm that there continues to be an expression of cultural identity to be found in specific Chicana literary texts dealing with the barrio and the city.

Elizabeth Ordóñez addresses the issue of cultural identity from the perspective of discourse analysis. In her study "The Concept of Cultural Identity in Chicana Poetry," she says, for example: "The woman writer – and the Chicana is no exception – in this way forges what has been named a 'double-voiced discourse'; she makes the invisible visible, gives voice to the muted."[2]

This discourse, in dealing with the barrio or city, repeatedly bespeaks an "I love you/I hate you" paradigm, which suggests the Chicana is often in a problematic, conflictive, ironic relationship to her space. Charles Glicksberg gives the following definition, which I still find most appropriate in discussing irony in Chicana literature: "The heart of irony is to be found in a contradiction which cannot be resolved and which cannot be endured and yet which is somehow lived."[3] It would appear that this ironic predicament is inherent in being a Chicana feminist and a writer, if we study selected works of several contemporary Chicana poets. The texts selected will reflect this ironic predicament (I love you/I hate you) and will provide examples of how humor (or irony) enables the Chicana to endure, as she perceives her existential dilemma. Her texts may represent individual, challenging, revolutionary acts, in which the very act of writing can be an act of faith itself.

Certainly, the barrio and the city have given birth to very distinct cultural/individual images in contemporary Chicana writing since the 1970s. Most Chicana poets expressed the same feelings of alienation and bewilderment as their male counterparts writing in the early and mid-1970s, when they considered the historical dispossession of lands, language, and culture. The following are some of many examples to be found of barrio/urban images in poetry alone.

Angela de Hoyos (San Antonio), one of the few Chicana writers publishing at that time (1970s), clearly is saddened by the lack of brotherhood and cultural understanding she experiences in the Southwest. Her classic poem "Hermano" ("Brother") is ironic, yet poignantly telling, as she describes San Antonio:

> "Remember the Alamo"
> (. . . and my Spanish ancestors
> who had the sense to build it.)
>
> I was born too late
> in a land
> that no longer belongs to me
> (so it says, right here in this Texas History).
>
> Ay, my San Antonio de Bexar
> city-queen of the border
> the long hand of greed
> was destined to seize you!
> . . . Did no one hear you when you fell,
> when those crude men ransacked you?
> Blind-folded they led you
> to a marriage of means
> while your Spanish blood
> smouldered within you!

Your sky no longer belongs to me,
Nor the Alamo, nor the Villita,
nor the river that by caprice
runs through your very center.
Nor the missions
– jewels of your past –
      San Juan de Capistrano
      Concepción
      San José
      La Espada
They belong to a pilgrim
who arrived here only yesterday
whose racist tongue says to me: I hate
Meskins. You're a Meskin. Why don't you
go back to where you came from?
Yes, amigo . . . ! Why don't I? Why don't I
resurrect the Pinta, the Niña, and the Santa María
– and you can scare up your little "Flor de mayo" –
so we can all sail back
to where we came from: the motherland womb.

I was born too late
or perhaps I was born too soon:
It is not yet my time;
this is not yet my home.

I must wait for the conquering barbarian
to learn the Spanish word for love:
hermano.[4]

In another poem, De Hoyos speaks of the alien environment encountered by Chicanos coming to the big city expecting improvement in their lives. The speaker in De Hoyos's poem "La Gran Ciudad" ("The Big City") is grossly disillusioned, finding instead a counterfeit Garden of Eden:

No one told me.
So how was I to know
that in the paradise
     of crisp white cities
snakes still walk upright?[5]

In the 1970s, the images of the city are often stark and surreal, such as in "North Avenue/1600 North" by Sandra Cisneros (Chicago). Cisneros describes a shocking reality in often-jarring images of downtrodden, blood-spittled streets. Nonetheless, the speaker admits to an unusual attraction and attachment to the city, describing it in erotic terms as a prostitute, an old lover that refuses to be forgotten.[6]

Rina García Rocha's poem, "The Truth in My Eyes," is also a jolting vision, where the speaker describes a walk down Twenty-sixth Street in the Barrio Latino (Chicago) in naturalistic terms, in stark description of rotting rats, ridden with maggots, lying on the open ground.[7]

On the other hand, "Guadalajara, U.S.A." by Tina Alvarez (Chicago/L.A.) speaks of an utterly conflictive world, voicing the young Chicana's identity crisis. The speaker has been brought from Mexico to live, first in Chicago and then Los Angeles. The father moves the family from Chicago to Los Angeles because he is unable to find work. The family traveled back and forth across the border every year, reinforcing her double heritage.[8]

What the speaker remembers are the conflicting attitudes of her new life; when she is in California, she is reminded to speak Spanish, not fifty-fifty; when she is in Mexico visiting relatives, she is told to show off her English, but never to forget she is Mexican. She feels she is an outsider, even in her native Mexico: "And going *de turista* in the summer . . ."[9]

This poem directly addresses the schizoid effect of acculturation for many Chicanas, and it speaks not only of a crisis of cultural identity, but also a crisis in the perception of self.[10] In the city, the speaker encounters racist nuns, but she contends with them even through high school. Her questioning of cultural values is renewed, however, when she wants to go to the university but her parents don't want her to go because she is a woman; the speaker wins out, and goes with at least her mother's blessing. The final lines of the poem recall the conflictive title itself: She lives a Mexican yet American existence, "Guadalajara, U.S.A."

And then, in "Beneath the Shadow of the Freeway" by Lorna Dee Cervantes (San Jose) we see the literal encroachment of the city upon the barrio, with freeways overshadowing yards as well as lives:

Across the street – the freeway,
blind worm, wrapping the valley up
from Los Altos to *Sal Si Puedes*.
I watched it from my porch
Unwinding. Every day at dusk

as Grandma watered geraniums
the shadow of the freeway lengthened.[11]

In this often-quoted poem, Cervantes describes the speaker's all-woman family, of mother, grandmother, and daughter, of which the daughter must become the "Buffer and Agent" between her barrio family and the outside world. Cervantes's speaker cannot dream of being Queen or Princess, as the two older women might, but turns instead to books and becomes the practical, determined "Woman of the Family" who trusts only her own resources.

Other early urban Chicana feminists who also offered telling poems about the city or barrio were Silvia González ("Chicana Evolution"),[12] Xelina ("Urban Life"),[13] and Inés Hernández Tovar (who wrote about the *Pachucas* that she scorned in her youth, in "Para Teresa").[14] These poems are often ironic or jarring, often with a poignant sense of remembering.

The occasional poem shows humor in dealing with barrio themes, such as places fondly remembered, as in "*El Burrito Cafe*" by Bernice Zamora (Colorado):

> Through the swinging doors
> That lead to your kitchen,
> I watch you taste
> The *menudo* you
> Prepare for drunks.
> Somehow, Augustina
> Godinez, the title
> *Chef* does not suit
> Your position.[15]

The images in "the *menudo* you / prepare for drunks" (*menudo* soup is a Chicano antidote or cure for hangovers), contrast sharply with the more formal image of a "Chef"; the result is a humorous clash of bicultural references.

In her poem "Metaphor and Reality," Zamora ironically contrasts rural and urban Chicano realities with the "scheme of things" of those who still have dreams of the majority culture's way of life. The American Dream is questioned: Is it metaphor or reality? Zamora writes:

> Working in canneries or
> picking beets is the

metaphor of being,
of being as it has been
in the scheme of things.

As it is, the dream remains
for you who sit easily with
Grendel and Godzilla
as they pick their teeth
with your children's bones
for you who sit easily with[16]

In the 1980s, we find Lorna Dee Cervantes's poem "Cannery Town in August," where women work in a surreal, dehumanizing environment:

All night it humps the air.
Speechless, the steam rises
from the cannery columns. I hear
the night bird rave about work
or lunch, or sing the swing shift
home. I listen, while bodyless
uniforms and spinach specked shoes
drift in monochrome down the dark
moon-possessed streets. Women
who smell of whiskey and tomatoes,
peach fuzz reddening their lips and eyes –
I imagine them not speaking, dumbed
by the can's clamor and drop
to the trucks that wait, grunting
in their headlights below.
They spotlight those who walk
like a dream, with no one
waiting in the shadows
to palm them back to living.[17]

The speaker in the following poem observes her marginalization even in a tourist location, such as the shore in Corpus Christi, Texas. The speaker identifies with the seabirds, who beg for food from the tourists' hands, much as the alienated, dispossessed Chicana (Chicano) must do in other cities, in a metaphorical sense. Nevertheless, there is a note of defiance in the last lines:

From Where We Sit: Corpus Christi

We watch seabirds flock the tour boat.
They feed from the tourist hand.

We who have learned the language
they speak as they beg

understand what they really say
as they lower and bite.[18]

Again, the city is a place where one can experience desolation and hunger. In "An Interpretation of Dinner by the Uninvited Guest," the speaker watches in secret from her second-floor apartment, as a family eats supper each day at six. She sees hands passing, setting, unfolding napkins, beginning the feast:

I am alone and hungry
and I watch this every night
from my voting booth room.
If I turned on the light
they would see me. But I never.
The hands would reattach themselves
and who knows what country
their bodies dwell in.[19]

Yet in "Freeway 280," Cervantes's speaker expresses hope that she may find herself in the abandoned gardens and orchards still found beside freeway fences:

Las casitas near the gray cannery,
nestled among wild *abrazos* of climbing roses
and man-high geraniums
are gone now. The freeway conceals it
all beneath a raised scar.

The barrio itself has disappeared because of the freeway, and she feels the loss, yet as she scrambles over a fence to a wild garden she says:

Maybe it's here
en los campos extraños de esta ciudad
where I'll find it, that part of me
mown under
like a corpse
or a loose seed.[20]

In the 1980s, Pat Mora's collection, *Chants,* also presents various urban images of acculturation, such as those in "Legal Alien" and "Elena." Mora (El Paso) writes of the alienating, conflictive condition inherent in being Chicana:

LEGAL ALIEN

Bilingual. Bi-cultural,
able to slip from "How's life?"
to *"Me'stan volviendo loca,"*
able to sit in a paneled office
drafting memos in smooth English,
able to order in fluent Spanish
at a Mexican restaurant.
American but hyphenated,
viewed by Anglos as perhaps exotic,
perhaps inferior, definitely different,
viewed by Mexicans as alien,
(their eyes say, "You may speak
Spanish but you're not like me" –
an American to Mexicans
a Mexican to Americans
a handy token
sliding back and forth
between the fringes of both worlds
by smiling
by masking the discomfort
of being pre-judged
Bi-laterally.[21]

Mora's urban lyric speaker copes by masking her discomfort with smiles, as she perceives herself as clearly a marginalized figure, neither Mexican nor

American, a hyphenated, truncated entity, facing prejudice from both cultures and never completely comfortable in either.

ELENA

My Spanish isn't enough.
I remember how I'd smile
listening to my little ones,
understanding every word they'd say
their jokes, their songs, their plots.
   Vamos a pedirle dulces a mamá. Vamos.
But that was in Mexico.
Now my children go to American high schools.
They speak English. At night they sit around
the kitchen table, laugh with one another.
I stand by the stove and feel dumb, alone.
I bought a book to learn English.
My husband frowned, drank more beer.
My oldest said, "Mamá, he doesn't want you
to be smarter than he is." I'm forty,
embarrassed at mispronouncing words,
embarrassed at the laughter of my children,
the grocer, the mailman. Sometimes I take
my English book and lock myself in the bathroom,
say the thick words softly,
for if I stop trying, I will be deaf
when my children need my help.[22]

  The speaker, Elena, in addition to feeling uneasy in a new culture where she cannot yet master the language, also experiences estrangement from her children and husband. The typical cultural image of the Mexican macho is delineated in this poem; as Elena learns more from books, including English, the husband feels threatened. This critical view of the structure of a traditional Mexican or Chicano family is frequent in Chicana feminist writing, especially since the mid-1970s.

  The borderlands cities of El Paso/Juárez are the backdrop for Mora's poem "Illegal Alien." Here, the Mexican domestic working in the speaker's home hastens introspection about self and cultural identity; the speaker feels impotent before the other woman's tale of physical abuse by her husband:

Socorro, you free me
to sit in my yellow kitchen
waiting for a poem
while you scrub and iron.

Today you stand before me
holding cleanser and sponge
and say you can't sleep at night.
"My husband's fury is a fire.
His fist can burn.
We don't fight with words
on that side of the Rio Grande."
. . . .
It is not cool words you need
but soothing hands.
My plastic band-aid doesn't fit
your hurt.
I am the alien here.[23]

In *The Second Street Poems* (1983), named after Second Street, which divides East and West San Jose, California, Beverly Silva addresses the issues of being Chicana in an urban barrio environment. The tone of her collection is often wistful, with ironic overtones, and clearly illustrates a fascination and preoccupation with her urban/barrio space. In her title poem "Second Street," Silva says:

with a fierce passion i have claimed you.
With a fierce pride i have named a book of poems for you.
As i stand here
balanced between East and West San José
weighing my life
you hold me.
. . . .
    Like a new lover
deftly withholding pleasure one moment
opening new dimensions of himself the next
you hold me.
    i walk the length of your pavement
writing poems.[24]

In her longer poem, "Pounding Down First Street," Silva measures her existence in terms of her relationship to her barrio/neighborhood and the city. This relationship varies and is filtered through her own struggles as student and divorced mother:

> First St.
> incredible dividing line
> between East and West
> the Los Gatos hills of my youth
> green as that young girl running off
> to be married.
> the East foothills
> bare as those struggling years
> as student and mother
> divorced and alone.[25]

Silva, in this same poem, describes how she loathes departing "this native land" even though her own daily routines impose limitations. There is a wistfulness in this poem, a desire to more fully enjoy the landscape or milieu:

> clenching the Arizona ticket
> avoiding a departure
> clinging to this native land
> with the same fierceness
> that carried me
> to a college degree.
> & for what?
> i haven't seen San Francisco
> in two years
> it's been five
> since i lay on the beach
> at Santa Cruz
> the sights of San José
> lie between the University
> and the welfare office . . .[26]

Silva further goes on to describe an evolution of self: "from this ghost of a woman / pounding First St. / a form was emerging / feeling coming from another language." Teaching others, hearing and speaking Spanish, she appears to flower. Finally, this positive evolution keeps her, for the moment, at home:

> i return the Arizona ticket
> buy a bicycle
> make a path to and from the school
> the tracks daily deepening
> pulling me ever tighter into this soil
> where i was born.
> & San José –
> wife, mother, student, woman alone,
> poet, teacher, lover,
> all i am and all i know
> is rooted in your streets.[27]

In the preceding poem, Silva appears to view her barrio and the city through soft-tinted lenses, her relationship tinged by this affinity she bears for her space. In the following poem, however, her view is more conflictive, although the barrio still is a source of inspiration for her:

I DREAM OF MEXICAN MURALS AND A COMMUNITY AFFAIR

> It's not an easy place to live
> on Second St.
> i moved into the manager's apartment
> after a knifing.
> i moved out of that apartment
> the complex, & all of Second St.
> after an assault
> & rental dispute hearings.
> the two and a half years between these events
> i dreamed of mexican murals & a community affair.[28]

In this poem, the speaker goes on to describe the day-to-day activities she observes from a window. She fills journal pages with her observations:

> those first days of nothingness & pain
> were spent at an open window

watching over an incredible under the freeway parking lot
owned by a next door dance hall
but used by everyone.
people passing through town slept in their cars
truckers parked for a few days
police had their check points here
lovers met on lunch hours or after work
others came in just to drink beer
prostitutes made their connections
old & young men stopped to piss beside the concrete posts
as if no one could see them
the mexican guys from apartments worked on their cars
usually all day Saturdays
leaving littered beer cans for the Sunday morning recycle collector
page after page of my journal
became filled with these events
i dreaded evening when i had to shut the drapes.[29]

The speaker eventually moves out of this particular neighborhood to one more tranquil, less economically depressed. She remains, however, haunted by dreams of the old neighborhood sights and sounds, and her idealistic visions. She appears to question the very integrity of her identity:

only at midnight i awaken to these dreams of mexican murals
& a community affair. & i cry out:
can this much of me be claimed
yet i walk away with nothing?[30]

Humor and whimsy are often the Chicana's resources when dealing with the urban milieu. Sandra Cisneros's work, for instance, offers varied responses, as she remembers the city or the barrio, as in the nostalgic "Good Hotdogs":

Fifty cents apiece
To eat our lunch
We'd run
Straight from school
Instead of home
Two blocks

Then the store
That smelled like steam
You ordered
Because you had the money
Two hotdogs and two pops for here
. . . .
We'd eat
Fast till there was nothing left
But salt and poppy seeds even
The little burnt tips
Of french fries
We'd eat
You humming
And me swinging my legs[31]

In ironic introspection, the urban Cisneros writes about writing, in "The Poet Reflects on Her Solitary Fate":

She lives alone now.
Has abandoned the brothers,
the rooms of fathers
and many mothers.

They have left her
to her own device.
Her nightmares and pianos.
She owns a lead pipe.

The stray lovers
have gone home.
The house is cold.
There is nothing on t.v.
She must write poems.[32]

The reader is left to ponder which space the poet/speaker needs to arm herself against: the outside, or the inside. She appears to defend herself with her poetry, as well as with a lead pipe. There is nonetheless, no self-pity here, only ironic self-evaluation: no distractions nor delays, no excuses, she must write poems.

Gloria Anzaldúa published *This Bridge Called My Back* with fellow lesbian writer Cherríe Moraga in the early 1980s. The book reflects an uncompromised definition or understanding of feminism by U.S. women of color. Moraga explains why she/they act, write and share the experiences in the collection of poetry, essays, narratives:

I am not talking here about some lazy faith, where we resign ourselves to the tragic splittings in our lives with an upward turn of the hands or a vicious beating of our breasts. I am talking about believing that we have the power to actually transform our experience, change our lives, save our lives. Otherwise, why this book? It is the faith of activists I am talking about.[33]

Some years later, Anzaldúa writes of the city in "Corner of 50th St. and Fifth Ave.," describing the common scene of police arrests, a crowd yelling insults at the man arrested:

Taking my usual walk
I run into sirens flashing red, turning
and a small crowd
watching the dark-haired man
with the thin mustache,
PR about 30,
maricón, a voice in the crowd shouts.[34]

The man, called a homosexual (*maricón*), is beaten on the bare buttocks by the uniformed police. The speaker in the poem concludes ironically:

the sirens turning turning
I wade through the thick air thinking
that's as close as they let themselves get
to fucking a man, being men.[35]

In Anzaldúa's poem "Nopalitos," however, home and the barrio are remembered bittersweetly. Home means familiar smells and sounds, cooking, memories, and sometimes reproaches:

It's that time of day
when the musty smell of dust hangs in the air
mingling with the scent of orange blossoms.[36]

Next door, the neighbor *señora* stirs a huge pot of *menudo,* while the speaker prepares cactus for cooking. She is reminded that she is one of them, yet she is not of them:

> I left and have been gone a long time.
> I keep leaving and when I am home
> they remember no one but me had ever left.
> I listen to the *grillos* more intently
> than I do their *regaños.*
> I have more languages than they,
> am aware of every root of my pueblo;
> they, my people, are not.
> They are the living, sleeping roots.[37]

These poems contrast perceptions of place, where the city and the barrio both may evoke feelings of marginalization, even when the mood may be nostalgic as in the barrio poem.

In the borderlands poems of this same collection (*Borderlands*), Anzaldúa has a very strong message at the end for her daughters. However marginal and dispossessed the Chicana may be, she is not to give in:

> And yes, they've taken our lands.
> . . . .
> But they will never take that pride
> of being *mexicana-Chicana-tejana*
> nor our Indian woman's spirit.
> . . . .
> Like old skin will fall the slave ways of
> obedience, acceptance, silence.
> Like serpent lightning we'll move, little woman.
> You'll see.[38]

In the 1990s, Demetria Martínez's poetry can represent the younger Chicana feminist writer's determination in the new decade. These poems often describe the barrio/city from a poignant or tragic point of view. In "New York Scrapbook," for instance, the speaker describes a subtle alienation or distancing as she walks along a New York street, the tourist's camera and map at the ready:

Fog rises in shudders
from the asphalt

an old man sells roses
and lightbulbs at the curbside

the young buy tickets
for a morning pornographic flick

a blind woman tilts her face toward the sky
and knows that blue has succumbed to grey

my knapsack lumpy with camera and map
your brown face in bank windows

among the driven and the beaten
we think we know our way

with only imagined destinations
between us and them[39]

Martínez's poem, "An El Paso Street by Night," offers a most depressing view of a city neighborhood, with references to contemporary border barrio realities such as "wetbacks,"[40] the exploitation of immigrant women, and other workers who are used, abused, and are paid slave wages:

Bronco Ballroom
Black Garter Lounge
Bueno Video
Wetbacks who scrounge
through two rusty trolleys
laid up on the tracks
touch this city's wet crotch,
you'll never go back.

Benzine dreams,
sweet sewage air,
blue motel sinkholes
choked with blonde hair.

In the next room a man
with another man's wife,
on this side of the border
she will recast her life.

She ends daylight savings,
turns back the hands,
an extra hour to fake
with this porcelain man.
Help Wanted he promised,
then fucked her backstage,
a Juarez extra scrubs sinks
at slavery wage.[41]

Martínez is one poet who clearly offers many examples of what Ordóñez refers to as "double-voiced discourse," where that which is invisible is made visible, where the speakers in these poems give voice to the muted. Martínez says, in her ironic poetry about the city and barrio, what is not spoken about, what is not generally pointed out. Her response to barrio and city realities is to "name the names," or to address what would ordinarily be repugnant or unmentionable. This critical stance, frequent in contemporary Chicana writing, includes feminist commentary on male/female relationships: In this decaying urban environment, women continue to be exploited.

In "Crossing Over," on the other hand, Martínez writes of other contemporary border city realities, such as the activities of the Sanctuary Movement and their anathema, the Department of Justice, Immigration and Naturalization Service. Some of the cruelties faced by refugee women and their children are the subject of this poem:

Somebody threw a baby
into the Rio Grande.
We scrub the scum off him
in the back of a station wagon
as we leave El Paso.
We tuck him, sleeping,
in a picnic basket
as we near the check point.
Officers see our fishing rods

and nod us through.
At midnight south of Albuquerque
we invent a name, a date of birth,
singing rock-a-bye-baby in English,
burying the placenta of his past.[42]

Martínez's outraged speaker questions the circumstances and policies leading to such sinister and tragic events:

Who's throwing babies
in the river?
What bastard
signs the release?

Who will break
the bastard's brains
and let this baby
keep his name?[43]

The Sanctuary volunteers, who evidence humaneness and understanding by their actions, are summarily called ". . . a sanctimonious band of renegades who advocate open violation of the law" by the Immigration authorities, according to Martínez.

In the introduction to *Making Face/Making Soul: Haciendo Caras,* Gloria Anzaldúa explains the concept for this anthology of the same title:

Among Chicanas/Mexicanas, *haciendo caras,* "making faces," means to put on a face, express feelings by distorting the face – frowning, grimacing, looking sad, glum or disapproving. For me, *haciendo caras* has the added connotation of making *gestos subversivos,* political subversive gestures, the piercing look that questions or challenges, the look that says, "Don't walk all over me," the one that says, "Get out of my face." . . . The masks, *las máscaras,* we are compelled to wear, drive a wedge between our intersubjective personhood and the persona we present to the world . . . After years of wearing masks we may become just a series of roles, the constellated self limping along with its broken limbs.[44]

These masks are removed by the writers in this collection, as in the poem "*La Dulce Culpa*" by Cherríe Moraga in which the speaker considers her sexuality and personhood in terms of inherited memories, a legacy of her mother's own passions, and a love unfulfilled.[45]

Alma Villanueva's poem "Friction" describes an exhausted speaker at a metropolitan airport, who with her young son finds temporary comfort underneath an artificial tree amidst the noise and crowd:

I'm so sleepy in the middle of
technology – planes loading
and leaving – planes landing,

they leave. And I have just
arrived with my careful baggage;
not too much, not too little –

the discipline of my soul . . .[46]

Legs outstretched on a red and dirty ottoman, sitting on hard black, plastic chairs, the speaker goes to sleep "under a leafy tree unvisited by birds, wind, sun and rain."

Other publications continue to include glimpses of urban and barrio life from the Chicana feminist perspective. Poets such as Barbara Brinson Curiel, Lorna Dee Cervantes, and Bernice Zamora join a trilogy of poets (Alicia Gaspar de Alba, María Herrera-Sobek, and Demetria Martínez) in breaking into the 1990s with new images of their respective "space."

One of the most delightful poems reflecting the clash of cultures is Barbara Brinson Curiel's "Recipe: *Chorizo con Huevo* Made in the Microwave." The poem is humorous, somewhat ironic as the speaker ruminates upon how a traditional food (*chorizo,* a spicy Mexican sausage, often cooked with eggs or potatoes) can now be prepared nontraditionally in a microwave oven. The speaker remembers her mother's disapproval long ago when at age eight the same speaker forsook *sopa de fideo* (a Mexican vermicelli dish) for peanut butter and jelly for lunch. She juxtaposes traditionally prepared dishes associated with fond memories of *how* mother/grandmother used to make them, and *where* (the Tucson barrio), versus the technological product, a microwave in an urban milieu, associated with timesaving appliances that may negate time-honored methods in Chicana culture.

I won't lie,
It's not the same.

When you taste it
memories of abuelita

feeding wood into the stove
will dim.

. . . .

You can turn away
from that eyebrow,
but there's no escaping the snarl
grandma will dish out
from her photo on the mantle.

It's the same hard stare
you closed your eyes to
on the day you brought
that microwave home.

Ni modo, pues.
. . . .
Eat your *chorizo con huevo*
with pale tortillas.
Remember grandma eating,
craving *chorizo* cooked
over an outdoor stove
in a Tucson summer.[47]

This same poet deals with discrimination and blatant "tokenism" in "18 Years Old, I Apply for a Job at a Bank across Town in Cow Hollow":

He pushed the application toward me,
joking about how much they all liked Betty –
the only dark-skinned girl
in that geography of white.
I filled out the form
knowing it was as much a gesture
as the hand he'd extend
as I left.[48]

The poetry of lesbian poet Alicia Gaspar de Alba includes a challenging antimythic explication of La Malinche, with erotic overtones. This is a progressive development of La Malinche's defense, so evident in urban Chicana and Mexicana feminist writing since the 1970s. Gaspar de Alba's poem "Malinchista, a Myth Revisited" is ironic as well:

La Malinche hated the way Cortés rubbed his cactus-
beard over her face and belly. The way his tongue
pressed against her teeth. She was used to smooth
brown lovers who dipped beneath her, who crouched
on the ground and rocked her in the musky space
between their chests and thighs.[49]

In the work of many Chicanas, we see again and again the cry for vindica-
tion of Malinche's name and honor. Malinche was Cortés's indigenous
interpreter when he arrived to conquer Tenochtitlan, the Aztec capital. She
has been denounced as a traitor to her people, as having assisted the Spaniards in their Conquest. Some Mexicans and Chicanos have linked Malinche's myth to *La Llorona*'s. *La Llorona* is a mythical woman figure who
appears at night, heard grieving for her children. The variants of the myth
include a Llorona who has killed her children, one who has simply lost her
children, one (Malinche-like) who grieves for her people, her lover, her
husband, etc. In the Chicano community, to be feminist or lesbian is to be
Malinche, or a traitor to the culture. So what does the mythical Malinche
cry about? Gaspar de Alba writes:

The woman shrieking along the littered bank of the
Río Grande is not sorry. She is looking for revenge.
Centuries she has been blamed for the murder of her
child, the loss of her people, as if Tenochtitlan
would not have fallen without her sin. History
does not sing of the conquistador who prayed
to a white god as he pulled two ripe hearts
out of the land.[50]

Gaspar de Alba's poem "Leaving 'The Killing Fields'" weaves urban images in the speaker's introspections on her own psychic/spatial/sexual
evolution:

I leave the movie and the dog-eared
shadows of trees, the afternoon
light, the smell of popcorn
remind me of you, white man
stalking my dreams like Jack
and his magic seeds. At night
I hear helicopters pumping over

the roof, radio waves, the click-
click of telegrams on your pink
tongue. Wherever you are,
you must hear the same sounds
you must remember the trench
we slept in, the hole that Alice
found, the rabbit chasing her
to a land far away from you.
Remember the eggshells littered
in the closet and my fingers
cake-sweet with blood. The cock
crowing in your belly warned you,
the gray hairs showing on your head,
the white space growing in our bed.
Five years ago I left you
wolfless: goodbye Peter, hello
Rita Mae Brown.[51]

Certainly, the urban Chicana poet (whether or not she originally was raised in a rural environment or not), has become much more explicit in her erotic imagery. She acknowledges her sexuality, whatever the space has become. We have especially from some poets like Anzaldúa, Moraga, and Gaspar de Alba evidence that lesbian writers share the same love/hate relationship with the city or the barrio that the work of other Chicanas bespeaks. The urban landscape can be merely the circumstantial backdrop for the Chicana's evolution, as in "Dark Morning Husband":

You meet a woman on the street
outside a gay bar. Blonde hair,
open red shirt, nipples
like tiny fists.
She looks you over down
the loose curve of shoulders
arms and hips. Your massive thighs
twitch in the dark.[52]

The barrio remembered may often include awareness of ever-present racism and feelings of alienation even in a familiar context, as experienced with established institutions such as the Catholic Church. María Herrera-Sobek's poem "Sunday Mass," for instance:

Sunday
was a time for *misa*
my wispy hand in yours
we walked the cobblestones.

"Oh dear, we are too early
the Anglo mass is on."
We wait our turn
The Mexican store
offers us quick shelter
from the onslaught
of our thoughts:
caramelos
colaciones
chocolates.

Sweet nothings
for our battered souls
It's ten o'clock
your forehead
sprinkled with
summer heat
begins to rain.

It's time to enter
the Mexican mass begins.

A house divided
by the colors of the rainbow
White Brown Black
Do not disturb the universe.
The blue-eyed God
wants it so.[53]

Mingled with bitter memories of going to Sunday Mass are the remembrances of sweets from the Mexican store where the speaker (the young child accompanied by a parent or an adult) took respite until the Mexican mass began.

A mother's fears is the focus of "My All-American Son," where she describes the dilemma of being "American Brown," in a world that appears to love-hate brown people, where brown people live out a precarious existence. She contemplates, from her own experience, what lies ahead for her son/children:

> Watching
> My all-American son
> Move in and out
> Of a white world
> Brown skin
> Glistening
> In a world
> That loves-hates
> Brown.
>
> Loves
> Toasted
> Blonde-brown
> Ocean-sprayed
> Sun-tanned
> Oiled
> Sleek
> Shiny
> Sun-soaked
> Brown.
> . . . .
> I know
> His stand is precarious
> One false move
> And he'll be
> Ejected
> Rejected
> Put in "his place."
>
> American Brown
> I ache for you.[54]

An award-winning collection from Lorna Dee Cervantes offers examples of a distinctive style, an evolution in this particular poet's relation to her space. Her earlier work was more direct in imagery and metaphor (see earlier examples from *Emplumada*, for instance); her recent publication tends to eerie turns in imagery, often a surreal tinge to the lines. In "Hotel" the impression is of reading not of a hotel, but of the speaker's self as if a hotel. The poem's several verses elucidate only a little about the place itself, and a great deal about the speaker's despair and yearning:

> I couldn't see in this light
> even if I wished. The black
> grillwork over black, cool upon coal,
> kisses me back in an icy press.
> Not wanting – anything – but to fall
> as the empty trash cans mingle
> below with the smell of feral cats.
> . . . .
> You had Irish eyes the color of old
> ice. What you lost was first love
> and a word for forever, like evergreen,
> oceanic, fossil. My bones could grind
> themselves to salt and I would still be
> this aging woman, this battered lifeline.
> History never has been kind to a loser.
> . . . .
> I had to leave before I could
> hear it: the sound of dishwater
> in a steamed house, the singing
> of water on white porcelain, cooling
> like clots seeping through a wound,
> our collision of tensions, a viscous
> rendered fat, divorced, releasing.[55]

In the poem "On Touring Her Hometown," the mood is also very distinct from Cervantes's earlier Freeway poems. Again as in the previous poem, a surreal sadness permeates the landscape, and the reader is unsure if it is "real/unreal," if the subject is truly the hometown or the speaker's self-identity:

I'm going away to where I'm from.
I'm fleeing from visions, fences
grinning from the post. Give me
a hole with a past to it. Fill up
this mess with your wicked engines.
. . . .
There's a place
in the mists of this city where a silence,
lean as ghosts, beckons, is archaic
in the workclothes of my otherness.
There is cedar, ash sage, an owl
on the grave of this town the width
of sin. And crying's like hating,
it won't ever pay. I'm going away
to where I'm from. I'm leaving,
last condor, last chance.[56]

The enigmatic mood of this recent collection by Cervantes is also captured in her poem "Macho," where she appears to be again addressing a
loved one, and seems to be describing a "real man":

Slender, you are, secret as rail
under a stairwell of snow, slim
as my lips in the shallow hips.
. . . .
You're a beautiful mess of thread and silk,
a famous web of work and waiting, an
angular stylus with the patience of lead.

Your potent lure links hunger to flesh
as a frail eagle alights on my chest,
remember: the word for *machismo* is *real.*[57]

The discourse of this particular poet, in this collection at least, has become more hermetic. That is, it is more difficult to decipher meanings, yet it
is still possible to gather impressions of the speakers' state of mind or mood.
The reader is left to ponder whether the *macho* in the poem exists, or if he is
only a projection of the speaker's hunger for this idealized man.
Even in these last poems, the reader can perceive the dialectical relation-

ship between rage and love, aesthetics and language. There is clearly a desire for some positive resolution, as evidenced by the themes borne out by Cervantes's subtitle, *Poems on Love and Hunger.*

In a sense, we can consider the Chicana feminist writer/artist as a *facilitator* in the teaching of specific Chicana literary texts. Her double-voiced discourse, her search of self and subsequent expression of cultural identity does indeed make the invisible visible, giving voice to the muted. The "I love you/I hate you" relationship with the barrio and city, is often expressed with humor, although most frequently the writer/space relationship is ironic, and therefore the discourse is ironic. Wayne C. Booth, in *Rhetoric of Irony,* tells us that irony is made evident to the understanding either by the delivery, the character of the speaker, or the nature of the subject.[58] By these criteria, these selected poems provide reasonable evidence that the Chicana feminist writer in the main continues to feel herself marginalized, in a conflictive state with regard to the barrio, the city, and her culture. The Chicana critic, María Inés Lagos-Pope says:

For Chicanos and women, literature has contributed to the development of a sense of identity and self-discovery, and at the same time that it has served as a means of attaining self-knowledge it has chronicled their struggle.[59]

Meanwhile, I believe that the Chicana feminist writer continues to seek new models and continues as well to translate her reality, often perceived in an urban environment, into mostly sensitive and frequently strong ironic images. The images of cultural identity evidenced in specific Chicana feminist texts include, often, an extremely critical position toward machismo.[60] However, this ironic predicament is the subject of another study; suffice it to say that the Chicana feminist typically is dissatisfied with imposed roles, and with the perpetuated subjugation of women within a male-dominated society. If there is, in some Chicana feminist writers, a loss of the bitter edge to the speakers' voices, there is also more often a sense of determination, through the very (individual) act of writing about her space, in forging her own future.

Is there a resolution to the Chicana feminist writer's existential dilemma? Indeed, is her dilemma any different from any other Chicano or other woman's dilemma, living in the United States? While the Chicana feminist writer may share the same concerns of many other Chicano writers (for example, dispossession of lands and culture, racism, alienation), she specifically suffers from what we have referred to as the phenomenon of triple colonization. If we must repeat to make this point: The Chicana is a member of a minority group within an industrialized, impersonal society; she is a woman; and she is oppressed once again by having to struggle within a macho-dominated culture. Chicano culture also comes complete with all its homophobic, *macho*-centric myths, namely, La Malinche, La Llorona, and a perception that homosexuality is anathema.

The Chicana feminist writer's texts can be considered political subversive gestures, the *gestos subversivos* that Gloria Anzaldúa defines. Chicana poems about the city or barrio give ample evidence of the poet's individual perception about, and rebellion against, her ironic circumstance. The Chicana feminist keeps on writing in order to save herself, the writing becoming an essentially hopeful (and revolutionary) act in itself. As Cherríe Moraga says: "It is the faith of activists I am talking about."

ACKNOWLEDGMENTS

The following poems or excerpts are reprinted with permission of the copyright holders.

"Corner of 50th St. and Fifth Ave.," "Nopalitos," and "Don't Give In Chicanita" by Gloria Anzaldúa are reprinted with permission from *Borderlands/La Frontera* (San Francisco: Aunt Lute Books, 1987).

"Cannery Town in August," "From Where We Sit: Corpus Christi," and "An Interpretation of Dinner by the Uninvited Guest" by Lorna Dee Cervantes are reprinted from *Emplumada,* by permission of the University of Pittsburgh Press, copyright 1981 by Lorna Dee Cervantes.

"Beneath the Shadow of the Freeway" and "Freeway 280" by Lorna Dee Cervantes are reprinted by permission of the publisher, *Latin American Literary Review* 5:10 (1977), Pittsburgh, Pennsylvania.

"Hotel," "On Touring Her Hometown," and "Macho" by Lorna Dee Cervantes are reprinted with permission from the publisher of *From the Cables of Genocide* (Houston: Arte Publico Press–University of Houston, 1991).

"Good Hotdogs" and "The Poet Reflects on Her Solitary Fate" by Sandra Cisneros are reprinted with permission from *My Wicked, Wicked Ways* (Berkeley: Third Woman Press, 1987) by the author and her agent, Susan Bergholz.

"Recipe: *Chorizo con Huevo* Made in the Microwave," and "18 Years Old, I Apply for a Job at a Bank Across Town in Cow Hollow," by Barbara Brinson Curiel are reprinted with permission from *Speak to Me From Dreams* (Berkeley: Third Woman Press, 1989).

"Hermano" by Angela de Hoyos is reprinted with permission from *Chicano Poems for the Barrio* (Bloomington: Backstage Books, 1975).

"La Gran Ciudad" by Angela de Hoyos is reprinted with permission from *Days of Milk and Honey* 1 (Oct. 1976).

"Malinchista, A Myth Revisited," "Leaving the Killing Fields," and "Dark Morning Husband" by Alicia Gaspar de Alba are reprinted with permission from *Three Times a Woman* (Tempe: Bilingual Press, 1989).

"Sunday Mass" and "My All-American Son" by María Herrera-Sobek are reprinted with permission from *Three Times a Woman* (Tempe: Bilingual Press, 1989).

"New York Scrapbook I," "An El Paso Street By Night," "Crossing Over, 1," and "Crossing Over, 3" by Demetria Martínez are reprinted with permission from *Three Times a Woman* (Tempe: Bilingual Press, 1989).

"Legal Alien," "Elena," and "Illegal Alien" by Pat Mora are reprinted with permission from the publisher of *Chants* (Houston: Arte Publico Press–University of Houston, 1984).

"Second Street," "Pounding Down First Street," and "i dream of mexican murals and a community affair" by Beverly Silva are reprinted with permission from *The Second Street Poems* (Ypsilante: Bilingual Press/Editorial Bilingüe, 1983).

"Friction" by Alma Villanueva is reprinted with permission from *Planet* (Tempe: Bilingual Press, 1993).

"El Burrito Cafe" and "Metaphor and Reality," by Bernice Zamora are reprinted with permission from *Restless Serpents* (Menlo Park: Diseños Literarios, 1976).

NOTES

1. Margarita Cota-Cárdenas, "The Chicana in the City as Seen in Her Literature," *Frontiers: A Journal of Women Studies* 6:1 (1981): 13–18. A Chicana is a woman of Mexican descent, living in the United States, but she may choose to call herself Mexican or Mexican American. The present study refers to some texts and findings from my earlier work but is intended to be an update and develops in new directions.

2. Elizabeth Ordóñez, "The Concept of Cultural Identity in Chicana Poetry," *Third Woman: Southwest/Midwest* 11:1 (1984): 75.

3. Charles Glicksberg, *The Ironic Vision in Modern Literature* (The Hague: Martinus Nijhoff, 1969), 258.

4. Angela de Hoyos, "Hermano," *Chicano Poems for the Barrio* (Bloomington: Backstage Books, 1975), n.p. The translation of the original bilingual poem is mine.

5. Angela de Hoyos, "La gran ciudad," *Days of Milk and Honey* 1 (October 1976): 23.

6. Sandra Cisneros, "North Avenue/1600 North," *Revista Chicano Riqueña* 6:3 (verano 1978): 27–28.

7. Rina García Rocha, "The Truth in My Eyes," *Hojas poéticas* 1 (1977): 2.

8. Tina Alvarez, "Guadalajara, U.S.A.," *Imágenes de la Chicana* 1 (1975): 7; see note 40.

9. "Guadalajara, U.S.A.," 7. "De turista" translates "as a tourist."

10. Gerda Lerner has addressed this cultural duality, saying that women live their social existence between women's culture and the general culture, "and, whenever they are confined by patriarchal restraint or segregation into separateness (which always has subordination as its purpose), they transform this restraint into complementarity . . . and redefine it." (*The Majority Finds Its Past* [New York: 1981], 52.)

11. Lorna Dee Cervantes, "Beneath the Shadow of the Freeway," *The Third Woman: Minority Women Writers of the United States,* ed. Dexter Fisher (Boston: Houghton Mifflin, 1980), 378–81. "Sal Si Puedes" is a barrio name which translates "Get Out If You Can."

12. Sylvia Gonzales, "Chicana Evolution," trans. Marcela Christine Lucero Trujillo, in Fisher, *The Third Woman,* 418–26.

13. Xelina, "Urban Life," in Fisher, *The Third Woman,* 384.

14. Inés Hernández Tovar, "Para Teresa," in Fisher, *The Third Woman,* 414–16.

15. Bernice Zamora, "El Burrito Cafe," *Restless Serpents* (Menlo Park: Diseños Literarios, 1976), 60.

16. Bernice Zamora, "Metaphor and Reality," 71.

17. Lorna Dee Cervantes, *Emplumada* (Pittsburgh: University of Pittsburgh Press, 1981), 6.

18. Cervantes, *Emplumada,* 33.

19. Cervantes, *Emplumada,* 34.

20. Cervantes, *Emplumada,* 39. "En los campos extranōs de esta ciudad" translates as "in the strange fields of the city."

21. Pat Mora, "Legal Alien," *Chants* (Houston: Arte Público Press, 1984), 52. "*Me'stan volviendo loca,*" translates "They're driving me nuts."

22. Pat Mora, "Elena," 50. "*Vamos a pedirle dulces a mamá. Vamos*" translates "Let's go ask Mama for candies. Let's."

23. Pat Mora, "Illegal Alien," 40.

24. Beverly Silva, "Second Street," *The Second Street Poems* (Ypsilanti: Bilingual Press/Editorial Bilingüe, 1983), 35.

25. Beverly Silva, "Pounding Down First St.," 41–45.

26. Silva, "Pounding Down First St.," 41–45.

27. Silva, "Pounding Down First St.," 41–45.

28. Beverly Silva, "i dream of mexican murals and a community affair," 65–67.

29. Silva, "i dream of mexican murals," 65–67.

30. Silva, "i dream of mexican murals," 65–67.

31. Sandra Cisneros, "Good Hotdogs," *My Wicked, Wicked Ways* (Berkeley: Third Woman Press, 1987), 10.

32. Cisneros, "The Poet Reflects on Her Solitary Fate," *My Wicked, Wicked Ways*, 35.

33. Cherríe Moraga, "Preface," *This Bridge Called My Back* (New York: Kitchen Table, Women of Color Press, 1983), xviii.

34. Gloria Anzaldúa, *Borderlands/La Frontera* (San Francisco, Aunt Lute Book Company, 1987), 145.

35. Anzaldúa, *Borderlands/La Frontera*, 145.

36. Anzaldúa, *Borderlands/La Frontera*, 112–13.

37. Anzaldúa, *Borderlands/La Frontera*, 112–13. "Gillos" are "crickets." "*Regaños*" means "scoldings."

38. Anzaldúa, "Don't Give In Chicanita," *Borderlands/La Frontera*, 202–3.

39. Demetria Martínez, "New York Scrapbook I," *Three Times a Woman: Chicana Poetry* (Tempe: Bilingual Press, 1989), 114. This poem is from her full-length collection, *Turning*, which is included in this book.

40. "Wetbacks" are undocumented workers or immigrants who cross the border. The term described those who literally got their backs wet crossing the Río Grande to come to the United States. This is considered to be a derogatory term.

41. Demetria Martínez, "An El Paso Street by Night," in *Three Times a Woman*, 112.

42. Demetria Martínez, "Crossing Over, 1," in *Three Times a Woman*, 118–19.

43. Demetria Martínez, "Crossing Over, 3," 118–19.

44. Gloria Anzaldúa, "Introduction," *Making Face/Making Soul: Haciendo Caras* (San Francisco: Aunt Lute Foundation Books, 1990), xv.

45. Cherríe Moraga, *Making Face/Making Soul: Haciendo Caras*, 118–19.

46. Alma Villanueva, *Planet* (Tempe: Bilingual Press, 1993), 56.

47. Barbara Brinson Curiel, *Speak To Me From Dreams* (Berkeley: Third Woman Press, 1989), 64–65. "*Ni modo, pues*" in this context means "What can you do?"

48. Barbara Brinson Curiel, 34–35.

49. Alicia Gaspar de Alba, "Malinchista, A Myth Revisited," in *Three Times a Woman*, 16–17.

50. Gaspar de Alba, "Malinchista," 16–17.

51. Gaspar de Alba, "Leaving 'The Killing Fields,'" in *Three Times a Woman*, 27.

52. Gaspar de Alba, "Dark Morning Husband," in *Three Times a Woman*, 21.

53. María Herrera-Sobek, "Sunday Mass," in *Three Times a Woman*, 77.

54. Herrera-Sobek, "My All-American Son," in *Three Times a Woman*, 79–80.

55. Lorna Dee Cervantes, "Hotel," *From the Cables of Genocide* (Houston: Arte Público Press, 1991), 38–39.

56. Cervantes, "On Touring Her Hometown," in *From the Cables of Genocide,* 41.

57. Cervantes, "Macho," in *From the Cables of Genocide,* 57.

58. This study does not pretend to discuss the many types of ironic discourse to be found in these various Chicana texts. Wayne C. Booth, *Rhetoric of Irony* (Chicago: University of Chicago, 1974), gives Quintilian's brief definition, saying that irony is made evident to the understanding either by the delivery, the character of the speaker, or the nature of the subject, 49.

59. María Inés Lagos-Pope, "A Space of Her Own: The Second Street Poems by Beverly Silva," *The Second Street Poems,* 11. This introductory essay gives an excellent sketch of the development of Chicana discourse.

60. The dilemma inherent in being Chicana is called the "triple oppression of Chicanas as colonized women," by Alfredo Mirandé and Evangelina Enríquez, in *La Chicana: The Mexican-American Woman* (Chicago: University of Chicago, 1979), 12–13. They are oppressed, according to Mirandé/Enríquez, as minority group members, as females, and as inheritors of a culture that is male (*macho*) dominated.

Frontiers 14:2 (1994): 51–80.

Reflections on Diversity among Chicanas

PATRICIA ZAVELLA

Second-wave feminists have been attempting to create a scholarship and conduct research in ways that no longer "privilege" the concerns of white, middle-class, or heterosexual women or take their experiences as the norm.[1] This agenda has often been born from struggle with those women seen as "other." Women of color have argued that race, class, and gender – including sexuality – are experienced simultaneously, and to only use a gender analysis for understanding women's lived experience is reductionist and replicates the silencing and social oppression that women of color experience daily.[2] The response by those feminist theorists who see women's common, biologically based experiences as the basis for the construction of theory has often been to include women's "many voices." Highly influenced by French feminist theory, this view sees that women from diverse class, ethnic, or racial groups have very different perspectives on so-called universal feminine experiences, and the project within feminist studies is to document, listen to, validate those voices. This viewpoint has produced somewhat of a quandary: On the one hand, we have an understanding of the great complexity of all women's experiences and know that there is variation among women on the basis of race, ethnicity, class, sexual preference, age, or abilities. Yet simply recognizing the richness of diversity can lead to an atheoretical pluralism where diversity seems overwhelming, and it is difficult to discern the basis of commonality and difference among women. Moreover, expanding the feminist canon to include other women can sometimes replicate stereotypes about internal similarities among the category of women being integrated. I believe we need to reflect on how women within a particular group vary from one another, and to research women's lives in ways that identify the sources of diversity without resorting to mechanistic conclusions that class, race, or gender (and I include sexuality within a gender analysis) alone gives rise to difference. That is, we should analyze how race, class, or gender are socially constructed yet not essentialize any of the categories of oppression.[3]

Further, I believe we must begin our analysis with the historically specific structural conditions constraining women's experiences. We can then link these conditions to the varieties of ways in which women respond to and construct subjective representations of their experiences. This suggestion helps us to avoid the problematic assumption of much recent feminist scholarship: beginning with historical material conditions rather than with "experience" embeds "women's diversity" as a theoretical priority and frees us from the artificial task of deriving diversity from prior commonality. In a sense, then, feminists of color are challenging one of the basic assumptions in women's studies – the notion that feminist theory should be grounded in women's experience in which there are commonalities. Instead, we ask that the structure in which women's experiences are framed become the primary analytical locus, which may generate profound differences between white women and women of color, and among Chicanas in particular.

The diversity among Chicanas can initially be seen by the terms of ethnic identification we have claimed for ourselves. When referring to ourselves within a white context, we often prefer more generic terms, like Las Mujeres or the combination Chicana/Latina, in opposition to Hispanic, which is often seen as inappropriate because of its conservative political connotations. When speaking among ourselves, we highlight and celebrate all of the nuances of identity – we are Chicanas, Mexicanas, Mexican Americans, Spanish Americans, Tejanas, Hispanas, Mestizas, Indias, or Latinas, and the terms of identification vary according to the context. This complexity of identification reflects the conundrum many Chicanas experience: On the one hand, together we are seen by others as a single social category, often Hispanic women. Yet the term *Hispanic,* imposed by the Census Bureau, is seen as inappropriate by many women who prefer to identify themselves in oppositional political terms. As Chicanas, we have common issues and experiences with other women of color in the United States, and we therefore often feel a strong sense of affinity with their struggles. On the other hand, we are a very diverse group of women, with diverse histories, regional settlement patterns, particular cultural practices, sexual preferences, and occasionally radically dissimilar political outlooks, and our solidarity as Chicanas can be undermined by these differences among us.

My purpose here is to contextualize the notion of diversity among Chicanas and sketch out a conceptual framework for making sense of the commonalities and differences among us. My discussion has two parts: In the first I concentrate on the structural commonalities among Chicanas, based on the subordination engendered by the intersection of race, class, and gender but that are different for particular groups of women; later, I discuss how we Chicanas have constructed our lives, our sense of selves in opposition to the many forms of subordination. We must also examine how Chicano culture is socially constructed in ways that are misogynist, homophobic, or internalize racism and class prejudices.

I suggest that our understanding of difference among Chicanas will be enhanced through close attention to women's social location within the social structure, that is, in looking at the social spaces created by the intersection of class, race, gender, and culture.[4] The term *social location* differs from and complements that of Renato Rosaldo's useful concept of "positioned subject," where the observer/writer/ethnographer is self-reflective of her own social status and takes responsibility for uncovering the power relations within the culture – including her own participation within changing cultural processes. Rosaldo cautions us that cultural analyses by positioned subjects are always provisional.[5] My use also differs slightly from the notion of "crossing borders" suggested by Gloria Anzaldúa, who emphasizes how Chicanas construct a sense of self, a liberating critical consciousness, in oppositional terms.[6] Instead, I am emphasizing the dialectical process in which historical conditions, including cultural traditions, and the social construction of self occurs. That is, I am emphasizing the processes that constrain Chicanas' sense of self, the structures of oppression that make being a "positioned subject" or "crossing borders" problematic.

DECONSTRUCTING DIVERSITY

To begin formulating a framework on diversity among Chicanas, it is important to first deconstruct the stereotypic thinking that comes from outsiders. Stereotypes often have a grain of truth but mask gross generalizations or ignorance of the diversity not only among different groups of women of color but within groups. Some of these stereotypes include the assumption that all Chicanas speak Spanish or that we have such a rich culture – when our culture has been repressed. Other assumptions that I've heard include that Chicanas have such loving, big families; in fact, like other groups, Chicanas experience familial breakdown or abuse toward women.

Probably one of the most insidious stereotypes regarding Chicanas is the notion that culture is determinant of behavior. Because Chicanas are racially distinct and have Spanish language as an ethnic signifier, we seem obviously culturally different than white North Americans. This often leads to the assumption that there is a coherent Chicano cultural heritage: that the values, norms, customs, rituals, symbols, material items (such as women's religious altars) form part of a "tradition" that all Chicanos are socialized into. Moreover, this thinking goes, Chicanos mechanistically base their behavior and decisions on these traditional norms. This stereotype was given new life with Oscar Lewis's notion of a "culture of poverty" based on fieldwork with Puerto Rican and Mexican families, in which people were said to have a whole host of maladaptive cultural traits.[7] This equation of racial status and poverty conditions with culture has been critiqued for being static, ahistorical, and simplistic. More importantly, this view of culture as determinant is really a different version of "blaming the victim," where Chicanas' own cultural heritage is seen as limiting their educational, social, or political aspirations. It is unfortunate that this view has cropped up in feminist thinking as well.

RECONSTRUCTING COMMONALITY

A way to move beyond stereotypic views and reconstructing how Chicanas have common experiences is through a historical perspective. History helps us to understand how particular stereotypes became hegemonic, and how Chicanas have become marginalized and invisible in the popular, political, and scholarly discourses. Although I cannot go into historical detail here, I would like to sketch out a framework that helps us to understand the similarities among Chicanas and helps clarify the sources of diversity among us, based on class, race, gender, and culture.

Some initial historical reorientations are important to point out: Spanish colonizers "discovered" America and the civilizations of indigenous peoples, and Spanish soldiers settled in what is now northern New Mexico in the early sixteenth century, long before the so-called original settlers landed on Plymouth Rock. The history of the Americas, then, is of Spanish, not English origin. Second, the conquest and racial mixtures with indigenous peoples set in motion the "colonized" status of Chicanos today. An important conceptual point is that Chicanas did not enter this country the same way that many white immigrant groups did. European immigrants were pushed out of their countries of origin for important economic and political reasons and then, depending on where they settled and the historical period, found more or less receptive communities in which to settle. As nonracialized peoples, they were able to choose the ethnic signifiers that were important to retain.

Chicanas have been integrated into American society through involuntary means, and internal class, racial, ethnic, and gender divisions within Spain and then within the colonies have been reconstituted through industrial development.[8] Mexican women became U.S. citizens by default after the U.S.-Mexican war, during which the border literally migrated to them – imposing on them a foreign language and sociolegal system. Through a variety of legal and informal mechanisms, Mexicans were displaced from their land and propelled into the bottom of the working class, were disenfranchised and segregated into barrios. Their language and customs were denigrated or even outlawed.[9] Many of the mechanisms that institutionalized racism, sexism, and working-class status that incorporated Chicanos into North American society continue today. This common historical legacy is a powerful basis of solidarity among Chicanas.

DIVERSITY COMPOUNDED

Attention to history, though it does point out the sources of common experiences, also begins our exploration of diversity among Chicanas. History helps us understand the regional settlement patterns of different groups of Chicanas that were then replenished through waves of migration: Women of Mexican descent originally settled in South Texas, northern New Mexico and California in the Southwest, and later migrant streams created settlements in the Midwest, Northwest Coast, and, more recently, on the East Coast. Other recent Latin-American immigrant women have settled in large cities – San Francisco, Los Angeles, New York, Washington, D.C., Miami – so that Chicano communities are becoming more heterogeneous. Settlement and migration history also helps us to understand the interethnic relations – both conflictual and cooperative – between groups of Chicanos. For example, in California researchers have found that Mexican immigrants who settled here in previous waves of migration have established economic "niches," in particular industries or occupations, and then felt threatened by compatriots who migrated more recently.[10]

Closely related to settlement patterns is the notion of culture-region, a geographic and sociopolitical area where historical processes – including isolation, waves of industrialization, urbanization, and discrimination toward racialized others – have segregated racial/ethnic groups and enabled historical actors to construct particular terms of ethnic identification in opposition to the dominant society.[11] The notion of culture-region helps highlight the particular racial mixtures that occurred – the mestizas from the unions of Spanish men and Indian women in the Southwest, the African and Spanish mixtures near the Caribbean – and helps us to understand the contours of cultural syncretism: Women from the gulf region show Puerto Rican, Cuban, and African influences whereas Chicanas from desert regions demonstrate more indigenous influences. There are also regional differences regarding the preferred terms of ethnic identification among women: *Chicana* in California, *Mexican American* or *Mexicana* in Texas, *Spanish American* in New Mexico, although there is a good deal of mixing of terms as well.[12]

One implication of culture-region is that generation is important: Whether women are of the first generation (that is, born in Mexico) or of subsequent generations born in the United States or are recent immigrants has implications for language use, cultural knowledge, and the process of identification. A Chicana's generation affects whether she feels a sense of identification and solidarity with other Chicanas, whether she feels marginalized, or whether she feels as if she is more "American" than Chicana.

Beyond historical settlement patterns, this framework attends to important internal differences within Chicano populations. Class is clearly an important demarcation: the overwhelming majority of Chicanos are of working-class origins, although with the recent economic crisis in Mexico, a few more middle-class and professional women are migrating to the United States. These women often have higher median incomes and higher educational levels, in contrast to those women who have migrated from rural, underdeveloped areas of Mexico. The class status of Chicanas can take on insidious overtones: Foreign-born Chicanas from elite, upper-class backgrounds clearly have very different life chances than those from the working class yet are often categorized as Hispanic and inflate the Affirmative Action statistics about the presence of underrepresented minorities. Class is often a source of tension among Chicanas, coinciding with political disagreements.

Racial physical features are also important: Whether women have fair or dark skin and hair; Indian, African, or European features or some combination thereof bears upon how Chicanas are treated and how they reflect upon their racial/ethnic status. Although some change is occurring regarding the preferred body image, our society still values images of women who are white – and blond in particular – and who have European features. Research shows that women who have dark skin, especially with indigenous features, face the worst treatment from society at large. Individuals within

Chicano communities may reflect this devaluation, or even internalize it, so that physical features are often noted and evaluated: Skin color in particular is commented on, with *las güeras* (light-skinned ones) being appreciated and *las prietas* (dark-skinned ones) being admonished and devalued. In contrast to white ethnic women, it is impossible for most Mexican women to "blend in," to opt out of their racial/ethnic status and pass for white. Thus we see examples all the time of U.S. citizens being mistaken for undocumented immigrants and being deported because of the color of their skin.

Sexuality is also a significant demarcation of social location. Whether women establish lesbian, heterosexual, or bisexual relationships is central to their identity and experience. Within our heterosexist society, Chicana lesbians and bisexuals, particularly those of working-class origin, face extreme marginalization from both the dominant and Chicano society. Paraphrasing Cherríe Moraga, being queer and of color is "as rude as women can get."[13] Sexuality, then, forms the basis of, and identity in which, community building is necessary against physical assaults and for survival. Sexual preference has generated political disagreements and conflict among lesbians, bisexual, and heterosexual Chicanas, and some lesbians are creating what Emma Perez calls a lesbian "uninvited discourse" with a separate "lengua y sitio" (language and space).[14]

These aspects of social location – class, gender, race/ethnicity, and sexual preference – all are indications of social inequality and reflect power relations in which Chicanas are often relatively powerless. Yet specifying women's social locations also means taking into consideration various ethnic or cultural attributes that create "borders" over which women cross in their daily lives. These attributes include nativity – whether Chicanas were born in the United States (and, if so, what generation) or in Mexico, and whether immigrants arrived as children and were socialized in the United States or received their education, socialization, and sense of identity in rural villages or urban centers of Mexico. Language use is critical and closely related to nativity. If Chicanas are born in the United States, particularly if they are reared in integrated communities, they are more likely to speak mainly English and without a Spanish accent, whereas Chicanas reared in Mexico or in segregated barrios in the United States are likely to be bilingual, predominantly Spanish speakers, or have Spanish heavy accents when speaking in English. Whether one was reared in the barrios or grew up isolated from other Chicanos has great implications for cultural knowledge and sense of self. Religion is also significant. The majority of Chicanas come from a Roman Catholic heritage in which religious rituals and practices are often the center of women's social activities and are forms of social control of women's sexuality. Finally, women's sexuality, in particular, but other activities as well are controlled through Chicano cultural forms involving the polar opposites of macho male, aggressive sexual license, and passive female chastity.

To understand how culture has placed constraints on the experiences of Chicanas, we need to distinguish between "traditional culture" – cultural knowledge as ideology – and culture in process. Cultural ideologies, as Rosaldo points out, are often forms of social control that seem most brittle when under attack.[15] When "culture" is evoked to remind recalcitrant women to be proprietous (for example, when working mothers are reminded of the importance of familism), Chicanos are orchestrating cultural ideology as cultural determinism.[16]

In contrast to a view of culture as determinant, Chicana and Chicano scholars have formulated a view of culture that is much more fluid and is embedded in an American historical context in which differential power relations between classes, Anglos and Chicanos, men and women, or heterosexuals and homosexuals are taken into consideration. This perspective also critiques the ways in which Chicano culture is exoticized and devalued. Further, this view sees culture as socially constructed by actors influenced by both "traditional" cultural norms and the audience of cultural "performances," so that culture is always interactive within particular situations.[17] This perspective focuses on cultural variation and the nuances of culture in process, particularly in daily life by "ordinary" Chicanas. In other words, I'm calling for a perspective that sees the dialectics of how the social structure and culture provide a context for the ways that Chicanas construct their identities. The implications are that ethnographic work should focus on particular subcultural groups and communities among Chicanos. Some of the more recent Chicano ethnographic work has had this focus – on lesbians and gay Chicanos who contest heterosexist traditions, on the elderly of northern New Mexican villages who construct oppositional discourse, on gangs and low-riders in southern California who form alternative support systems, on high school youth in south Texas who resist authority, on south Texas men who resist ethnographic characterizations, or on middle-aged women workers in northern California who consider alternative work and family-based culture.[18] Comparisons between Chicanos within these different social locations reveal important variations of experience. More ethnographies of various communities of Chicanas would heighten our sense of diversity.

I am suggesting that in addition to class, race, and sexual preference, "traditional" culture provides a context in which Chicanas are in positions or situations in relation to other women and men that allow greater or lesser autonomy. Further, these women strategize within this context to construct a sense of self and try to live their lives in opposition to these constraints. Although the limitations on Chicanas' lives can delineate "borders" by which women construct a sense of self in their lives, I am emphasizing that there are "locations" created by the intersection of class, race, gender, sexuality, and culture and that women sometimes cannot "cross" some "borders" that constrain their lives.

I believe that we should construct feminist studies that reflect the myriad of social locations among Chicanas, which specify relationships – both personal and structural – that sustain them. I believe that this is the starting point for understanding the social and cultural symbolic representations and consciousness that women express through literature, art, and daily activity.

It might be helpful to use my own experience to illustrate how culture-region and culture in process is integral to social location: I have been repeatedly told, "You're so different from other Mexicans" – a puzzling, objectifying idea, especially to a child. I am fourth generation, born in the United States in a working-class, predominantly English-speaking family. My cultural heritage is from the northern New Mexico culture-region, my family descended from peasant farmers who migrated from Tierra Amarilla, New Mexico, to Trujillo Creek in southern Colorado. My grandparents were coal miners and farmers. I remember that when I was a child my grandmother used to say we were "Spanish American" (often used synonymously with "Hispano"), the term used in the northern New Mexico culture-region to distinguish Mexican Americans from Indians, whites, and Mexicans from Mexico. Although my parents' native language was Spanish, they were punished for speaking Spanish in school, and we used English at home. (Some of us eventually took Spanish classes in an attempt to regain "our" language.) The Spanish language was all around us, but it was mainly the language of adult kin, who used it when speaking of things they wanted hidden from the children – unfortunately a common occurrence under conditions of language repression.

My father joined the air force to escape the racism and lack of economic opportunities in Laredo, Texas, on the border between the United States and Mexico. As an "air force brat" I was born on an air base in Tampa, Florida. My grandmother's home in Colorado Springs was our home base, but we made annual forays to rural Maine and rural South Dakota (twice) before my family migrated to southern California. We were often one of few Mexican families on the base, so I never lived in barrios. With many experiences of racism (particularly in schools, where I heard the refrain that I was so different from other Mexicans), I grew up feeling marginalized from whites and isolated from other Chicanos. Because we moved so much, I was often the new kid in school, and teachers frequently assumed that because I was Mexican I would be a Spanish speaker and would not perform well. My schooling, then, was in contesting the racist and sexist assumptions about my abilities, and I became a "scholarship girl." I was often puzzled at being called Mexican. Although my racial features are clearly Mexican, I had never been to Mexico, nor did I know any relatives who were living there. Yet my grandmother and mother are staunch Catholics, and part of my sense of being Chicana comes from chafing from the misogyny of Catholic rituals and doctrine.

I am part of the limited class mobility occurring among Chicanos: I am of the first generation that received a higher education, the only Ph.D. among my large extended family, the only writer. I was fortunate to take part in the Chicano movement and Chicana movement, which shaped my consciousness and identity as a Chicana feminist. My social location, then, of working-class, English-speaking Hispana Catholic background, clearly demarcates my experiences from those of other Chicanas. My experiences in constructing culture in process (feminist parenting, for example) embody the contradictions generated from my now privileged social location.

CHANGING DEMOGRAPHY

If anything, the heterogeneity of Chicanas will only increase in the future. Stepped-up migration from Mexico and some class mobility mean that the class polarization will become more pronounced. More Chicanas are entering higher education and professional occupations; others – women from rural Central American and Latin American countries are entering this country, often without documentation, at the bottom margins of the social structure. In California, but also in other settlement areas like Washington, Miami, and New York, Chicano communities are becoming global cities with polyglot organizations and neighborhoods.

Let me conclude by returning to the notion of identity, which captures the heart of the problematic of understanding Chicanas. I have suggested that we pay attention to the history of particular groups of Chicanas, where they settled or migrated to, how their communities were formed, how there are key, structurally based differences among Chicanas. For each woman, this means understanding her social location structurally and culturally. Instead of lumping all Chicanas together into separate sections of a course on women, we might better ask, what purpose does it serve to categorize all of these very disparate groups? Whose interests get served? When is it appropriate to think of these women as Chicanas, and when it is better to specify a particular regional form of identity?

Regarding curriculum development, I have found that "social location" is helpful for white and other students as well. In trying to develop feminist curriculum to include Chicanas, we might think about when it is useful to make comparisons between women with different cultural backgrounds but in similar social locations. In a course on women and work, for example, we might contrast Chicana and Jewish working-class factory workers. At other times, our strategy might be to contrast women from very different social locations: the poetry and novels of Alice Walker and Ana Castillo, both women who searched for their historic roots. More importantly, what identity does a particular Chicana claim, and why? It is obvious that we have much work before us in understanding diversity among all women and in struggling to develop solidarity with women of different social locations. Yet it is exciting to envision a feminist studies in which women "on the margins" are demanding that the "center" be reconstituted.

NOTES

1. For a critique of this perspective and examples of more historically grounded feminist studies, see Micaela di Leonardo, ed., *Gender at the Crossroads of Knowledge: Feminist Anthropology in the Postmodern Era* (Berkeley: University of California Press, 1991); Faye Ginsburg and Anna Lowenhaupt Tsing, eds., *Uncertain Terms: Negotiating Gender in American Culture* (Boston: Beacon Press, 1990); and Sandra Morgen, ed., *Gender and Anthropology: Critical Reviews for Research and Teaching* (Washington, D.C.: American Anthropological Association, 1989).

2. See Gloria Anzaldúa, ed., *Making Face, Making Soul: Haciendo Caras* (San Francisco: Aunt Lute Foundation, 1990); bell hooks, *Feminist Theory from Margin to Center* (Boston: South End Press, 1984); Aida Hurtado, "Relating to Privilege: Seduction and Rejection in the Subordination of White Women and Women of Color," *Signs* 14:4 (1989); Gloria Joseph, "The Incomplete Ménage à Trois: Marxism, Feminism, and Racism," in *Women and Revolution: A Discussion of the Unhappy*

Marriage of Marxism and Feminism, ed. Lydia Sargent (Boston: South End Press, 1981); and Amy Swerdlow and Hanna Lessinger, eds., *Class, Race, and Sex: The Dynamics of Control* (Boston: G. K. Hall, 1983).

3. See Karen Brodkin Sacks, "Toward a Unified Theory of Class, Race and Gender," *American Ethnologist* 16:3 (1989): 534–50.

4. For a discussion of "social location" that compares ethnographic data from two research sites, see my article: "Mujeres in Factories: Race and Class Perspectives on Women, Work and Family," in Leonardo, *Gender at the Crossroads of Knowledge.*

5. Renato Rosaldo, *Culture and Truth: The Remaking of Social Analysis* (Boston: Beacon Press, 1989).

6. Gloria Anzaldúa, *Borderlands/La Frontera: The New Mestiza* (San Francisco: Spinsters/Aunt Lute Foundation, 1987).

7. For a critique of this view, see Leonarda Ybarra, "Empirical and Theoretical Developments in Studies of the Chicano Family," in *The State of Chicano Research on Family, Labor and Migration: Proceedings of the First Stanford Symposium on Chicano Research and Public Policy,* ed. Armando Valdéz, Albert Camarillo, and Tomas Almaguer (Stanford: Stanford Center for Chicano Research, 1983).

8. See Tomas Almaguer, *Racial Fault Lines: The Historical of White Supremacy in California* (Berkeley: University of California Press, 1994).

9. Mario Barrera, *Race and Class in the Southwest: A Theory of Racial Inequality* (Notre Dame: University of Notre Dame Press, 1979); Albert Camarillo, *Chicanos in a Changing Society* (Cambridge: Harvard University Press, 1979).

10. Wayne A. Cornelius, Richard Mines, Leo R. Chavez, and Jorge G. Castro, *Mexican Immigrants in Southern California: A Summary of Current Knowledge* (San Diego: University of California, Center for U.S.-Mexican Studies, Research Report Series 40, 1982).

11. Ernesto Galarza sketches out some Chicano culture-regions. See "Mexicans in the Southwest: A Culture in Process," in *Plural Society in the Southwest,* ed. Edward H. Spicer and Raymond H. Thompson (New York: Interbook, 1972).

12. For literature on the process of ethnic identification for Chicanos as a whole, see: John A. García, "Yo Soy Mexicano . . . : Self-Identity and Sociodemographic Correlates," *Social Science Quarterly* 62:1 (1981): 88–98; Ramón Gutierrez, "Unraveling America's Hispanic Past: Internal Stratification and Class Boundaries," in *Proceedings of the All-U.C. Invitational Conference on the Comparative Study of Race, Ethnicity, Gender and Class,* ed. Sucheng Chan (Santa Cruz: University of California, 1987); Susan E. Keefe and Amado M. Padilla, *Chicano Ethnicity* (Albuquerque: University of New Mexico Press, 1987); José E. Limon, "The Folk Performance of Chicano and the Cultural Limits of Political Ideology," in *"And Other Neighborly Names": Social Process and Cultural Image in Texas Folklore,* ed. Richard Bauman

and Roger D. Abrahams (Austin: University of Texas Press, 1981); and Joseph V. Metzgar, "The Ethnic Sensitivity of Spanish New Mexicans: A Survey and Analysis," *New Mexico Historical Review* 49:1 (1974): 49–73. For discussion of how race/ethnicity and gender are intertwined in ethnic identification, see Anzaldúa, *Borderlands/La Frontera;* Cherríe Moraga, *Loving in the War Years, lo que nunca pasó por sus labios* (Boston: South End Press, 1983); and Maxine Baca Zinn, "Gender and Ethnic Identity Among Chicanas," *Frontiers* 5:2 (1981): 18–24.

13. Moraga, *Loving in the War Years.*

14. Emma Perez, "Speaking from the Margin: Uninvited Discourse on Sexuality and Power," in *Building with Our Hands: New Directions in Chicana Studies,* ed. Beatriz Pesquera and Adela de la Torre (Berkeley: University of California Press, 1993). For other works on Chicana/Latina lesbians, see Norma Alarcón, Ana Castillo, and Cherríe Moraga, eds., *The Sexuality of Latinas,* special issue of *Third Woman* (1989); and Juanita Ramos, ed., *Compañeras: Latina Lesbians (An Anthology)* (New York: Latina Lesbian History Project, 1987).

15. Rosaldo, *Culture and Truth.*

16. Beatriz Pesquera, "Work and Family: A Comparative Analysis of Professional, Clerical and Blue-Collar Chicana Workers" (Ph.D. dissertation, University of California, Berkeley, 1986).

17. Américo Paredes, "On Ethnographic Work Among Minority Groups: A Folklorist's Perspective," *New Scholar* 6:1/2 (1977): 1–32.

18. Tomas Almaguer, "The Cartography of Homosexual Desire and Identity among Chicano Men," *Differences: A Journal of Feminist Cultural Studies* 3 (Summer 1991); Charles L. Briggs, *Competence in Performance: The Creativity of Tradition in Mexicano Verbal Art* (Philadelphia: University of Pennsylvania Press, 1988); Douglas E. Foley, *Learning Capitalist Culture, Deep in the Heart of Tejas* (Philadelphia: University of Pennsylvania Press, 1990); José Limon, "Carne, Carnales, and the Carnivalesque: Bakhtinian Batos, Disorder and Narrative Discourses," *American Ethnologist* (August 1989); Diego Vigil, *Barrio Gangs: Street Life and Identity in Southern California* (Austin: University of Texas Press, 1988); Patricia Zavella, *Women's Work and Chicano Families: Cannery Workers of the Santa Clara Valley* (Ithaca: Cornell University Press, 1987).

Frontiers 12:2 (1991): 73–85.

Writing, Politics, and *las Lesberadas*

Platicando con *Gloria Anzaldúa*

ANNLOUISE KEATING

A self-described "Chicana *tejana* feminist-dyke-*patlache* poet, fiction writer, and cultural theorist" from the Rio Grande Valley of south Texas, Gloria Anzaldúa has played a pivotal role in redefining U.S. feminist movement.[1] She is the coeditor of *This Bridge Called My Back: Writings by Radical Women of Color* and editor of *Making Face, Making Soul/Haciendo Caras: Creative and Critical Perspectives by Women of Color.* She lectures nationally and internationally and has taught creative writing, Chicano/a studies, and feminist theory at several U.S. colleges and universities. Anzaldúa and her works have won numerous awards, including the Before Columbus Foundation American Book Award for *This Bridge,* the Lambda Lesbian Small Book Press Award for *Haciendo Caras,* an NEA Fiction Award, and the Sappho Award of Distinction.

The following conversations with Gloria Anzaldúa took place at the University of Arizona on October 25 and 26, 1991, during her residence as a Rockefeller visiting scholar, in which she presented a series of lectures and workshops. Anzaldúa discusses her motivation for editing *This Bridge* and *Haciendo Caras;* the differences between unity and solidarity; the interconnections between spirituality and politics; sexuality; and writing.

THIS BRIDGE AND HACIENDO CARAS

ANNLOUISE: It's been over ten years since *This Bridge Called My Back* was first published.[2] Has its impact on both feminists of color and white feminists' thinking met your expectations? Exceeded them?

GLORIA: I think that it did meet my expectations. Before I started *This*

Bridge I had gone through a very frustrating time with the middle-class white women who were the heads of the writing groups and writing organizations that I was involved in – the Feminist Writers' Guild, the women's writers union. In grad school I had been virtually ignored and told who I was; nobody wanted to listen to what I wanted to say, and I felt invisible. When I left Austin in '77 and went to San Francisco the same thing happened. I would go to these consciousness raising meetings at the Y, and I would be the only Chicana. These women's organizations were on the one hand saying "How do you define yourself?" But before I could even open my mouth they'd start defining who I was. Or they would interrupt when I was talking. Or they would let me talk, but then they would repeat what I had said but they would completely misread and mishear everything I had said. So finally Merlin Stone was doing a workshop at Willow, and she had a couple of scholarships for working-class or women of color who couldn't afford the prices for a weekend retreat at this out-of-the-way, nice, scenic, middle-class inn.

I went, and Merlin and I were getting along fine. But I started noticing that the people who ran the retreat were looking at me funny, and they switched me from my single room into a collective bunk-bed room, where I was one of the only ones. Merlin and I figured that they had found out I was not a paying member like the other women – there were about twelve of us – and they started treating me differently. Like I didn't deserve a room to myself and I didn't deserve to eat what they ate. Their remarks were really racist, and they weren't even aware of it. One evening I was so angry that I couldn't sleep. I went into the kitchen to make some tea and thought, "They're not going to be around begrudging me my cup of tea." Merlin also had insomnia and she was bothered by the same thing, so we talked. It was at her encouragement that I started doing *This Bridge*.

I put the soliciting letter together and started telling people about it. Things were kind of slow, so I asked Cherríe [Moraga], about six months after I started, to join me, and we started the project in '78 or '79. In '80 we were going along, and neither of us could afford the costs that it takes when you're putting a book together. Not only xeroxes but phone calls and postage and time, you know. I got very very ill and almost died. At the end of March the doctor told me not to take on any heavy duties or major projects. But that summer we had to put the book together. So those and other similar frustrations compelled me to do *Haciendo Caras* nine years later.[3]

I actually started *Haciendo Caras* in the fall of '88 when I started grad school. The frustrations this time around came out of my search for materials to teach a women-of-color class, and once again I had to search for articles, essays, stories, and poems. I couldn't rely on teaching *This Bridge* again because people had been teaching it in a number of classes. One student told me that she had had it in four of her undergrad and grad classes. So I thought, well, I have to do it. There wasn't anything out there. There were single anthologies of particular cultures, Native American, etc., etc. So I started looking at magazines, quarterlies. I'd go to the library, look at my bookshelves, ask other people, and put together a reader for this class. I had been waiting for someone to do a similar kind of work, and nobody did.

So I got the idea of using this as a book – mostly a textbook for women's studies classes or classes like the one that you teach – but I wanted original things as well. Very early on in fall of '88 when I was putting together the reader I had already decided that it was going to be a book. So I started asking people to submit. I had all these wonderful essays planned, but although some people came through, others didn't. So it doesn't have as many poems, stories, and essays originally written for the book as I had wanted it to. I think it's not time for them to publish; they can't take the risk, or something else is holding them back. Those nine years I thought there *has* to have been some improvements, right? And the fact that *Bridge* had become a widely read book in the women's community said to me that people were listening to the voices of women of color – that white women were listening and that women of color were listening to each other. But it seemed to me that more of the dialogue in *This Bridge* was addressed to the white women, the white feminists. In *Haciendo Caras* I wanted us to be talking to each other more. And sometimes that's true and other times it's not.

AL: You mean that sometimes it seems that the writers are addressing themselves to white women?

G: Well, some of it – like the Anmiach who wrote the poem to her birthmother. She's talking directly to her birthmother, but I think incidentally she was also talking to her white adopted mother as the other negative, and I don't know how fair that was. Papusa in her letter – when she wrote me this letter because she couldn't write the essay that I wanted her to write about her antiracism work that she does in Iowa – I think she's talking to us. It's addressed to *us.*

AL: "Us" being?

G: Us, the people in *Haciendo Caras* – the women-of-color contributors. Chela Sandoval's report on the NWSA conference against racism, I think it's speaking to white women, and it's also speaking to us, so there's a change from *Bridge* in that there's more of the debate among women of color. You've read it. What do you think?

AL: Yeah. I think sometimes the debate is more among women of color. Your essay "En Rapport, In Opposition" very much is. Others seem to be self-expression; they're just going out, and some seem addressed to whoever reads it – María Lugones's piece, for example.

G: A more general audience? For me, one of the differences is that in *Bridge* we were reacting against the white feminists' theories and words, and it was more of a reactive kind of book. *Haciendo Caras* feels to me like yes, that part is still there, but now we've gone off on our own paths and we're utilizing that energy to work things out amongst ourselves. We're still bridging with white women, but a lot of the energy is just staying here.

AL: As you say in the preface, you're building a culture.

G: Yes. But that's just my vision of the book. I may have read it in a way entirely different from you or from other people because my particular reading was that I had certain themes that I wanted linked so that I could create a whole out of all these disparate voices and all these hundreds and hundreds of concerns. That I could somehow focus, highlight, certain areas so that then I could say, "These are the concerns of the book; this is what these women are saying." As an editor, to create an entity out of all these different arms and legs and eyes and ears – that's always hard because there's bound to be things that you have to leave out in creating a picture of this total entity, so if it had been a different editor it would have been a different book. Even if it had been the same same pieces in the book, if somebody else had edited and written the preface, the introduction – you know what I mean? Because the title pulls it together, *Haciendo Caras,* making our own identities.

AL: Yes. And the order that you arranged the pieces in.

G: Right, and the order they fall in. I really didn't want to intercede or interpret too much so I didn't do a little intro for each section, like we did with *Bridge.* I also didn't want to do a typical introduction where you say, "This author does thus and thus and thus; and the next author . . ." I wanted to create another little essay out of all the things that were in the book and my own ideas; I wanted it to be different from your typical introduction. A professor at University of California who saw a preliminary draft of the manuscript told me that I was centering myself too much in the essay, that I should take three-quarters of myself out of the intro. But I said when people ask me about the process of putting together *Bridge* they want to know: "How did you do it?" "What was your process?" So I went ahead and did it my way.

UNITY/SOLIDARITY

AL: I think your approach anchors the collection; it tells your position. In "En Rapport, In Opposition" you say that you've "come to suspect that unity is another Anglo invention like their one sole god and the myth of the monopole."[4] This essay was first published four years ago. Do you still feel this way?

G: Yes. I especially feel this way when I go to Hispanic Heritage Week events. Once a year in different universities they have Hispanic Heritage Week and their big thing, you know, is "Latinos unidos," "Jamás serán vencidos," and I think, why is there such an emphasis put on unity? What about just plain being in solidarity with each other? What about just maintaining our own separate ethnic groups yet coming together and interacting? You know, the Chileans, the Mexicanos, the Chicanos, the newly arrived, the Puerto Ricans . . . Why does it have to be this Hispanic umbrella, or this Latino/Latina umbrella? Why this thing about unity, and why – after five hundred years haven't we achieved it? And the reason we haven't achieved it is because we're so different – geographically, culturally, and even linguistically. If you're from Brazil or from the Caribbeans, you may not speak Spanish. So then I started thinking that if we never achieve unity we're going to have such a sense of failure. Such a sense of "Oh we've been struggling for years and we can't unite; there must be something wrong with Chicanos who can't get it together to present a united front." And if you take the Chicanos there's differences between the California ones, the ones in Arizona, in New Mexico, in Texas, in the Midwest. Yes, we have a lot of common stuff, but it's a big imposition, a big burden, to put on an ethnic group that they should get their shit together and unite. White people aren't united. They may be united under capitalism or some kind of system that forces everybody to be under it.

And so I thought what is it in our mentality – and I say "our" because I've been trained in the Western way of thinking – that there has to be some kind of hierarchical order, and at the very top there is the One: the one law, the one god, the one universe, the one language, the one absolute? And that absolute may be "Do unto others as you would have them do unto you"; or it could be what the physicists are now searching for, the one general law that everything that happens in the universe – biologically, physically, and everything else – will fall under this one law.

Then I look at the U.S. Americanization of the total planet through the media of television and radio (mostly television). People go into these little villages like in Vietnam or Australia, and you will have everybody watching, including the people of color. I read an article about how the Aborigines in Australia really like some of these movies like *Rocky* and *Rocky II* because they see that Stallone looks a little ethnic, and for a while he's winning against the other guys, which the Aborigines see as the whites. The underdog is the hero with his bombs and his guns. So there's this whole gathering of the whole peoples' minds on the planet. It's very attractive – anything American from Coca Cola to Levis. And then I think maybe in terms of capitalism and in terms of the commodity market that such a unity through clothes could be possible, but I don't think politically or aesthetically or psychologically or any of the other ways. I don't think it can happen.

AL: So you see unity as homogenizing or monolithic?

G: Yes. I see it as homogenizing because it is used as the big umbrella where everyone can take shelter. And that big umbrella, if you don't achieve it – if you can't get under that umbrella and achieve unity – it becomes a club against you because then why are you as a black or a Latin or an Indian so divisive that you can't achieve any kind of unity with your own people?

AL: So it just erases differences?

G: *Sí.* And it also says that we can't live separately and be connected, and I think we can live separately, and we can also connect and be together. But I would rather call that "in solidarity," "in support of each other," "*en conocimiento,*" rather than unity. Because I think unity always privileges one voice, one group. Whereas with solidarity everybody has their own space and can say their own thing and recognize that here's another group that has their own thing and says their own thing. But there's connections, commonalities as well as differences. And the differences don't get erased, and the commonalities don't become all-important; they don't become more important than the differences or vice versa.

AL: And also people can say things *to each other* in terms of each particular group as well as speaking to bigger groups?

G: Yes, yes. And then I think of the human personality. It's supposed to be one. You know, you're one entity – one person with one identity. And that's not so. There are many personalities and subpersonalities in *you,* and your identity shifts every time you shift positions. The other thing – and I'm fictionalizing this; it's a story called "La Entrada de Ajenos a la Casa," "The

Entry of Foreigners into the House" or "Foreigners Coming in the House" –
it's about the body and all the organisms that live in the body: the E. coli in
the stomach – the bacteria – the plaque in your teeth. In just the forehead
area there are literally millions of little organisms that live in your skin, and
the root of each eyelash has a particular different organism from the one in
your forehead. So that you, AnnLouise, are not just AnnLouise. You're all
the different organisms and parasites that live on your body and also the
ones that live in symbiotic relationship to you. And then the animals, too.
You look at the cows and there'll be little birds picking the ticks off the cows,
and there'll be a water buffalo with a little bird sitting on its back. So who
are you? You're not a single entity. You're a multiple entity.

AL: So you're really talking about an incredible interconnectedness?

G: Yes, and I'm talking about it not just on the biological level – the
personal or human level – but these different groups. It's so wrong for me to
emphasize a unity when there's no such thing. You know? Your hands right
now have all these living things on the surface, not to talk about all your
insides! Anyway, the story is about having a wart. The story is about a
woman who becomes aware that she's not a single entity.

AL: *Prieta?*

G: It's *Prieta*. It's one of the lesser finished stories, so I don't know if it's
going to make it into the book.[5] So it's not just on the political level of
uniting groups of people under one thing, but our own *body* is not one
entity. So you can take it from the microcosm to the macrocosm, from the
microorganism to the system of planets, our Milky Way cosmos, which
again is only one . . .

SPIRITUALITY/POLITICS

AL: In the same essay you discuss the importance of spirituality to women
of color. How do you integrate spirituality with your political views?

G: I think that most of us, *all* of us men and women of all colors, go
around thinking that this is who and what we are, and we only see maybe
three-quarters or maybe not even three-quarters of ourselves. There's a
component that is very much part of the unconscious – part of the spirit
world – that's also part of us, but we've been told it's not there so we don't
perceive it. A little child is taught what to see physically. If we were taught to
see differently we would probably see people from other dimensions sitting
in the armchair, you know. Interlapping universes. But we're not taught to
see that way. There's certain traditions like the shamanist tradition – some

of the other spiritual traditions that you actually *learn* to experience the interpenetration of those other worlds. According to the Olmacs, the Toltecs, the Mayans, the Aztecs, and others, this physical reality is one facet or facade of the spirit world. This is a mask for the spirit world, so that you and I are masks for the spirit. We're just the costume; we're just the clothes. And if you can take the mask off or go behind the mask, you are let into a connection with this other reality, of the spirit.

I think with me it always happens with trauma, with a traumatic shock of some kind that opens me so brutally – I'm just cracked open by the experience – that for a while things come inside me, other realities, other worlds. Like when I was mugged I became aware of things that had to do with the landscape and the trees and this particular ravine where it happened. I could almost hear their vibrations because every living thing has vibrations, has a speed of vibrating. And somewhere really, really, really far back in our history I think someone got really scared of this connection with the spirit and the spiritual world, put down the wall, and concentrated on using our hands rather than our imaginations to achieve certain things. So like in the poem "Interface," Leyla can achieve things with her imagination. She doesn't need to move dirt; she doesn't need a crane. We went a technological route rather than a spiritual route. If you want to move from here to New York you get on a plane. But had we gone in the other direction, all we'd have to do is think "I am now in New York between Third and whatever," and there we would be. And I think this is why shamanism is so intriguing to people and intriguing to me, because you achieve that through your imagination, through your soul. Your soul is actually there. And when you dream, your soul is really – if you're dreaming about Manhattan – it's really there. And then you travel back to your body.

So here we go as feminists wanting to be practical and wanting to make a difference and wanting to make some changes, and we're looking at everything that gives us strength: having roots, having a historical past that we can connect with and say, "This is the route that my particular group has walked, and I can see how what happened in the past has affected the present and therefore affected me and who I am and how I feel about myself." So we've dug into the past for a history and models and women and stories that can give us some sort of ground to walk on, some sort of foundation, some sort of place to take off from and also to find positive stuff that will feed us, that will inspire us. And I think when you start connecting with your past racial history and your own childhood personal history, and you have all these ideas about feminism and the rights of women, the rights of all people, trying to make the world a little cleaner and a little safer and stop the destruction. And you want it so badly that that desire opens you up to being exposed to things that will give you the strength to survive and accomplish this. And as these pathways open – in these channels, tunnels, cracks, whatever you want to call them – you come up against an awareness that the universe is alive. It pulsates; everything's alive: nature, and trees, and the sky, and the wind.

Once you connect with that, you feel like you are part of interconnecting organisms – vegetable, animal, mineral – and that they all have some kind of consciousness. If this pulsating rhythm, vibration, is some kind of awareness, of aliveness, then that's a consciousness. So you start looking at rocks in a different way – at birds – and when they appear and when they don't appear, and you let your imagination act as a brain, as a center like in a computer there's a center that connects and sorts through all the data and comes out with what you want. I think the imagination does that, and it will look at the clouds and project certain images in the clouds so that you see certain patterns, and the clouds stop being some kind of weather phenomena and become part of this force that pulsates, that's everywhere. That's the spirit and the spirituality, and it's real and you know it. Sometimes it comes through you as a result of a shock. Sometimes it comes through you as a result of a dream or something that you read. But it's such a popular thing right now, in California anyway, that some people pretend that they've experienced this, and they go through what I call this pseudo-spiritual New Age awareness – the pseudo witches, but it's just a performance. And then there are other real people who don't need to do that, who in some way have seen the fourth or the quarter part of their personality that's been hidden from them, the spiritual part, the unconscious part. They don't need to go through any of those fancy retreats and elaborate rituals and drumming and going into ecstatic states. They just all of the sudden see it. It's like turning around and looking at your shoulder and realizing that you'd only been seeing half an arm. Does that make sense to you?

AL: Definitely.

G: But right now in the academy with high theorists, it's very incorrect to talk about that part because they're afraid that that part is something innate, and therefore they'll be labeled essentialists. Because the women who talk about spirituality a lot of times will talk about *la diosa*, the goddess, and how women are innately nurturing, and how they're peaceful. But they're not. It's all learned. Right?

AL: Right.

G: So they equate that kind of essentialism with spirituality, and I don't. And maybe in the past there is that in my writing . . .

AL: Can you say more about the interconnection between "masks," physical reality, and the spirit world?

G: Well, I think the different personas that we are – the you that's with me right now has one face; the you that's going to be with other people tomorrow will have a slightly different one; but basically there's the you. Basically there's you.

AL: But it's all these parts.

G: Yeah. But the masks are integral to you. The concept of the Olmacs and the Toltecs and the Mayans is slightly different. For example, their statues of a person inside a jaguar's head, or emerging from the mouth of the eagle, illustrate their belief that there's always the human behind the animal. But behind the human there's the animal. This concept of the mask is their philosophy of life, their belief that this is the adornment for the spirit; this is how the spirit dresses itself. And behind this mask – this outer reality, this house, my clothes, my face, me – is a spiritual entity. Okay, that was *their* explanation. To me, the masks are no longer necessary. You know, when people would do the deer dance, they would wear the deerskin. I don't think that we need that mask. I think we recognize that our flesh is spiritualized and that instead of "here is the so-called real world and there's a wall, a partition, and then over here is the world of the spirit and the world of the ideals, that's totally noncorporeal and that we're the corporeal manifestation of *that* world" – which is what the ancients believed in; there was a separation there. In *Prieta* I'm trying to do away with the separation and say it's here and now, and at the blink of an eye. I don't know if you ever read "*El Paisano* Is a Bird of Good Omen," where the roadrunner blinks, and Andrea (who's now Prieta) blinks and suddenly she's not sitting there on the fence post but is over in the lagoon. And when she's watching those little kids playing with the lizard and they have the horned toad – and the blink of the eye she is those lizards and that horned toad and those ants and she's feeling the bites.[6] I think that we don't need that partition. Does that make sense to you?

AL: Yeah. It's not that the "spiritual" is somewhere else; it's just that right now we don't see it because of the way we're looking.

G: Because of the way we have been taught what reality is and what reality is not.

AL: Right. Because what we've been trained to see influences what we believe and therefore how we act.

G: Yeah. And the analogy that I have read is a dog whistle that humans can't hear, or the frequencies in a radio station. Certain species will pick up a wide range of these frequencies, and others won't. And the body itself can tune into all these stations . . . if we knew how.

AL: But nobody's really cared or learned how, right?

G: Yeah, so that a very large percentage of our brain goes unused, a very large percent of the reality that we could take in through the senses is not used because we've been trained that this is only what we can see. And so the people who can see like this are either crazy or they're shamans or creative people.

AL: That's similar to what I believe. . . . There's this tree I communicate with, and I resist it. I really resist it, and what'll happen is that as I resist it when I'm working, my writing . . . I can't write. Or things will start to go wrong around the house, and I'll say okay and I'll go outside and just sit there and say –

G: "Talk to me."

AL: Yeah. But the rational side can always say, "Oh this is just yourself talking to yourself." But the other part says, "Well, yes it could be that, but it just seems like something more."

G: Yeah, because I think that that self is extended to the tree. The self does not stop with just you, with your body. I think the self can penetrate other things and they penetrate you. And your remark that you can't prove it – it's not rational; it's not scientific – goes back to the concept of objectivity, which has been one of the ruling models of our lives, even before science. But it started with science, that you have to test it. It has to show some kind of physical manifestation or else –

AL: – it's not real.

G: And that theory of objectivity, which has been proven false over and over by its own scientists makes us separate because it privileges the eyes, the visual, and causes distance and separation. So the other part of yourself that's objective says, "Oh no. You can't be experiencing this. It's just you talking to another part of you. It's just your imagination taking off." And so here come other people that say what happens in your imagination is just as real as what happens when you walk down the street. What happens in a fantasy, *that* reality has as much validity as external reality. A work of fiction, when you're working at creating a story, what happens to those people and the setting is just as much *real* as what happens to your mother and your brother . . . you know?

AL: Yes.

G: And that's one of the points that I try to make in *Prieta,* that there's just not *one* reality; there's all these different realities, and why should one reality – which is external life – be privileged over the others? Some cultures really pay a lot of attention to their dreams and their rituals and the imaginative part of their lives, which is considered other dimensions of reality. But those are very few tribes on the planet and they are being killed off, like the Aborigine in Australia that have their dream time. And it's just us that privilege the mechanical, the objective, the industrial, the scientific.

At a recent conference I took the pamphlet entitled "Alternative Responses to the Columbus Sesquicentennial" with a map of the U.S. and Mexico and South America, and I got up in front of the crowd and I turned it over and said, "Who's to say that up is up and down is down? We're whirling on an axis but we're also going around the sun. So why should the U.S. and Canada be upstairs – top – and South America and Africa and Australia be down here?" Just like why does the U.S. take it upon itself to call itself America?

I feel the same way about waking life – which is external reality plus some other alternate states because you can be sitting there and go off into alternate states, you know, fantasies of thinking about yesterday, memories and things that have nothing to do with external reality. But the other division is between the dream life and waking life, and we spend eight hours sleeping and dreaming and the rest of time in waking reality and going off into alternate states. When you're writing, for example, you go off in alternate states. What's to say that on the other side, the dream eagle – the dream self – is not looking at external reality as the dream, and the dream as real? Because sometimes to me the dreams make more sense in the way they connect, associatively like a poem, than this outer reality. . . . It's getting too wild, right?

AL: Not at all. Well, I don't think so. But some people object to spirituality; they see it as passive. If you're going to say there's all these other realities, someone could take the step of saying, "So external reality doesn't matter; oppression doesn't matter because you have all these other worlds." And you don't do that. You have definite spiritual beliefs yet maintain a very strong political agenda, and I think that's very rare. How do you manage to do that?

G: Because I look at us and we're flesh and blood. We're corporeal. We occupy weight and space, three-dimensionally. We're not some kind of thought energy that's disembodied. We're embodied in the flesh. So there must be a purpose to this stage that we're living in, to this corporeal stage which we lose after we die and we don't have before we're born. The things that we really struggle with and need to work out, we need to work out on the physical plane. So we can't escape. Just because those other realities are there, we can't just escape and say, "Oh, this is just a play on some kind of stage and it doesn't really matter." It might be a play on the stage, but it's a matter of life and death. So these things can only be worked out in physical reality.

AL: Like in *Bridge*, "theory in the flesh."

G: Yes.

AL: Also, if there's this kind of interconnection that goes with this kind of spiritual whatever, then that's another way that people who are so different in so many ways can connect, through this other level. Does that make sense?

G: *Sí.*

AL: I think I picked that up from your writing.

G: Yes. What I call "*almas afines.*" That we're kindred spirits.

LESBERADAS

AL: In *Borderlands/La Frontera* you claim that your lesbianism is chosen; for some it is genetically inherent, but you "*made the choice to be queer.*"[7] Now, Cherríe Moraga, in a review of your book, interprets this statement to refer to your political decision to identify yourself as lesbian, and her view makes sense.[8] But I hadn't interpreted it that way when I first read your essay. So what did you mean, what kind of choice were you referring to?

G: I was thinking back to how much are we born with knowing and being. How much of the basic personality, the basic self, is there genetically – is just born? And how much of it has been taught, especially about sexuality and being female and being Chicana, being white, being whatever class. I got to thinking that there's got to be a middle road, and this thinking has been since *Borderlands*. There has to be a middle way, that you can't get polarized between "You are born into this world as a blank slate and everything that's written on your body has been put there by society, including your sexual preference" and the other extreme that "You are born female and therefore you're nurturing and you're giving and you're peaceful; you don't kill, you don't violate." I wasn't a dumb person: I knew who was getting the strokes and who was getting the slaps; the boys would always be privileged. Heterosexuality was a patriarchal institution and the woman would always have to constantly struggle, even if she was coupled with a very progressive feminist-oriented male. His training would be to be the macho, and however much he would fight it some of it would bleed through, just like we fight against the passivity and all the things we were told we were. As a thinking woman, I looked at the model of the heterosexual couple. I would never be able to stand putting up with that kind of shit from a man. Or if I did put up with it I would be very ashamed of myself and feel very bad about myself.

So the only viable choice for me was lesbianism. Because in lesbianism there would be *some* power things – if my lover happened to be white she would have some privilege; if I was older I'd have some power – but I had more of a chance to have a meaningful relationship with a woman than I would with a man. This is common sense. You look at all the countries on the planet and how the heterosexual model is the ruling model and how some men have four or five wives and the wife never has power unless she's an upper-class woman, and then she has to do other things to keep that power – manipulate and conform. Or a businesswoman who's an executive has to play the game in order to obtain that position, and it's a very rare woman who can keep her gender identity female as traditional female identity. So the women who've become equal to men in terms of power, it's been at a great cost to them, and they negate a lot of stuff. Sometimes they repress feelings, you know? They get ulcers . . . not that the men have it that easy, but across the planet heterosexuality benefits the male, so isn't it logical for you to want a different relationship?

AL: Definitely.

G: And if desire is something that you learn . . . just like heterosexuality was taught us, you know, you're supposed to like this little boy if you're a little girl. This is some of the stuff that I'm talking about in "She Ate Horses."[9] If desire is something that you're not born with, something that you acquire – that sexual hunger to connect, to touch somebody, to be touched by somebody – if that can be learned, it can also be unlearned and relearned. So that if there are political lesbians out there (a lot of political lesbians came out in the seventies because that was a viable alternative), there were other lesbians like Cherríe who at a very early age were attracted, lusting, after women. With both types, there was a resistance to the teaching that we should desire men. But with people like Cherríe, that took on a very emotional kind of manifestation very early on. They got turned on by girls. And with the political lesbian you were a lesbian in your head first and then you started looking at women differently because of these theories about sexuality: Is sexuality learned? Is heterosexuality learned? Is lesbianism learned? And through the theory you got to the body and the emotion and the closeness with women.

After *Borderlands* came out I got to thinking that yes, some of us do choose. It's a very conscious thing: "I'm going to give up men; I'm going to go to women; I'm going to come out of the closet and declare my lesbianism." With other people, it's very unconscious. They don't even know they've made the choice. They think it's just natural to be a lesbian or to be a heterosexual woman, but there have been all these processes and decisions made all along the way that you're not even aware of, that you don't remember. Okay so here we are now in 1991, and I don't think a person is born queer; I don't think every person is born queer. I think there may be some genetic propensity towards most things: music, having a good ear for music. I don't know if there are any queer genes, but if there are they'll be discovered. So some of it might be biological; some of it might be learned; and some of it might be chosen. My position will probably change in a year or two, but that's where I'm at with it.

AL: So it's more than a political decision to *identify* yourself as lesbian; you were deciding a lifestyle?

G: Yes. But now in retrospect I look back and remember the kind of closeness that I've had with women from the time I was real little even though I was taught that women were spiteful and competed against each other and it wasn't worth it to make friends with women, that only men could be your friends. *Todo eso.* And then when I was teaching high school all the Chicana *jotitas* and the Chicana *marimachas* and all the Chicana *maricones* would hang around with *me,* and all the Chicana *maricones* would follow me around, and they'd show me the love letters that their lovers had sent them. The same thing happened later with my friends when I would go up to the Y and do the consciousness-raising feminist stuff, when I thought I was the only straight woman and there were all these diesel dykes. One time I turned around and asked a friend, "If I become a dyke will I have to drive a motorcycle and be like them?" You know it's sexist for me to say that, but that was the thought I had. And then one day I looked around and I reviewed my life from this other way station where I had stopped. Did I give you the analogy of the train and the tracks and the terrain as being the self?

AL: No.

G: The train will stop at this way station, which might be Boston, and stay a few years and then get on the road again and stop at another way station. In this way station you were a heterosexual; in this way station you were a lesbian. You look back down the tracks and you look at your past and all the events in your life and your friends, and you're now looking at them through lesbian eyes. So you're reinterpreting the past.

When I became a lesbian I looked back at my life and realized that all along I had had these signals that I was one of them too. So, when I became a political lesbian that I thought *I* had chosen, had I really chosen it or had I been one all along but repressed it? When I was writing *Borderlands* I had the lesbian perspective, but my thinking had not evolved to the place where I believed that when you realize that you like women, that you want to have primary relationships with women, that you want to have carnal relationships with women, you can still make the choice to stay with men. Many of us have done that. You can become a lesbian and be a lesbian for twenty years and then decide that you want to be sexual with a man. I don't know if that changes your lesbian identity, but . . . you make a choice. If you know you're a lesbian and you're married and have kids you say, "Okay I'm going to be with my husband and I'll be a straight woman as much as I can and be with my kids." Or you can say, "I'm going to leave my husband; I'm going to come out as a lesbian and take this path," depending on how much courage you have. But I think that there's only certain places where you can make that choice, and those are the places of ambiguity, of change, where you're in *nepantla* – you can go either way. Once you're on this track, you're pretty much a lesbian and you think like a lesbian and you live with lesbians and your community is lesbians, and the heterosexual world is foreign and that's the path you and I – well I don't know about you – but that's the path I'm on.

But I will get to these *nepantla* places where I have the choices. I can say, "I'm not going to be political anymore; I'm just going to retreat into my writing." I don't think I'll ever be that way, but people have made that choice. So it's not that I'm invalidating what I said in *Borderlands*. That was my thinking then and I was in that particular track, but the train has kept going and I've stopped at other way stations. The way station that I last stopped, had to do with my class changes, going from a *campesino* working class into an intellectual, academic, artistic class. With the money and royalties and speaking engagements coming in, I am now entering a middle class, which was like the *nepantla* space with the *Coatlicue* state right in the middle of it; it was so agonizing. And at the next way station I will look back at our conversation, and at *Borderlands* and *Prieta* and *Bridge* and *Haciendo Caras* and whatever other books I write and I will say "I am now this identity." The old identities are still part of me: the straight woman is in me; the white woman is in me; the nonpolitical woman is in me. But basically my personality has always been a resisting personality, going against what's not fair. It wasn't fair the way my culture treated girls. It wasn't fair the way the white culture treats ethnic groups. So there's this strong sense in me of "It's not fair and I'm going to fight against it because it's not fair."

AL: You have the poem where you talk about "the other side" – always on the other side – in *Compañeras*.[10] And also you use that metaphor in *Borderlands* of being on the other side. What can you say about that?

G: It's almost like the differences in me from other women started at a very early age. When I was three months old I started menstruating. The effect wasn't just psychological, but it was also biological and physical. My body suffered. I was in pain. I had breasts when I was six years old – these same breasts that I have now – which my mother would wrap up so the little kids wouldn't notice. She would tie a little rag in my panties, so that if I bled it wouldn't be all over the place. And I had to make excuses at P.E. that I couldn't bathe with the other kids because they would see that I had pubic hair. So I was marked very early, and it was very painful for me to be so different because I already felt different because of my race and being a farmworker. In the valley if you worked the fields you're a much lower Chicana than if you worked in a department store or in an office. It was a very class thing. So there are already differences between women and between the different ethnic groups and white people. Those differences are painful. Well, with me they really went all the way to the bone, the body. And because I was wide open as a child everything came in. People would say something in the wrong tone of voice and I would take it *so* personally that I would be devastated for the rest of the week. (And I have a poem called "*la vulva es una herida abierta*," "The Vulva Is an Open Wound." I'll give you a copy because I was going to read it, but when I decided that I wanted the audience to laugh rather than to cry I decided not to read it because they'd be crying. They would have gone away real sad.) I had very thin skin; everything came in.

AL: How does your childhood go with being on the other side?

G: When I went to school I saw that I was so different from the other kids – en masse – because I could pick up knowledge. They called me "the brain." I was a dumb Mexican who was smart. It was such a shock to the teachers that I was smart because I was supposed to be dumb like the other kids. I always felt separate in school, and this was like a hundred percent Chicano with only the teachers being white. I already felt on the other side.

AL: Separate, different? Not belonging.

G: Yes. Not belonging. Always on the other side. When I got to high school it happened literally because I was placed in accelerated classes, and all the other Chicanas except one guy were in different classes. The only time we got together was in P.E., homeroom, and health. But the white kids never spoke to me, and the teachers never spoke to me. I'd sit in one corner, or in the middle, or in the front, or the back, and it didn't matter.

AL: You were always on the other side.

G: I was always on the other side. The kids that would have been there for me in high school I couldn't really be friends with because I didn't spend the majority of my classes with them. I would just see them at P.E. I had a few friends that were – peripheral friends. And I went to a consolidated school where people from the country were bussed in, so they were all strangers except for the kids who lived in the town. But then I went to college in an all girls' school – Texas Women's University – where I witnessed a first lesbian experience: two women making love to each other. There were two dorm rooms with a connecting bath, and one day both of the bathroom doors were opened and there they were making out on the bed, two women naked. I was shocked and ran out of the bathroom. Then I had my first experience with an epileptic. I didn't know my roommate was an epileptic, and one day she just fell on the floor and was doing these strange things. But before she fell she started coming towards me with her hands shaking and this *really* funny energy coming from her and this look in her eyes, and I thought she wanted to strangle me. Nobody had explained it to me; I hadn't seen an epileptic before. All in the course of the same semester.

So I started looking at both kinds of queerness: the queerness of making love with another woman and this strange energy that a person could go into convulsions. I started connecting with differences then. I no longer felt like I was the only one on the other side. In some way I had an affinity to the queer women and to the epileptic woman. I realized that I wasn't the baddest little girl in the world because before I thought that I was the worst. I had thought that there was something really wrong with me, that I must be so sinful to have this happen to me that, I must *deserve* to have this kind of pain and problem and that there was nobody else like me. Then I realized that there were other people not exactly like me but that had these so-called sicknesses, so I started feeling better about being on the other side because now there were a few others on the other side. And I already knew about the race and class stuff by then, but you can be working class, middle class, upper class, and you can be sitting there and look perfectly healthy and normal; it's invisible. And the epilepsy is also not noticeable until a person is going through it, and two lesbians can be walking down the street and could pass. You can't tell unless they were making love or declared it in some way through their clothes or their lifestyle. But I always felt like my difference was visible, even though it was hidden – that somehow people could see I was marked, and that mark, that *seña*, everybody could see – and they could see that I was abnormal, subhuman or whatever. It was agonizing. So if I'm before an auditorium and I'm speaking, I still feel like I'm on the other side, even though I try to get rid of the lectern and not to have any barriers, and I try to be as open as I can. There's a little part of me that feels that I'm different.

AL: You do have a certain vulnerability when you speak.

G: I think that some people choose to cloak themselves in a kind of self-defensive way and act real cool. Or you can just be honest and say, "I'm vulnerable." We're all vulnerable up there on stage; it's just that some of us wear armor and some of us do not. And I want to take as much of it off as I can. I still know that I have my shields.

AL: Paula Gunn Allen describes homosexuals as "perverse" and defines "perversity" as "transformationality . . . the process of changing from one condition to another – *lifelong* liminality."[11] It seems that you see homosexuality in a similar fashion: as *difference,* and because it's difference you can make these changes.

G: *Sí.* It's like saying, "Okay. If I am queer and I am different, then I'm going to make those differences strengths and not liabilities." It's going to be a pleasure being that and not a chore.

AL: And because "I'm 'outside' of certain cultural inscriptions, change becomes more possible?"

G: Yes. It's almost like "I'm going to be hung anyway, and if I'm going to be hung I might as well be hung for multiple deeds." It's almost like once you've transgressed – once you've crossed the line, once you've broken the law – the punishment is the same if you do it for a few things as if you do it for many. (Probably it's not, but that's my rationalization.) If I've already broken one inscription, gone against one law and regulation, then I just have to gather up my courage and go against another one and another one and another one. If I'm gonna be hung for all the things.

AL: Then that goes with the "*lesberada.*" You used the term in a speech you gave at the 1988 NWSA Lesbian Plenary session.[12] I wonder if you could elaborate on how the term applies to your definition/view of lesbians.

G: I see us as outlaws but not in the way that the S/M people see themselves as outlaws. The *lesberada/lesberado* may have started as a stigma – the outsider, the outlaw from the greater society. It's taking that stigma and turning it around and saying, "As a *lesberada,* as a *lesberado,* I am proud of who I am." A kind of camping up of that identity. Of really doing it in – yahooing and throwing the lasso. Like the cowboy. If I'm going down, I'm going to go down not with a whimper but with a bang. That kind of attitude is behind the *lesberada*. I guess it goes back to the western movies I would watch and the westerns I would read. That's why I'm partial to popular genres – horror, mystery, spy, detective, romance, westerns, science fiction. *Los desperados* were always these few marginalized cowboys, the "bad guys." So if I'm going to be a bad guy, I want to do it in style and I want to reverse the meaning for it and make it a sign for younger lesbians that would say "I want to be that too."

AL: Allen also claims that dykes have both masculine and feminine energy. You say a similar thing in *Borderlands*, when you talk about homosexuals as being "hieros gamos," both male and female.[13]

G: The *hieros gamos* comes from alchemy where the marriage was an inner marriage of what they called the masculine force and the feminine force, and the marriage of the two was called the "inner marriage, the *hieros gamos.*" I'm not sure if there's such a thing as masculine and feminine energy now. And I'm not so sure that that's an essential thing we're born with, but we're socialized into having male energy and female energy. We're socialized into there being assertive "male" ways – a male way of walking, a male way of *thrusting* into space – and there's a female way of being receiving and nurturing and giving and all that. With us the femininity didn't take completely.

AL: With dykes?

G: Yeah and with some strong women, the feminists. It did not take.

AL: That cultural training?

G: Yeah. And so we also learned the "male" mode. Maybe not in their style, but "We're just as proud; we're just as strong; we can thrust through space and assert ourselves." In the valley, we're called "*mita' y mita'.*" That's what I talk about in *Borderlands:* half a month we're a man and have a penis, and half a month we're women and have periods. That's what a lesbian is, that's what a dyke is. But instead of it being split like that I think of it as something that's integral.

AL: That works together?

G: It works together. And sometimes if the situation warrants for you thrusting out – forcing your words out because you're being excluded or oppressed – then you have that energy to do it. And in other situations you will have the energy to be a receptacle, to just take things in. And right now women privilege the feminine and say the aggressive masculine is all wrong, all bad. The men say femininity is inferior and *they're* superior. And I think they're both wrong. It takes the two.

AL: You're rejecting that either/or thinking.

G: Yeah. It's like my theory of identity: All these people are on the stage, and they take turns taking center. It's the same thing with that kind of energy. In certain situations you don't need certain kinds of energy, you need other kinds. But when you're short and get in lines – like with me, I was always ignored by the white person or the man behind the counter. I had to learn to say "EXCUSE ME. I WAS HERE FIRST." You don't do that in my culture; it's very bad for a woman to do that, but I've learned to go and ask.

AL: I don't always go and ask. I'm learning, but it's hard.

G: Well we've been socialized not to.

WRITING

AL: In one of the workshops you distinguished between an "individual we" and a "collective we." What did you mean?

G: Because we're seen by the dominant culture as generic people, as a generic tribe, we've begun to see ourselves that way too – as a representative of a group rather than as individuals. When you're seen like that all your life, when you speak (at least when I speak) I find myself going from the personal "I" to the collective "we." I know that it's politically incorrect to be representing other people, but in this particular chapter of my dissertation, "The Poet as Critic, the Poet as Theorist," I talk in more detail about why this is true. One reason is because there are so many people – women especially – that identify with the ethnic writer because that ethnic experience is not represented in the dominant literature.

AL: When you say "women" you mean women of color?

G: Women of color. We never see ourselves in these books; we don't see ourselves represented. So along comes Cherríe Moraga or me or any of the other Chicanas – Sandra Cisneros – and the Chicanas say, "Oh, that's *me* you're writing about," or "That happened to my mother." They really identify. What happens is that these women – and this is all women of color and maybe even white women such as yourself – we start getting a sense of who we are and a sense of our mission and a sense of the political work we have to do by reading Audre Lorde, by reading these women. We no longer look towards the so-called *politicos* – the politicians, the leftists – the guys that before were telling us what's wrong with the family, or with capitalism, or the economic system. Instead, the women are looking at women of color, and not just Chicanas but also Audre Lorde, Leslie Silko, Paula Gunn Allen, the Asian writers. If we have commonalities with them, if we've had similar experiences we *identify*, so part of the reading process is formulating an identity for the reader. Also, if we don't happen to agree, to identify with certain passages of a book or with certain people or with certain books – we *dis*-identify. As readers dis-identifying is also a way of formulating an identity . . . by saying, "That's not me." We find ourselves represented or not represented. I am a reader as a well as a writer, and that process happens to me; it happens to all women who read. So as a writer and as a reader I know that when I say "we" sometimes it's a singular "we" that I use in order to make a connection with the readers. But sometimes it's a plural "we."

AL: Meaning speaking for?

G: For *them*. Speaking to them and for them and with them. It's much more speaking *with* them, than *for* them.

AL: Doris Sommer has done some work on that – in Third World testimonials the women speak *within* rather than *for* the community.

G: Yes. I see it more as a dialogue between the author, the text, and the reader. And then if the reader happens to write about the reading, it's a dialogue between the author, the text, the reader, and the reader-as-writer.

AL: And do you learn as you're writing?

G: Yes. That's when I get insights. Sometimes I get them when I'm speaking, but mostly when I'm writing. I discover what I'm trying to say as the writing progresses. And this is more true with fiction and poetry because I allow more freedom for those words to come. Whereas in a creative essay – yes, it's creative and I have some freedom, but also I know that I'm theorizing.

AL: When you write a creative essay do you know where you're going to end up?

G: No. And this is the problem with the graduate classes that I've taken. They want an abstract, an idea, or an outline. I don't work that way. For example, in writing *Lloranas* they expected me to finish one chapter. And I said, "This is the way I write: I write all the chapters at the same time and bring them up through the second draft, the third draft all together." So I don't have just one finished thing because I don't know where things are going to go. They don't understand that process because they plan a book: They perfect the introduction, then the first chapter, then the second . . . I don't work that way. All the pieces have to be on the table, and I'm adding and subtracting pieces and I'm shifting them around. So there tends to be a lot of repetition in my work. I put the same thing in two or three chapters because ultimately I don't know where it's going to end up. And that frustrates them. So I made that a part of the process, I talk about the "repetition compulsion."

AL: Would you say that it's repetition with variation by the time you get to the final draft?

G: Yes. You start at the center and you spiral around. When you come back to that point where that particular idea is mentioned, you touch on it but you extend it in some way – you go off on another tangent, you elaborate on it, I might put it in Spanish, or whatever – so that it gets more and more complex. But because with a computer it's very easy to copy, I may have the exact same passage in another chapter, which I'll later rework to fit that chapter.

AL: I do that too.

G: You do that too? And I thought I was one of the few who had that process because I do the same thing with the novel. It was hard for my publisher to understand. She understands that now, that I can't really finish "She Ate Horses" until I finish some of the other stuff.

AL: You're learning as you write; you have to figure out where things are going to go. It wouldn't work if you just tried to finish one thing. I think you get a better whole by doing it your way.

G: I think it becomes more integral, more of a single entity rather than disparate parts. The parts are still there but they're . . .

AL: Different?

G: Yeah. And I have to have a central metaphor like *La Llorana* or *Prieta*. Within that central metaphor are these things like working with the interface between the different realities – *nepantla* space. *Nepantla* is kind of an elaboration of "Borderlands." The little "b" is the actual Southwest borderlands or any borderlands between two cultures, but when I use the capital B it's like a mestiza with a capital M. It's a metaphor, not an actuality.

AL: A metaphor that doesn't apply specifically to *one* thing but that can apply to many things?

G: Right. *Sí*. But I found that people were using "Borderlands" in a more limited sense than I had meant it. So to elaborate on the psychic and emotional borderlands I'm now using "*nepantla*" – which is the same thing. But with *nepantla* there's more of a connection to the spirit world. There's more of a connection to the world after death and to psychic spaces like between air and water. As I mentioned before, the world of external reality and behind it is the other world – *el mundo de mas allar* – so there's more of a spiritual, psychic, supernatural, and indigenous connection to Borderlands by using the word *nepantla*.

NOTES

1. I follow bell hooks in using the term "feminist movement" rather than *the* Feminist movement. To my mind, the former phrase is less monolithic than the latter; also, it more fully captures both the unity and the diversity among contemporary feminists.

2. Cherríe Moraga and Gloria Anzaldúa, eds., *This Bridge Called My Back: Writings by Radical Women of Color* (New York: Kitchen Table Press, 1983).

3. Gloria Anzaldúa, ed., *Making Face, Making Soul/Haciendo Caras: Creative and Critical Perspectives by Women of Color* (San Francisco: Aunt Lute Foundation, 1990).

4. Gloria Anzaldúa, "En Rapport, In Opposition," in *Haciendo Caras,* 142–48.

5. *Prieta and the Ghost Woman* (San Francisco: The Children's Book Press, 1995).

6. Gloria Anzaldúa, "*El Paisano* Is a Bird of Good Omen," in *Cuentos: Stories by Latinas,* ed. Alma Gomez, Cherríe Moraga, and Mariana Romo-Carmona (New York: Kitchen Table Press, 1983).

7. Gloria Anzaldúa, *Borderlands/La Frontera: The New Mestiza* (San Francisco: Spinsters/Aunt Lute, 1987), 19, her emphasis.

8. Cherríe Moraga, "Algo secretamente amado," *Third Woman: The Sexuality of Latinas* 4 (1989): 151–56.

9. The first version of "She Ate Horses" was published in *Lesbian Philosophies and Cultures,* ed. Jeffner Allen (Albany: State University of New York Press, 1990), 371–88.

10. Gloria Anzaldúa, "*Del otro lado,*" in *Compañeras: Latina Lesbians,* ed. Juanita Ramos (New York: Latina Lesbian History Project, 1987), 2–3.

11. Paula Gunn Allen, in Jane Caputi, "Interview With Paula Gunn Allen," *Trivia* 16 (1990): 50–67, 56.

12. Gloria Anzaldúa, "Bridge, Drawbridge, Sandbar or Island: Lesbians-of-Color *Hacienda Alianzas,*" in *Bridges of Power: Women's Multicultural Alliances,* ed. Lisa Albrecht and Rose M. Brewer (Philadelphia: New Society, 1990), 216–31.

13. Gloria Anzaldúa, *Borderlands/*La Frontera, 19.

Frontiers 14:1 (1993): 105–30.

Gender, Race, and Culture

Spanish-Mexican Women in the Historiography of Frontier California

ANTONIA I. CASTAÑEDA

Historians, whether writing for a popular or a scholarly audience, reflect contemporary ideology with respect to sex, race, and culture. Until the mid-1970s, when significant revisionist work in social, women's, and Chicano history began to appear, the writing of California history reflected an ideology that ascribed racial and cultural inferiority to Mexicans and sexual inferiority to women.[1] Not only do ideas about women form an integral part of the ideological universe of all societies, but the position of women in society is one measure by which civilizations have historically been judged.[2] Accordingly, California historians applied Anglo, middle-class norms of women's proper behavior to Mexican women's comportment and judged them according to their own perceptions of Mexican culture and of women's positions within that culture.

This essay pays a good deal of attention to the popular histories of frontier California because of the inordinate influence that have had on the more scholarly studies. In particular, the factual errors and stereotypes in the work of Hubert Howe Bancroft, Theodore H. Hittell, and Zoeth Skinner Eldredge have been propagated not only by other nineteenth- and twentieth-century popularizers but also by scholars – in the few instances where they include women at all. Although historians of the Teutonic, frontier hypothesis, and Spanish borderlands schools barely mention women, an implicit gender ideology influences their discussions of race, national character, and culture. The more recent literature in social, women's, and Chicano history breaks sharply with the earlier ideology and corollary interpretations with respect to race and culture or gender and culture, but it has yet to construct an integrative interpretation that incorporates sex-gender, race, and culture.

THE POPULAR HISTORIES OF THE LATE NINETEENTH CENTURY

Women were not treated with the greatest respect: in Latin and in savage countries they seldom are; hence, as these were half Latin and half savage, we are not surprised to learn that the men too often idled away their time, leaving the women to do all the work and rear the family.[3]

Written by lawyers, bankers, and other prominent men who came to California in the aftermath of the Mexican War and the gold rush, the multivolume popular histories of the late nineteenth century provide the first composite description and interpretation of Spanish-Mexican California.[4] These histories fundamentally reflect the political and socioracial ideology that informed both the war with Mexico and the subsequent sociopolitical and economic marginalization of Mexicans in California.[5] With respect to women, they reaffirm the contradictory but stereotypic images found in the travel journals and other documents written by entrepreneurs, merchants, adventurers, and other members of the advance guard of Euro-American expansion between the 1820s and 1840s.[6]

In the tradition of the patrician historians whose romantic literary style set the standards and popular patterns from the end of the nineteenth century until well into the twentieth, Bancroft, Hittell, and other popularizers intersperse their voluminous histories of California with musings about race, religion, national character, savagery, and civilization.[7] Riddled with the nationalistic fervor of the post–Civil War decades and with an unquestioning belief in Nordic racial superiority, these historians predictably conclude that the Anglo-Saxon race and civilization are far superior to the Latin race and Spanish Mexican civilization that had produced in California, according to Bancroft, "a race halfway between the proud Castillian and the lowly root digger," existing "halfway between savagery and civilization."[8] Only Amerindians ranked lower than the minions of Spain.

In the works on early colonial development, the discussion of women is only incidental to the larger consideration of specific institutions – the mission, *presidio*, and *pueblo* – or of great men – the governors. Thus, for example, a brief discussion of the maltreatment of Amerindian women in the mission system has no importance beyond its illustration of institutional development and Spanish brutality, which, in the tradition of the "Black Legend," spared not even women.[9] Similarly, Bancroft treats sexual and other violence against native women primarily in relation to the bitter conflict between the institutions of church and state, and attributes it to the moral degeneration of the racially mixed soldier-settler population.

Bancroft and his colleagues also introduce individual elite women to their readers. The portraits of two in particular set the tone for the consistent romanticization of "Spanish" as opposed to "Mexican" women. A prototype of the tempestuous Spanish woman, Eulalia Callis, high-born Catalán wife of the doughty Governor Fages, was dubbed the "infamous governadora (governor's wife)" for refusing Fages her bed upon his refusal to relinquish the governorship and return the family to Mexico.[10]

Even more important in the development of the "Spanish" stereotype was Concepción Arguello, the young daughter of Don José Arguello, Commandant at the Presidio of San Francisco. Prototype of the tragic maiden, Doña Concepción became betrothed to the Russian ambassador and chamberlain, Nickolai Petrovich Resanov, in 1806.[11] Resanov had sailed to California from Alaska aboard the brig *Juno,* seeking to trade the ship's entire cargo for foodstuffs desperately needed to stave off starvation and mass desertions in Sitka. But Governor Arrillaga, bound by Spain's policy of prohibiting trade with foreigners, refused to negotiate. Undaunted, Resanov wooed the young Concepción and, upon her acceptance of his proposal of marriage persuaded her father to intercede with the governor, who finally agreed to the trade.

Resanov left for Alaska and thereafter for Russia, promising to return as soon as he had the Czar's permission to marry, but he died while in Russia. Doña Concepción continued to await his return, for she did not learn of his death until many years later. After a life spent in nursing and charitable work, she became, in 1851, the first novice in the newly established Dominican convent in Monterey. She took her vows as Sister María Dominica in 1852 and died five years later at age sixty-six.[12]

Bancroft's commentary addresses not only the diplomatic and political strategy evident in Resanov's courtship and proposal of marriage but also the character of the Californians, both male and female: "What wonder that court life at St. Petersburg was fascinating, or that this child, weary of the sun-basking indolence of those about her, allowed her heart to follow her ambitions."[13] This aura of exotic drama and romance informs all later descriptions of "Spanish" women, in popular and scholarly works alike.

Bancroft also briefly discusses women in the context of colonial settlement and the family. He records the arrival of the first group of Spanish-Mexican women and families in 1774 and the overland journeys of the Anza and Rivera soldier-settler families in 1775–1776 and 1781 respectively. He also comments on Governor Borica's efforts to attract single women to the distant frontier and on the arrival of the *niñas de cuna,* the ten orphan girls brought to Alta California in 1800 as future marriage partners for single presidial soldiers.[14]

In general, the popular historical accounts of the Spanish period (1769–1821) are notable for their absence of pejorative gender-specific sexual ste-reotypes. Instead, pejorative stereotypes are generalized to the entire group and focus on race. In accounts of Mexican California (1822–1846), the popular historians divide women into two classes: "Spanish" and "Mexican." Although the vast majority of Californians, including the elite, were *mestizo* or *mulato* and Mexican, not Spanish, in nationality, women from longtime Californian elite, landowning families, some of whom married Europeans or Euro-Americans, were called "Spanish." Women from more recently arrived or nonelite families were called "Mexican." "Spanish" women were morally, sexually, and racially pure; "Mexican" women were immoral and sexually and racially impure. These sexual stereotypes not only reveal the convergence of contemporary political and social ideological currents but also underscore the centrality of the politics of sex to the ideological justifi-cation of expansion, war, and conquest. The dominant social Darwinism of the late nineteenth century, which used scientific theory to rationalize Nor-dic racial superiority and male sexual supremacy, also held that a society's degree of civilization could be judged by the status and character of its women. The Victorian True Woman, like her predecessor the Republican Mother, represented the most advanced stage of civilized society.[15] Physically and mentally inferior to men but possessed of the cardinal female virtues – piety, purity, submissiveness, and domesticity – she was confined to the home, where she could neither threaten nor challenge the existing order. She was the norm by which historians judged Mexican women, individually and collectively, and thus one of the norms by which they judged Mexican society. Like other reductionist representations of Mexicans in the literature that treats the Mexican period as a "backdrop to the coming of Old Glory," pejorative stereotypes of Mexicanas thus served a political purpose.[16] The worst stereotypes of women appeared in the histories of the Mexican rather than the Spanish period not just because the primary sources were written largely by white men who visited and/or lived in Mexican, not Spanish, California, but because the war was fought with Mexico.

The most extensive treatment of Mexican women appears in Bancroft's interpretative social history, *California Pastoral,* in which he devotes an entire chapter to "Woman and Her Sphere."[17] By virtue of publishing the earliest work of this genre, Bancroft became the main source for the stereotypes of women in Mexican California in subsequent histories.

In the work of Bancroft, Hittell, and their modern successors, the portrayals of Mexican men, the wartime foes, are uniformly stereotypic and pejorative, focusing both on their racial origins and on a national character formed by Spanish tyranny, absolutism, and fanaticism. Bancroft describes Mexicans as "droves of mongrels" deriving from a "turgid racial stream" and concludes that they were "not a strong community either physically, morally, or politically." He depicts life in Mexican California as a long, happy holiday in a lotus land where "to eat, to drink, to make love, to smoke, to dance, to ride, to sleep seemed the whole duty of man."[18]

His stereotypes of women, however, are contradictory and reveal greater gradation. Women's position in Mexican society, especially, is treated contradictorily. "The Californians, violent exercise and lack of education makes them rough and almost brutal. They have little regard for their women, and are of a jealous disposition . . . they are indifferent husbands, faithless and exacting and very hard taskmasters," Bancroft says at one point. Yet several pages later he comments, "There was strong affection and never a happier family than when a ranchero, dwelling in pastoral simplicity saw his sons and his sons' sons bringing to the paternal roof their wives and seating them at the ever-lengthening table."[19]

Bancroft's Mexican women are dunces and drudges. They work laboriously and continuously; bear twelve, fifteen, and twenty children; and are subject to being prostituted by their husbands, who "wink at the familiarity of a wealthy neighbor who pays handsomely for his entertainment." Women have no recourse to laws, which men make and women obey. At the same time, however, Bancroft quotes earlier writers to the effect that "the women are pretty, but vain, frivolous, bad managers, and extravagant. They are passionately fond of fine, showy dresses and jewelry . . . their morality is none of the purest; and the coarse and lascivious dances show the degraded tone of manners that exist." Nevertheless, infidelity is rare because Californianas fear the swift and deadly revenge exacted by jealous husbands.[20]

Bancroft based his negative images of Mexican women on the accounts of Richard Henry Dana and others who visited California in the 1840s, on the eve of the war with Mexico. But he also recorded a positive image derived from the writings of Alfred Robinson and other Euro-Americans who traveled to California in the 1820s and 1830s to ply the hide and tallow trade and who married elite *Californianas* and settled there.[21]

Robinson's accounts expressed similar negative stereotypes of men but presented positive portrayals of "Spanish" or "Californio" women. Robinson, who married María Teresa de la Guerra y Noriega, wrote that "the men are generally indolent and addicted to many vices . . . yet . . . in few places of the world . . . can be found more chastity, industrious habits and correct deportment than among the women."[22] Similar images appeared in literary pieces written on the eve of the Mexican War by individuals who had no firsthand experience of California. In this literature, Spanish-speaking women invited the advances of Euro-American men whom they anxiously awaited as their saviors from Mexican men. For example, "They Wait for Us," published in Boston at the time that John C. Frémont's outlaw band was raising the Bear Flag at Sonoma in June 1846, treats Mexican women as the symbol for the country about to be conquered:

THEY WAIT FOR US

The Spanish maid, with eyes of fire
At balmy evening turns her lyre,
And, looking to the Eastern sky,
Awaits our Yankee Chivalry
Whose purer blood and valiant arms,
Are fit to clasp her budding charms.

The *man*, her mate, is sunk in sloth –
To love, his senseless heart is loth:
The pipe and glass and tinkling lute,
A sofa, and a dish of fruit;
A nap, some dozen times by day;
Sombre and sad, and never gay.[23]

The meaning is clear – Mexicans cannot appreciate, love, direct, or control their women/country.

Forty years later, Bancroft and Hittell underscored this theme in the primary sources. "It was a happy day," writes Bancroft, "for the California bride whose husband was an American." According to Hittell, Californian *señoritas* eagerly sought American husbands, who "might not touch the guitar as lightly," but "made better husbands than those of Mexican blood."[24] The chaste, industrious Spanish beauty who forsook her inferior man and nation in favor of the superior Euro-American became embedded in the literature. The negative image that Bancroft et al. picked up from the English-language primary sources was reserved for Mexican women: *fandango*-dancing, *monte*-dealing prostitutes, the consorts of Mexican bandits.[25] These dual stereotypes became the prototypic images of Spanish-speaking women in California. They were the grist of popular fiction and contemporary newspapers throughout the latter part of the nineteenth and early twentieth centuries, and they resurfaced in the popular historical literature of the twentieth century, including the few works that focused specifically on women of Spanish California.

THE MAKERS OF MODERN HISTORIOGRAPHY:
THE TEUTONIC HISTORIANS

While Bancroft, Hittell, and other popularizers stereotyped women in their sweeping general histories of California, their scholarly contemporaries, the Teutonic historians, barely mentioned women at all. As professional historical scholarship took root in the post–Civil War era, the question of gender became a nonissue.[26]

Rather, the new scientific historians, reflecting the period's conservative, organic nationalism, were concerned principally with explaining the origin, nature, and Old World antecedents of Euro-American institutions in the United States. Their studies focused on political institutions, the pivotal structures perceived both as the sources of a nation's order and coherence and as the hallmarks that distinguished one civilization from another. They dichotomized such institutions into free and nonfree, defining democratic institutions based on representative government as free and superior, and institutions based on monarchies as unfree and inferior.[27] The Teutonics divided contemporary New World civilizations deriving from European origins accordingly.

For these historians, deification of the national state was closely linked to glorification of Anglo-Saxon people and institutions. Euro-American civilization in the United States, according to the Teutonic germ theory of history, was characterized by superior, free institutions transplanted from medieval England and Germany by Anglo-Saxons, the superior Caucasian race, and destined to expand to the entire North American continent. The Teutonics did not question the earlier romantic historians' interpretation of continental expansion as God-ordained manifest destiny; instead, they re-cast the same view in terms of evolutionary theory.[28] In the inexorable sweep of Anglo-Saxons across the continent, inferior races and civilizations were to be swept aside.

The Teutonic historians' emphasis on Old World antecedents focused their attention on the eastern region of the United States rather than on the Far West, which had but recently been incorporated into the Union. The few early scholarly studies of colonial California and the Southwest focused on Spanish institutional development.[29] For post–Civil War historians con-cerned with nationalism and national unification, the important question was how to explain the Spanish Mexican institutions rooted in California and the Southwest. A corollary question was how to incorporate the new region intellectually and ideologically into the history of the United States.[30]

While imbued with the more objective scientific approach to historical research being taught at Johns Hopkins and other graduate schools, schol-arly studies were nevertheless informed by the racist attitudes that saturated the primary sources and popular histories, particularly those of the Mexi-can War era, and by the colonial legacy of the Black Legend. In explaining the Spanish presence and institutions in the region ceded to the United States, the Teutonic historians concluded that Spain had failed to implant permanent institutions in this area, for two reasons. First, Spanish politi-cal institutions were not free. Second, Spanish cohabitation with inferior Amerindian and Negroid races in the Americas had produced an even more inferior, mongrelized population incapable of self-government.[31] The low level of population across New Spain's vast northern region, its inability to pacify Amerindian groups fully, and its lack of strong agricultural, commer-cial, or industrial development were offered as proof positive that Spanish institutions had been a dismal failure. Spain's colonizing institutions, the missions, *presidios,* and *pueblos,* were not adequate to develop the region, nor did they leave a lasting influence on the people or landscape.

While the Teutonics' major documentary sources were Euro-American, they also cited French, English, and Russian travel accounts to California and the writings of Franciscan missionaries.[32] The anti-Spanish sentiments of French, English, and Euro-American expeditionary forces, as well as these countries' continued interest in acquiring California, are obvious in the logs, journals, and reports of Jean François Galaup de La Perouse, George Vancouver, William Shaler, and other foreigners who visited Span-ish California.[33] The reports, petitions, and correspondence of the mission priests, most of whom were peninsular Spaniards, cast aspersions on the racially mixed soldiers and settlers sent to this remote outpost of the empire. Historian Manuel Servín suggests that in California, prejudice and discrimination against persons of mixed blood can be traced to the pejorative racial attitudes of peninsular Franciscans and other *españoles* during the Spanish colonial era.[34]

Since women were not a formal part of institutional life, the Teutonic historians did not discuss them.[35] Frank W. Blackmar, for example, who relies heavily on Bancroft for his description of colonial California, makes only passing reference to women in his discussion of the institution of the mission and the social and political life of the Spanish colonies.[36] But popular and amateur historians of the time continued to include women in their works, stereotyping Mexican women on the basis of both sex and race, as we have seen. These stereotypes take on additional significance when we recognize that, as Rodman Paul recently stated, the West, particularly California, that most romanticized, mythologized, and distorted of western states, "is a primary meeting ground of professional historiography, popular interests, and popular writers."[37]

Throughout the late nineteenth and early twentieth centuries, then, even as Frederick Jackson Turner successfully challenged the germ theory of Euro-American history, the history of California remained the province of popular historians, journalists, and writers. Professional historians, now writing within the developing frontier hypothesis school of historiography, continued the Teutonics' neglect of women.

Nonetheless, ideas about gender and race formed a part of their intellectual subsoil. As the United States moved from expansionism to imperialism by going to war against Spain and by preparing to absorb former Spanish colonies, race and culture became pivotal political issues for imperialists and anti-imperialists alike. In addition, increased immigration from southern and eastern Europe occasioned considerable discussion about the assimilability of certain races and ethnic groups as well as alarm over the high birthrate among the new immigrants. At the same time, social and political theorists were alarmed by the decline in the birthrate among the white middle class; the potential threat that women's greater economic independence posed to the existing social order; and the women's rights movement. The survival and destiny of the Anglo-Saxon race, they determined, rested with women. In particular, eugenicist theorists like Karl Pearson and Havelock Ellis glorified an ideal of motherhood that required women's self-sacrifice for the good of the race. Though it rested on social function rather than on biological constraint, the eugenicist ideal denied women's individuality, removed them as potential economic competitors, and silenced their potential political voices.[38]

TURNER'S FRONTIER HYPOTHESIS AND THE FANTASY
SPANISH HERITAGE

As the mission revival movement and the rediscovery of California's "Spanish" past gained force toward the end of the nineteenth century, Frederick Jackson Turner's presidential address to the American Historical Association in 1893 redefined Euro-American history and civilization. By the early twentieth century, Turner's concept, the "frontier hypothesis," had supplanted the Teutonic germ theory of history and American institutions.[39]

Instead of looking to Old World antecedents to explain the development of representative government and Euro-American civilization, Turner focused on the New World itself, whose environment alone explained the differences between the civilizations of Europe and America. In his view, expansion into new areas recreated the conditions of primitive social organization as successive waves of trappers, traders, miners, farmers, and cattlemen adapted to and molded the environment on continuous frontiers – "the meeting point between savagery and civilization." The men engaged in this continuous process were imbued with a "rugged individualism" that, combined with frontier conditions, promoted democracy and representative government. From the very beginning, then, the frontier was a democratizing agent. Departing from the Teutonic emphasis on Anglo-Saxon racial origins, Turner argued that "in the crucible of the frontier [redemptioners of non-English stock] were Americanized, liberated and fused into a mixed race, English in neither nationality nor characteristic."[40] American development represented a severance, a discontinuity with European origins, patterns, and institutions.

While on the one hand Turner conceived of Euro-American history as discontinuous from European origins, on the other hand his reinterpretation merely shifted the emphasis on institutional origins from the Old to the New World – from the German forest to the American wilderness – and stressed the impact of the new environment on diverse groups of Caucasian males. It left intact the Teutonics' basic assumptions about representative government, democratic institutions, race, culture, gender, and economics. In both interpretations, neither women nor non-Caucasian men were active participants in the creation of democratic institutions. That both were legally prohibited from direct participation in such institutions was not an issue; rather, their exclusion was consistent with theories of biological and social evolution.

Joan Jensen and Darlis Miller have identified four major stereotypes of Euro-American women in the Turnerian literature of the western frontier: gentle tamers, sunbonneted helpmeets, hell raisers, and bad women.[41] The first two types were extolled as bastions of the pioneer family; the second two were condemned as libertines, created by the same frontier influence that liberated men. But in the Turnerian studies that extol and stereotype Euro-American women, Spanish Mexican women were entirely absent – a fact hardly surprising in view of the school's racist attitudes toward non-Caucasian peoples and its ignoring of what Richard Hofstadter called "the shameful aspects of Western development, including the arrogance of American expansion, the pathetic tale of the Indians, anti-Mexican [and] anti-Chinese nativism."[42]

With respect to Mexicans, the revisionist frontier historians, if they addressed the pre-American period at all, retained the Teutonic interpretation of Spanish institutional failure while dismissing the Mexican period as an unimportant interlude between the Spanish and North American eras. Maintaining the stereotype of indolent Mexicans, Frederic L. Paxson argued that in losing California, Mexico has "paid the penalty under that organic law of politics which forbids a nation to sit still when others are moving," and thus "determined the inevitability of the United States War with Mexico and the Conquest of California and the South West."[43]

Having thus easily dismissed the obstacles that Indians and Mexicans, as prior occupants, represented to acquisition of the land base, the frontier historians focused their white, male-centered studies on the "Westward Movement" of Anglo-American pioneers into Oregon, Utah, the Pacific Northwest, and, most particularly, gold-rush California. Most recently, historians reexamining the literature of the frontier and the West have concluded that the initial success of Turner's thesis was due largely to the fact that he told an emerging industrial nation rising to world power what it wanted to hear. "Turner," states Michael Malone, "told a maturing nation . . . that it was not an appendage of a decadent Europe, but rather was a unique and great country in its own right."[44]

Meanwhile, Anglo Westerners were searching for roots in the land they now occupied. To collect, exhibit, and publish their past the new westerners organized local county and state historical societies, museums, and journals during the late nineteenth and early twentieth centuries. And, in the tradition of the earlier historical literature, the histories published by these institutions were romantic, provincial, nationalistic, and rife with filial piety.[45]

But in California, the search for roots that fit into national history ran into hardpan – the Indians and Mexicans on the land. While the United States Army and the federal government had largely removed the Indians from their midst, historically minded Californians still had to deal with Mexicans and with the fact of Spanish Mexican colonization and institutions on the slopes that they now called home.[46] Whereas their scholarly Teutonic forebears had dismissed Spain and its institutions, the new westerners now took an interest in the region's "Spanish" past. In Spain's Caucasian racial origins and former imperial grandeur they found an acceptable European past for one particular class of the former Mexican citizens in their midst, whose blood flowed in some of their own veins. In the now decaying Spanish missions and their "laudable" effort to Christianize the native population they found one institution worthy of preserving – at least structurally – for posterity.

The mission revival movement, which initiated a Spanish Mediterranean architectural style for public and private buildings, dates from this period. Historical societies and journals published histories of the missions and *pueblos,* along with reminiscences of the halcyon days in the former Spanish colony.[47] Preservationists targeted first the missions, then the *adobes.* Leading Anglo denizens in towns up and down the state organized "fiesta days" that included parades, music, food, rodeos, and a *fandango* (dance) or two. In Santa Barbara, Helen Hunt Jackson's novel *Ramona* was converted into a play that was performed year after year. Some of the descendants of California's "best Spanish families," who aided and abetted both the creation and the perpetuation of the Spanish myth, joined these celebrations.[48]

The majority of Anglo Californians seeking to understand their past probably did not read the scholarly studies of the frontier historians. The newspapers, novels, and nonprofessional histories that they did read continued the romanticized "Spanish" stereotypes first applied to *mestizas* in the primary sources and in Bancroft. In these works, women were featured prominently, and even males were now romanticized.[49]

The gratuitous determination that Mexican California's landowning class, some of whom still had kinship and/or economic ties to the new westerners, were pure-blooded Spaniards was a principal feature of the newly fabricated "fantasy Spanish heritage," to use Carey McWilliams's term.[50] Taking some of their cues from contemporary newspaper stories that "the best families were of Castillian stock, many of them pure in blood and extremely fair of skin," the new popularizers created a new racial and social history for the landowning class that the Euro-American conquest had displaced and now appropriated. In these fabulous histories, "The men went to Old Spain or Mexico for their wives and there was but little mixture of the high-bred Spanish families with the Mexicans and Indians." In *Spanish Arcadia,* which focuses on the Mexican period, Nellie Van de Grift Sánchez wrote that the Californios "kept their white blood purer than did the Mexicans or South Americans" and thus, "as a race, are greatly superior to the Mexicans."[51]

Dispossessed of their lands and politically disenfranchised, the former rancheros represented no threat to Euro-American supremacy and thus could be safely romanticized. The new popular histories converted Mexican rancheros into "the California Dons," dashing, silver-saddled *caballeros* who roamed baronial estates from dawn to dusk in a remote Spanish past. The new Dons, however, continued to be inept; incapable of hard work, they lacked the genius or moral strength to develop California's lush, fertile land. (Gertrude Atherton, who published short stories, novels, and popular histories in the late nineteenth and early twentieth centuries, entitled one collection of short stories about Mexican California *The Splendid Idle Forties.*[52])

The women of Spanish California, however, according to these novels and histories, surpassed the men. Like the primary sources of the 1840s, the new popularizers concluded that women were men's superiors in "modesty, moral character, and sound common sense."[53] California's "Spanish" (read Caucasian) daughters were industrious, chaste, and morally as well as racially pure. In short, they could be claimed as the pure-blooded "Spanish" grandmothers of many a Euro-American frontier family. But Mexican women fared less well. While the literature seldom specifically discusses Mexican women, a designation that included nonelite Californianas and Mexicanas who came during the gold rush, it implies that they were licentious women – common prostitutes who, like their male counterparts, deserved to be wiped out. Thus popular historical interpretations of California's Spanish Mexican past essentially dichotomized Californianas the same way the scholarly frontier historians dichotomized and stereotyped Anglo-American women – as good and bad women. For Californianas, however, the values of good and bad were explicitly related to their race and culture or class.

Meanwhile, among professional historians, Spain's presence in the American Southwest resurfaced as a historiographical issue. In the early decades of the twentieth century a reexamination of the history of colonial institutions in the old Spanish borderlands by a young scholar named Herbert Eugene Bolton led to a reinterpretation of those institutions and to a "new" school of historiography.

THE SPANISH BORDERLANDS SCHOOL

In the 1930s Turner's frontier thesis came under increasing scrutiny and attack. A new generation of revisionist historians argued that national development resulted not from a single cause but from many, from economic and class forces as well as from ideas rooted in East Coast intellectualism rather than western individualism.

The Great Depression, too, provoked a reexamination of the social unanimity implicit in Turner's interpretation of United States history. The climate of national questioning, internationalism, and a Good Neighbor Policy toward Mexico and Latin America prompted scholars to tackle once more the history of California, the Southwest, and the Far West. At the University of California at Berkeley, Herbert Eugene Bolton and his students developed a new revisionist school, the Spanish borderlands school of historiography. The new school revised the Teutonics' original theory of Spanish institutional failures by turning it on its head. Basing their arguments on a concept of "a Greater America" and on archival research in unmined Spanish language collections, Bolton and his students argued that, contrary to prevalent scholarly wisdom, which they characterized as nationalistic, chauvinistic, and distorted, Spanish institutions had not failed.[54]

Examining the Spanish borderlands in the broad context of European exploration, exploitation, and colonization of the American continents from the sixteenth to the nineteenth centuries, Bolton conceptualized Spain's far northern frontiers as integral parts of Euro-American history. He concluded that, with the exception of New Mexico, Spain's movement into its far northern frontier was defensive in nature. He argued further that Spain's frontier institutions – the mission, *presidio*, and *pueblo* – not only were admirably suited to frontier conditions and defensive needs but also had exerted a lasting impact on the landscape and had paved the way for subsequent Euro-American colonizers. Missions and ranchos had broken ground for subsequent Anglo-American agricultural and pastoral development. Spanish *pueblos* had been the nucleus of major urban centers throughout the West. Spanish laws had influenced western mining, water, and community property rights, and Spanish terminology continued in use throughout the western states.[55]

Rejecting both the Hispanophobia of the Teutonics and the strident nationalism of the Turnerians, the borderlands school effectively refuted the allegation of Spain's institutional failure. Nevertheless, Bolton and his students retained their predecessors' definitions of the makers and nature of history. Caucasian males engaged in exploration and in the development of religious, political, military, and economic institutions make history. But the Spaniards, whom the Teutonics had disparaged as a cruel, greedy, bigoted nonwhite lot of miscreants, the Boltonians lauded as valiant, daring, heroic Europeans.[56] Where the Teutonics had seen institutional failure, the Boltonians saw a seedbed for Spanish civilization.

In either view, however, women and nonwhite males do not contribute to history. While the Boltonians did address the exploitation of the Indians, their discussion revolved around the mission's efficacy as a frontier institution, not around the lot of the Indian.[57] The early Spanish borderlands studies rarely mention racially mixed soldiers and settlers. When Bolton does briefly discuss California's *mestizo* and *mulato* colonists, he reaffirms Bancroft's views of their idle but kindly, hospitable, and happy character; and, like the contemporary popular historians, he makes a racial distinction between Californians and Mexicans: "Californians were superior to other Spanish colonists in America, including Mexicans," a superiority that he attributes to "the greater degree of independence, social at least if not political," caused by their isolation from Mexico and to their "good Castillian blood."[58] Women, who (to the historians) were neither intrepid explorers, barefooted black-robed missionaries, nor valiant lancers for the king, do not figure in Spanish borderlands studies. Until very recently, mention of women was limited to scattered references to intermarriage in the Americas, to women's relationship to the men who founded Spanish institutions, or, in the case of Amerindian women, to the institution of the mission itself.

Though Bolton touches briefly on the cultural significance of marriage between Spanish *conquistadores* and Amerindian women in the early conquest of the Americas, borderlands discussions of California native women center on their relation to the mission. Borderlands descriptions of rapacious attacks on Amerindian women by soldiers focus not on the women but on the conflict over authority that these attacks exacerbated between officials of church and state.[59] Until recently borderlands historians, like the

Teutonics, attributed the problems of Spanish institutional development to the despicable behavior of the common soldiers, which was in turn blamed on their socioracial origins. In the 1970s, however, borderlands historians began to examine the experiences and contributions of the racially mixed *soldado de cuera* (leather-jacket soldier) and *poblador* (settler), who derived largely from the lower social classes of colonial Spanish society. Although this new generation of historians has dealt more equitably with the issue of race, it has still focused exclusively on soldiers and male settlers.[60]

Just as the early Boltonians dismissed the common soldier, so they dismissed the racially mixed wives of the artisans, soldiers, settlers, and convicts – women who endured difficult ocean voyages or who trekked over desert wastelands to settle Alta California. The only women systematically included are the wives of the governors, principally Eulalia Callis, with her marital strife, her "scandalous behavior," and the problems that she caused the missionaries.[61]

Although the borderlands school studies end with the close of the Spanish colonial era, Bolton makes brief reference to Mexican women in connection with Euro-American expansion into the old Spanish borderlands in the 1820s and 1830s. Though he shows an awareness of the importance of intermarriage and miscegenation to frontier development, and of the significance of Mexican women's economic roles as property owners and consumers on the borderlands, he joins the popular historians in his uncritical acceptance of Euro-American males' claims that Mexican women preferred them to Mexican males.[62] While noting that James Ohio Pattie was a notorious braggart, Bolton nevertheless paraphrases Pattie's report that "at a *fandango* in Taos, the gateway to New Mexico, the American beaux captured not only all the señoritas, but the señoras as well. The jealous *caballeros* drew their knives." And, "in California, long before the Mexican War," wrote Bolton, "it was a customary boast of a señorita that she would marry a blue-eyed man."[63] Thus Bolton accepts the distorted view that equated California women with the land that promised "freedom-loving, adventure-loving, land-hungry Americans" romance, exoticism, and adventure.[64]

PRESIDARIAS, POBLADORAS, CALIFORNIANAS, CHICANAS: REINTERPRETING SPANISH MEXICAN WOMEN IN FRONTIER CALIFORNIA

Within the last two decades, social historians and feminist historians have illuminated nineteenth-century U.S. social, women's, Chicano, borderlands, and family history; and recent studies on colonial women in Mexico and Latin America have yielded information and analysis pertinent to women in Spanish Mexican California.[65] Yet even this new body of literature fails to deal directly with Spanish Mexican women on the remote outposts of empire. There are no published book-length scholarly studies of Mexicanas on nineteenth-century frontiers, and the periodical literature is sketchy and impressionistic rather than grounded in substantive primary research.

Recent studies of women in the Far West reflect a historiography in the initial stages of development. Current works include edited and annotated compilations of primary materials, most specifically of "westering" Anglo women's diaries and journals; descriptive works with varying degrees of analysis within the context of social, economic, and family history; and edited anthologies.[66]

Descriptive studies, including those of Sandra L. Myres and Julie Roy Jeffrey, have emphasized the perspective of Euro-American women and, in a neo-Turnerian version of the frontier as place (environment) and process, have viewed Amerindian and Mexican women as part of the new environment to which Yankee, midwestern, and southern white women pioneers must adapt.[67] Glenda Riley and Annette Kolodny have probed Euro-American women's images of Amerindians; and Sandra Myres has described Anglo women's response to Mexicans.[68] These works find that Anglo women generally shared Anglo men's racial antipathy to Amerindians and Mexicans, though they tended to be more sympathetic to women of other racial and cultural groups.[69] Proximity sometimes served to break down barriers, and in some instances Anglo women struck up friendships with Amerindian and Mexican women based on "mutual respect and trust."[70] Three anthologies, *New Mexico Women: Intercultural Perspectives* (1986), *The Women's West* (1987), and *Western Women: Their Land, Their Lives* (1988), address the critical, albeit thorny, issues of race, sex, class, and cultural interaction in the frontier West and Southwest.[71]

In many respects, however, these initial efforts continue to mirror the larger problems of the earlier historiography. That is, the new scholarship lacks a clear framework to examine the historical experience of women whose race and culture are not Anglo North American. Moreover, it often reflects the underlying assumptions and race and class biases of the earlier historiography. Historians of women in the frontier West, for example, have not yet grappled with defining the term *frontier* from a non-Anglo perspective, nor have they yet tackled the roles of English-speaking women in the imposition of Anglo hegemony. The new scholarship has indeed focused on gender, but its concept of gender ignores nonwhite, non–middle-class experiences on the frontier. And the lack of an integrative conceptual framework particularly hampers attempts to address the question of race and the nature of interracial contact, including interracial marriage.

Thus, Myres, Riley, and Susan Armitage find a "more peaceful version of Indian-white contact" in the diaries and journals of literate Anglo women, but they fail to reconcile this version with the brutality and violence that Amerindian and Mexican women experienced during the Anglo North American conquest of the western frontier.[72] Although the underlying assumption that westering Anglo women were less violent than Anglo men may in fact be true, it is also true that Anglo women benefited directly from male violence that occurred before their own arrival in a particular region: frontier wars, army massacres, and the violence during the California gold rush.[73] Anglo women may have neither committed nor witnessed this violence, but they reaped its fruits: removal of Amerindians and Mexicans from the land base. And in addition to general violence rife in a society under conquest, Amerindian and Mexican women also suffered sexual violence.[74] Gerda Lerner and other feminist scholars have concluded that under conditions of military and/or political conquest, rape, abduction, and other acts of sexual violence against women of the conquered group are acts of domination.[75] Although Albert Hurtado and other scholars studying the history of Amerindian people in California have begun to address sexual violence, historians of women in the frontier West have not examined this subject, which is pivotal to the history of Amerindian and Mexican women.[76] While certainly women of all races and classes in the West experienced domestic violence, conquest and racism intensified sexual assault. Because racial inferiority was equated with sexual impurity – even prostitution – nonwhite women could be raped with impunity, just as they could be enslaved, killed, or worked to death like beasts of burden.

Anglo attitudes toward Mexican women have been the subject only of brief essays. In "Californio Women and the Image of Virtue," David Langum concludes that the pejorative stereotypes of Mexican women were class based, derived from the perceptions of lower-class Mexican women by upper-class Yankees like Richard Henry Dana.[77] But Dana did have the opportunity to observe elite Californianas, and Langum does not address Dana's underlying gender ideology. Furthermore, Langum's class explanation is merely an extension to women of Cecil Robinson's earlier interpretation of pejorative stereotypes of Mexicanos, an interpretation that has already been refuted.[78] In "The Independent Women of New Mexico," Janet Lecompte attributes Anglos' negative views of Nuevo Mexicanas' morality to sexist Anglo behavioral norms conditioned by the relatively constricted position of women in North American society and culture, and by the corollary view of womanhood as the upholder and symbol of American morality.[79] Unfortunately Lecompte does not develop the gender-based argument, not does she fully address the issue of race.

Jane Dysart, Darlis Miller, and Rebecca Craver have published the only studies to date on the subject of interracial marriage.[80] These works describe but do not analyze significant historical, political, economic, and cultural issues inherent in interracial marriage and assimilation; and despite their recognition that intermarriage existed before the Anglo North American conquest, their point of departure is generally North American culture and society. Yet intercultural contact, interracial marriage, and *mestizo* children were part of Mexican women's historical reality long before the arrival of Anglo Americans on the landscape; this subject, especially, requires examination within a broader context.[81] Moreover, in the early periods of contact, when whites sought to establish trapping, trading, and other commercial relations with Indians and Mexicans, intermarriage and consensual unions were as much economic as they were sexual or romantic alliances. White men who married or lived with nonwhite women were assimilated into the women's culture. This pattern was conditioned by sex ratio, itself a manifestation of the particular stage of contact, which we must take into account before we can generalize about intermarriage and assimilation. In her exemplary study of the Spanish-Mexican women of Santa Fe, 1820–1880, Deena González grounds her examination of interracial marriage in Spanish-Mexican patterns of racial and cultural contact, while also charting the economic changes that her subjects experienced with the change of legal and political institutions from Mexican to Anglo-American patterns.[82]

Earlier studies of nineteenth-century Chicano history include general discussions of Chicanas, particularly in relation to labor and the family, but they do not incorporate gender as a category of analysis. Those of Albert Camarillo, Richard Griswold del Castillo, and Ricardo Romo begin on the eve of the Mexican American War and center on the development of Chicano communities in California's urban centers during the latter half of the nineteenth and early twentieth centuries.[83] Griswold del Castillo's more recent study on the Chicano family also begins after the U.S. war with Mexico, as does the earliest social history of the Californios; and Roberto Alvarez's anthropological examination of family migration in Baja and Alta

California focuses mainly on the period after 1880.[84] Recent social and frontier histories of Spanish and Mexican California and the Southwest, whether they derive from the Spanish borderlands school or from Mexican historical studies, either ignore women entirely or discuss them in very general terms.[85] For colonial California, one unpublished dissertation and three brief articles on marriage and childrearing patterns and on race, all by Gloria Miranda, constitute the totality of recent scholarly studies.[86]

But there is new scholarship in colonial Mexican and Latin American women's and family history that is invaluable to the study of Spanish-speaking women in eighteenth- and nineteenth-century California. Ramón Gutiérrez's *When Jesus Came, the Corn Mothers Went Away* offers a singularly important point of departure for an examination of gender and marriage in colonial New Mexico.[87] Although Gutiérrez's is the only recent study that focuses on New Spain's northern frontier, Patricia Seed's *To Love Honor and Obey in Colonial Mexico* examines the changing laws and conflicts over marriage choice.[88] Sylvia Arrom's *The Women of Mexico City, 1790–1857* and Asunción Lavrin's work on nuns and women's wills address the status of colonial women in law, in the patriarchal family, in religious orders, and in social, economic, and political life.[89] The new scholarship revises earlier interpretations of Mexicanas as passive, male-dominated, and powerless. While most of these studies do not focus on frontier women, they provide a well-defined sociocultural and political context for such discussion by illuminating gender-specific Spanish colonial and Mexican laws and policies.

And there are rich sources for the study of frontier Spanish Mexican women.[90] Though the standard archival sources for the Spanish colonial period are official reports, correspondence, diaries, and journals written by male missionaries and military authorities, they yield factual information about women's work and life in the missions and *presidios,* as well as insights into the gender ideology of the era. And although few Spanish-speaking women were literate, they did have petitions and letters penned for them.[91] There are also quantifiable sources: censuses, court records, and mission registers of baptisms, marriages, and deaths. The marriage registers reveal the extent of interracial marriage between Amerindian women and Spanish-*mestizo* men. Both ecclesiastical and military records document the violence that soldiers committed against Amerindian women.[92]

For the Mexican period, civil, criminal, and ecclesiastical court records reveal that women sued and were sued for divorce (legal separation), for land, and for custody of children and godchildren, as well as for numerous social transgressions.[93] Court records document a significant increase in domestic violence against women; they also document violence by women. Court records, official reports, and correspondence yield information about race relations. *Libros de solares* (books of lots) record women's ownership of town lots, and there are also documents proving women's receipt and ownership of Mexican land grants. Before secularization in 1836, interracial marriages – now of Mexican women with European and Euro-American men – may be traced through mission registers.

For the era just before and after the American conquest, there are further quantifiable sources, in addition to the journals and correspondence of Anglo men and women, contemporary newspapers, and the literature of the gold rush. The records of the Land Grant Commission detail Mexican women's loss and retention of land grants. Extant Ayuntamiento (later City Council) records and Sole Trader records permit examination of Mexican women's economic life, as do the federal manuscript censuses. Women's wills and probate court records reveal the nature and disposition of women's property. Justice of the peace and parish records document interracial marriage. Justice of the peace and superior court records document crimes with which women were charged, crimes of which women were the victims, and indentures of children. Hubert Howe Bancroft's collection includes narratives from eleven Mexican women that provide significant information and insight into women's lives, work, family, race relations, and politics up to the 1870s, when the women were interviewed. Finally, family collections and papers in various repositories throughout the state contain women's correspondence, diaries, and journals of elite, literate Californianas and, in some cases, middle-class Mexican women who came to California in the latter half of the nineteenth century.[94]

The threads of Spanish Mexican women's history run throughout these sources. What is missing is an approach to the history of the frontier that integrates gender, race, and culture or class as categories of historical analysis. An integrative ethnohistorical approach would enable us to examine women's roles and lives in their societies of origin, as well as to describe and interpret how conquest changed their lives and restructured economic and social relationships not only between the sexes but also among persons of the same sex. For example, although we know that Spanish Mexican and Anglo-American societies were stratified along gender, as well as racial and class lines, research is wanting on the nature or extent of male domination and the subordination of women in Amerindian societies before 1769. Feminist anthropologists have suggested that male domination was not universal in the Americas, and that foraging societies – such as those that existed in California – were essentially egalitarian, but this hypothesis has not been tested. Nor have historians compared gender stratification and patriarchy in Spanish Mexican and Euro-American frontier California. I have suggested here that violence toward women is part of the politics of domination. Likewise, pejorative stereotypes and the deracination of *mestiza* women reveal the intersection of ideologies of gender, sexuality, and race in the politics of conquest. But it is premature to generalize about women and race relations, intermarriage, and assimilation on the frontiers of expansion. We have not yet done the research.

For three centuries, American frontiers were bloody battlegrounds of European and Euro-American expansion and conquest and of Amerindian resistance. Impoverished Spanish-speaking *mestiza, mulata,* and other *casta* women who migrated to Alta California in the eighteenth century came as part of soldier-settler families recruited and subsidized to populate the military forts in imperial Spain's most remote outpost. These women began the process of reproducing Hispanic culture and society on this frontier. Their daughters and granddaughters continued it as the region changed from Spanish to Mexican political control. A developing agropastoral economy built on trade and Amerindian labor gave rise to greater social stratification and the beginning of class distinctions. By the mid-1840s the great-granddaughters of the first generation of women, then in the midst of their own childbearing years, themselves experienced war, conquest, and displacement. Many of them became part of the menial wage labor force of a new, expanding, capitalist economy and society that bought their labor as cheaply as possible while it devalued their persons racially, culturally, and sexually. It is time to reexamine the history of these women within a conceptual framework that acknowledges the sex-gender, race, and culture or class issues that inhered in the politics and policies of frontier expansion, and to reinterpret the terms that define our changing reality on this frontier – presidarias, pobladoras, Californianas, Chicanas.

NOTES

1. For comprehensive bibliographies on the Spanish Mexican frontier, see John Francis Bannon, *The Spanish Borderlands Frontier, 1531–1821* (New York: Holt, Rinehart, and Winston, 1970), 257–87; Oakah L. Jones Jr., *Los Paisanos: Spanish Settlers on the Northern Frontiers of New Spain* (Norman: University of Oklahoma Press, 1979), 309–32; David J. Weber, *The Mexican Frontier, 1821–1846* (Albuquerque: Uni-

versity of New Mexico Press, 1982), 377–407; Weber, "Mexico's Far Northern Frontier, 1821–1846: A Critical Bibliography," *Arizona and the West* 19 (autumn 1977): 225–66; and Weber, "Mexico's Far Northern Frontier: Historiography Askew," *Western Historical Quarterly* 7 (July 1976): 279–93.

The following (not exhaustive) list includes titles discussing Spanish Mexican women in early biographies, family histories, and histories of ranchos: Susanna Bryant Dakin, *A Scotch Paisano: Hugo Reid's Life in California, 1832–1852* (Berkeley: University of California Press, 1939); Bess Adams Garner, *Windows in an Old Adobe* (1939; reprint Claremont, Calif.: Bronson Press, 1970); Henry D. Hubbard, *Vallejo* (Boston: Meador Publishing Company, 1941); Terry E. Stephenson, "Tomas Yorba, His Wife Vicenta, and His Account Book," *The Quarterly Historical Society of Southern California* 23 (March 1944): 126–55; Myrtle McKittrick, *Vallejo: Son of California* (Portland, Ore.: Bindfords and Mort Publishers, 1944); Susanna Bryant Dakin, *The Lives of William Hartnell* (Stanford, Calif.: Stanford University Press, 1949); Angustias de la Guerra Ord, *Occurrences in Hispanic California*, trans. Francis Price and William Ellison (Washington, D.C.: Academy of Franciscan History, 1956); Edna Deu Pree Nelson, *The California Dons* (New York: Appleton-Century-Crofts, 1962); *The 1846 Overland Trail Memoir of Margaret M. Hecox*, ed. Richard Dillon (San Jose, Calif.: Harlan-Young Press, 1966); Madie Brown Emparan, *The Vallejos of California* (San Francisco: Gleeson Library Association, 1968); and Virginia L. Carpenter, *The Ranchos of Don Pacífico Ontiveros* (Santa Ana, Calif.: Friis Pioneer Press, 1982).

For a discussion of race as a central theme in the history of the West and a review of the historical literature, see Richard White, "Race Relations in the American West," *American Quarterly* 38 (1986): 396–416. Herbert Eugene Bolton criticized American historiography for its nationalistic chauvinism in "The Epic of Greater America," *American Historical Review* 38 (April 1933): 448–74. See also White, "Race Relations in the American West," and Weber, "Mexico's Far Northern Frontier: Historiography Askew." For a review of pervasive ideas about female inferiority, see Rosemary Agonito, *History of Ideas on Women: A Sourcebook* (New York: Perigree Brooks, 1977).

2. Eileen Power, *Medieval Women*, ed. M. M. Postan (London, New York, Melbourne: Cambridge University Press, 1975), 9.

3. Hubert Howe Bancroft, *California Pastoral, 1769–1848* (San Francisco: The History Company, 1888), 305; Theodore S. Hittell, *History of California*, 4 vols. (San Francisco: The History Company, 1897), 2:469–511; see especially Hubert Howe Bancroft, *History of California*, 7 vols. (San Francisco: The History Company, 1886–1890); and Zoeth Skinner Eldredge, *History of California*, 5 vols. (New York: The Century Company, 1915).

4. Franklin Tuthill, *The History of California* (San Francisco: H. H. Bancroft and Company, 1866); Lucia Norman, *A Popular History of California from the Earliest Period of Its Discovery to the Present Time* (1867; reprint San Francisco: A. Roman, AGT, Publisher, 1883); J. M. Guinn, *A History of California and an Extended History of Los Angeles and Environs Also Containing Biographies of Well Known Citizens of the Past and Present,* 3 vols. (Los Angeles: Historic Record Company, 1915).

5. Thomas R. Hietala, *Manifest Design: Anxious Aggrandizement in Late Jacksonian America* (Ithaca, N.Y.: Cornell University Press, 1985); Reginald Horsman, *Race and Manifest Destiny: The Origins of Racial Anglo-Saxonism* (Cambridge, 1981); Frederick Merk, *A Reinterpretation of Manifest Destiny and Mission in American History* (New York: Alfred Knopf, 1963); *The Mexican War: Was It Manifest Destiny?* ed. Ramon Eduardo Ruiz (New York: Holt, Rinehart and Winston, 1963).

6. For a discussion of the contradictory but stereotypic images of women in Euro-American travel literature, see Antonia I. Castañeda, "Anglo Images of Nineteenth Century Californianas: The Political Economy of Stereotypes," in *Between Borders: Essays on Mexicana/Chicana History,* ed. Adelaida del Castillo (Encino, Calif.: Floricanto Press, 1990).

7. For a discussion of the early traditions of United States historical writing, see Michael Kraus and Davis D. Joyce, *The Writing of American History,* rev. ed. (Norman: University of Oklahoma Press, 1985): 92–135; John Higham, *History: Professional Scholarship in America* (New York: Harper and Row, 1965): 3–25, 68–74, 148–49; and David Levin, *History as Romantic Art: Bancroft, Prescott, Motley and Parkman* (Stanford, Calif.: Stanford University Press, 1959).

8. Bancroft, *California Pastoral,* 180; see also Edward N. Saveth, "The Conceptualization of American History," in *American History and the Social Sciences,* ed. Edward N. Saveth (London: The Free Press of Glencoe, 1964), 10–11.

9. The Black Legend refers to an anti-Spanish policy perpetrated by Spain's European enemies accusing the Spanish monarch of brutal tyranny more extreme than that of their own absolutist regimes. See James J. Rawls, *Indians of California: The Changing Image* (Norman: University of Oklahoma Press, 1984), 42–43, 55, 64; *The Black Legend: Anti-Spanish Attitudes in the Old World and the New,* ed. Charles Gibson (New York: Alfred A. Knopf, 1971); and Phillip Wayne Powell, *Tree of Hate: Propaganda and Prejudice Affecting United States Relations with the Hispanic World* (New York: Basic Books, 1971).

10. For discussion of Eulalia Callis, see Bancroft, *History of California* 1:389–93, and Eldredge, *History of California* 1:5–8.

11. Bancroft, *History of California* 2:64–78; footnote 23, 78; Bancroft, *California Pastoral,* 331–32; Richard A. Pierce, *Resanov Reconnoiters California: A New Translation of Resanov's Letters, Parts of Lieutenant Khvostov's Log of the Ship Juno, and*

Dr. Georg von Langsdorff's Observations (San Francisco: The Book Club of San Francisco, 1972), 15–23, 69–72.

12. Bancroft, *History of California* 2:77–78; footnote 23, 78; and Susanna Bryant Dakin, *Rose, or Rose Thorn? Three Women of Spanish California* (Berkeley: The Friends of the Bancroft Library, 1963), 25–56.

13. Bancroft, *History of California* 2:72.

14. Bancroft, *History of California* 1:224, 257–69, 341–45, 603; footnote 6, 603; and footnote 13, 606.

15. For discussion of Nordic superiority in North American history, see Kraus and Joyce, *The Writing of American History*, 136, 145, 165; Bert James Lowenberg, *American History in American Thought* (New York: Simon and Schuster, 1972), 347–49, 371–75, 380–98, 458–65; Levin, *History as Romantic Art*, 85–87; and Edward Saveth, *American Historians and European Immigrants, 1875–1925* (New York: Russell and Russell, 1965), 90–92.

For discussion of male supremacy, see Mary P. Ryan, *The Empire of the Mother: American Writing about Domesticity, 1830–1860* (New York: Harrington Park Press, 1985); Carroll Smith-Rosenberg, *Disorderly Conduct: Visions of Gender in Victorian America* (New York: Oxford University Press, 1985); Mary Beth Norton, "The Evolution of White Women's Experience in Early America," *The American Historical Review* 89 (June 1984): 593–619; Lorna Duffin, "Prisoners of Progress: Women and Evolution," in *The Nineteenth Century Woman: Her Cultural and Physical World*, ed. Sara Delamont and Lorna Duffin (New York: Barnes and Noble Books, 1978), 57–91; Agonito, *History of Ideas on Women*, 251–63; Susan Phinney Conrad, *Perish the Thought: Intellectual Women in Romantic America, 1830–1860* (New York: Oxford University Press, 1976), 15–41; and Linda K. Kerber, *Women of the Republic: Intellect and Ideology in Revolutionary America* (1980; reprint New York: W. W. Norton & Company, 1986).

16. Weber, *The Mexican Frontier, 1821–1846*, 17.

17. Bancroft, *California Pastoral*, 305–34; Bancroft, *History of California*, vols. 2, 3, and 4.

18. Bancroft, *California Pastoral*, 76–79, 292–93; Bancroft, *History of California* 2:69.

19. Bancroft, *California Pastoral*, 279–80, 305.

20. Bancroft, *California Pastoral*, 279–80, 322; Hittell, *History of California* 2:491.

21. With few exceptions, Euro-Americans who left published accounts of Mexican California in their memoirs, journals, and correspondence described Mexican men in racist terms and consistently expressed expansionist sentiments toward U.S. acquisition of California. Bancroft draws heavily upon these published sources, and he also had access to numerous unpublished manuscripts of similar sentiment. See

Castañeda, "Anglo Images of Nineteenth Century Californianas"; see also notes 78 and 79.

22. Alfred Robinson, *Life in California* (1846; reprint Santa Barbara: Peregrine Press, 1970), 51, and as quoted in Bancroft, *California Pastoral*, 326.

23. "They Wait for Us," as quoted in Horsman, *Race and Manifest Destiny*, 233.

24. Bancroft, *California Pastoral*, 312; Hittell, *History of California* 2:179.

25. In Spanish-Mexican California, *el fandango* was a specific dance, while *un fandango* referred to an informal dancing party. Euro-Americans used the term loosely and applied it to all dances and any dancing occasion. *Monte* is a card game. See Lucille K. Czarnowski, *Dances of Early California Days* (Palo Alto: Pacific Books, 1950), 16, 22.

26. For early critiques of sexism in the historical scholarship, see "Part I: On the Historiography of Women," in *Liberating Women's History: Theoretical and Critical Essays*, ed. Berenice A. Carroll (Urbana: University of Illinois Press, 1976), 1–75; Gerda Lerner, *The Majority Finds Its Past: Placing Women in History* (New York: Oxford University Press, 1979).

27. Discussion of the Teutonic hypothesis is based primarily on Kraus and Joyce, *The Writing of American History;* Lowenberg, *American History in American Thought;* George Callcott, *History in the United States, 1800–1860: Its Practices and Purpose* (Baltimore: The Johns Hopkins Press, 1970); John Higham, *Writing American History: Essays on Modern Scholarship* (Bloomington: University of Indiana Press, 1970); Holt W. Stull, *Historical Scholarship in the United States and Other Essays* (Seattle: University of Washington Press, 1967); and Saveth, *American Historians and European Immigrants.*

28. Kraus and Joyce, *The Writing of American History*, 165; Callcott, *History in the United States, 1800–1860*, 154, 162, 165–72; Levin, *History as Romantic Art*, 78, 82–85, 121–37.

29. Frank W. Blackmar, *Spanish Institutions in the Southwest* (1891; reprint Glorieta, N.M.: Rio Grande Press, 1976).

30. Kraus and Joyce, *The Writing of American History*, 92–135, 164–209; Higham, *History*, 151–52, 167; Lowenberg, *American History in American Thought*, 131–32, 200–220, 328, 424.

31. Blackmar, *Spanish Institutions in the Southwest;* Lewis Hanke, ed., *Do the Americas Have a Common History? A Critique of the Bolton Theory* (New York: Alfred A. Knopf, 1964).

32. Rawls, *Indians of California*, 32–43.

33. *Jean Francois Galaup de La Perouse, A Voyage Round the World in the Years 1785, 1786, 1787, and 1788*, ed. M. L. A. Milet-Mureau, 3 vols. (London: J. Johnson, 1798), 2:202–4, passim; George Vancouver, *Vancouver in California, 1792–1794: The*

Original Account of George Vancouver, Early California Travel Series, Nos. 9, 10, and 22, ed. Marguerite Eyer Wilbur (Los Angeles: Glen Dawson, 1953–54), 19, 243–48; William Shaler, *Journal of a Voyage between China and the Northwestern Coast of America Made in 1804 by William Shaler* (Claremont, Calif.: Saunders Studio Press, 1935).

34. Manuel Patricio Servín, "California's Hispanic Heritage," *The Journal of San Diego History* 19 (1973): 1–9.

35. Trained in the Teutonic school, Henry Adams sometimes rebelled against its canons; see "The Primitive Rights of Women," in his *Historical Essays* (New York: Charles Scribner's Sons, 1891), 1–41.

36. Blackmar, *Spanish Institutions in the Southwest,* 112–51, 255–79.

37. Rodman W. Paul and Michael P. Malone, "Tradition and Challenge in Western Historiography," *The Western Historical Quarterly* 16 (January 1985): 27.

38. Saveth, *American Historians and European Immigrants,* 32–65; Richard Hofstadter, *Social Darwinism in American Thought* (1944; reprint New York: George Braziller, Inc., 1959), 170–200; Duffin, "Prisoners of Progress: Women and Evolution," 57–91.

39. Frederick Jackson Turner, *The Frontier in American History* (1920, reprint New York: Robert E. Krieger Publishing Company, 1976), 1–38. Turner's "The Significance of the Frontier in American History" first appeared in the *American Historical Association, Annual Report of the Year 1893* (Washington, D.C., 1894), 199–227. Discussion of Turner and the frontier hypothesis of American history is based on the following: Ray Allen Billington, *America's Frontier Heritage* (New York: Holt, Rinehart, and Winston, 1966); *The Frontier Thesis: Valid Interpretation of American History?* ed. Ray Allen Billington (1966, reprint New York: Robert E. Krieger Publishing Company, 1977); *The Turner Thesis: Concerning the Role of the Frontier in American History,* ed. George Rogers Taylor (Lexington: D.C. Heath and Company, 1956); Richard Hofstadter, *The Progressive Historians: Turner, Beard, Parrington* (New York: Alfred A. Knopf, 1968); Earl Pomeroy, "The Changing West," in *The Reconstruction of American History,* ed. John Higham (London: Hutchinson & Co., 1962), 64–81.

40. Turner, *The Frontier in American History,* 3, 23.

41. Joan M. Jensen and Darlis A. Miller, "The Gentle Tamers Revisited: New Approaches to Women in the American West," *Pacific Historical Review* 49 (May 1980): 173–213.

42. Hofstadter, *The Progressive Historians,* 104.

43. Frederick Logan Paxson, *The Last American Frontier* (New York: The MacMillan Company, 1910), 107.

44. Michael P. Malone, ed., *Historians and the American West* (Lincoln: University of Nebraska Press, 1983), 5.

45. See, for example, "California Historical Society, 1852–1922," *California Historical Society Quarterly* 1 (July–October 1922): 9–22.

46. Rawls, *Indians of California*, 137–70; Patricia Nelson Limerick, *The Legacy of Conquest: The Unbroken Past of the American West* (New York: Norton, 1987), 44–45, 82.

47. See, for example, "Society of Southern California: Fifteen Years of Local History Work," *Historical Society of Southern California Publications* (hereafter cited as HSSCP) 4 (1898): 105–10; Walter Bacon, "Value of a Historical Society," HSSCP 4 (1899): 237–42; and Marion Parks, "In Pursuit of Vanished Days: Visits to the Extant Historic Adobe Houses of Los Angeles County," Part 1, *Historical Society of Southern California Annual Publications* (hereafter cited as HSSCAP) 14 (1928): 7–63; Part 2, HSSCAP 14 (1929): 135–207.

48. Helen Hunt Jackson, *Ramona* (1884; reprint Boston: Little, Brown and Company, 1922); Richard Griswold del Castillo, "The del Valle Family and the Fantasy Heritage," *California History* 59 (spring 1980): 2–15.

49. Tirey L. Ford, *Dawn and the Dons: The Romance of Monterey* (San Francisco: A. M. Robertson, 1926); Nellie Van de Grift Sánchez, *Spanish Arcadia* (San Francisco, Los Angeles, Chicago: Powell Publishing Company, 1929); Sydney A. Clark, *Golden Tapestry of California* (New York: Robert M. McBride and Company, 1937).

50. Carey McWilliams, *North from Mexico: The Spanish-Speaking People of the United States* (1948; reprint New York: Greenwood Press, 1968), 35–47.

51. Mabel Clare Craft, "California Womanhood in 1848," *San Francisco Chronicle*, January 23, 1898, 12–13. Van de Grift Sánchez, *Spanish Arcadia*, 237.

52. Charlotte S. McClure, *Gertrude Atherton* (Boston: Twayne Publishers, 1979); Lawrence Clark Powell, *California Classics: The Creative Literature of the Golden State* (Los Angeles: Ward Ritchie Press, 1971), 103–14. For discussion of Anglo images and stereotypes of *Californianos* that mention but do not focus on women, see James D. Hart, *American Images of Spanish California* (Berkeley: Friends of the Bancroft Library, 1960); Harry Clark, "Their Pride, Their Manners, and Their Voices: Sources of the Traditional Portrait of Early Californians," *California Historical Society* 52 (spring 1974): 71–82; David J. Langum, "Californios and the Image of Indolence," *The Western Historical Quarterly* 9 (April 1978): 181–96; and David J. Weber, "Here Rests Juan Espinosa: Toward a Clearer Look at the Image of the 'Indolent' Californios," *The Western Historical Quarterly* 10 (January 1979): 61–68.

53. Van de Grift Sánchez, *Spanish Arcadia*, 375.

54. Bolton, "The Epic of Greater America"; Bolton, *Wider Horizons of American*

History (1930; reprint New York: D. Appleton-Century Company, 1939), 55–106. For a critique of the Bolton theory, see Hanke, *Do the Americas Have a Common History?*

55. Bolton, "The Mission as a Frontier Institution in the Spanish American Colonies," in his *Wider Horizons of American History,* 107–48; Bolton, *The Spanish Borderlands: A Chronicle of Old Florida and the Southwest* (New Haven, Conn.: Yale University Press, 1921), 7–10; Bolton, "Defensive Spanish Expansion and the Significance of the Spanish Borderlands," in *Bolton and the Spanish Borderlands,* ed. John Francis Bannon (Norman: University of Oklahoma Press, 1964), 32–66.

56. John W. Caughey, "Herbert Eugene Bolton," in *Turner/Bolton/Webb: Three Historians of the American Frontier,* ed. Wilbur Jacobs, John W. Caughey, and Joe B. Frantz (Seattle: University of Washington Press, 1965), 49; David J. Weber, "Turner, the Boltonians, and the Borderlands," *American Historical Review* 91 (February 1986): 68.

57. Bolton, "The Mission as a Frontier Institution"; Bolton, *The Spanish Borderlands,* 188–91, 192–202, 215–17, 279–87; Charles E. Chapman, *A History of California: The Spanish Period* (New York: The MacMillan Company, 1930), 352–96.

58. Bolton, *The Spanish Borderlands,* 294. The reciprocal influence between popular and scholarly history is worth noting in the case of Bolton and Van de Grift Sánchez, professional and popular historians who worked together. See John Francis Bannon, *Herbert Eugene Bolton: The Historian and the Man* (Tucson: University of Arizona Press, 1978), 171, 173.

59. Bolton, "Defensive Spanish Expansion and the Significance of the Borderlands," 61, 63; Bolton, "The Epic of Greater America," 452.

60. Jones, *Los Paisanos*; Max L. Moorhead, "The *Soldado de Cuera:* Stalwart of the Spanish Borderlands," and Leon G. Campbell, "The First *Californios:* Presidial Society in Spanish California, 1769–1822," in *The Spanish Borderlands: A First Reader,* ed. Oakah L. Jones Jr. (Los Angeles: Lorrin L. Morrison, 1974), 85–105 and 106–18.

61. Donald A. Nuttall, "The Gobernantes of Upper California: A Profile," *California Historical Quarterly* 51 (fall 1972): 253–80.

62. Bolton, "Epic of Greater America," 452; Bolton, "Significance of the Borderlands," 56–58. Bolton, "Spanish Resistance to Carolina Traders," in *Bolton and the Spanish Borderlands,* ed. John Francis Bannon (Norman: University of Oklahoma Press, 1964), 148.

63. Bolton, "Significance of the Borderlands," 56, 58.

64. Bolton, "Significance of the Borderlands," 54.

65. For theories of gender and discussion of gender as a category of social and historical analysis in women's history, see Linda J. Nicholson, *Gender and History: The Limits of Social Theory in the Age of the Family* (New York: Columbia University

Press, 1986); Smith-Rosenberg, *Disorderly Conduct*, 11–52; Linda Gordon, "What's New in Women's History," and Carroll Smith-Rosenberg, "Writing History: Language, Class, and Gender," in *Feminist Studies-Critical Studies*, ed. Teresa de Lauretis (Bloomington: Indiana University Press, 1986), 20–30 and 31–54; Joan Kelly-Gadol, "The Social Relation of the Sexes: Methodological Implications of Women's History," in *Sex and Class in Women's History*, ed. Judith L. Norton, Mary P. Ryan, and Judith Walkowitz (London: Routledge and Kegan Paul, 1983), 1–15; and Catharine A. MacKinnon, "Feminism, Marxism, Method, and the State: An Agenda for Theory," in *Feminist Theory: A Critique of Ideology*, ed. Nannerl O. Keohane, Michelle Z. Rosaldo, and Barbara C. Gelpi (Chicago: The University of Chicago Press, 1982), 1–30.

For early discussion of Chicana history, see Rosaura Sánchez, "The History of Chicanas: Proposal for a Materialist Perspective," in *Between Borders: Essays on Mexicana/Chicana History*, ed. Adelaida del Castillo (Encino, Calif.: Floricanto Press, 1990); Mario García, "The Chicana in American History: The Mexican Women of El Paso, 1880–1920 – A Case Study," *Pacific Historical Review* 49 (May 1980): 315–37; and María Linda Apodaca, "The Chicana Woman: An Historical Materialist Perspective," in *Women in Latin America: An Anthology from Latin American Perspectives* (Riverside, Calif.: Latin American Perspectives, 1979), 81–100.

For studies that use gender as a category of historical analysis with respect to Spanish-speaking women in the present West and Southwest, see Ramón Gutiérrez, *When Jesus Came, the Corn Mothers Went Away: Marriage, Sexuality and Power in New Mexico, 1500–1846* (Stanford, Calif.: Stanford University Press, 1991); Sarah Deutsch, *No Separate Refuge: Culture, Class, and Gender on an Anglo-Hispanic Frontier in the American Southwest, 1880–1940* (New York: Oxford University Press, 1987); Salomé Hernández, "Nuevo Mexicanas as Refugees and Reconquest Settlers," in *New Mexico Women: Intercultural Perspectives*, ed. Joan M. Jensen and Darlis Miller (Albuquerque: University of New Mexico Press, 1986), 41–70; Deena González, "The Spanish-Mexican Women of Santa Fe: Patterns of Their Resistance and Accommodation, 1820–1880" (Ph.D. diss., University of California, Berkeley, 1985); and Antonia I. Castañeda, "*Presidarias y Pobladoras*: Spanish-Speaking Women in Monterey, California, 1770–1821" (Ph.D. diss., Stanford University, 1990).

66. For a review of the historical literature and citations relative to new approaches to the history of women in the frontier West, see Glenda Riley, "Frontier Women," in *American Frontier and Western Issues: A Historiographical Review*, ed. Roger L. Nichols (New York: Greenwood Press, 1986), 179–98; Sandra L. Myres, "Women in the West," in *Historians and the American West*, ed. Michael Malone (Lincoln: University of Nebraska Press, 1983), 369–86; Jensen and Miller, "The Gentle Tamers Revisited"; and Glenda Riley, "Images of the Frontierswoman: Iowa

as a Case Study," *Western Historical Quarterly* 8 (1977): 189–202. For a discussion of literary stereotypes in historical portraits of frontier women, see Sandra L. Myres, *Westering Women and the Frontier Experience, 1800–1915* (Albuquerque: University of New Mexico Press, 1982), 1–11; see also William Cronon, Howard Lamar, Katherine G. Morrissey, and Joy Gitlin, "Women and the West: Rethinking the Western History Survey Course," *The Western Historical Quarterly* 17 (July 1986): 269–90; and Susan Armitage, "Women and Men in Western History: A Stereoptical Vision," *The Western Historical Quarterly* 16 (October 1985): 381–95.

For studies taking more inclusive, multicultural approaches to women in the West, see del Castillo, ed., *Between Borders; Western Women: Their Land, Their Lives,* ed. Lillian Schlissel, Vickie Ruiz, and Janice Monk (Albuquerque: University of New Mexico Press, 1988); *The Women's West,* ed. by Susan Armitage and Elizabeth Jameson (Norman: University of Oklahoma Press, 1987); Joan M. Jensen and Gloria Ricci Lothrop, *California Women: A History* (San Francisco: Boyd and Fraser Publishing Company, 1987); and Jensen and Miller, eds., *New Mexico Women.*

For examples of edited and annotated source material on women in the West, see *Ho for California: Women's Overland Diaries from the Huntington Library,* ed. Sandra L. Myres (San Marino: Henry E. Huntington Library and Art Gallery, 1980); *A Victorian Gentlewoman in the Far West: The Reminiscences of Mary Hallock Foote,* ed. Rodman W. Paul (San Marino: The Huntington Library, 1980); *Let Them Speak for Themselves: Women in the American West, 1849–1900,* ed. Christine Fischer (New York: E. P. Dutton, 1977); and Dame Shirley (Louise A. K. S. Clappe), *The Shirley Letters* (1854–1855; reprint Santa Barbara and Salt Lake City: Peregrine Smith, Inc., 1970).

67. For generally descriptive studies, see Myres, *Westering Women;* Lillian Schlissel, *Women's Diaries of the Westward Journey* (New York: Schocken Books, 1982); and Julie Roy Jeffrey, *Frontier Women: The Trans-Mississippi West, 1840–1900* (New York: Hill and Wang, 1979).

For women and the family in California and the Far West, see Richard Griswold del Castillo, *La Familia: Chicano Families in the Urban Southwest, 1848 to the Present* (Notre Dame, Ind.: University of Notre Dame Press, 1984); Robert L. Griswold, *Family and Divorce in California, 1850–1890* (Albany: State University of New York Press, 1982); and John Mack Faragher, *Women and Men on the Overland Trail* (Yale University Press, 1979).

68. Annette Kolodny, *The Land before Her: Fantasy and Experience of the American Frontiers, 1630–1860* (Chapel Hill: University of North Carolina Press, 1984); Glenda Riley, *Women and Indians on the Frontier, 1825–1915* (Albuquerque: University of New Mexico Press, 1984); Sandra L. Myres, "Mexican Americans and Westering Anglos: A Feminine Perspective," *New Mexico Historical Review* 57 (1982): 414–30.

69. Ibid.

70. Riley, *Women and Indians on the Frontier*, 224.

71. Jensen and Miller, eds., *New Mexico Women*; Armitage and Jameson, eds., *The Women's West*; Schlissel, Ruiz, and Monk, eds., *Western Women: Their Land, Their Lives.*

72. Susan Armitage, "Through Women's Eyes: A New View of the West," in Armitage and Jameson, *The Women's West*, 17.

73. Limerick, *The Legacy of Conquest.*

74. Albert L. Hurtado, *Indian Survival on the California Frontier* (New York: Yale University Press, 1989), 169–92; Antonia I. Castañeda, "Sexual Violence in the Politics and Policies of Conquest: Amerindian Women and the Spanish Conquest of Alta California," in *Building with Our Hands: New Directions in Chicana Studies*, ed. Adela de la Torre and Beatríz M. Pesquera (Berkeley: University of California Press, 1993); Castañeda, "Anglo Images of Nineteenth Century *Californianas.*"

75. Gerda Lerner, *The Creation of Patriarchy* (New York: Oxford University Press, 1986); see also Susan Brownmiller, *Against Our Will: Men, Women and Rape* (1975; reprint Toronto: Bantam Books, 1976); Christine Ward Gailey, "Evolutionary Perspectives on Gender Hierarchy," in *Analyzing Gender: A Handbook of Social Science Research*, ed. Beth B. Hess and Myra Marx Ferree (Newbury Park: Sage Publications, 1987), 32–67; Carole J. Sheffield, "Sexual Terrorism: The Social Control of Women," in Hess and Ferree, *Analyzing Gender*, 171–89; Jalna Hanmer and Mary Maynard, "Introduction: Violence and Gender Stratification," in *Women, Violence and Social Control*, ed. Jalna Hanmer and Mary Maynard (Atlantic Highlands, N.J.: Humanities Press International, Inc., 1987), 1–12; see also Anne Edwards, "Male Violence in Feminist Theory: An Analysis of the Changing Conceptions of Sex/Gender Violence and Male Dominance," and David H. J. Morgan, "Masculinity and Violence," in Hanmer and Maynard, *Women, Violence and Social Control*, 13–29 and 180–92.

76. See note 74.

77. David Langum, "Californio Women and the Image of Virtue," *Southern California Quarterly* 59 (fall 1977): 245–50.

78. Cecil Robinson, *With the Ears of Strangers: The Mexican in American Travel Literature* (Tucson: University of Arizona Press, 1963); Ramond A. Paredes, "The Mexican Image in American Travel Literature, 1831–1869," *New Mexico Historical Review* 52 (January 1977): 5–29; Paredes, "The Origins of Anti-Mexican Sentiment in the United States," *New Scholar* 6 (1977): 139–65; Doris L. Meyer, "Early Mexican American Responses to Negative Stereotyping," *New Mexico Historical Review* 53 (January 1978): 75–91; David J. Weber, "Scarce More than Apes: Historical Roots of Anglo-American Stereotypes of Mexicans in the Border Region," in *New Spain's Far Northern Frontier: Essays on Spain in the American West, 1540–1821*, ed. David J. Weber (Albuquerque: University of New Mexico Press, 1979), 295–307.

79. Janet Lecompte, "The Independent Women of Hispanic New Mexico, 1821–1846," *The Western Historical Quarterly* 12 (January 1981): 17–35; see also James H. Lacy, "New Mexico Women in Early American Writings," *New Mexico Historical Review* 34 (January 1959): 41–51; and Beverly Trulio, "Anglo American Attitudes toward New Mexican Women," *Journal of the West* 12 (April 1973): 229–39.

80. Jane Dysart, "Mexican Women in San Antonio, 1830–1860: The Assimilation Process," *The Western Historical Quarterly* 7 (October 1976): 365–75; Darlis A. Miller, "Cross-Cultural Marriages in the Southwest: The New Mexico Experience, 1846–1900," *New Mexico Historical Review* 57 (October 1982): 335–59; Rebecca McDowell Craver, *The Impact of Intimacy: Mexican-Anglo Intermarriage in New Mexico, 1821–1846* (Southwestern Studies, Monograph No. 66, El Paso: Texas-Western Press, 1982); see also Kathleen Crawford, "María Amparo Ruíz Burton: The General's Lady," *Journal of San Diego History* 30 (summer 1984): 198–211.

81. González, "The Spanish-Mexican Women of Santa Fe," 111–53; Antonia I. Castañeda, "*Presidarias y Pobladoras,*" chapter 5.

82. González, "The Spanish-Mexican Women of Santa Fe"; for comparative purposes and studies of differing quality, see Sylvia Van Kirk, *Many Tender Ties: Women in Fur Trade Societies, 1670–1870* (Norman: University of Oklahoma Press, 1980); Walter O'Meara, *Daughters of the Country: The Women of the Fur Traders* (New York: Harcourt, Brace, and World, 1968); and William R. Swagerty, "Marriage and Settlement Patterns of Rocky Mountain Trappers and Traders," *The Western Historical Quarterly* 49 (1980): 159–80.

83. Albert Camarillo, *Chicanos in California: A History of Mexican Americans in California* (San Francisco: Boyd and Fraser Publishing Company, 1984); Ricardo Romo, *East Los Angeles: History of a Barrio* (Austin: University of Texas Press, 1983); Camarillo, *Chicanos in a Changing Society: From Mexican Pueblos to American Barrios in Santa Barbara and Southern California, 1848–1930* (Cambridge: Harvard University Press, 1979); Richard Griswold del Castillo; *The Los Angeles Barrio, 1850–1890: A Social History* (Berkeley: University of California Press, 1979); see also Leonard Pitt, *The Decline of the Californios: A Social History of the Spanish-Speaking Californians, 1846–1890* (Berkeley: University of California Press, 1971); Gloria E. Miranda, "Racial and Cultural Dimensions in Gente de Razón Status in Spanish and Mexican California," *Southern California Quarterly* 70 (fall 1988): 235–64; Miranda, "Hispano-Mexicano Childrearing Practices in Pre-American Santa Barbara," *Southern California Historical Quarterly* 65 (1983): 307–20; Miranda, "Gente de Razón Marriage Patterns in Spanish and Mexican California: A Case Study of Santa Barbara and Los Angeles," *Southern California Historical Quarterly* 63 (1981): 1–21.

For Chicano histories that treat pre–twentieth-century New Mexico, Texas, or the entire Southwest and include discussion of women, see David Montejano, *An-*

glos and Mexicans in the Making of Texas, 1836–1986 (Austin: University of Texas Press, 1987); Arnoldo De León, *They Called Them Greasers: Anglo Attitudes toward Mexicans in Texas, 1821–1900* (Austin: University of Texas Press, 1983); Gilberto Miguel Hinojosa, *A Borderlands Town in Transition: Laredo, 1755–1870* (College Station: Texas A&M University Press, 1983); Mario T. García, *Desert Immigrants: The Mexicans of El Paso, 1880–1920* (New Haven, Conn.: Yale University Press, 1981); and Alicia V. Tjarks, "Comparative Demographic Analysis of Texas, 1777–1793," *Southwestern Historical Quarterly* 77 (January 1974): 291–338.

84. Griswold del Castillo, *La Familia*; Pitt, *The Decline of the Californios;* Roberto Alvarez Jr., *Familia: Migration and Adaption in Baja and Alta California, 1800–1975* (Berkeley: University of California Press, 1987).

85. See note 60.

86. Gloria Elizarraras Miranda, "Family Patterns and the Social Order in Hispanic Santa Barbara, 1784–1848" (Ph.D. diss., University of Southern California, Los Angeles, 1978); Miranda, "Racial and Cultural Dimensions in Gente de Razón Status"; Miranda, "Hispano-Mexicano Childrearing Practices"; Miranda, "Gente de Razón Marriage Patterns."

87. Gutiérrez, *When Jesus Came, the Corn Mothers Went Away;* see also Ramón Gutiérrez, "Honor Ideology, Marriage Negotiation, and Class-Gender Domination in New Mexico, 1690–1846," *Latin American Perspectives* 44 (winter 1985): 81–104.

88. Patricia Seed, *To Love, Honor, and Obey in Colonial Mexico: Conflicts over Marriage Choice, 1574–1821* (Stanford: Stanford University Press, 1988).

89. Sylvia M. Arrom, *The Women of Mexico City, 1790–1857* (Stanford: Stanford University Press, 1985); Asunción Lavrin, "Women in Convents: Their Economic and Social Roles in Colonial Mexico," in *Liberating Women's History: Theoretical and Critical Essays,* ed. Berenice A. Carroll (Urbana: University of Illinois Press, 1976), 250–77; Asunción Lavrin and Edith Couturier, "Dowries and Wills: A View of Women's Socioeconomic Role in Colonial Guadalajara and Puebla, 1640–1790," *Hispanic American Historical Review* 59 (May 1979): 280–304; *Latin American Women: Historical Perspectives,* ed. Asunción Lavrin (Westport, Conn.: Greenwood Press, 1978).

90. The sources identified in the following discussion are selective and representative. Each archival repository, including city and county libraries, museums, and historical societies, must be examined and/or reexamined for materials pertinent to women and must be approached with gender-specific questions.

91. The standard archival sources for Spanish-Mexican California history that contain transcripts and/or abstracts of government reports and correspondence, censuses, transcripts of hearings, petitions, letters, testimonies, etc. include the bound volumes of *The Archives of California,* 63 vols., and the microfilm copy of

the multivolume *Archivo de la Nación,* Bancroft Library, University of California, Berkeley, California; see also *The Writings of Junipero Serra,* 4 vols., ed. Antonine Tiebesar (Washington, D.C.: Academy of Franciscan History); *Writings of Francisco de Lasuen,* 2 vols., ed. Finbar Kinneally (Washington, D.C.: Academy of American Franciscan History, 1965).

92. The Mission Archives at Mission Santa Barbara, Santa Barbara, California, include, among numerous other sources, the extant *Books of Marriage, Books of Baptism,* and *Books of Death* for each mission, marriage testimonies, petitions for dispensation of consanguinity, mission censuses, sermons, official reports, and correspondence. Also, individual missions may have additional archival material.

93. For the Mexican period, see *Archives of California,* as well as the "Vallejo Collection" and the reminiscences of individual women in the manuscript collection, including Catarina Avila de Ríos, Angustias de la Guerra Ord, Apolinaria Lorenzana, Felipa Osuna de Marrón, Juana Machado de Ridington, Eulalia Pérez, María Inocenta Pico, Mariana Torres, Dorotea Valdez, Rosalía Vallejo de Leese, Bancroft Library, Berkeley, California. For the civil and criminal court records for the northern district of Mexican California, and the Libros de Solares for Monterey, see *The Monterey Archives,* 16 vols., Office of the County Recorder and Clerk, Salinas, California; see also the Monterey Collection, San Marino, California.

94. María Ignacia Soberanes de Bale, Papers and Correspondence, Bale Family Papers, Manuscript Collection, Bancroft Library, Berkeley, California; *Records of the Land Grant Commission,* Archives of the State of California, Sacramento, California.

Frontiers 11:1 (1990): 8–20.

Gender, Labor History, and Chicano/a Ethnic Identity

SARAH DEUTSCH

It is commonplace now, if not universal, to recognize that gender issues are inseparable from those of culture, class, and race.[1] That recognition has both arisen from and influenced works on Chicano history as it has other fields. Recently, Douglas Monroy and Ramón Gutiérrez, in their elegant prizewinning books on colonial California and New Mexico respectively, made gender and the political economy of sex central to their arguments about imperialism, conquest, race, and ethnicity.[2] In addition, a flurry of publications that focus more specifically on Chicanas has altered our picture of ethnicity, race, and class in the American West.[3]

Yet this common recognition still leaves some gaps in the literature, alongside some resisters. This article originated in an attempt to convince that remnant, not a uniformly sympathetic audience, of the importance of gender analysis even where it seems most unlikely.[4] I chose as examples what seemed at the time to be unrelated arenas and methodologies: the social history of Chicano labor and a literary analysis of ethnic identity as expressed in selected second-generation Chicano autobiographies. Indeed, few if any works have managed to encompass both these sites of analysis, even in their more general sense. Works on shifting definitions of race or ethnicity for Chicanos have assumed that no difference existed in men's and women's experience.[5] Works on labor mobilization and strikes, even in works about women or works that note differences between men and women, have tended to have little room for an analysis of the formation of ethnic identity as it varied on gender lines.[6] These gaps resulted in part from differences in focus, from lack of sources, and also from the state of the field at the time.[7]

This article marks a provisional and tentative attempt to explore how these two seemingly unrelated paths – the first path being labor history, and the second the construction and reconstruction of identity among non–working-class Chicanos and Chicanas – might converge. The locations of struggle differ in the two sets of literature, the actors differ in their social locations, and the texts those actors produce differ. Yet both Chicano labor history and autobiographies are concerned with issues of identity and consciousness. They both make clear that identity and consciousness are constructed and emerge through contest and struggle. The different facets of identity central to each literature illuminate each other. Chicano labor historians' focus on the construction of "a" class identity and mobilization has made it difficult to understand the differences in behavior of men and women on the same site. On the other hand, the autobiographies often center exactly on articulating the gender differences in the meaning of being Chicano/a. While their middle-class insights cannot be directly transferred to Chicano and Chicana workers, they can warn us against taking ethnic identity as a given and redirect us to those working-class movements and texts for clues as to the ways in which the construction of a gendered ethnicity might help explain variations in labor strategies. In other words, what the two literatures together clarify is that the identity being constructed through struggle on any given site involved gender as well as class and ethnicity, and that struggles occurred within as well as between groups.

LABOR HISTORY

It is essential to begin this exploration by examining the way in which labor history has treated men and women workers. When I was at the Lowell Conference on industrial history a few years ago, I was struck by the differences in the treatment of women's and men's labor history. The theme of the conference that year was immigration, ethnicity, and the Industrial Revolution. In the morning, at the session on immigrant workers, two men told stories of men and unions. The male workers they described seemed to exist entirely outside of families or, at least, without women – a situation not impossible, but unlikely. Because there was little sense of a family economy or sexual division of labor, there was little explanation of how these men could afford to leave their jobs or strike, or even of why their language and organizing styles took the particular gendered forms they did.

In the afternoon session on women, work, and ethnicity, three women described the complex interrelationships of work and family for women workers of various ethnic groups in various industries. As had the men in the morning, they discussed the formative influences of ethnic background on the workers' behavior. But there was no "story" here, no chronological narrative; there were "uprisings," but there was no movement history of growing or developing consciousness or change over time.

This sense of the different social locations of men and women in relation to work, due to ideologies of family and gender, had led to an exaggerated split in the labor histories of men and women, the development of different methodologies and languages – institutional vs. family history – different ways of understanding labor history and class consciousness, as gender specific. But the differences in consciousness, in identity, between women and men workers is not so neat and clean.[8] After all, men exist in families, too. Margaret Rose's study of the United Farm Workers (UFW) makes clear the centrality of family structure and dynamics in determining the shape and strategies of the UFW. The innovation of sending whole families east, instead of just young men, to publicize the boycott, for example, arose from the realities of lonely male organizers who kept abandoning their posts to return to their families.[9] Similarly, even migrant men remote from home, as was clear with the Chicano miners I studied in northern Colorado in the 1920s, made organizing and investment decisions within a network of kinship relations, as, indeed, they had often been sent forth from the family to do. Insurance records of the Rocky Mountain Fuel Company showed these miners sending wages to parents and wives in Mexico, New Mexico, and southern Colorado.[10] In short, men's and not just women's labor organizations grew out of a particular framework of a family economy and a sexual division of labor.

On the other hand, women's consciousness and forms of protest, as Vicki Ruiz's study of cannery workers demonstrates, also have a historical dynamic; they are influenced by past as well as present events. Her cannery workers learned from the series of protests they launched in the 1930s, and that politicizing lesson affected their demands and organizing skills. The knowledge thus gained allowed them to take advantage of the labor shortage in World War II to achieve unprecedented benefits in the way of childcare, for example.[11]

Beyond the simple corrective of recognizing that men have families and that women have histories, however, still lies the question of the ways in which men's and women's separate consciousness did derive from differences in their work situations and influenced each other. Differences in time, space, and industry all affected the consciousness of women and men, sometimes in the same family. In this context, I cannot help wondering, for example, what David Montejano's powerful argument in *Anglos and Mexicans in the Making of Texas* would have looked like had he included women and gender as a category of analysis.[12] Montejano uses a modes-of-production analysis to argue that race and ethnic relations took their shape from shifting economic relations of production – from a move from pastoral to agricultural to industrial. The inclusion of women, who were often engaged in a different mode of production from the men with whom they lived, might have had a profound impact on his argument.

Montejano may have assumed, as scholars traditionally have, that women derived their class status and consciousness vicariously, from men. But increasingly historians recognize, first, that when women were working for wages, whether in the home or outside of it, that work brought relations of production to bear directly on their notions of themselves and their place in the world. And second, they recognize that even for women not engaged in wage work, class has a different meaning when experienced differently. When Texas Chicanas were domestic servants, for example, they derived a sense of their identity as workers from a hierarchical, personalist relationship with Anglo women, certainly a different sense of "worker" and a different set of race relations than a male industrial worker experienced; similarly, if men were farm laborers and women were pecan shellers, they, too, were in different modes of production.[13] If men and women lived together, these distinct consciousnesses would affect each other in ways obscured or denied if women's experience is ignored.[14]

On the other hand, even when women were not engaged in wage labor, their activities affected men's strategies and consciousness. In southern Colorado and northern New Mexico, for example, only Spanish Mexican village women's maintenance of food production made possible migrant men's ability to slip in and out of wage labor.[15] Only their maintenance of the relations and material production that sustained the village made it possible for the men to continue to conceive of themselves as villagers, and not simply as wageworkers.

The varying sexual division of labor within families at different sites, due, in part, to the nature of local industries, may, in fact, have contributed to site-specific senses of identity as Chicanos, Chicanas, and workers. These identities, in turn, may help to explain the different labor strategies and demands generated on different sites. In the coal-mining camps of southern Colorado in the early years of this century, Chicano miners joined other miners of different ethnic backgrounds in a major strike. The new sense of identity emerging in the mines, symbolized by this new cross-ethnic alliance as well as by splits among local Hispanics, owed itself in part to the local ethnic and sexual structure of labor. In the coal-mining camps, the women depended totally on their husband's or son's wage. They had no produce gardens as they had back home, and their very residences were occupied at the company's will.[16]

Women's consciousness, like men's, emerged in a particular context, a particular set of economic and social relations that varied by industry as well as region and era. In the coalfields, women had supported the strike and the men's demands. In agriculture in the 1930s, when beet workers struck in northern Colorado, women supported this strike, also. But this time their relation to the strike differed. In the beet fields women worked alongside the men. But men received the wages for the women's labor. Beet labor demands could have included a demand for an individual instead of a family wage; they did not. Unlike the coal miners' demands, however, they did include a demand for garden lots with adequate water. In conjunction with other demands, these gardens would have recreated a village structure of symbiotic male and female labor and a separate, autonomous productive base for women without denying the centrality of the family to all areas of their life.[17] Examining the sexual division of labor and its impact on consciousness, even when women seem most invisible and distanced from the workplace, illuminates workplace as well as homeplace strategies for men and women and for the group as a whole.

Not only do the material circumstances of each sex help govern the choices and identity of the other, but the meaning with which work experience is endowed depends, to some extent, on the individual players involved and their responses. Patricia Zavella and Emma Perez have both documented a range of Chicano attitudes toward Chicana wage, work even within the same industry and era, from those men who would not permit their wives to work outside the home, to those who expected them to help support the family in that way.[18] The women themselves displayed similar conflicts.

This is not to deny that larger forces had a powerful effect on family strategies and women's sense of identity as women and as workers. It is merely to recognize that that effect is complex and varied. The assumption that wage work brings autonomy, for example, and a shift in consciousness from identity by family role to identity by workplace role, has long come under fire.[19] In her study of Chicana cannery workers in the 1930s, Ruiz found that waged work did seem to increase the women's weight in consumer decision making at home and helped women develop peer networks alongside kinship ones. Moreover, as the two cases of coal and beet work indicate, it may have increased their voice in mixed-sex labor organizations. Yet the low wages also came permeated with domination by bosses, often but not always male. An individual wage, in this context, would not have resolved Chicana beet workers' dilemma. Increased autonomy in the form of an independent income could accompany, rather than oppose, subordination and dependence. Patricia Zavella found that Chicana cannery workers more recently, despite their individual wages, identified themselves by their family roles rather than their work roles. They felt ambivalent about what work meant to their identity when it did not pay enough to make them independent of their family, had they desired such independence, and when it did not free them from discrimination, long hours, sexual harassment, and dangerous conditions at work.[20]

In short, the relation of experience to consciousness, of behavior, to ideology remains harder to grasp than that. Whether women were visible at the work site or not, the sexual division of labor had an impact on the strategies of both sexes and the way in which they experienced class. How, for example, do we understand what it means about Chicanas' consciousness when Chicanas were more militant, judged by strike action, in 1930s San Antonio, than were Chicanos?[21] And how do we make sense of the fact that in 1910, Anglo and Spanish Mexican male census takers in northern New Mexico found only ten women with occupations for every one hundred men, while a local Spanish-Mexican woman found seventy-nine women with occupations for every one hundred men? What are the implications for the group's ethnic and labor consciousness of the fact that she recognized women's productive labors in home fields and gardens and the men and Anglo women did not?[22]

Devra Weber's article in *Oral History Review* on striking California Chicana farmworkers of the 1930s reveals not only that women were militantly conscious of their position as workers, but that their definition of "worker" was gendered, as was their experience of the strike. According to Weber, men and women had different memories of key demands and leaders as well as of their own roles. To the women, the central issue was food and the provision of it to their community, and the central striking group was women in concert. To the men, the central issue was wages, and they did not recall the female bar owner who played a central role in the strike stories of the women. The strike's meaning changed according to the sex of the striker.[23] That meaning was bound up with their different identities as workers, providers, and community builders.

Traveling still deeper into the Chicano working-class consciousness, Margaret Rose's study of women in the United Farm Workers reveals significant differences not just between women and men but among women as to the meaning of work and activism and as to aspirations and self-definition. Helen Chávez and Dolores Huerta pose quite different models for the younger women of the movement as well as for Anglo consumers of boycott literature.[24] According to Rose, Dolores Huerta, with her unconventional life, her numerous scattered children, and her activism, is a model that young women organizers seek to emulate only as part of a life-stage. When they look to lifelong models, they prefer Chávez, the behind-the-scenes reluctant player, solidly married to a strong male figure.

At issue here is not simply their identity as workers or as women, but their identity as Chicanas as apart from Chicanos and as apart from Anglo women. These women constructed a distinctly female ethnic identity. That construction interpenetrated their interpretation of themselves as women workers. At the same time, the racial and ethnic dynamics that helped determine their opportunities as Chicana workers also contributed to their construction of their identity. Moreover, as Margaret Rose's work implies, their definitions of what it was to be a Chicana varied among themselves.[25]

ETHNIC IDENTITY

It is here that a closer examination of the impact of gender on the construction of ethnic identity might prove helpful. Susan Glenn has convincingly argued in *Daughters of the Shtetl* that one generation of Jewish immigrant women's sense of themselves as Jewish women in a modernizing world explains why their patterns of labor activism differed from those of male and other female workers in the early twentieth century. Vicki Ruiz has shown that Chicana workers, too, felt the allure of modernity in the form of popular culture, and that it altered their sense of what it meant to be Chicana.[26] Working-class texts tend to be silent on explicit, articulated definitions of a particularly Chicana ethnic identity. Working-class Chicanas have had few opportunities to create literary vehicles of self-expression. Scholars have approached these issues for working-class Chicanas indirectly, through an examination of behavior and language – when they moved out of the home, wore makeup, or had different memories of strikes. The middle-class authors who do produce autobiographical examinations of ethnic identity, on the other hand, rarely focus on workplace struggles and identity. The different social locations of these classes are crucial to the nature of the texts they produce. Nonetheless, as self-conscious reconstructions of self for a public audience, the autobiographies may provide the best entry point for examining the ways in which ethnic consciousness grows differently from the lived experience and social locations of men and women.

It also grows from differences among women. In the past two years or so, a spate of articles by prominent feminist scholars has addressed the salience of differences among women in the creation of women's identities, the importance of recognizing that ethnic differences, definitions, and identities arise in part from relations of power among women as well as between men and women. Norma Alarcón has argued, in regard to "the psychic and material violence that gives shape to" one's understanding of one's own position, that "not all of this violence comes from men."[27]

Beyond calling for the removal of what I would call Monolithic Woman, the portrayal of women as though they all shared the same experiences and oppressions, most of these writers point away from a focus on a single ethnic group or sex as a narrative strategy. Gerda Lerner has urged us to write history focused on the interweaving of sex, race, class, and cultural systems as they mutually reinforced each other.[28] Elizabeth Fox-Genovese similarly, though for different reasons, has warned about the dangers and pitfalls encountered on the way to making the marginal central by focusing solely on one group's construction of its identity. Too often an analysis of the construction of ethnic identity loses sight of larger relations of power. Citing works that depicted such a thoroughly successful slave community that the realities of dominance and oppression receded into the deep background, Fox-Genovese reasserts the shaping impact of the dominant group's power over social relations and also over notions of identity.[29]

Yet by treating the dominant group's actions, whether of women or men or both, as generating responses by all others, such a narrative reinforces the dominance of the one group and distorts the history of those other groups. It allows the dominant group to set the agenda and write the text for all groups. Textual analysis of autobiographies and oral testimony allows us to escape some of the dangers of a narrative built around the dynamics of domination.

Autobiographical texts by people outside the dominant group recenter the narrative without losing sight of relations of power. Such relations are inescapable, for example, in Richard Rodriguez's *Hunger of Memory,* where he argues that it was the realities of cultural power in the United States that led him to choose assimilation to fulfill first the expectations of his upwardly mobile first-generation family and then his own. Despite their different conclusions, the work of Cherríe Moraga, Gloria Anzaldúa, and Olivia Castellano also consciously presents their social location between classes and ethnic groups. Castellano recently described the rage that motivates her: "When nothing on either side of the two cultures, Mexican or Anglo-American, affirms your existence, that is how rage is shaped."[30] Her sense of herself as a Chicana was intimately bound to the negative messages of the two cultures that dominated her and could not be understood without examining both.

Moreover, however hard-pressed they may have been, Chicanas and other groups were driven also by their own needs, desires, and heritage. Alma Garcia has argued that Chicana feminism, for example, emerged from dynamics within the Chicano movement rather than from contagion by a largely Anglo, middle-class women's movement. And Deena Gonzáles has shown how Spanish Mexican women of New Mexico managed to use a court system in which they had no direct representation for their own ends.[31] Anglo males, and occasionally Anglo females, and sometimes even Chicanos, hardly unified, may have called the tune, but those who danced had usually learned their steps from someone else.[32]

In short, both external and internal forces combined to shape Chicano and Chicana experiences of class, gender, and ethnicity, and individuals experienced their class, gender, and ethnicity not as autonomous categories but as entangled and interdependent. That interdependence ensured that, while gender was not the only significant factor in the shaping of individual experience and ethnic identity, it was a crucial one. In this essay, for this difficult topic, my hope is to be suggestive rather than definitive, to lay out one possible approach among many, and to make clear by that path what the issue might have to offer in a fuller examination of more or different texts using this or another focus. Here I examine the construction of ethnic identity through symbolic reconstructions of history in autobiographical writings of second-generation Chicanas and Chicanos.

The reconstruction of the past, in particular, a story of origins, is often a strategy for creating a unified, distinct group identity or even nationalism in the present. In the years immediately following the American Revolution, for example, the United States sought to distance itself from England by leaping across time and laying claim to both the wilderness and classical Rome as its immediate forebears. England, in this account, contributed little to the new republic. Similarly, one hundred years later, Japan, seeking to distance itself from the West and legitimize its ascendancy in the East, rewrote Chinese history into a narrative that would logically culminate in

Japan rather than in a Far East dominated by China.[33] In the same vein, John Chávez explored, without gender analysis, Chicano uses of "Aztlán" in *The Lost Land*.[34]

The autobiographies of both Chicanos and Chicanas – specifically those of Cherríe Moraga, Gloria Anzaldúa, Richard Rodriguez, and Oscar Zeta Acosta – reconstruct the Mexican and Chicano past to aid in the creation of their own identities. It is this self-conscious restructuring of the past that makes these autobiographies particularly useful vehicles for examining the ways in which ethnic identity is constructed, just as national myths illuminate notions of national identity among their promulgators.

Few would claim that any of the four authors – two lesbian feminists, one conservative gay male, and one counterculture hero – is typical of Chicanos, but their typicality is not at issue here. It may well have been, in part, the contested nature of their sexual politics and identity that drove them to print or helped provide them, and not other Chicano authors, with a market, for there are few other second-generation autobiographies of the era available, and none that focus so clearly on the construction of identity. These would certainly be fragile pillars for an argument about the nature of ethnic identity for all Chicanos and Chicanas. I am using these autobiographies rather to support an argument that ethnic identity is gendered and resists totalizing tendencies. And I am posing one possible method for analyzing the gendered nature of ethnic identity in particular cases by focusing on the selves these authors constructed and articulated in these texts rather than outside them. In a sense, these autobiographies are manifestos of ethnic identity specific to place, generation, class, and sexuality. My focus, however, is far more limited. Reading four autobiographies of a single generation, with similarities in context and experience, allows a comparison of the ways they reconstruct the past. All these authors wrote after the Chicano movement had begun, though they had widely different relations to that movement, and all use some aspects of that movement ideology (including the choice of symbols) in their writings. All are educated and middle class in distinction to their own parents and in ways that stem directly from their status as second-generation.[35]

All four of these authors represent themselves as multiply identified and torn between their Anglo and Chicano heritage, their middle-class opportunities and attributes, and their identity with a working-class past. Indeed, as distinct from the workers discussed in the first part of this essay, it is in part their class position itself that seems to make their ethnic identity problematic. Their ethnic identity and consciousness become bound up with social mobility between races and between classes in a land where to be middle class assumes some identification with a dominant cultural and not just an economic group.

The authors call on the same set of symbols – Malinche, Aztlán, and the Virgin of Guadalupe – to resolve these tensions, but the men and women do so differently.[36] Symbols are always created by someone for some purpose. There was never a time when these symbols were not appropriated, and they have no meaning apart from their use. Malinche, or Malintzin, was the native Mexican woman sold to Cortés who became his consort. Aztlán is the territory claimed by the Chicano movement as their ancient southwestern homeland straddling the current international border between Mexico and the United States. The Virgin of Guadalupe is the version of Mary who appeared miraculously, with a Mexican face, to an Indian, Juan Diego, in 1531.[37] Each of the authors is selective in the symbols used, and appropriates the symbols for his or her own end.

Moraga and Anzaldúa call on both Malinche and Aztlán to construct a Chicana identity. Part of the feminist Chicana agenda, in which they participate, has been to appropriate and redefine Malinche or Malintzin.[38] While they describe Malintzin in vivid, concrete terms, Aztlán, to these two authors, is instead often a shadowy, imprecise place, a falsely romanticized past.[39] The two symbols are linked. Cherríe Moraga describes Aztlán in its usual ideal terms, but then turns the table and calls it a dream: "*Pero, es un sueno.* This safety / of the desert. / My country was not like that. / Neither was yours. / We have always bled / with our veins / and legs / open / to forces / beyond our control."[40] For Chicana feminists, Aztlán was the place where Malintzin was always already betrayed, rather than simply betrayer. Caught between two patriarchal cultures, sold by her mother that her mother might curry favor with her brother, Malintzin, also called La Vendida, was the sell-out who had already been sold, been alienated.[41] Similarly, Anzaldúa claims, "Not me sold out my people but they me. *Malinali Tenepas,* or Malintzin, has become known as *la Chingada* – the fucked one. . . . Not me sold out my people but they me." To see Malintzin as the betrayer, in this view, is to ignore the power relations within and not just between cultures. Anzaldúa demands "an accounting with all three cultures – white, Mexican, Indian." To be female, to be Chicana, in this view, is to be multiply-identified.

Knowing that redefining these symbols has placed her outside of the Chicano movement's definition of ethnicity, Anzaldúa proclaims, "And if going home is denied me then I will have to stand and claim my space, making a new culture – *una cultural mestiza* – with my own lumber, my own bricks and mortar and my own feminist architecture."[42] Anzaldúa and Moraga have rejected Aztlán as defined by the male-dominated Chicano movement, or as they have constructed that definition. Their own lived experience and their interpretation of that experience differ from the men's; they are not the displaced rulers, and Malinche serves as a symbol of that difference and the power relations bound up in it. Instead of using Aztlán, as the land stolen from men by their own women and the men of another culture, Moraga and Anzaldúa construct their own ethnic origins in the woman Malintzin, the site of cultural contest and mixing. In her, they create their own "homeland," their own female ethnic identity.

Moreover, having constructed Malinche as on the border between cultures, for Anzaldúa and Moraga, lesbianism becomes an extension of their Chicana identity, another borderland, another betrayal of Chicano men, of their own. In describing the fear she inspires in her mother, Moraga explains,

The line of reasoning goes:

Malinche sold out her indio people by acting as courtesan and translator for Cortez, whose offspring symbolically represent the birth of the bastardized mestizo-Mexicano people. My mother then is the modern-day Chicana, Malinche marrying a white man, my father, to produce the bastards my sister, my brother, and I are. Finally, I – a half-breed Chicana – further betray my race by choosing my sexuality which excludes all men, and therefore most dangerously, Chicano men.

I come from a long line of Vendidas.

I am a Chicana lesbian. My own particular relationship to being a sexual person; and a radical stand in direct contradiction to, and in violation of, the women [*sic*] I was raised to be.[43]

By refusing to be "the women [she] was raised to be," Moraga has rejected the prescribed roles she sees available for her in Chicano culture. She is betraying not her ethnicity, but that particular construction of Chicano culture, and substituting for it a Chicana culture, a culture redefined to include her. She is not simply a lesbian, but "a Chicana lesbian." "Chicana" here means Malintzin, the borderlands within, not Aztlán, the mythically pure, monocultural territory. Like Malinche's, their sexuality is a betrayal that does not gain them the dominant culture's acceptance or place them within the dominant culture. Instead, it is another enactment of dual marginalization.

Oscar Zeta Acosta's use of the same symbols stems more directly from the Chicano movement. In *The Revolt of the Cockroach People,* he uses the semi-autobiographical novel's centerpiece trial to give the jury a Chicano history lesson. Aztlán is more concrete here, "the northern deserts, the land we now call the Southwest. It is the ancient land of Aztlán, the original home of the *aztecas.*"[44] While also fighting for freedom and autonomy, Acosta's battle differs from Anzaldúa's and Moraga's. "What the hell are we fighting for?" His main character rages during a dispute with fellow activists. "For land and to live just like we want."[45] Anzaldúa and Moraga fight in the borderlands, not over the borderlands; Acosta's character fights for reconquest.

The greater definition of place in Acosta's book is reinforced by his use of the land for recuperation. He presents a primal connection to the land, a sexual connection. Out in the California desert, he recalls, "I kiss the dirt. I eat the sand. I roll over so that I am flat on my ass, stretched out with my palms to the skies. . . . I am at peace. Content with my commitment to the earth."[46] Like a warrior battling over territory, after the above-mentioned court case, Acosta declares, "Now is the time to forget those days and nights of fighting with the pigs. And now is the time of women."[47] Sex, like the land, becomes restorative, a necessary breather for an embattled activist lawyer.[48] Women become part of the scenery.

In light of his own characterization of Malinche as the one who "to her everlasting disgrace, provides him [Cortés] with her brown body and her strange words," Acosta's depiction of his main character's sexuality is significant.[49] Aggressive heterosexuality and reconquest are linked. Those Chicanos who do not join Acosta in his battle are given derogatory labels, as was one judge, "a short faggoty Mexican."[50] Anzaldúa and Moraga identify with Malintzin and internalize the borderlands, viewing themselves, like Malintzin, as caught between and being the site where diverse strands cross. Acosta does not internalize the borderland; he has sex with it. He poses his relation to the lost land as reconquest through sex with all contemporary Malinches. Not Cortés this time but Acosta will have Malinche.[51]

Acosta, too, struggles with his ethnic identity. Indeed, early in the book, Acosta's hero confesses that he has avoided Mexican women: "I haven't thought of myself as a member of a group since I was with the Baptists in 1956. A dozen years have come and gone. . . . All through schools, jobs and bumming, I haven't even held the hand of a Mexican woman, excepting whores who are all the same anyhow." "Am I ashamed," he asks himself, "of my race?"[52] In the context of his prior rejection of Chicanas as lovers, his turning to Chicanas as sexual partners represents his return to Chicano ethnicity. Not simply his sexual prowess, but his sexual partners help define the meaning of Chicano – women are the site of his struggle; his struggle is externalized.

Moraga explains this difference in ethnic identity and the dilemma for Chicano men by their validation and privilege in their Chicano homes and their potential privilege in the Anglo world. "The pull to identify with the oppressor was never as great in me," she writes, "as it was in my brother. For unlike him, I could never *become* the white man, only the white man's *woman*" (Moraga's emphasis).[53] It is not simply deep sexism that separates Acosta from Anzaldúa and Moraga. As a male struggling between patriarchal societies, Acosta cannot be Malintzin; Anzaldúa and Moraga, similarly, cannot usurp Cortés's role.

In both Acosta's and Rodriguez's work, the temptation to identify with the oppressor can be overwhelming, particularly for that segment of the second generation whose parents had achieved a precarious perch in the middle class. Both depict main characters experiencing success in the Anglo world. For Acosta, the temptation is heterosexualized, personified in a variety of sexual partners. In Rodriguez's *Hunger of Memory*, however, Malinche does not appear. Instead Rodriguez provides her opposite: the asexual Virgin of Guadalupe. This asexual figure Rodriguez can outgrow.

Rodriguez claims that the Anglo Catholic church "excited more sexual wonderment than it repressed."[54] The Mexican religion of his home was, in contrast, feminized, soothing, full of fairy tales. When he remembered his family's religion, he heard "the whispering voices of women." "Whereas at school the primary mediator was Christ," he recalls, "at home that role was assumed by the Mexican Virgin," and "the superstitious Catholicism of home provided a kind of proletarian fairy-tale world." On the other hand, "The *gringo* church, a block from our house, was a very different place. In the *gringo* church Mary's statue was relegated to a side altar, imaged there as a serene white lady who matter-of-factly squashed the Genesis serpent with her bare feet." Jesus, not Mary, reigned supreme, and even Mary was fearless, bold, and white.

Since Rodriguez's agenda is assimilation to Anglo culture, neither a search for Aztlán nor a rehabilitation or even repudiation of Malintzin would serve his purpose. Instead he poses the Mexican church as childlike and the Anglo one as adult and manly. As a child, he identifies with the "shy Mexican Mary" who "appeared, I could see from her picture, as a young Indian maiden – dark just like me." It is the Anglo church and the Anglo world, however, that Rodriguez chooses as an adult, claiming that in the realities of the distribution of power in the United States, that choice is synonymous with "coming of age" and "becoming a public man."[55] Choosing the Virgin of Guadalupe, identifying with the Chicano culture as he defines it, would lock him forever in a marginal, privatized, childlike, and domestic realm.

Anzaldúa also calls on the Virgin of Guadalupe. Unlike Rodriguez, however, Anzaldúa uses the Virgin not as a symbol of childlike faith, but as "a synthesis of the old world and the new, of the religion and culture of the two races in our psyche, the conqueror and the conquered. . . . the symbol of our rebellion against the rich, upper and middleclass [sic]; against their subjugation of the poor and the *indio*."[56] The difference in usage demonstrates the malleability of symbols and of definitions of Chicano culture. At the same time, even with this definition of the Virgin as rebel, not submissively shy, it still fits with Rodriguez's agenda of assimilation and participation in the dominant power structure to reject her.

These four autobiographies point to a stark contrast between Chicana and Chicano definitions of ethnicity. With a recuperated Malinche rather than Aztlán as the archetypal Chicana image, the Chicana encompasses opposites, racial mixing, ambivalence, power, and powerlessness. Anzaldúa goes back still further, before Cortés, to find an Aztec goddess, Coatlihue, to provide an "Indian women's history of resistance" and to affirm just where the betrayal surrounding Malintzin lies: "The worst kind of betrayal lies in making us believe that the Indian woman in us is the betrayer."[57] Anzaldúa argues for a Chicana identity that recognizes a plural personality, "tolerance for ambiguity," and synthesis. Rodriguez and Acosta, on the other hand, seem to demand choice.[58]

IMPLICATIONS

The point of this skimming analysis of four autobiographical writings is not to provide a definitive statement on the difference between Aztlán and Malinche as gendered usable pasts, but to draw attention to the way in which the construction of ethnic identity is gendered, in this case differing by the substantial distance between Acosta's reconquest and Anzaldúa's and Moraga's incorporation. In discussions about the growth of ethnic consciousness, such gender distinctions must be attended to, and their meaning for the group as a whole sought. The fundamental differences in social location within their own group and between groups of women and men critically affected their definition of their interests, their strategies, and their agendas. They stood, as male and female, symbolically as Malinche and her brother, in different relation to the distribution of power both in their own society and in relation to the dominant society. Their position in relations between the groups inevitably, therefore, also differed. This social and cultural location intimately affected their sense of their own and the group's best interests and their interpretation of the actions resulting from contact between the groups as well as their interpretation of the meaning of their ethnic identity.

Moreover, it is unlikely that the effects of the different meanings of ethnic identity were limited to private constructions of the self. Rather, they bring us back to public outcomes, such as the labor and community actions addressed earlier. For these varying interpretations would intimately affect strategies of resistance and of assertion chosen by women and men. Strikes and other workplace contests, which combine resistance and assertion, would have been crucibles for the articulation of that interpretation of identity and its transformation, as the interpretation would be contested by employers, coethnics, and other strikers from different groups. The different memories of Devra Weber's informants, the different interpretations of census takers, and the different levels of activism in depression Texas all bespeak differences between the self-definition of Chicanas and the definitions others bestowed on them. Gendered definitions of ethnicity must be examined, not assumed away by labor historians, just as social location must not be elided by cultural historians.[59]

The two models I have provided here use two quite different methodologies: a standard social historical analysis and a cultural analysis borrowing from new cultural criticism. Both recognize the multiplicity of ethnic identity; both look at men and women in relation to each other and to other "others." Joan Scott has urged social historians alienated by the textuality and the language of new literary theory not totally to reject it.[60] Instead, we can use it to listen to old sources in new ways, to find new entry points to the lived experience of those about whom we write, to look at the relation between language and behavior, expression and identity, and to look at the multiple ways in which power is expressed, exercised, and diffused. Surely it is, after all, in part through language that groups create and recreate each other, themselves, and their past.

NOTES

1. See, for example, Gerda Lerner, "Reconceptualizing Differences Among Women," *Journal of Women's History* (winter 1990): 106–22; Elizabeth Fox-Genovese,

"Between Individualism and Fragmentation: American Culture and the New Literary Studies of Race and Gender," *American Quarterly* 42 (March 1990): 7–34; and Nancy A. Hewitt, "Beyond the Search for Sisterhood: American Women's History in the 1980s," in *Unequal Sisters: A Multi-Cultural Reader in U.S. Women's History,* ed. Ellen Carol Du Bois and Vicki L. Ruiz (New York: Routledge, Chapman & Hall, Inc., 1990), 1–14.

2. Douglas Monroy, *Thrown Among Strangers: The Making of Mexican Culture in Frontier California* (Berkeley: University of California Press, 1990); Ramón A. Gutiérrez, *When Jesus Came, the Corn Mothers Went Away: Marriage, Sexuality, and Power in New Mexico, 1500–1846* (Stanford: Stanford University Press, 1991).

3. Gloria Anzaldúa, *Borderlands/La Frontera: The New Mestiza* (San Francisco: Spinsters/Aunt Lute Book Company, 1987), 2, 77, 194–95. See also Alarcón, "The Theoretical Subject(s), of *This Bridge Called My Back* and Anglo-American Feminism," in *Making Face, Making Soul: Haciendo Caras: Creative and Critical Perspectives by Women of Color,* ed. Gloria Anzaldúa (San Francisco: Aunt Lute Foundation, 1990), 359: "This exploration [of common differences] appears impossible without a reconfiguration of the subject of feminist theory, and her relational position to a multiplicity of others, not just white men"; and Tey Diana Rebolledo, "The Politics of Poetics: Or What Am I, a Critic, Doing in This Text Anyhow?" in Anzaldúa, ed., *Making Face,* 352: "We have grown up and survived along the edges, along the borders of so many languages, worlds, cultures and social systems that we constantly fix and focus on the spaces in between. . . . Categories that try to define and limit this incredibly complex process at once become diminished for their inability to capture and contain." See also Adelaida R. Del Castillo, ed., *Between Borders: Essays on Mexicana/Chicana History* (Encino, Calif.: Floricanto Press, 1990). This volume is an excellent collection of essays, many originally given at a 1983 conference, including material on Mexicanas in Mexico and in the United States and essays by Gutiérrez, Monroy, Ruiz, Weber (essay cited below), Perez, Antonia Castañeda, Louise Ano Nuevo Kerr, and many others.

4. At a panel on Chicano history at the OAH in 1991 where, though Vicki Ruiz was the chair, I was the only female presenter, and the only Anglo member of the panel.

5. See, for example, Mario T. García, "Mexican Americans and the Politics of Citizenship: The Case of El Paso, 1936," *New Mexico Historical Review* 59 (April 1984): 187–204, and *Mexican Americans: Leadership, Ideology, & Identity, 1930–1960* (New Haven: Yale University Press, 1989); and David Montejano, *Anglos and Mexicans in the Making of Texas, 1836–1936* (Austin: University of Texas Press, 1987).

6. See, for example, Vicki L. Ruiz, *Cannery Women/Cannery Lives: Mexican Women, Unionization, and the California Food Processing Industry, 1930–1950* (Albuquerque: University of New Mexico Press, 1987); Devra Anne Weber, "Raiz Fuerto:

Oral History and Mexicana Farm Workers," *Oral History Review:* 17:2 (fall 1989): 47–62, and "Mexican Women on Strike: Memory, History and Oral Narratives," in Castillo, ed., *Between Borders,* 175–200, which is particularly rich in its implications for this topic; and Sarah Deutsch, *No Separate Refuge: Culture, Class, and Gender on an Anglo-Hispanic Frontier in the American Southwest, 1880–1940* (New York: Oxford University Press, 1987).

7. Some new studies illuminate precisely these congruences, for example, Deena J. González, *Resisting Colonization: The Spanish-Mexican Women of Santa Fe, 1820–1880;* and Irene Ledesma, "Unlikely Strikers: Mexican American Women's Strike Activity in Texas, 1919–1977 (Ph.D. diss., Ohio State University, 1992).

8. A few recent studies have attempted to bridge this gap, some of them in progress on Chicano history, for example, Margaret Eleanor Rose, "Women in the United Farm Workers: A Study of Chicana and Mexicana Participation in a Labor Union, 1950–1980" (Ph.D. dissertation, UCLA, 1988); see also Susan A. Glenn, *Daughters of the Shtetl: Life and Labor in the Immigrant Generation* (Ithaca: Cornell University Press, 1990); Mary H. Blewett, *Men, Women, and Work: Class, Gender, and Protest in the New England Shoe Industry, 1780–1910* (Urbana: University of Illinois Press, 1988); and Eileen Boris and Cynthia R. Daniels, eds., *Homework: Historical and Contemporary Perspectives on Paid Labor at Home* (Chicago: University of Illinois Press, 1989), also Ava Baron, ed., *Work Engendered: Toward a New History of American Labor* (Ithaca: Cornell University Press, 1991).

9. Rose, "Women in the United Farm Workers."

10. Deutsch, *No Separate Refuge.*

11. Ruiz, *Cannery Women/Cannery Lives,* for example, 82.

12. Montejano, *Anglos and Mexicans in the Making of Texas, 1836–1986.*

13. See Vicki Ruiz, "By the Day or the Week: Mexicana Domestic Workers in El Paso," in Vicki L. Ruiz and Susan Tiano, eds., *Women on the U.S./Mexico Border: Responses to Change* (Boston: Allen and Unwin, 1987), 61–76; Evelyn Nakano Glenn, "The Dialectics of Wage Work: Japanese-American Women and Domestic Service, 1905–1940," *Feminist Studies* 6:3 (fall 1980): 466–60; and Julia Kirk Blackwelder, *Women of the Depression: Caste and Culture in San Antonio, 1929–1939* (College Station: Texas A&M University Press, 1984) on pecan shellers.

14. See, for example, Joan Scott's article on French garment workers in Joan Scott, *Gender and the Politics of History* (New York: Columbia University Press, 1988). Tamara Hareven is one of the few scholars to recognize women's productive labor at the same time that she recognizes the importance of male family relations to male workplace strategies, but her analysis is hindered by her refusal to recognize the distinct interests of men and women in the families and the conflict that often resulted. These ideas are worked out more fully in Sarah Deutsch, "Confronting

Capitalism: Comparative Perspectives on Capitalism and Gender in Modern America, 1870–1940" (unpublished paper delivered at the Conference on Rural Women and the Transition to Capitalism, Northern Illinois University, March 1989).

15. Deutsch, *No Separate Refuge.*

16. Deutsch, *No Separate Refuge.*

17. Deutsch, *No Separate Refuge.*

18. Patricia Zavella, *Women's Work and Chicano Families: Cannery Workers of the Santa Clara Valley* (Ithaca: Cornell University Press, 1987); Emma Perez, at the Eighth Berkshire Conference on the History of Women.

19. Capitalism, according to many historians and social scientists, liberated women from dependence on the family. Through individualized earning or a cash market for women's production, it bestowed a measure of autonomy. Deutsch, *No Separate Refuge;* MariJo Wagner, " 'Helping Papa and Mamma Sing the People's Songs': Children of the Populist Party," in *Women and Farming: Changing Roles, Changing Structures,* ed. Wava G. Haney and Jane B. Knowles (Boulder: Westview Press, 1988), 319–38; Laura F. Klein, "Contending with Colonization: Tlingit Men and Women in Change," *Women and Colonization,* ed. Mona Etienne and Eleanor Leacock (New York: Praeger Publishers, 1980), 88–108; Kathy Peiss, *Cheap Amusements: Working Women and Leisure in Turn-of-the-Century New York* (Philadelphia: Temple University Press, 1986); and Joan Jensen, *Loosening the Bonds: Mid-Atlantic Farm Women, 1750–1850* (New Haven: Yale University Press, 1986), can all be taken as supporting this viewpoint to a limited extent. In reaction to this theory – as pertaining more to middle-class than to working-class women – and in response to an older vision of urban capitalism wreaking its disintegrating havoc on working-class and immigrant families fresh from the countryside, generating a quivering pathological mass of impoverished city-dwellers, historians and social scientists retorted that capitalism instead had reinforced the family's bonds. These scholars argued that when confronted with the strategies of resourceful new recruits, wage work and market activity still occurred in the framework of and for the support of a family. See, for example, Virginia Yans McLaughlin, *Family and Community: Italian Immigrants in Buffalo, 1880–1930* (1971, reprint, ed., Ithaca: Cornell University Press, 1977); Judith E. Smith, "Our Own Kind: Family and Community Networks in Providence," in *A Heritage of Her Own: Toward a New Social History of American Women,* ed. Nancy F. Cott and Elizabeth H. Pleck (New York: Simon and Schuster, 1979), 396–407; Tamara Hareven, "Family Time and Industrial Time: Family Work in a Planned Corporation Town, 1900–1924," *Journal of Urban History* 1:3 (May 1975): 366–84; among others. Certainly in the beet fields of northern Colorado, the wage rates were so low that the pooled labor of the entire family barely provided enough wages for the individuals to survive. Most women's wages were far

too low for independent living. I suppose one could call that cementing the family bond, but the concept clearly bears further examination. Deutsch, *No Separate Refuge.*

20. Ruiz, *Cannery Women/Cannery Lives;* Zavella, *Women's Work and Chicano Families;* Deutsch, *No Separate Refuge.*

21. Ruiz, *Cannery Women;* Blackwelder, *Women of the Depression* (both pecan shellers and garment workers). Rosaura Sánchez, "The History of Chicanas: A Proposal for a Materialist Perspective," in *Between Borders,* 1–29, examines (on p. 19) Ruiz's attempt to reconcile traditionally defined Mexican family roles with Mexican women's labor activism. Sánchez adds, "The question here would be whether it is in fact family roles that lead to labor activism or whether it is a particular type of production which leads both to particular family roles and to a particular type of exploitation which calls for resistance." Though they both mention the strains on the family that women's activism produced, neither Ruiz nor Sánchez examines the way in which what these women mean by "Chicana," the attributes that word encompasses, may differ from the men's definition and may change in the course of their labor experience.

22. Deutsch, *No Separate Refuge,* 54. It was not simply an issue of whether or not the women were paid for their labor, as many of the men listed with occupations also were not paid. The norm would be not listing the women, as happened with Anglo farm women; what was significant was that the Spanish Mexican woman did list them.

23. Weber, "Raiz Fuerto." The same could be said of Barbara Kingsolver's *Holding the Line* and the film *Salt of the Earth.*

24. Rose, "Women in the United Farm Workers."

25. Rose, "Women in the United Farm Workers"; for variations in women's definitions of their ethnicity, see also Sylvia Junko Yanagisako, *Transforming the Past: Tradition and Kinship Among Japanese Americans* (Stanford: Stanford University Press, 1985); and Micaela di Leonardo, *Varieties of Ethnic Experience: Kinship, Class, and Gender Among California Italian-Americans* (Ithaca: Cornell University Press, 1984).

26. Glenn, *Daughters of the Shtetl;* Vicki L. Ruiz, "Star Struck: Acculturation, Adolescence and Mexican American Women," in *Building with Our Hands: New Directions in Chicana Studies,* ed. Adela de la Torre and Beatríz Pasquera (Berkeley: University of California Press, 1993), and also in Elliott West and Paula Petrik, eds., *Small Worlds: Childhood and Adolescence in American History, 1850–1950* (Lawrence: University of Kansas Press, 1992).

27. Norma Alarcón calls for "a reconfiguration of the subject of feminist theory,

and her relational position to a multiplicity of others, not just white men" (Norma Alarcón, "The Theoretical Subject(s)," 359).

28. Lerner, "Reconceptualizing Differences Among Women."

29. Fox-Genovese, "Between Individualism and Fragmentation." See also Maria C. Lugones and Elizabeth V. Spelman, "Have We Got a Theory for You! Feminist Theory, Cultural Imperialism and the Demand for 'the Woman's Voice,' " *Women's Studies International Forum* 6 (1983): 573–81; and Hewitt, "Beyond the Search for Sisterhood."

30. Richard Rodriguez, *Hunger of Memory: The Education of Richard Rodriguez: An Autobiography* (Boston: David R. Godine, 1982); Anzaldúa, *Borderlands/La Frontera;* Cherríe Moraga, *Loving in the War Years: lo que nunca paso por sus labios* (Boston: South End Press, 1983); Olivia Castellano, "Canto, locura y poesia," *The Women's Review of Books* 7:5 (February 1990): 18–20.

31. Alma Garcia, "The Development of Chicana Feminist Discourse, 1970–1980," in Ruiz and DuBois, *Unequal Sisters,* 418–31; González, *Resisting Colonization.*

32. For the best bibliography of this literature, see Ruiz and DuBois, *Unequal Sisters.* In addition, see Asian Women United of California, *Making Waves: An Anthology of Writings By and About Asian American Women* (Boston: Beacon Press, 1989); and Anzaldúa, ed., *Making Face, Making Soul.* See also, Linda Gordon, "On 'Difference,' " *Genders* 10 (spring 1991): 91–111 for a critique of concentrating on cultural aspects of differences among women to the exclusion of recognizing similarities in women's experiences relative to structures of power.

33. See Stefan Tanaka, *Japan's Orient: Rendering Pasts into History* (Berkeley: University of California Press, 1993).

34. See John R. Chávez, *The Lost Land: The Chicano Image of the Southwest* (Albuquerque: University of New Mexico Press, 1984), on the uses of Aztlán. There is no gender analysis in the book.

35. I am grateful to one of *Frontiers's* anonymous readers (number 6) for pointing out the similarities and the need to explain these similarities to the reader. I also find it significant that these are four of the five second-generation autobiographies available. It seems to me that it makes a statement about the market, about what images of Chicanos the book-buying and book-publishing market is willing to buy. We have, on the one hand, the macho, Chicano, wild animal (Acosta), and the darling of the right, a conservative, "tamed"?, "Hispanic" (Rodriguez). On the other hand, the alternative feminist press has provided a market for the most "different," and so we have two Chicana lesbian feminists to "represent" Chicanas to us. Oral history collections are far more wide-ranging in their representation of Chicanos than autobiographies are. On Rodriguez's sexuality, which is not explicitly defined

in *Hunger of Memory,* in distinction to the other books, see, for example, Richard Rodriguez, "Late Victorians: San Francisco, Aids, and the Homosexual Stereotype," *Harper's Magazine* (October 1990): 57–66. Here, again, Rodriguez does not explicitly identify himself as gay, but is ironically admonished by his dying friend as "the only one spared" AIDS because " 'You are too circumspect' " (65).

36. José Limón, in a valuable and fascinating essay on another symbol, La Llorona, has analyzed why so many of these symbols are female and the very different significance of the symbols in terms of their counter-hegemonic potential. His gender analysis is centered on the symbol, rather than the purveyors of the symbol. José E. Limón, "La Llorona, The Third Legend of Greater Mexico: Cultural Symbols, Women, and the Political Unconscious," in del Castillo, ed., *Between Borders,* 399–432.

37. José Limón claims that her importance as a symbol of and for national Mexico grew mainly in the seventeenth century (Limón, "La Llorona," 399–403).

38. Norma Alarcón, "Chicana's Feminist Literature: A Re-vision through Malintzin/or Malintzin: Putting Flesh Back on the Object," in *This Bridge Called My Back: Writings by Radical Women of Color,* ed. Cherríe Moraga and Gloria Anzaldúa (New York: Kitchen Table/Women of Color Press, 1981), 182–90.

39. See Chávez, *The Lost Land: The Chicano Image of the Southwest.*

40. Moraga, *Loving,* 45. See also Tey Diana Rebolledo, 353.

41. Moraga, *Loving,* 98–99.

42. Anzaldúa, *Borderlands/La Frontera,* 21–22.

43. Moraga, *Loving,* 117. And see Anzaldúa, *Borderlands,* 18–20.

44. Oscar Zeta Acosta, *The Revolt of the Cockroach People* (1973; New York: Vintage Books, 1989), 160.

45. Acosta, 207.

46. Acosta, 70–71.

47. Acosta, 164.

48. Acosta, 191–94. And, for example, after his return from Mexico, during which absence an activist has been killed, he defensively declares to his peers, "Just because I go around and screw who I want to, you think I'm not in this fight whole hog?" (Acosta, 207).

49. Acosta, 160.

50. Acosta, 49.

51. The book's sex scenes and objectifications of women are too numerous to delineate here, but for some examples, see pp. 62, 130, 164, 221. It is not clear whether "gringas" also count as Malinches here. While Acosta reclaims Chicanas, he does not abandon Anglo women.

52. Acosta, 29–31.

53. Moraga, *Loving*, 92.

54. Rodriguez, 84–86, 87.

55. Rodriguez, 7.

56. Anzaldúa, *Borderlands*, 30–31.

57. Anzaldúa, *Borderlands*, 22, 41–51.

58. This dichotomy shows up in daily practice. At a Latino Studies Conference at Oberlin in the spring of 1990, the scholars held a discussion on the topic, "What is a Latino?" They soon found themselves discussing terminology. Some of the men present argued for the term Latino to encompass Cubans, Chicanos, and Puerto-riqueños. Some of the women, who came from Colorado and New Mexico, pointed out that the choice of such a term as a monolith would alienate many people who self-identified as Spanish American or Mexican. They argued for a more inclusive strategy and a tolerance for diverse labeling. The men argued that such a strategy would weaken the Latino cause, and they reconstructed the debate to label the women's strategy as a feminist strategy and their own as a Latino strategy.

59. Gordon, "On 'Difference,'" on the tendency of those scholars focusing on cultural differences to ignore power relations.

60. Joan Scott, *Gender and the Politics of History*. At the same time, such methods must not simply be an excuse to look once again at the dominant group, whether men or Anglos. They must not solely study other groups through representations of gender or of Chicanos instead of privileging the experience and self-representations of Chicanos and Chicanas themselves. The theories brought to bear must not emerge simply as bonding exercises among Anglo theorists, male or female, as both María Lugones and Barbara Christian have labeled them, but must have roots in the lived experience, the social location of Chicanas and Chicanos. Lugones and Spelman, "Have We Got a Theory for You," 573–81; Barbara Christian, "The Race for Theory," in *Making Face*, 335–45.

Frontiers 14:2 (1994): 1–22.

Traditional and Nontraditional Patterns of Female Activism in the United Farm Workers of America, 1962 to 1980

MARGARET ROSE

One of the most inspiring social movements of the post–World War II era was the historic struggle for the unionization of California farm workers that began in the early 1960s. Studies of the United Farm Workers of America, AFL-CIO (UFW), and the farmworker insurgency that developed during this period have focused on its male leadership and provided a patriarchal interpretation of its origins.[1] Perpetuating this view, a recent history textbook noted, "A thirty-five-year-old community organizer named Cesar Estrada Chavez set out single-handedly to organize impoverished migrant farm laborers in the California grape fields."[2] Such male-centered interpretations have distorted the history of the UFW and the role of women in its development. The following pages document the heretofore "invisible" participation of Mexicanas and Chicanas in the founding and management of the UFW and analyze the impact of gender on this union. Women's commitment to the union, however, was not uniform. To illustrate the wide range of women's contributions to the UFW, this investigation contrasts the experiences of the rare women, such as Dolores Huerta, whose style of leadership fit a "male" model of labor organizing, with the more common but no less vital endeavors of women such as Helen Chávez, whose activism fit a more "female" model of collective action – that is, work performed, often behind the scenes, in an auxiliary or supportive fashion.

During the past two decades scholarship in women's labor history has uncovered the diversity and distinctiveness of women's working-class heritage.[3] Most of this work has concentrated on Anglo or ethnically European women, and more recently on black women in the South.[4] The protests of Chicanas and Mexicanas in UFW campaigns demonstrate a continuity with women in other labor struggles in the United States. Thanks to a growing body of research that emerged during the 1980s, the experiences of women of Mexican heritage can also be considered in relationship to the past and contemporary struggles of their ethnic sisters – striking Mexicana laundresses in El Paso at the turn of the century, Mexican cannery operatives in California in the 1930s and 1940s, the wives of Mexican miners who formed women's auxiliaries in copper strikes during the 1950s, militant garment workers at Farah in the 1970s, and female employees in *maquiladoras* (export-oriented, in-process assembly plants operating along the U.S.-Mexican border).[5] Indeed, Chicanas and Mexicanas have a rich and detailed labor history and have frequently resorted to collective action to resist unjust working conditions. The present inquiry examines how ideologically defined gender roles have shaped such activism within the UFW.[6]

UFW women have taken two different paths to trade unionism.[7] Observers of the UFW are most familiar with the career of Dolores Huerta, the union's cofounder and first vice-president. Yet Huerta's union activism is atypical. She rebelled against the conventional constraints upon women's full participation in trade union activism, competing directly with male colleagues in the UFW. Her activism resembles that of other well-known Chicana labor leaders of earlier generations, such as Emma Tenayuca and Luisa Moreno; it can only be labeled "nontraditional." A more "traditional" model is that of Helen Chávez, wife of UFW president César Chávez. Chicanas and Mexicanas adopting this approach juggle the competing demands of family life, sexual division of labor, and protest in a unique blend of union activism. But their contribution to union building is obscured because it occurs in the context of domestic responsibilities.[8] Despite her marriage to a prominent labor reformer, Chávez can be readily likened to hundreds of other Mexicanas and Chicanas who participated in strikes and picket lines but remained anonymous and forgotten.

Huerta's and Chávez's differing experiences of and attitudes toward politicization, union work, visibility, and domesticity illustrate two distinct ways in which Chicanas and Mexicanas attain and exercise power in this trade union. And their personal backgrounds indicate how class and generational distance from Mexico, in addition to gender, influence women's opportunities and social expectations for themselves.

Superficially, it would seem that these two Mexican American women share much in common. Both grew up during the Depression era; Helen Chávez, née Fabela, was born in Brawley, California, in 1928 and Dolores Huerta, née Fernández, in Dawson, New Mexico, in 1930.[9] Both women wed in the surge of marriages in the post–World War II years. Chávez married in 1948 at age twenty; Huerta married one day shy of her twentieth birthday, in Stockton, California, in 1950.[10] As practicing and devout Hispanic Catholics, both women valued large families: Helen Chávez bore eight children, Dolores Huerta eleven.[11]

Yet despite these similarities, notable differences in the two women's lifestyles and personal histories reflect the complexity and diversity of the experience of the Mexican American woman in the twentieth century. Huerta, on her mother's side of the family, was a third-generation New Mexican; her maternal grandmother was born in Las Cruces, her grandfather in Carrizozo. Both her mother and her father were born in Dawson, a small mining town in the northern part of the state. Helen Chávez was a first-generation Mexican American. Her mother was from Sombrete, Mexico, her father from San Jacinto, Mexico; the two immigrated separately to the United States in the years after the Mexican Revolution and married in Los Angeles, California, in 1923. In terms of bilingualism, economic opportunity, education, and social class, Huerta's family was more assimilated than Chávez's into North American society.[12]

Chávez's parents were farm workers who lived first in the Imperial Valley in California, not far from the Mexican border, and later moved to the San Joaquin Valley in central California, eventually settling in a small rural agricultural community south of Delano. Forced to quit high school after the death of her father, Chávez worked in the fields and vineyards full time in order to help her widowed mother provide for the family of five children. Chávez's poverty and lack of education typify the experience of immigrant Mexican farmworker women, who often had even less education, spoke no English, and had to make the difficult adjustment of living and working in a foreign country and culture. Huerta, on the other hand, had a more middle-class upbringing, particularly after her mother moved to Stockton, California, where she operated a hotel with her second husband. Huerta's comfortable lifestyle and family resources enabled her to graduate from high school and community college, a rare accomplishment for Mexican-heritage women in the years just after World War II.[13]

Both class and ethnicity affected the opportunities and social outlets open to these women during the 1950s. The years after the war were a time of civic pride and growing political awareness in the Mexican American community.[14] For Helen Chávez, politicization began with her membership in the Community Service Organization (cso), a grassroots Mexican American self-help group that established a chapter in San Jose, California, in 1952.[15] A young mother, Chávez became involved through her husband's interest in the CSO. As was customary for this generation of women, her activities were essentially auxiliary; she helped in the office, mimeographing fliers or sorting the mail, but usually she worked at home in the evenings, after her domestic chores were done and the children were asleep. "If we were going to have a meeting," she recalled, "I would address all the envelopes or address postcards, whatever had to be done."[16] The voluntarism of Helen Chávez and other women behind the scenes made the CSO one of the most successful associations for Mexican Americans in California during this time.

Huerta also began with traditional, female-defined activities in community-based philanthropy and volunteer work for Mexican American groups, but by the late 1950s she evolved into a more nontraditional activist leader. Huerta's middle-class resources, particularly her education, gave her valuable skills and confidence, aiding this transformation. Her association with the CSO began in 1955, when a chapter was established in Stockton, California. At first she performed a variety of traditionally "female" tasks – making arrangements for CSO meetings, participating in voter registration drives, and teaching citizenship classes for individuals in the community – as opposed to the "male" tasks of organizing new chapters and serving as an elected officer.[17] Soon, however, she moved into a more demanding position of responsibility and authority: that of paid legislative advocate for the CSO in Sacramento, an unusual pursuit for most women in the 1950s, and particularly so for ethnic women.[18] Through the CSO Huerta also became interested in the poverty and exploitation of farmworkers, in 1958 becoming a charter member of a local group, the Agricultural Workers Association (AWA), and serving as an elected official of the AFL-CIO–sponsored Agricultural Workers Organizing Committee (AWOC), founded in Stockton in 1959.[19] Huerta's active participation in the AWA caused opposition from male colleagues:

But Father McCullough [an AWA founder] didn't want me to be involved. He said farm labor organizing was no place for a woman. So I kind of worked under cover, doing the work through my husband [Ventura] and my brother [Marshall].[20]

This gender-based reaction indicated that Huerta was challenging the customary division that separated acceptable volunteer activity for women from the traditionally male-dominated world of highly politicized union organizing.

A similar contrast appears in the types of work the two women performed in the National Farm Workers Association (NFWA), the precursor to the UFW, founded in 1962. Helen Chávez's work, like that of most Chicanas and Mexicanas in the UFW, was administrative and supportive. Yet her participation, and that of other female family members and friends, was vital in building the union and carried risks. "The registration crew will most likely be made up of women," noted César Chávez in a letter to a colleague. "I have most of mine and Helen's relatives on the hook, but they are a little afraid of getting evolved [sic] and being black-balled. Will most likely keep their names out in the beginning so as to protect them."[21] During subsequent demonstrations and strikes, Helen, along with other Chicanas and Mexicanas and their children, joined picket lines to demand union recognition in the face of taunts, intimidation, and threats of physical harm.

After the NFWA was on more solid ground, Helen was persuaded to quit her work in the fields to assume office duties. Hesitating because of her lack of training, she accepted the responsibility reluctantly. "We wanted her [Helen] to learn the credit union bookkeeping," recalled Dolores Huerta years later. "[During one of our board meetings], he [César] yelled at her [Helen] one night into the kitchen, 'You're going to be the assistant book-keeper.' She yelled back, 'No, I won't either,' but we voted her the job. Boy was she mad! But you should see her books. We've been investigated a hundred times and they never find a mistake."[22] For over twenty years she has managed the UFW's credit union. Since she is the only full-time staff member, without Helen Chávez this union service probably would not have survived. While this work is essential to the institutional apparatus of the UFW, it has been underrated because it is an area traditionally reserved for women and one that does not attract the public attention given to strikes and organizing campaigns.[23] In her association with the union Helen Chávez did not seek a policy-making role. Although she wielded considerable informal influence over her husband, and by extension the UFW, this influence was exercised in the privacy of her home.

Huerta's service to the union, on the other hand, has clearly been nontraditional. As a cofounder of the union with César Chávez, and as first vice-president, Huerta has held a decision-making post in the UFW from the outset.[24] She was also the union's first contract negotiator, founding the negotiations department and directing it in the early years. "[César] Chávez left the negotiations up to Dolores Huerta," observed one commentator.[25] Collective bargaining talks such as the mid-1960s Christian Brothers negotiations were demanding, drawn out, and tedious. "They were difficult," Huerta recalled, "and this is where persistence pays off, you just have to keep hammering away. You may have to have five meetings to change two words . . . this is where César gets uptight. He never really quite trusted what I did until he started to negotiate himself; then he found it was pretty hard to get the kind of language that I had gotten, and he started respecting what I had done."[26] As she assumed responsibilities and stances that were traditionally held by white males, Huerta encountered criticism based on both gender and ethnic stereotypes. One grower representative reacted to Huerta's forceful negotiating style and uncompromising positions, "Dolores Huerta is crazy. She is a violent woman, where women, especially Mexican women, are usually peaceful and calm."[27] Such comments indicate the depth of her challenge to the political, social, and economic power of California agribusiness, as well as to the ideology of male dominance.

Another major responsibility for Huerta was the directorship of the boycott in New York City, the largest grape distribution center in the U.S., and her service as East Coast boycott coordinator in 1968 and 1969. Her leadership there contributed to the success of the boycott in mobilizing labor unions, political activists, community organizations, religious supporters, women's clubs, peace groups, student protestors, and concerned consumers behind the union. "The whole thrust of our boycott is to get as many supporters as you can," she declared. "You have to get organizers who can go out to the unions, to the churches, to the students and get that support. You divide an area up – in New York we split it up into eight sections – and each organizer is responsible for an area. We get supporters to help us picket and leaflet; we go after one chain at a time, telling the shoppers where they can find other stores."[28] The power of this grassroots coalition forced the Coachella and Delano grape producers to negotiate the historic table grape contracts in 1970. Huerta's executive abilities and influence were also apparent when she returned to New York to administer the lettuce, grape, and Gallo wine campaigns from 1973 to 1975.[29] The pressure of revived cross-class and cross-cultural cooperation in New York and across the nation led to the passage of the Agricultural Labor Relations Act, the first law to recognize the collective bargaining rights of farmworkers in California.[30] During the late 1970s Huerta's leadership was spotlighted again; she assumed the directorship of the Citizenship Participation Day Department (CPD), the political arm of the UFW, which she administered until 1982.[31] In all these capacities, Huerta has served on the executive board of the UFW and participated in the highest levels of policy making in the union. She has proved a formidable strategist in the political contests for power within the union and has had a direct influence on guiding the UFW.

Chávez's and Huerta's differing approaches to trade union activism are also revealed in their relationship to the public world. Helen Chávez has always preferred to remain out of the public eye – a personal choice, but also the result of a more traditional Mexican upbringing, lack of confidence due to limited education, and the fact that English is her second language, characteristics she shares with immigrant Mexicanas, many of whom speak only Spanish and have even less schooling. The most visible aspect of her life has been her four arrests, two of which were widely reported. The first occurred in the Delano area in 1966, when she was arrested with the celebrated group of "forty-four," many of whom were members of the clergy, for shouting "*huelga*" (the Spanish word for "strike"). "Being in jail didn't scare me," she explained, "because I know that what I'm doing is right and that I'm doing it for people who have worked and sacrificed so hard."[32] The second highly publicized incident took place in Arizona in 1978, when she was arrested with her husband for violating an all-encompassing ban on picketing issued by a local magistrate. The two Chávezes underwent arrest to test the constitutionality of the ruling. "It was a disgusting, filthy jail," she recalled. "I went there and I started cleaning up the place where I had to stay. Mopping. And it was the worst jail I had been in."[33] Although her acts of civil disobedience have been few, her example has encouraged other Mexicanas and Chicanas to undergo arrest, thus expanding the social sphere for wives, grandmothers, aunts, and daughters in addition to women fieldworkers in the UFW. Significantly, however, Helen Chávez shuns public appearances on her own and feels very uncomfortable in this role. One of her rare solo ventures occurred in Los Angeles at a fundraiser in 1976. "I will not speak [formally to the audience] because I have not spoken in front of a crowd," she told a reporter who was covering the event.[34] Instead, opting for the more traditional practice of female hospitality, Chávez chose to greet people personally in a reception line.

In contrast, Dolores Huerta's educational background and middle-class resources gave her self-confidence and made her, from her earliest association with the union, a sought-after public speaker. She has addressed countless labor, student, religious, women's, political, antiwar, environmental, and consumer groups. Through print, radio, and television, she has raised much-needed funds as well as public awareness of the UFW struggles.[35] Huerta has also been a very able lobbyist and advocate on behalf of farmworkers before national, state, and local governmental committees. In frequent appearances before congressional bodies, she has forcefully argued the union's position on a wide range of issues from amending migration labor laws to the health problems of fieldworkers to immigration policy. In 1984 she testified before a House committee:

The Simpson-Mazzoli bill is a thinly disguised effort to stop labor organizing among farm workers. The other provisions of this bill, legalization, that would apply to so few it would be meaningless, sanctions[,] that would be another political tool in the hands of the Immigration Service, would be used as they have always used their power: against unionization.[36]

Although an altered version of the bill eventually passed, the UFW's opposition to a guest worker provision prevailed. Probably Huerta's greatest asset has been her constant presence in the public eye as a representative of the UFW and the ease with which she has related to diverse constituencies, such as student, religious, labor, women's, and ethnic groups. A four-day trip to Michigan in 1974 typifies her total immersion in and dedication to *la causa*.

In addition to boycott day, Dolores participated in a rally on the University of Michigan [Ann Arbor] campus, an Ecumenical Service in Detroit, a reception of trade union women, sponsored by the Coalition of Labor Union Women (CLUW) and a Mexican Independence Day Celebration in Pontiac, Michigan. Dolores appeared on two television programs, radio programs and did taped interviews. On the boycott day rally we got news coverage on 2 Detroit T.V. stations, a newspaper story, several radio stations and three feature articles were written on Dolores.[37]

Huerta, in contrast to Chávez, clearly relishes the demands of a public life.

Finally, the contrast between Chávez's traditionalism and Huerta's non-traditionalism appears in their divergent attitudes toward domesticity and home life. Chávez described her role as follows:

I felt that my job was at home taking care of my children. That was the most important thing to me and I felt, as a woman, [that] that's very important to a child. You have children and I think that your children should be raised by you, not by a babysitter.[38]

Despite the fact that Chávez went to work in the onion fields and grape vineyards to support her family during difficult economic times while her husband organized fieldworkers, and despite her management of the UFW credit union, she still maintains that a woman's proper place is in the home. This value reflects the aspiration of many working-class Chicanas and recently immigrated Mexicanas who desired to care for their families like middle-class Anglo wives and mothers but were denied this opportunity because of economic need. Like black women, who were also forced to work, they were pushed into the labor force by the inferior wages their husbands earned in a racially segmented labor market.[39]

Huerta's perception of domesticity contrasts greatly with that of Chávez. To accommodate her hectic work and travel schedule and frequent residential changes, she made unorthodox child care arrangements, often leaving her children with nonfamily members and union supporters for extended periods of time. "You have to make a decision," she once told a reporter, "that if working with people, the people have the priority and the family must understand."[40] In another interview during a fundraising trip to Chicago, Huerta indicated her total commitment to the union. "There is so much to be done. My life is the union, every minute of it."[41] Like other prominent female labor leaders – Mother Jones, Lucy Parsons, Emma Tenayuca, and Luisa Moreno – Huerta reversed the traditional female priorities, placing personal autonomy and trade union activism before family life.[42]

Women who did not conform to the conventional model of femininity and domesticity were often subject to criticism and, at the very least, ambivalence.[43] While Chávez was praised by women in the union for keeping her family together under trying circumstances, Huerta, like her well-known predecessors, endured criticism from family, union colleagues, and the public at large for her nontraditional attitudes toward her personal and family life. "You could expect that I would [get criticism from] farmworkers themselves, but it mostly comes from middle-class people," she explained in an interview. "They're more hung-up about these things than the poor people are, because the poor people have to haul their kids around from school to school, and women have to go out and work and they've got to either leave their kids or take them out to the fields with them. So they sympathize a lot more with my problems in terms of my children."[44] Huerta's distinct perceptions of wifehood and motherhood have also contributed to her two divorces. "I knew that I wasn't comfortable in a wife's role but I wasn't clearly facing the issue," she acknowledged. "I hedged, I made excuses, I didn't come out and tell my husband that I cared more about helping other people than cleaning our house and doing my hair."[45] Where many women might have resented household tasks, Huerta simply disregarded them.

One might argue that these differences with regard to politicization, work, public visibility, and domesticity merely reflect Huerta's and Chávez's differing personalities; and, indeed, personality does play a role in their choices. However, because the great majority of Chicanas and Mexicanas in the UFW follow Helen Chávez's path to union activism, a deeper process than temperament seems to be indicated here. That path is influenced by complex factors – class, cultural values, social expectations, views of motherhood, childrearing, and the sexual division of labor.[46]

Female UFW volunteers – such as María Luisa Rangel, who moved her family of nine to Detroit, Michigan, in 1968 for the grape boycott, or Juanita Valdez, who transplanted her eight children to Cincinnati, Ohio, in 1970 for the lettuce campaign, or Herminia Rodríguez, who relocated her family of six to Washington, D.C., in 1973 for the renewed grape, lettuce, and Gallo wines boycotts – have all participated as part of a family unit and juggled the competing interests of family, work, and union activism on behalf of the UFW.[47] Chicanas and Mexicanas who manage the *campesino* (service) centers located primarily in rural communities throughout California continue in the Helen Chávez tradition.[48] Female administrators of other union programs, such as Antonia González at the Agbayani Village (retirement home for farmworkers), also emulate this pattern.[49] Because their contribution to union building has blended with domestic responsibilities, it remains largely hidden from public view and goes unrecognized.

In contrast, Dolores Huerta's style of union activism attracts widespread attention and conveys the inaccurate impression that women in the UFW see in her a model for their own trade unionism. In actuality, Huerta's approach is a rare phenomenon. Women, usually U.S.-born, who rose to positions of prominence in the boycott, such as Jessica Govea, director of the Montreal operation, and Hope Lopez, head of the Philadelphia effort, were exceptions like Dolores Huerta. In June 1969, out of forty-three boycott coordinators in major cities, thirty-nine were men and five were women. The elevation of those five to power was accomplished in spite of ambivalent and in some cases even hostile male attitudes toward women with authority. Recognizing their uncommon and tentative status, Hope Lopez, whose ascent to the upper echelons of the union hierarchy was facilitated by the chronic shortage of male candidates and the crisis atmosphere of the union's early years, noted, "Of course, the real test for the female farmworkers will come after we win this strike. The female farmworker will either continue to help the administration of labor or she will be sent back to the labor room."[50] Chicanas and Mexicanas who aspire to nontraditional positions of power and decision making, such as women in the ranch committees (local union governance bodies), are also few in number and encounter obstacles to and gender-based criticism of their participation in this traditionally male-dominated activity. Ranch committee women Mary Magaña, Carolina Guerrero, and Cleo Gómez demonstrated stamina and determination in resisting opposition from male family members and co-workers who did not readily accept women's participation at this level. Organizer Jessie de la Cruz remembered,

It was very hard being a woman organizer. Many of our people my age and older were raised with the old customs in Mexico: where the husband rules, he is king of his house. The wife obeys, and the children, too. So when we first started it was very, very hard. Men gave us the most trouble – neighbors there in Parlier! They were for the union, but they were not taking orders from women, they said. When they formed the ranch committee at Christian Brothers – that's a big wine company, part of it is in Parlier – the ranch committee was all men.[51]

Dolores Huerta's example encourages women struggling in such male-dominated areas of the union. But the admiration for her model also over-shadows more traditional types of women's union activism, so that the essential contribution of the rank-and-file female union activists remains taken for granted.

The irony of this situation is that Huerta is an atypical, and perhaps impractical, model of female trade unionism in the UFW today. Huerta's activism most closely resembles the example of César Chávez, who

approached the work of helping the poor to help themselves in the only way his nature allowed with a single-mindedness that made everything else in his life – home, family, personal gain – secondary. For Chavez, nothing short of total immersion in the work of forcing change was enough. If his wife inherited virtually the entire responsibility for raising their children, . . . Chavez remained unshaken in his belief that the promotion of the greater good made every sacrifice necessary and worthwhile.[52]

Given the existing sexual division of labor in the union and in society, few women are able or willing to relegate their personal lives or families to a secondary position in order to pursue union organizing. Thus, the more common form of female participation, à la Helen Chávez, remains "invisible" – unrecognized and unappreciated by union members as well as historians. Far from being a "single-handed" effort, the UFW was built and sustained by rank-and-file union members and supporters, including a great many Chicanas and Mexicanas. To appreciate fully the contribution of thousands of ordinary women to the process, researchers need to develop an expanded definition of union activism that takes into account the commitment of women who combine family responsibilities with labor activism.

NOTES

I would like to thank Nancy Gabin, Carol Groneman, and the anonymous readers at *Frontiers* for their thoughtful criticisms and suggestions.

1. For early popular treatments of the UFW, see John Gregory Dunne, *Delano, The Story of the California Grape Strike* (New York: Farrar, Straus and Giroux, 1966); Eugene Nelson, *Huelga: The First Hundred Days of the Great Delano Grape Strike* (Delano, Calif.: Farm Worker Press, 1966); Peter Matthiessen, *Sal Si Puedes: Cesar Chavez and the New American Revolution* (New York: Random House, 1970); Mark Day, *Forty Acres: César Chávez and the Farm Workers* (New York: Praeger Press, 1971); and Joan London and Henry Anderson, *So Shall Ye Reap* (New York: Thomas Crowell Company, 1970). A second wave of literature about the UFW appeared during the mid-1970s and was written primarily by reporters who had covered the story firsthand; see, for example, Ronald B. Taylor, *Chavez and the Farm Workers* (Boston: Beacon Press, 1975); Jacques E. Levy, *César Chavez: Autobiography of La Causa* (New York: W. W. Norton, 1975); Dick Meister and Anne Loftis, *A Long Time Coming: The Struggle to Unionize America's Farm Workers* (New York: MacMillan, 1977); Sam Kushner, *Long Road to Delano* (New York: International Publishers, 1975). A quick review of the titles reveals the emphasis on César Chávez, president of the UFW. For the most scholarly work to appear on the UFW (which also includes analyses of previous farm labor insurgencies), see Linda C. Majka and Theo J. Majka, *Farm Workers, Agribusiness, and the State* (Philadelphia: Temple University Press, 1982). While this monograph is the most analytical and interpretive work, it very rarely mentions the participation of Dolores Huerta, cofounder and first vice-president of the union, in contrast to the earlier, firsthand, journalistic accounts. See also J. Craig Jenkins, *The Politics of Insurgency: The Farm Worker Movement in the 1960s* (New York: Columbia University Press, 1985).

2. Quoted in James Kirby Martin, et al., *America and Its People, from 1865*, vol. 2 (Glenview, Ill.: Scott Foresman and Company, 1989), 930.

3. Alice Kessler-Harris, *Out to Work: A History of Wage-Earning Women in the United States* (Oxford: Oxford University Press, 1982); Susan Levine, "Labor's True Woman: Domesticity and Equal Rights in the Knights of Labor," *Journal of American History* 70:2 (September 1983): 323–39; Jacquelyn Dowd Hall, "Disorderly Women: Gender and Labor Militancy in the Appalachian South," *Journal of American History* 73:2 (September 1986): 354–82; Nancy Gabin, "'They Have Placed a Penalty on Womanhood': The Protest Actions of Women Auto Workers in Detroit-Area UAW Locals, 1945–1947," *Feminist Studies* 8:2 (summer 1982): 373–98; Ruth Milkman, *Gender at Work: The Dynamics of Job Segregation by Sex during World*

War II (Urbana: University of Illinois Press, 1987); Susan Porter Benson, *Counter Cultures: Saleswomen, Managers, and Customers in American Department Stores, 1890–1940* (Urbana: University of Illinois Press, 1986); Patricia Cooper, *Once a Cigar Maker: Men, Women, and Work Culture in American Cigar Factories, 1900–1919* (Urbana: University of Illinois Press, 1987).

4. Jacqueline Jones, *Labor of Love, Labor of Sorrow: Black Women, Work, and the Family from Slavery to the Present* (New York: Basic Books, 1985); Dolores E. Janiewski, *Sisterhood Denied: Race, Gender, and Class in a New South Community* (Philadelphia: Temple University Press, 1985); Karen Tucker Anderson, "Last Hired, First Fired: Black Women Workers during World War II," *Journal of American History* 69 (June 1982): 82–97; Lois Rita Helmbold, "Downward Occupational Mobility during the Great Depression: Urban Black and White Working Class Women," *Labor History* 29:2 (spring 1988): 135–72. Asian and Native American women have received the least historical treatment of all ethnic women. See for example Sylvia Van Kirk, *Many Tender Ties: Women in Fur-trade Society, 1670–1870* (Norman: University of Oklahoma Press, 1980); and Evelyn Nakano Glenn, *Issei, Nisei, War Bride: Three Generations of Japanese American Women in Domestic Service* (Philadelphia: Temple University Press, 1986). For a more recent historiographical article on women of color in an understudied region see Elizabeth Jameson, "Toward a Multicultural History of Women in the Western United States," *Signs* 13:4 (summer 1988): 761–91.

5. Mario T. García, "The Chicana in American History: The Mexican Women of El Paso, 1880–1920 – A Case Study," *Pacific Historical Review* 49 (May 1980): 315–37; Vicki L. Ruiz, *Cannery Women, Cannery Lives: Mexican Women, Unionization, and the California Food Processing Industry, 1930–1950* (Albuquerque: University of New Mexico Press, 1987); Sarah Deutsch, *No Separate Refuge: Culture, Class, and Gender on an Anglo-Hispanic Frontier in the American Southwest, 1880–1940* (New York: Oxford University Press, 1987); Rosalinda M. González, "Chicanas and Mexican Immigrant Families 1920–1940, Women's Subordination and Family Exploitation," in *Decades of Discontent, 1920–1940,* ed. Lois Scharf and Joan M. Jensen (Westport, Conn.: Greenwood Press, 1983), 59–84; Michael Wilson, with commentary by Deborah Silverton Rosenfelt, *Salt of the Earth* (Old Westbury, N.Y.: The Feminist Press, 1978); Laurie Coyle, Gail Hershatter, and Emily Honig, "Women at Farah: An Unfinished Story," in *Mexican Women in the United States: Struggles Past and Present,* ed. Magdalena Mora and Adelaida R. Del Castillo (Los Angeles: UCLA Chicano Studies Research Center Publications, 1980), 117–43; Patricia Zavella, *Women's Work and Chicano Families: Cannery Workers of the Santa Clara Valley* (Ithaca, N.Y.: Cornell University Press, 1987); Vicki L. Ruiz and Susan Tiano, eds.,

Women on the U.S.-Mexico Border: Responses to Change (Boston: Allen & Unwin, 1987).

6. For a fuller explanation of this idea, see Margaret Eleanor Rose, "Women in the United Farm Workers: A Study of Chicana and Mexicana Participation in a Labor Union, 1950–1980" (Ph.D. diss., University of California, Los Angeles, 1988).

7. Although dealing with different places, times, and industries, the following articles have influenced my interpretation: Louise A. Tilly, "Paths of Proletarianization: Organization of Production, Sexual Division of Labor, and Women's Collective Action," *Signs* 7:2 (winter 1981): 400–417; and Temma Kaplan, "Female Consciousness and Collective Action: The Case of Barcelona, 1910–1918," *Signs* 7:3 (spring 1982): 545–66.

8. Maxine Baca Zinn, in "Political Familism: Toward Sex Role Equality in Chicano Families," *Aztlan* 6:1 (1975): 13–27, notes the phenomenon of family participation in the struggle for Chicano civil rights. See also Kessler-Harris, *Out to Work*, passim.

9. Interview with Helen Chávez, Keene (La Paz), California, July 12, 1983, 1 (hereafter Chávez Interview). Helen Chávez was born January 21, 1928. Interview with Dolores Huerta, 2, Keene (La Paz), California, February 4, 1985, 69 (hereafter Huerta Interview 2). Huerta was born April 10, 1930.

10. For statistical data on the increased marriage rate in the postwar years, see U.S. Department of Commerce, Bureau of the Census, *A Statistical Portrait of Women in the United States* (Washington, D.C.: Government Printing Office, 1976), 15–20. For Chávez's courtship and marriage, see Levy, *César Chavez*, 86–87, and Chávez Interview, 9. Huerta's first marriage was noted in the local newspaper; see *Stockton Record*, April 20, 1950.

11. Chávez Interview, 11. The following is a list of Helen Chávez's children's birth order and birth dates.

Fernando	February 20	1949
Sylvia	February 15	1950
Linda	January 22	1951
Eloise	May 13	1952
Anna	September 11	1953
Paul	March 23	1957
Elizabeth	February 15	1958
Anthony	August 12	1959

The list of Huerta's children was compiled from the following sources: Huerta Interview, 2, 80–81, 88–92; Interview with Dolores Huerta, 5, Keene (La Paz), California, February 19, 1985, 172–73 (hereafter Huerta Interview, 5); Lori Head Survey

(La Paz) June 12, 1984, 4; Alicia Huerta Hernández Survey (La Paz), June 12, 1984, 4. Head and Hernández are Huerta's daughters.

Celeste	1951	First Marriage
Lori	1952	
Fidel	1956	Second Marriage
Emilio	1957	
Vincent	1958	
Alicia	1959	
Angela	1963	
Juanita	1970	Third Relationship
María Elena	1972	
Ricky	1973	
Camilla	1976	

12. Richard Griswold Del Castillo, *La Familia: Chicano Families in the Urban Southwest, 1848 to the Present* (Notre Dame, Ind.: University of Notre Dame Press, 1984), 96–106. The author discusses the variations between native-born Mexican American and immigrant Mexican families in terms of bilingualism, assimilation, employment patterns, economic conditions, and cultural values. New Mexican Hispanics have considered their history and experience distinct from that of immigrant Mexican families; for an exploration of their past, see Nancie L. González, *The Spanish-Americans of New Mexico: A Heritage of Pride* (Albuquerque: University of New Mexico Press, 1967), 1–85. For biographical data see Interview with Dolores Huerta, 1, Keene (La Paz), California, March 16, 1984, 1–8, 14, and 39 (hereafter Huerta Interview, 1), and Chávez Interview, 1–3, 5–6.

13. Huerta graduated from Stockton High School in 1947 and later went on to Stockton Junior College, where she was awarded an Associate Arts degree (a two-year program); see *Who's Who in Labor* (New York: Arno Press, 1976), 283, and *Stockton Record*, April 20, 1950. See also Jean Murphy, "Unsung Heroine of La Causa," *Regeneración* 1:10 (1971): 20. For statistics on college attendance for Spanish-surnamed women, see U.S. Department of Commerce, Bureau of the Census, *Population Characteristics of Selected Ethnic Groups in Five Southwestern States* (Washington, D.C.: G.P.O., 1960), 2. Graduation from high school and college attendance were rare accomplishments for Latinas, as revealed by this census report conducted in 1960. Even in these later years, only 14.2 percent of Spanish-surnamed women in the Southwest completed four years of high school. This number contrasted with a figure of 31.2 percent for Anglo women. Latinas who achieved between one and three years of college fell dramatically, to 3.2 percent. The corresponding figure for Anglo women was 13 percent. Huerta's family provided her with advantages and exposure not generally available to Mexican American women of her generation.

14. Rodolfo Acuña, *Occupied America: A History of Chicanos,* 2nd ed. (New York: Harper & Row, 1981), 329–30.

15. Dunne, *Delano,* 66–67. On these pages, Fred Ross, an organizer for the CSO, explained that he got the Chávezes' name as prospective recruits from a Mexican American public health nurse employed at a well-baby clinic visited by Helen Chávez. See also Matthiessen, *Sal Si Puedes,* 43–50; and Levy, *César Chavez,* 97–99.

16. Quoted in Chávez Interview, 23. For an analysis of the CSO, see Ralph Guzmán, *The Political Socialization of the Mexican American People* (New York: Arno Press, 1976), 137–43.

17. Huerta is mentioned by name as a contact person in a newspaper article describing a regional CSO meeting in Stockton; see *Stockton Record,* July 25, 1958.

18. Huerta's activity as the CSO legislative representative is noted in CSO *Reporter,* n.d. (circa 1959), Ernesto Galarza Collection, box 13, folder 8, p. 2, Department of Special Collections, Stanford University (hereafter Galarza Collection, Stanford).

19. London and Anderson, *So Shall Ye Reap,* 39–78 and 79–98. The authors have devoted a chapter to the Agricultural Workers Association (AWA) in which they mention the activities of Dolores Huerta. London and Anderson also discuss the AFL-CIO–sponsored Agricultural Workers Organizing Committee (AWOC), founded in 1959, in which Huerta participated. The director of AWOC notes the hiring of Dolores Huerta and her election to the office of secretary of AWOC; see Correspondence from Norman Smith to Don Vial, July 13, 1959, AWOC Collection, box 2, folder 7, Archives of Labor and Urban Affairs, Walter P. Reuther Library, Wayne State University, Detroit, Michigan (hereafter ALUA).

20. Quoted in Levy, *César Chavez,* 145.

21. Quoted in letter from César Chávez to Fred Ross, May 2, 1962, Fred Ross Collection, box 3, folder 6, ALUA.

22. Quoted in Barbara L. Baer and Glenna Matthews, " 'You Find a Way': The Women of the Boycott," *The Nation,* February 23, 1974, 237.

23. Helen Chávez, along with her husband, was an original member of the credit union; see Articles of Incorporation of Farm Workers Credit Union, July 21, 1963, UFW Small Collection, box 4, no folder, ALUA. (The original document is now stored in the archive's vault. Note: Most of the UFW collection is unprocessed.) Statistics collected by the National Credit Union Administration for 1985 reported a membership figure of 2,389 and listed the total number of loans issued for the year as 273; see National Credit Union Administration, Financial Statement for UFW, 1985, 3–4.

24. Huerta was the only woman elected to the National Farm Workers Association, the precursor to the UFW. She was a vice-president. The other original officers were César Chávez, general director; Manuel Chávez, secretary-treasurer; Gilbert

Padilla and Roger Terrones, vice-presidents. See César Chávez to Fred Ross, January 24, 1963, Fred Ross Collection, box 3, series I, folder 11, Correspondence, 1963, ALUA.

25. Quoted in Taylor, *Chavez*, 217. Huerta explained that she used the ILWU [Longshoreman] pineapple-worker contracts for Hawaiian workers as her model. For an example of early UFWOC contracts, see Collective Bargaining Agreement between DiGiorgio and United Farm Workers Organizing Committee, January 13, 1966, Anne Draper Collection, box 20, folder 173, Department of Special Collections, Stanford University (hereafter Draper Collection, Stanford). For a winery contract, see United Farm Workers Organizing Committee (hereafter UFWOC), box 2, folder: Almaden Vineyards Contract, 1967, ALUA. The Almaden contract was negotiated by Huerta after a card check election held June 28, 1967. A minimum wage of $1.80 plus standard UFWOC benefits were guaranteed; see *El Malcriado*, August 16, 1967.

26. Taylor, *Chavez*, 217.

27. Quoted in Barbara L. Baer, "Stopping Traffic: One Woman's Cause," *The Progressive* 39:9 (September 1975): 39–40. For an opposite opinion, see Kushner, *Long Road*, 185.

28. Taylor, *Chavez*, 229–30.

29. For Huerta's involvement in the 1968 boycott, see a sample of her correspondence with New York union leaders: letter from Dolores Huerta to Patrick Gleason (Retail Food Clerks), January 18, 1968, in UFWOC, New York Boycott, acc #376, box 6, folder 6, Huerta Correspondence, 1968, ALUA. Huerta generated a tremendous amount of publicity on the strike and boycott; see, for instance, [New York] *International* (official publication of the Seafarers' International Union of North America) 1:2 (February 1968). Vivid accounts of Huerta's participation in the negotiations with Delano grape growers in 1970 appear in Levy, *Cesar Chavez*, 313–25, and Day, *Forty Acres*, 161–68. Huerta again headed the New York boycott effort and coordinated the East Coast boycott operations in 1973. For a typical staff meeting and local coordinators' reports, see Minutes, Staff Meeting, May 22, 1973, UFW New York Boycott Office (acc 6/25/78), box 1, folder: Weekly Meetings – Minutes, ALUA. For a report on success in the chain store campaign, see *East Coast Boycott News*, July 27, 1973, UFW Chicago Boycott Office (acc 2/3/76), box 2, folder: Dolores Huerta File, ALUA.

30. Majka and Majka, *Farm Workers*, 233–47. See also Meister and Loftis, *A Long Time Coming*, 215–28.

31. Huerta's assumption of the directorship of the CPD is noted in an open letter to UFW supporters; see "Dear Brothers and Sisters from the Northern California Boycott Staff," n.d. [circa April 1978], Anne Loftis Collection, box 8, folder 2, De-

partment of Special Collections, Stanford University (hereafter Loftis Collection). For César Chávez's congratulatory comments on Huerta's legislative achievements as director of the CPD, see *Acta de cuarta convención constitucional de la unión de campesinos de América*, AFL-CIO, Agosto 12, 1979, Salinas, California, 24–25 [Proceedings of the Fourth Constitutional Convention of the UFW].

32. Quoted in Chávez Interview, 33. For the first arrest of Helen Chávez in 1965, see *Bakersfield Californian*, October 20, 1965. See also Levy, *Cesar Chavez*, 192–93.

33. Quoted in Chávez Interview, 33–34. Accounts of her Arizona arrest with her husband, César Chávez, were reported in several newspapers; see *Yuma Daily Sun*, June 14, 1978, and *Los Angeles Times*, June 25, 1978. See also Majka and Majka, *Farm Workers*, 253.

34. *Los Angeles Times*, February 2, 1976.

35. For example, after her address to the delegates, Huerta was presented with a $10,000 check by the Amalgamated Clothing Workers of America at their convention held in Miami in 1968; see [Washington, D.C.] *AFL-CIO News*, June 8, 1968, UFWOC box 9, folder: *AFL-CIO News*, 1968, ALUA. In addition, Huerta has made countless speeches and commentaries on radio and television. See, for example, transcript, PBS, "The Advocates," March 8, 1973, "Should You Support the National Lettuce Boycott?" Dolores Huerta, discussant, vertical files, Chicano Studies Center Research Library, UCLA.

36. Quoted from U.S. Congress, House, Subcommittee on Labor Standards of the Committee on Education and Labor, *Hearings on Immigration Reform and Agricultural Guestworkers*, 98th Cong., 2nd sess., April 11, and May 3, 1984, 21–27, especially 21. For earlier examples of her testimony, see U.S. Congress, Senate, Subcommittee on Migratory Labor of the Committee on Labor and Public Welfare, *Amending Migratory Labor Laws: Hearings on S.1864, S.1865, S.1866, S.1867, and S.1868*, 89th Cong., 1st and 2nd sess., March 16, 1966, 690–95. See also U.S. Congress, House, Special Subcommittee on Labor of the Committee on Education and Labor, *Extension of National Labor Relations Act to Agricultural Employees: Hearing on H.R. 4769*, 90th Congress, 1st sess., May 1, 4, 5, 8, 9, and 12, 1967, 81–91.

37. Report on Activities for International Boycott Day, September 14, 1974, UFW Boycott Central (acc May 1977), box 2, folder: Michigan, Detroit 1974, ALUA. [Detroit] *Sunday News*, September 15, 1974. [Detroit] *SolidaridadMotor City-Boycott*, November 1974, UFW Cleveland, Ohio Boycott (acc 1/17/75), box 1, folder: Boycott Newsletters, 1973–74, ALUA.

38. Chávez Interview, 23–24.

39. Zavella, *Women's Work and Chicano Families*, 154–59. The author also notes women's ambivalence over work and family roles. For black women see Jacqueline Jones, *Labor of Love*, passim.

40. Quoted in typed transcript of interview with Dolores Huerta by Ron Taylor at the AFL-CIO convention in Miami, 1974, Ron Taylor Collection, series II, box 9, folder 21, ALUA.

41. Quoted in *Chicago Tribune*, April 19, 1975.

42. James J. Kenneally, *Women and American Trade Unions* (St. Albans, Vt.: Eden Press Women's Publications, Inc., 1978), 92–118; Carolyn Ashburgh, *Lucy Parsons: American Revolutionary* (Chicago: Charles Kerr Publishing Co., 1976), passim; "Living History: Emma Tenayuca Tells Her Story," *The Texas Observer*, October 28, 1983: 7–15; Ruiz, *Cannery Women*, 104–5, 107–8, 113, 116, 119.

43. Kessler-Harris, *Out to Work*, 235. Hall, "Disorderly Women," 354–82.

44. Quoted in [San Bernardino, Calif.] *El Chicano* 7:34 (January 25, 1973): 3. In addition, Huerta cites her father's opposition to her unconventional family and personal life. Huerta's second husband, Ventura Huerta, vigorously opposed her nontraditional attitudes and child care practices. Huerta alludes to her disagreements with her husband over the care of their children in Barbara L. Baer and Glenna Matthews, " 'You Find a Way,' " 234. See also Huerta Interview, 1, 43–49.

45. Quoted in Baer, "Stopping Traffic," 39.

46. Kessler-Harris, *Out to Work*, passim. Milkman, *Gender at Work*, passim.

47. Margaret Rose, " 'From the Fields to the Picket Line: Huelga Women and the Boycott,' 1965–1975," *Labor History* (summer 1990): 271–93.

48. Rose, "Women in the United Farm Workers," chapter 6.

49. Interview with Antonia Guajarda González, Delano, California, October 7, 1983.

50. Quoted from rough draft of typed text, no title, "The female farmworker is as unique . . ." [by Hope Lopez], March 20, 1970, UFW, Philadelphia Boycott Office, box 5, folder 13, ALUA.

51. For quotation from de la Cruz, see Ellen Cantarow, "Jessie Lopez De La Cruz: The Battle for Farmworkers' Rights," in *Moving the Mountain: Women Working for Social Change,* ed. Ellen Cantarow, Susan Gushee O'Malley, and Sharon Hartman Strom (Old Westbury, N.Y.: The Feminist Press, 1980), 136–37. For ranch committee women, see Rose, "Women in the United Farm Workers," chapter 7. For the difficulties of other working women in the male-dominated world of trade unionism, see Ruth Milkman, "Women Workers, Feminism and the Labor Movement since the 1960s," in *Women, Work and Protest: A Century of U.S. Women's Labor History,* ed. Ruth Milkman (Boston: Routledge & Kegan Paul, 1985), 306.

52. Quoted in Cletus E. Daniel, "Cesar Chavez and the Unionization of California Farm Workers," in *Labor Leaders in America,* ed. Melvyn Dubofsky and Warren Van Tine (Chicago: University of Illinois Press, 1987), 360.

Frontiers 11:1 (1990): 26–32.

Mexican American Women Grassroots Community Activists

"Mothers of East Los Angeles"

MARY PARDO

The relatively few studies of Chicana political activism show a bias in the way political activism is conceptualized by social scientists, who often use a narrow definition confined to electoral politics.[1] Most feminist research uses an expanded definition that moves across the boundaries between public, electoral politics and private, family politics; but feminist research generally focuses on women mobilized around gender-specific issues.[2] For some feminists, adherence to "tradition" constitutes conservatism and submission to patriarchy. Both approaches exclude the contributions of working-class women, particularly those of Afro-American women and Latinas, thus failing to capture the full dynamic of social change.[3]

The following case study of Mexican American women activists in "Mothers of East Los Angeles" (MELA) contributes another dimension to the conception of grassroots politics. It illustrates how these Mexican American women transform "traditional" networks and resources based on family and culture into political assets to defend the quality of urban life. Far from unique, these patterns of activism are repeated in Latin America and elsewhere. Here as in other times and places, the women's activism arises out of seemingly "traditional" roles, addresses wider social and political issues, and capitalizes on informal associations sanctioned by the community.[4] Religion, commonly viewed as a conservative force, is intertwined with politics.[5] Often, women speak of their communities and their activism as extensions of their family and household responsibility. The central role of women in grassroots struggles around quality of life, in the Third World and in the United States, challenges conventional assumptions about the powerlessness of women and static definitions of culture and tradition.

In general, the women in MELA are longtime residents of East Los Angeles; some are bilingual and native born, others Mexican born and Spanish dominant. All the core activists are bilingual and have lived in the community over thirty years. All have been active in parish-sponsored groups and activities; some have had experience working in community-based groups arising from schools, neighborhood watch associations, and labor support groups. To gain an appreciation of the group and the core activists, I used ethnographic field methods. I interviewed six women, using a life history approach focused on their first community activities, current activism, household and family responsibilities, and perceptions of community issues.[6] Also, from December 1987 through October 1989, I attended hearings on the two currently pending projects of contention – a proposed state prison and a toxic waste incinerator – and participated in community and organizational meetings and demonstrations. The following discussion briefly chronicles an intense and significant five-year segment of community history from which emerged MELA and the women's transformation of "traditional" resources and experiences into political assets for community mobilization.[7]

THE COMMUNITY CONTEXT:
EAST LOS ANGELES RESISTING SIEGE

Political science theory often guides the political strategies used by local government to select the sites for undesirable projects. In 1984, the state of California commissioned a public relations firm to assess the political difficulties facing the construction of energy-producing waste incinerators. The report provided a "personality profile" of those residents most likely to organize effective opposition to projects:

middle and upper socioeconomic strata possess better resources to effectuate their opposition. Middle and higher socioeconomic strata neighborhoods should not fall within the one-mile and five-mile radii of the proposed site. Conversely, older people, people with a high school education or less are least likely to oppose a facility.[8]

The state accordingly placed the plant in Commerce, a predominantly Mexican American, low-income community. This pattern holds throughout the state and the country: three out of five Afro-Americans and Latinos live near toxic waste sites, and three of the five largest hazardous waste landfills are in communities with at least 80 percent minority populations.[9]

Similarly, in March 1985, when the state sought a site for the first state prison in Los Angeles County, Governor Deukmejian resolved to place the 1,700-inmate institution in East Los Angeles, within a mile of the long-established Boyle Heights neighborhood and within two miles of thirty-four schools. Furthermore, violating convention, the state bid on the expensive parcel of industrially zoned land without compiling an environmental impact report or providing a public community hearing. According to James Vigil Jr., a field representative for Assemblywoman Gloria Molina, shortly after the state announced the site selection, Molina's office began informing the community and gauging residents' sentiments about it through direct mailings and calls to leaders of organizations and business groups.

In spring 1986, after much pressure from the 56th assembly district office and the community, the Department of Corrections agreed to hold a public information meeting, which was attended by over seven hundred Boyle Heights residents. From this moment on, Vigil observed, "the tables turned, the community mobilized, and the residents began calling the political representatives and requesting their presence at hearings and meetings."[10] By summer 1986, the community was well aware of the prison site proposal. Over two thousand people, carrying placards proclaiming "No Prison in ELA," marched from Resurrection Church in Boyle Heights to the Third Street bridge linking East Los Angeles with the rapidly expanding downtown Los Angeles.[11] This march marked the beginning of one of the largest grassroots coalitions to emerge from the Latino community in a decade.

Prominent among the coalition's groups is "Mothers of East Los Angeles," a loosely knit group of over four hundred Mexican American women.[12] MELA initially coalesced to oppose the state prison construction but has since organized opposition to several other projects detrimental to the quality of life in the central city.[13] Its second large target is a toxic waste incinerator proposed for Vernon, a small city adjacent to East Los Angeles. This incinerator would worsen the already debilitating air quality of the entire county and set a precedent dangerous for other communities throughout California.[14] When MELA took up the fight against the toxic waste incinerator, it became more than a single-issue group and began working with environmental groups around the state.[15] As a result of the community struggle, AB58 (Roybal-Allard), which provides all Californians with the minimum protection of an environmental impact report before the construction of hazardous waste incinerators, was signed into law. But the law's effectiveness relies on a watchful community network. Since its emergence, "Mothers of East Los Angeles" has become centrally important to just such a network of grassroots activists including a select number of Catholic priests and two Mexican American political representatives. Furthermore, the group's very formation, and its continued spirit and activism, fly in the face of the conventional political science beliefs regarding political participation.

Predictions by the "experts" attribute the low formal political participation (i.e., voting) of Mexican American people in the United States to a set of cultural "retardants" including primary kinship systems, fatalism, religious traditionalism, traditional cultural values, and mother country attachment.[16] The core activists in MELA may appear to fit this description, as well as the state-commissioned profile of residents least likely to oppose toxic waste incinerator projects. All the women live in a low-income community. Furthermore, they identify themselves as active and committed participants in the Catholic Church; they claim an ethnic identity – Mexican American; their ages range from forty to sixty; and they have attained at most high school educations. However, these women fail to conform to the predicted political apathy. Instead, they have transformed social identity – ethnic identity, class identity, and gender identity – into an impetus as well as a basis for activism. And, in transforming their existing social networks into grassroots political networks, they have also transformed themselves.

TRANSFORMATION AS A DOMINANT THEME

From the life histories of the group's core activists and from my own field notes, I have selected excerpts that tell two representative stories. One is a narrative of the events that led to community mobilization in East Los Angeles. The other is a story of transformation, the process of creating new and better relationships that empower people to unite and achieve common goals.[17]

First, women have transformed organizing experiences and social networks arising from gender-related responsibilities into political resources.[18] When I asked the women about the first community, not necessarily "political," involvement they could recall, they discussed experiences that predated the formation of MELA. Juana Gutiérrez explained:

Well, it didn't start with the prison, you know. It started when my kids went to school. I started by joining the Parents Club and we worked on different problems here in the area. Like the people who come to the parks to sell drugs to the kids. I got the neighbors to have meetings. I would go knock at the doors, house to house. And I told them that we should stick together with the Neighborhood Watch for the community and for the kids.[19]

Erlinda Robles similarly recalled:

I wanted my kids to go to Catholic school and from the time my oldest one went there, I was there every day. I used to take my two little ones with me and I helped one way or another. I used to question things they did. And the other mothers would just watch me. Later, they would ask me, "Why do you do that? They are going to take it out on your kids." I'd say, "They better not." And before you knew it, we had a big group of mothers that were very involved.[20]

Part of a mother's "traditional" responsibility includes overseeing her child's progress in school, interacting with school staff, and supporting school activities. In these processes, women meet other mothers and begin developing a network of acquaintanceships and friendships based on mutual concern for the welfare of their children.

Although the women in MELA carried the greatest burden of participating in school activities, Erlinda Robles also spoke of strategies they used to draw men into the enterprise and into the networks.[21]

At the beginning, the priests used to say who the president of the mothers guild would be; they used to pick 'um. But, we wanted elections, so we got elections. Then we wanted the fathers to be involved, and the nuns suggested that a father should be president and a mother would be secretary or be involved there [at the school site].[22]

Of course, this comment piqued my curiosity, so I asked how the mothers agreed on the nuns' suggestion. The answer was simple and instructive:

At the time we thought it was a "natural" way to get the fathers involved because they weren't involved; it was just the mothers. Everybody [the women] agreed on them [the fathers] being president because they worked all day and they couldn't be involved in a lot of daily activities like food sales and whatever. During the week, a steering committee of mothers planned the group's activities. But now that I think about it, a woman could have done the job just as well![23]

So women got men into the group by giving them a position they could manage. The men may have held the title of "president," but they were not making day-to-day decisions about work, nor were they dictating the direction of the group. Erlinda Robles laughed as she recalled an occasion when the president insisted, against the wishes of the women, on scheduling a parents' group fundraiser – a breakfast – on Mother's Day. On that morning, only the president and his wife were present to prepare breakfast. This should alert researchers against measuring power and influence by looking solely at who holds titles.

Each of the cofounders had a history of working with groups arising out of the responsibilities usually assumed by "mothers" – the education of children and the safety of the surrounding community. From these groups, they gained valuable experiences and networks that facilitated the formation of "Mothers of East Los Angeles." Juana Gutiérrez explained how preexisting networks progressively expanded community support:

You know nobody knew about the plan to build a prison in this community until Assemblywoman Gloria Molina told me. Martha Molina called me and said, "You know what is happening in your area? The governor wants to put a prison in Boyle Heights!" So, I called a Neighborhood Watch meeting at my house and we got fifteen people together. Then, Father John started informing his people at the Church and that is when the group of two to three hundred started showing up for every march on the bridge.[24]

MELA effectively linked up preexisting networks into a viable grassroots coalition.

Second, the process of activism also transformed previously "invisible" women, making them not only visible but the center of public attention. From a conventional perspective, political activism assumes a kind of gender neutrality. This means that anyone can participate, but men are the expected key actors. In accordance with this pattern, in winter 1986 an informal group of concerned businessmen in the community began lobbying and testifying against the prison at hearings in Sacramento. Working in conjunction with Assemblywoman Molina, they made many trips to Sacramento at their own expense. Residents who did not have the income to travel were unable to join them. Finally, Molina, commonly recognized as a forceful advocate for Latinas and the community, asked Frank Villalobos, an urban planner in the group, why there were no women coming up to speak in Sacramento against the prison. As he phrased it, "I was getting some heat from her because no women were going up there."[25]

In response to this comment, Veronica Gutiérrez, a law student who lived in the community, agreed to accompany him on the next trip to Sacramento.[26] He also mentioned the comment to Father John Moretta at Resurrection Catholic Parish. Meanwhile, representatives of the business sector of the community and of the 56th assembly district office were continuing to compile arguments and supportive data against the East Los Angeles prison site. Frank Villalobos stated one of the pressing problems:

We felt that the Senators whom we prepared all this for didn't even acknowledge that we existed. They kept calling it the "downtown" site, and they argued that there was no opposition in the community. So, I told Father Moretta, what we have to do is demonstrate that there is a link (proximity) between the Boyle Heights community and the prison.[27]

The next juncture illustrates how perceptions of gender-specific behavior set in motion a sequence of events that brought women into the political limelight. Father Moretta decided to ask all the women to meet after mass. He told them about the prison site and called for their support. When I asked him about his rationale for selecting the women, he replied:

I felt so strongly about the issue, and I knew in my heart what a terrible offense this was to the people. So, I was afraid that once we got into a demonstration situation we had to be very careful. I thought the women would be cooler and calmer than the men. The bottom line is that the men came anyway. The first times out the majority were women. Then they began to invite their husbands and their children, but originally it was just women.[28]

Father Moretta also named the group. Quite moved by a film, *The Official Story,* about the courageous Argentine women who demonstrated for the return of their children who disappeared during a repressive right-wing military dictatorship, he transformed the name "Las Madres de la Plaza de Mayo" into "Mothers of East Los Angeles."[29]

However, Aurora Castillo, one of the cofounders of the group, modified my emphasis on the predominance of women:

Of course the fathers work. We also have many, many grandmothers. And all this is with the support of the fathers. They make the placards and the posters; they do the security and carry the signs; and they come to the marches when they can.[30]

Although women played a key role in the mobilization, they emphasized the group's broad base of active supporters as well as the other organizations in the "Coalition Against the Prison." Their intent was to counter any notion that MELA was composed exclusively of women or mothers and to stress the "inclusiveness" of the group. All the women who assumed lead roles in the group had long histories of volunteer work in the Boyle Heights community; but formation of the group brought them out of the "private" margins and into "public" light.

Third, the women in "Mothers of East L.A." have transformed the definition of "mother" to include militant political opposition to state-proposed projects they see as adverse to the quality of life in the community. Explaining how she discovered the issue, Aurora Castillo said,

You know if one of your children's safety is jeopardized, the mother turns into a lioness. That's why Father John got the mothers. We have to have a well-organized, strong group of mothers to protect the community and oppose things that are detrimental to us. You know the governor is in the wrong and the mothers are in the right. After all, the mothers have to be right. Mothers are for the children's interest, not for self-interest; the governor is for his own political interest.[31]

The women also have expanded the boundaries of "motherhood" to include social and political community activism and redefined the word to include women who are not biological "mothers." At one meeting a young Latina expressed her solidarity with the group and, almost apologetically, qualified herself as a "resident," not a "mother," of East Los Angeles. Erlinda Robles replied:

When you are fighting for a better life for children and "doing" for them, isn't that what mothers do? So we're all mothers. You don't have to have children to be a "mother."[32]

At critical points, grassroots community activism requires attending many meetings, phone calling, and door-to-door communications – all very labor-intensive work. In order to keep harmony in the "domestic" sphere, the core activists must creatively integrate family members into their community activities. I asked Erlinda Robles how her husband felt about her activism, and she replied quite openly:

My husband doesn't like getting involved, but he takes me because he knows I like it. Sometimes we would have two or three meetings a week. And my husband would say, "Why are you doing so much? It is really getting out of hand." But he is very supportive. Once he gets there, he enjoys it and he starts in arguing too! See, it's just that he is not used to it. He couldn't believe things happened the way that they do. He was in the Navy twenty years and they brainwashed him that none of the politicians could do wrong. So he has come a long way. Now he comes home and parks the car out front and asks me, "Well, where are we going tonight?"[33]

When women explain their activism, they link family and community as one entity. Juana Gutiérrez, a woman with extensive experience working on community and neighborhood issues, stated:

Yo como madre de familia, y como residente del Este de Los Angeles, seguiré luchando sin descanso por que se nos respete. Y yo lo hago con bastante cariño hacia mi comunidad. Digo "mi comunidad," porque me siento parte de ella, quiero a mi raza como parte de mi familia, y si Dios me permite seguiré luchando contra todos los gobernadores que quieran abusar de nosotros. (As a mother and a resident of East L.A., I shall continue fighting tirelessly, so we will be respected. And I will do this with much affection for my community. I say "my community" because I am part of it. I love my "raza" [race] as part of my family; and if God allows, I will keep on fighting against all the governors that want to take advantage of us.)[34]

Like the other activists, she has expanded her responsibilities and legitimated militant opposition to abuse of the community by representatives of the state.

Working-class women activists seldom opt to separate themselves from men and their families. In this particular struggle for community quality of life, they are fighting for the family unit and thus are not competitive with men.[35] Of course, this fact does not preclude different alignments in other contexts and situations.[36]

Fourth, the story of MELA also shows the transformation of class and ethnic identity. Aurora Castillo told of an incident that illustrated her growing knowledge of the relationship of East Los Angeles to other communities and the basis necessary for coalition building:

And do you know we have been approached by other groups? [She lowers her voice in emphasis.] You know that Pacific Palisades group asked for our backing. But what they did, they sent their powerful lobbyist that they pay thousands of dollars to get our support against the drilling in Pacific Palisades. So what we did was tell them to send their grassroots people, not their lobbyist. We're suspicious. We don't want to talk to a high salaried lobbyist; we are humble people. We did our own lobbying. In one week we went to Sacramento twice.[37]

The contrast between the often tedious and labor-intensive work of mobilizing people at the "grassroots" level and the paid work of a "high salaried lobbyist" represents a point of pride and integrity, not a deficiency or a source of shame. If the two groups were to construct a coalition, they must communicate on equal terms.

The women of MELA combine a willingness to assert opposition with a critical assessment of their own weaknesses. At one community meeting, for example, representatives of several oil companies attempted to gain support for placement for an oil pipeline through the center of East Los

Angeles. The exchange between the women in the audience and the oil representative was heated, as women alternated asking questions about the chosen route for the pipeline:

"Is it going through Cielito Lindo [Reagan's ranch]?" The oil representative answered, "No." Another woman stood up and asked, "Why not place it along the coastline?" Without thinking of the implications, the representative responded, "Oh, no! If it burst, it would endanger the marine life." The woman retorted, "You value the marine life more than human beings?" His face reddened with anger and the hearing disintegrated into angry chanting.[38]

The proposal was quickly defeated. But Aurora Castillo acknowledged that it was not solely their opposition that brought about the defeat:

We won because the westside was opposed to it, so we united with them. You know there are a lot of attorneys who live there and they also questioned the representative. Believe me, no way is justice blind. . . . We just don't want all this garbage thrown at us because we are low-income and Mexican American. We are lucky now that we have good representatives, which we didn't have before.[39]

Throughout their life histories, the women refer to the disruptive effects of land use decisions made in the 1950s. As longtime residents, all but one share the experience of losing a home and relocating to make way for a freeway. Juana Gutiérrez refers to the community response at that time:

Una de las cosas que me caen muy mal es la injusticia y en nuestra comunidad hemos visto mucho de eso. Sobre todo antes, porque creo que nuestra gente estaba mas dormida, nos atrevíamos menos. En los cincuentas hicieron los freeways y así, sin más, nos dieron la noticia de que nos teníamos que mudar. Y eso pasó dos veces. La gente se conformaba porque lo ordeno el gobierno. Recuerdo que yo me enojaba y quería que los demás me secundaran, pero nadia quería hacer nada. (One of the things that really upsets me is the injustice that we see so much in our community. Above everything else, I believe that our people were less aware; we were less challenging. In the 1950s – they made the freeways and just like that they gave us a notice that we had to move. That happened twice. The people accepted it because the government ordered it. I remember that I was angry and wanted the others to back me but nobody else wanted to do anything.)[40]

The freeways that cut through communities and disrupted neighborhoods are now a concrete reminder of shared injustice, of the vulnerability of the community in the 1950s. The community's social and political history thus informs perceptions of its current predicament; however, today's activists emphasize not the powerlessness of the community but the change in status and progression toward political empowerment.

Fifth, the core activists typically tell stories illustrating personal change and a new sense of entitlement to speak for the community. They have transformed the unspoken sentiments of individuals into a collective community voice. Lucy Ramos related her initial apprehensions:

I was afraid to get involved. I didn't know what was going to come out of this and I hesitated at first. Right after we started, Father John came up to me and told me, "I want you to be a spokesperson." I said, "Oh no, I don't know what I am going to say." I was nervous. I am surprised I didn't have a nervous breakdown then. Every time we used to get in front of the TV cameras and even interviews like this, I used to sit there and I could feel myself shaking. But as time went on, I started getting used to it.

And this is what I have noticed with a lot of them. They were afraid to speak up and say anything. Now, with this prison issue, a lot of them have come out and come forward and given their opinions. Everybody used to be real "quietlike."[41]

She also related a situation that brought all her fears to a climax, which she confronted and resolved as follows:

When I first started working with the coalition, Channel 13 called me up and said they wanted to interview me and I said OK. Then I started getting nervous. So I called Father John and told him, "You better get over here right away." He said, "Don't worry, don't worry, you can handle it by yourself." Then Channel 13 called me back and said they were going to interview another person, someone I had never heard of, and asked if it was OK if he came to my house. And I said OK again. Then I began thinking, what if this guy is for the prison? What am I going to do? And I was so nervous and I thought, I know what I am going to do!

Since the meeting was taking place in her home, she reasoned that she was entitled to order any troublemakers out of her domain:

If this man tells me anything, I am just going to chase him out of my house. That is what I am going to do! All these thoughts were going through my head. Then Channel 13 walk into my house followed by six men I had never met. And I thought, Oh, my God, what did I get myself into? I kept saying to myself, if they get smart with me I am throwing them ALL out.[42]

At this point her tone expressed a sense of resolve. In fact, the situation turned out to be neither confrontational nor threatening, as the "other men" were also members of the coalition. This woman confronted an anxiety-laden situation by relying on her sense of control within her home and family – a quite "traditional" source of authority for women – and transforming that control into the courage to express a political position before a potential audience all over one of the largest metropolitan areas in the nation.

People living in Third World countries as well as in minority communities in the United States face an increasingly degraded environment.[43] Recognizing the threat to the well-being of their families, residents have mobilized at the neighborhood level to fight for "quality of life" issues. The common notion that environmental well-being is of concern solely to white middle-class and upper-class residents ignores the specific way working-class neighborhoods suffer from the fallout of the city "growth machine" geared for profit.[44]

In Los Angeles, the culmination of postwar urban renewal policies, the growing Pacific Rim trade surplus and investment, and low-wage international labor migration from Third World countries are creating potentially volatile conditions. Literally palatial financial buildings swallow up the space previously occupied by modest, low-cost housing. Increasing density and development not matched by investment in social programs, services, and infrastructure erode the quality of life, beginning in the core of the city.[45] Latinos, the majority of whom live close to the center of the city, must confront the distilled social consequences of development focused solely on profit. The Mexican American community in East Los Angeles, much like other minority working-class communities, has been a repository for prisons instead of new schools, hazardous industries instead of safe work sites, and one of the largest concentrations of freeway interchanges in the country, which transports much wealth past the community. And the concerns of residents in East Los Angeles may provide lessons for other minority as well as middle-class communities. Increasing environmental pollution resulting from inadequate waste disposal plans and an out-of-control "need" for penal institutions to contain the casualties created by the growing bipolar distribution of wages may not be limited to the Southwest.[46] These conditions set the stage for new conflicts and new opportunities, to transform old relationships into coalitions that can challenge state agendas and create new community visions.[47]

Mexican American women living east of downtown Los Angeles exemplify the tendency of women to enter into environmental struggles in defense of their community. Women have a rich historical legacy of community activism, partly reconstructed over the last two decades in social histories of women who contested other "quality of life issues," from the price of bread to "Demon Rum" (often representing domestic violence).[48]

But something new is also happening. The issues "traditionally" addressed by women – health, housing, sanitation, and the urban environment – have moved to center stage as capitalist urbanization progresses. Environmental issues now fuel the fires of many political campaigns and drive citizens beyond the rather restricted, perfunctory political act of voting. Instances of political mobilization at the grassroots level, where women often play a central role, allow us to "see" abstract concepts like participatory democracy and social change as dynamic processes.

The existence and activities of "Mothers of East Los Angeles" attest to the dynamic nature of participatory democracy, as well as to the dynamic nature of our gender, class, and ethnic identity. The story of MELA reveals, on the one hand, how individuals and groups can transform a seemingly "traditional" role such as "mother." On the other hand, it illustrates how such a role may also be a social agent drawing members of the community into the "political" arena. Studying women's contributions as well as men's will shed greater light on the networks dynamic of grassroots movements.[49]

The work "Mothers of East Los Angeles" do to mobilize the community demonstrates that people's political involvement cannot be predicted by their cultural characteristics. These women have defied stereotypes of apathy and used ethnic, gender, and class identity as an impetus, a strength, a vehicle for political activism. They have expanded their – and our – understanding of the complexities of a political system, and they have reaffirmed the possibility of "doing something."

They also generously share the lessons they have learned. One of the women in "Mothers of East Los Angeles" told me, as I hesitated to set up an interview with another woman I hadn't yet met in person,

You know, nothing ventured nothing lost. You should have seen how timid we were the first time we went to a public hearing. Now, forget it, I walk right up and make myself heard and that's what you have to do.[50]

POSTSCRIPT

In 1992, the final defeat of the proposed prison resulted from sustained political battles at several levels: mass community protests in the streets, litigation in the courts, and lobbying within the legislature. Madres del Este de Los Angele, Santa Isabel incorporated into a neighborhood-based non-profit community organization. See Mary Pardo, *Mexican American*

Women Activists: Identity and Resistance in Two Los Angeles Communities (Philadelphia: Temple University Press, 1998).

NOTES

Another version of this paper was accepted for presentation at the 1990 International Sociological Association meetings held in Madrid, Spain, July 9, 1990.

1. See Vicky Randall, *Women and Politics, An International Perspective* (Chicago: University of Chicago Press, 1987), for a review of the central themes and debates in the literature. For two of the few books on Chicanas, work, and family, see Vicki L. Ruiz, *Cannery Women, Cannery Lives, Mexican Women, Unionization, and the California Food Processing Industry, 1930–1950* (Albuquerque: University of New Mexico Press, 1987), and Patricia Zavella, *Women's Work & Chicano Families* (Ithaca, N.Y.: Cornell University Press, 1987).

2. For recent exceptions to this approach, see Anne Witte Garland, *Women Activists: Challenging the Abuse of Power* (New York: The Feminist Press, 1988); Ann Bookman and Sandra Morgan, eds., *Women and the Politics of Empowerment* (Philadelphia: Temple University Press, 1987); and Karen Sacks, *Caring by the Hour* (Chicago: University of Illinois Press, 1988). For a sociological analysis of community activism among Afro-American women see Cheryl Townsend Gilkes, "Holding Back the Ocean with a Broom," *The Black Woman* (Beverly Hills, Calif.: Sage Publications, 1980).

3. For two exceptions to this criticism, see Sara Evans, *Born for Liberty, A History of Women in America* (New York: The Free Press, 1989); and Bettina Aptheker, *Tapestries of Life, Women's Work, Women's Consciousness, and the Meaning of Daily Experience* (Amherst: The University of Massachusetts Press, 1989). For a critique, see Maxine Baca Zinn, Lynn Weber Cannon, Elizabeth Higginbotham, and Bonnie Thornton Dill, "The Costs of Exclusionary Practices in Women's Studies," *Signs* 11:2 (winter 1986).

4. For cases of grassroots activism among women in Latin America, see Sally W. Yudelman, *Hopeful Openings: A Study of Five Women's Development Organizations in Latin American and the Caribbean* (West Hartford, Conn.: Kumarian Press, 1987). For an excellent case analysis of how informal associations enlarge and empower women's world in Third World countries, see Kathryn S. March and Rachelle L. Taqqu, *Women's Informal Associations in Developing Countries, Catalysts for Change?* (Boulder, Colo.: Westview Press, 1986). Also, see Carmen Feijoó, "Women in Neighbourhoods: From Local Issues to Gender Problems," *Canadian Woman Studies* 6:1 (fall 1984) for a concise overview of the patterns of activism.

5. The relationship between Catholicism and political activism is varied and not

unitary. In some Mexican American communities, grassroots activism relies on parish networks. See Isidro D. Ortiz, "Chicano Urban Politics and the Politics of Reform in the Seventies," *The Western Political Quarterly* 37:4 (December 1984): 565–77. Also, see Joseph D. Sekul, "Communities Organized for Public Service: Citizen Power and Public Power in San Antonio," in *Latinos and the Political System,* ed. F. Chris Garcia (Notre Dame, Ind.: University of Notre Dame Press, 1988). Sekul tells how COPS members challenged prevailing patterns of power by working for the well-being of families and cites four former presidents who were Mexican American women, but he makes no special point of gender.

6. I also interviewed other members of the Coalition Against the Prison and local political office representatives. For a general reference, see James P. Spradley, *The Ethnographic Interview* (New York: Holt, Rinehart and Winston, 1979). For a review essay focused on the relevancy of the method for examining the diversity of women's experiences, see Susan N. G. Geiger, "Women's Life Histories: Method and Content," *Signs,* 11:2 (winter 1982): 334–51.

7. During the last five years, over three hundred newspaper articles have appeared on the issue. Frank Villalobos generously shared his extensive newspaper archives with me. See Leo C. Wolinsky, "L.A. Prison Bill 'Locked Up' in New Clash," *Los Angeles Times,* July 16, 1987, sec. 1, p. 3; Rudy Acuña, "The Fate of East L.A.: One Big Jail," *Los Angeles Herald Examiner,* April 28, 1989, A15; Carolina Serna, "Eastside Residents Oppose Prison," *La Gente UCLA Student Newspaper* 17:1 (October 1986): 5; and Daniel M. Weintraub, "10,000 Fee Paid to Lawmaker Who Left Sickbed to Cast Vote," *Los Angeles Times,* March 13, 1988, sec. 1, p. 3.

8. Cerrell Associates, Inc., "Political Difficulties Facing Waste-to-Energy Conversion Plant Siting," Report Prepared for California Waste Management Board, State of California (Los Angeles, 1984): 43.

9. Jesus Sanchez, "The Environment: Whose Movement?" *California Tomorrow* 3:3/4 (fall 1988): 13. Also see Rudy Acuña, *A Community Under Siege* (Los Angeles: Chicano Studies Research Center Publications, UCLA, 1984). The book and its title capture the sentiments and the history of a community that bears an unfair burden of city projects deemed undesirable by all residents.

10. James Vigil Jr., field representative for Assemblywoman Gloria Molina, 1984–1986, personal interview, Whittier, Calif., September 27, 1989. Vigil stated that the Department of Corrections used a threefold strategy: political pressure in the legislature, the promise of jobs for residents, and contracts for local businesses.

11. Edward J. Boyer and Marita Hernandez, "Eastside Seethes over Prison Plan," *Los Angeles Times,* August 13, 1986, sec. 2, p. 1.

12. Martha Molina-Aviles, administrative assistant for Assemblywoman Lucille Roybal-Allard, 56th assembly district, and former field representative for Gloria

Molina when she held this assembly seat, personal interview, Los Angeles, June 5, 1989. Molina-Aviles, who grew up in East Los Angeles, used her experiences and insights to help forge strong links among the women in MELA, other members of the coalition, and the assembly office.

13. MELA has also opposed the expansion of a county prison literally across the street from William Mead Housing Projects, home to two thousand Latinos, Asians, and African Americans, and a chemical treatment plant for toxic wastes.

14. The first of its kind in a metropolitan area, it would burn 125,000 pounds per day of hazardous wastes. For an excellent article that links struggles against hazardous waste dumps and incinerators in minority communities and features women in MELA, see Dick Russell, "Environmental Racism: Minority Communities and Their Battle against Toxics," *The Amicus Journal* 11:2 (spring 1989): 22–32.

15. Miguel G. Mendívil, field representative for Assemblywoman Lucille Roybal-Allard, 56th assembly district, personal interview, Los Angeles, April 25, 1989.

16. John Garcia and Rudolfo de la Garza, "Mobilizing the Mexican Immigrant: The Role of Mexican American Organizations," *The Western Political Quarterly* 38:4 (December 1985): 551–64.

17. This concept is discussed in relation to Latino communities in David T. Abalos, *Latinos in the U.S., The Sacred and the Political* (Indiana: University of Notre Dame Press, 1986). The notion of transformation of traditional culture in struggles against oppression is certainly not a new one. For a brief essay on a longer work, see Frantz Fanon, "Algeria Unveiled," *The New Left Reader,* ed. Carl Oglesby (New York: Grove Press, Inc., 1969), 161–85.

18. Karen Sacks, *Caring by the Hour.*

19. Juana Gutiérrez, personal interview, Boyle Heights, East Los Angeles, January 15, 1988.

20. Erlinda Robles, personal interview, Boyle Heights, Los Angeles, September 14, 1989.

21. Mina Davis Caulfield, "Imperialism, the Family, and Cultures of Resistance," *Socialist Revolution* 29 (1974): 67–85.

22. Robles, personal interview.

23. Robles, personal interview.

24. Gutiérrez, personal interview.

25. Frank Villalobos, architect and urban planner, personal interview, Los Angeles, May 2, 1989.

26. The law student Veronica Gutiérrez is the daughter of Juana Gutiérrez, one of the cofounders of MELA. Martín Gutiérrez, one of her sons, was a field representative for Assemblywoman Lucille Roybal-Allard and also central to community mobilization. Ricardo Gutiérrez, Juana's husband, and almost all the other family

members are community activists. They are a microcosm of the family networks that strengthened community mobilization and the Coalition Against the Prison. See Raymundo Reynoso, "Juana Beatrice Gutiérrez: La incansable lucha de una activista comunitaria," *La Opinion,* Agosto 6, 1989, Acceso, p. 1, and Louis Sahagun, "The Mothers of East L.A. Transform Themselves and Their Community," *Los Angeles Times,* August 13, 1989, sec. 2, p. 1.

27. Villalobos, personal interview.

28. Father John Moretta, Resurrection Parish, personal interview, Boyle Heights, Los Angeles, May 24, 1989.

29. The Plaza de Mayo mothers organized spontaneously to demand the return of their missing children, in open defiance of the Argentine military dictatorship. For a brief overview of the group and its relationship to other women's organizations in Argentina, and a synopsis of the criticism of the mothers that reveals ideological camps, see Gloria Bonder, "Women's Organizations in Argentina's Transition to Democracy," in *Women and Counter Power,* ed. Yolanda Cohen (New York: Black Rose Books, 1989): 65–85. There is no direct relationship between this group and MELA.

30. Aurora Castillo, personal interview, Boyle Heights, Los Angeles, January 15, 1988.

31. Castillo, personal interview.

32. Robles, personal interview.

33. Robles, personal interview.

34. Reynoso, "Juana Beatrice Gutiérrez," 1.

35. For historical examples, see Chris Marín, "La Asociación Hispano-Americana de Madres Y Esposas: Tucson's Mexican American Women in World War II," *Renato Rosaldo Lecture Series 1: 1983–1984* (Tucson, Ariz.: Mexican American Studies Center, University of Arizona, Tucson, 1985) and Judy Aulette and Trudy Mills, "Something Old, Something New: Auxiliary Work in the 1983–1986 Copper Strike," *Feminist Studies* 14:2 (summer 1988): 251–69.

36. Mina Davis Caulfield, "Imperialism, the Family and Cultures of Resistance."

37. Castillo, personal interview.

38. As reconstructed by Juana Gutiérrez, Ricardo Gutiérrez, and Aurora Castillo.

39. Castillo, personal interview.

40. Gutiérrez, personal interview.

41. Lucy Ramos, personal interview, Boyle Heights, Los Angeles, May 3, 1989.

42. Ramos, personal interview.

43. For an overview of contemporary Third World struggles against environmental degradation, see Alan B. Durning, "Saving the Planet," *The Progressive* 53:4 (April 1989): 35–59.

44. John Logan and Harvey Molotch, *Urban Fortunes* (Berkeley: University of California Press, 1988). Logan and Molotch use the term in reference to a coalition of business people, local politicians, and the media.

45. Mike Davis, "Chinatown, Part Two? The Internationalization of Downtown Los Angeles," *New Left Review,* 164 (July/August 1987): 64–86.

46. Paul Ong, *The Widening Divide, Income Inequality and Poverty in Los Angeles* (Los Angeles: The Research Group on the Los Angeles Economy, 1989). This UCLA-based study documents the growing gap between "haves" and "have nots" in the midst of the economic boom in Los Angeles. According to economists, the study mirrors a national trend in which rising employment levels are failing to lift the poor out of poverty or boost the middle class; see Jill Steward, "Two-Tiered Economy Feared as Dead End of Unskilled," *Los Angeles Times,* June 25, 1989, sec. 2, p. 1. At the same time, the California prison population will climb to more than twice its designed capacity by 1995. See Carl Ingram, "New Forecast Sees a Worse Jam in Prisons," *Los Angeles Times,* June 27, 1989, sec. 1, p. 23.

47. The point that urban land use policies are the products of class struggle – both cause and consequence – is made by Don Parson, "The Development of Redevelopment: Public Housing and Urban Renewal in Los Angeles," *International Journal of Urban and Regional Research* 6:4 (December 1982): 392–413. Parson provides an excellent discussion of the working-class struggle for housing in the 1930s, the counterinitiative of urban renewal in the 1950s, and the inner city revolts of the 1960s.

48. Louise Tilly, "Paths of Proletarianization: Organization of Production, Sexual Division of Labor, and Women's Collective Action," *Signs* 7:2 (1981): 400–417; Alice Kessler-Harris, "Women's Social Mission," *Women Have Always Worked* (Old Westbury, N.Y.: The Feminist Press, 1981): 102–35. For a literature review of women's activism during the Progressive Era, see Marilyn Gittell and Teresa Shtob, "Changing Women's Roles in Political Volunteerism and Reform of the City," in *Women and the American City,* ed. Catharine Stimpson et al. (Chicago: University of Chicago Press, 1981), 64–75.

49. Karen Sacks, *Caring by the Hour,* argues that often the significance of women's contributions is not "seen" because they take place in networks.

50. Castillo, personal interview.

Frontiers 11:1 (1990): 1–7.

Awareness, Consciousness, and Resistance

Raced, Classed, and Gendered Leadership Interactions in Milagro County, California

JOSEPHINE MÉNDEZ-NEGRETE

Mainstream scholars as well as Chicano scholars have begun their studies of leadership by expounding upon the attributes, ascribed and assigned, and characteristics of the individual. Assumptions found within these leadership theories are functional and conflict oriented. Most leadership arguments assume pluralist and managerial theories for understanding.[1] From these theoretical perspectives, leadership is perceived in terms of the individual.[2] Within the individualistic framework of leadership, women or individuals with ethnic affiliations are assumed capable of accessing and amassing a power base if they are willing to seize the opportunity, which is theoretically available to anyone. At the same time, common assumption exists that these populations lack the necessary individualistic attributes for leadership, and thus miss out on leadership opportunities.

As with conventional studies of leadership, a myriad of theoretical perspectives from a variety of disciplines have been used to examine Chicano leaders and leadership. Many Chicano scholars have replicated a male argument in leadership research, marginalizing women or minimizing their activism by placing their analysis in the context of a male perspective.[3] Evidence shows that women made significant contributions to the Chicano Movement, yet the exploits of Rodolfo "Corky" González, Reies Tijerina, José Angel Gutiérrez, and César Chávez, commonly known as the four horsemen of the Chicano Movement, abound today, while female leadership remains overshadowed. In the present, as in the past, culture and domestic everyday activities remain the expected realm of women, and leadership exercised within this sphere tends to be neither recognized nor valued. Even Mario García, in his most recent account of Mexican American leadership, places women in a male equation of gender, failing to address female leadership for its own value.[4]

In contrast, feminist theorists provide analyses that expand our current understanding of leadership.[5] They have advanced leadership understandings beyond the public world of politics and exclusive gendered domains.[6] For example, many Chicana scholars critique the limitations of the analyses of women's involvement in the *movimiento*.[7] They argue that these limitations are due to women's subordination by way of labor division and invalidation based on gender assignment. I propose that an examination of race, class, and gender oppression, embedded in the tensions and struggles waged by women leaders in their quest for social change, the quest that characteristically locates women at the center of leadership, can yield a more complex and rich analysis.

Using thirteen sociohistorical ethnobiographies collected from 1992 to 1994, I examine the ways in which Chicanas used raced, classed, and gendered interactions to carry out their leadership or activism. I explore how the women internalized, understood, and negotiated leadership interactions, and how their experiences serve to illustrate a reflective awareness of their social locations. I propose that they used a relational leadership strategy to carry out social justice and social change agendas.[8]

The women began with the assumption that their gender influences how they are treated or perceived within their other social locations. Some Chicanas in this sample defined their leadership interactions within a female consciousness, while others expressed their involvement within a feminist frame of reference.[9] Most participants rejected traditional notions of femininity, while some claimed a female consciousness. All framed their activism within their belief in justice, equality, and fairness, as understood through a multiplicity of social locations.

These activists and leaders used their knowledge of themselves, their respective social locations, and their social environments to gauge justice, equality, and fairness as they confronted issues embedded in their leadership interactions. Their recollected experiences with structures of inequality serve as a way to analyze Chicana leadership relationships.

The women in this study, whom I have identified with pseudonyms, have actively sought to create social change in Milagro County, through formal and informal leadership venues.[10] They have worked as program directors, elected officials, grassroots organizers, and business owners to create institutions of change, administer educational institutions, and serve as educators.

Chicana/Latino leaders, with some exceptions, have not been recognized and have largely remained invisible within the dominant society.[11] Yet, in matters of everyday life, these leaders have served as a source of empowerment and change for the Chicana/Latino community. César Chávez raised the consciousness of the United States to the plight of farmworkers. In coalition with liberal idealistic leaders – Jews, middle-class Euro-Americans, Catholic nuns and priests, and students who were a prominent force in this alliance – César Chávez and the United Farm Worker (UFW) members waged a struggle for human dignity and recognition of workers. Because Chávez fit traditional attributes of leadership, he was bestowed with recognition as a charismatic leader of a movement. To this day, Chávez is still considered a key and primary figure in the union's formation and evolution. On the other hand, Dolores Huerta, vice-president of the UFW, a leader within the union since its inception and instrumental in contract negotiations, policy formulations, and boycott actions, has not received the recognition afforded Chávez.[12] While a number of other Latino and Chicano men have received recognition as leaders by dominant and Raza communities, the contributions made by Chicana activists and leaders have been widely overlooked, with a few important exceptions.[13] For the most part, the androcentric nature of the historical visibility of Chicano leadership and activism obscures Chicana leadership.[14] While Ema Tenayuca and Luisa Moreno are noted for their progressive and union activism, and Josefina Fierro de Bright is recognized for her political involvement, notions of leadership are generally grounded on assumptions about a universal and male understanding of power and authority.[15] The inclusion of these women leaders only serves to complement or illustrate the exploits of masculine leadership and activism. Strength, rationality, and decisiveness are some of the characteristics expected of a person, generally male, who exercises leadership or holds a position of power.[16] These qualities often upstage contributions that Chicanas or Latinas bring into the leadership process, especially in their struggles to overcome the forces of racism, classism, and sexism or androcentrism.

SELECTION AND METHOD

Twenty-four of the twenty-six Chicanas/Latinos who participated in this study were selected using a reputational sampling technique; that is, they were selected based upon their recognized leadership roles in the Chicana/Latino community. The analysis in this article is based on the data collected from thirteen women who participated in the study. The process entailed conducting prefield interviews with twenty recognized Chicana leaders. Four questions guided the prefield interviews: (1) define a leader; (2) describe a leader; (3) what is leadership, to you?; and (4) given your definition and description of a leader, and your meaning of leadership, can you give me the names of five Chicanas and five Chicanos who fit your requirements for leadership? The four questions used in the prefield interviews were incorporated into the ethnobiographies. The prefield interviews yielded more than 126 names. Twelve men and twelve women were selected based on frequency of identification by those who participated in the preinterviews. About one-half of the twenty individuals who participated in the prefield interviews became members of the sample.

Participant observation fieldnotes and individual profiles extracted from each individual's life history served to identify multiple areas of raced, classed, and gendered interaction. Data were collected on the following: family of origin, family of birth, educational history, community definition and interactions, leadership trajectory, and attributes and qualities of leadership. Grounded theory and content analysis were used to complete the analysis. Grounded theory relies primarily on interviews and begins with the assumption that theory is developed in the field during the process of data gathering. Content analysis analyzes manifest and latent meaning in data, through which categories, patterns, and classifications emerge, in this case, to provide an explanation of leadership and activism derived from participant experience.

LEADERSHIP: WHAT IS IT?

Chicanas in this study concluded that leadership is more than believing or speaking a certain way; it is acting out a philosophy that creates change to benefit the many over the individual. For them, it is not enough to talk about change; leaders actively work to create it. Taking a stance and acting upon issues that have had a negative impact on others is part of their active involvement in creating and bringing about change. Moreover, key to their leadership is the ability to listen, to observe, and to keep an eye on the overall process, along with the flexibility to modify process. This notion of leadership is akin to that found in Carol Hardy-Fanta's study of political activists.[17]

According to Milagro County Chicana leaders, negotiation of leadership interactions is best undertaken when a leader is grounded in who she or he is, has a sound understanding of the community needs, and has firmly gauged personal and others' expectations of the issues from a common perspective. Enedina Gardea, an educational activist and community organizer, said that leadership means to "do what one can *para cambiar las cosas* (to change things) . . . *pa' mejorar* (to improve) people . . . *y ya que otros mejoran* (and when others improve) maybe I'll get a share *pero* (but) not for our benefit . . . *es para que mejoremos todos* (it's so all of us improve)." For her, and the other Chicanas interviewed, leadership is not about personal gain, although this can be an end result of exposure and recognition. Without exception, the participants in this study expressed their belief that their leadership approach placed priority on that which benefits the greatest number of people.

In Milagro County, a leader is expected to understand herself or himself, the community, and issues faced in everyday interactions. Sonia Melgoza, a community organizer, political activist, and recognized leader, said it best when she explained that to exercise leadership one must "be where the people are at: dress like the people, speak like the people, be one of the people." It is not enough to exercise leadership with others; leadership begins at home. Reflecting the consensus of women leaders in this study, Melgoza explained that everything starts at home: "Leadership begins with the exercise of justice, fairness, and equality within the leader's private world." According to Melgoza, the domestic sphere is a site of change.

Chicanas experience, practice, and perform leadership differently from their male counterparts. For these participants, a preferred strategy for exercising leadership is not to stand or act alone, but to work collaboratively. Bela Ambriz, past political activist, vice-mayor, and current president of Milagro County's Board of Supervisors, summarized Chicana leadership as a process that takes place among others: "Leadership is being able to be out there, not as a stand-alone person, but as a person who can work to meet common objectives with groups of people." In leadership, a preferred mode of interaction is working with a group and in the direction of the group, instead of working individually. For Ambriz, leadership originates within a shared vision for the common good of all involved.

Taking the group into account and engaging in relational processes of interaction, where each individual is accepted as an integral part of the process, does not release those in leadership from "taking charge or being willing to lead in certain events, situations, or incidents," according to Jessie Ronstedt, a community and mental health activist and founder of an institute for the study of the family. Elaborating, she suggested that leadership means knowing when to lead "without being asked to guide, mentor, support, and direct." Further, she observed, "Enabling others to act should be emphasized, rather than doing for, which is a disabling leadership; one must take equal responsibility for change." In leadership interactions there is an ownership for your contributions and a respect for those who contribute to the leadership process. Leadership does not happen through the charm or special attributes of an individual; it evolves in interaction with others. Ethel Mesina, a feminist activist and administrator, saw leadership as, "Joining people who are already involved in what they already want to do, and somehow empowering them to do it." In Chicana leadership, collective strategies drive their action. Although not always in the front lines, the women in the study directly weave their notion of leadership into the continuum of their everyday life. They see struggle as an integral aspect of improving the quality of life for their group and community, understanding that improvement of the group and the community results in a better environment for themselves and their families. Self-sacrifice is not a word in these women's leadership vocabularies or interactions because their driving concepts are resistance, struggle, and change.

For these Chicana leaders, power relations are a constant part of their interactions as they struggle with and negotiate leadership. In their everyday relationships, Chicanas confront external forces (outside the Chicano community's sphere of influence) and internal structures that impinge upon their leadership. Gender status places Chicanas in conflict with misperceptions held about them by dominant groups as exotic, foreign, and willing to collude with patriarchal power. They also have to contend with cultural expectations centered on their gender as they struggle with stereotypes of *marianismo,* such as submissiveness, abnegation, and passivity.[18] Chicanas are also expected to manage domestic responsibilities and public life. While none of the Chicanas in this study expressed suppression or limitations on their involvement at the request of their partners, they recalled the need to negotiate gender relations and incorporate their domestic responsibilities into their involvement. The Chicanas in this study indicated that, while the demarcation between private and public worlds of action was not always clear, the so-called private realm did limit and shape their perception of leadership insofar as leadership is embedded in the everyday gendered interactions of their lives, as discussed below.

GENDER RELATIONS: NOTIONS OF DIFFERENCE

The women in the study recalled that gender relations have been part of their consciousness as women. While the means were not always clear, the

women were expected to be molded within patriarchal notions of femininity, domesticity, and *marianismo*. While being imparted with traditional
messages of being *niña* (girl) or being *mujer* (woman), they spoke of experiencing a gender structure of subordination, regardless of their generation.
Cici Amaro, a planner and political and community activist, recalled the
gendered interactions and expectations within her family: "My brother was
treated very differently, although he was ten years younger. It was a whole
different scenario for my brother. He knocked heads a lot with my dad. I
became the go-between that protected my brother. Still, my brother could
do things that we [my sister and me] would never have imagined because he
was a man." Notions of difference guided Amaro's understanding of her
brother's position as a boy in the family as she spoke of negotiating feelings
of nurturance and protection for a brother for whom she was expected to
assume responsibility. The conflict of having to protect her brother from
the problems generated through his own behavior was also intensified by
the parental attitude that "boys will be boys."

Kelly Chaidez Navoni (who grew up with a Mexican-descent mother and
an American Indian father) recalled from her childhood, "Boys were much
more valued than girls." Providing a cultural explanation for that behavior,
she added: "Even in my father's culture – the Native American [she did not
specify a tribe] – boys were always much more free to do what they wanted,
to be what they wanted: they got more attention, they got more things, their
opinion mattered. That was the way it was." Both in Chaidez Navoni and
Amaro's interactions, boys were more valued and occupied a central place
in the everyday life of the family. Reflecting on her gendered interactions,
her socialization as a girl still influenced Chaidez Navoni's perception of
herself as an adult woman who is a leader. This is particularly clear in her
position as president of an otherwise mostly male membership. She finds
herself constantly having to examine and reflect on the gendered interactions that surface among the membership and mediating any differences
that might surface because of these interactions.

As the eldest of three siblings, Dora Aguilar, an activist and retired administrator, recalled experiencing divergent gender socialization. She explained: "I remember my dad saying, 'You should have been a boy.' I would
be the one willing to work on the car, or I was out working in the yard – I
didn't want to wash dishes. If I went out and watered the lawn, I didn't have
to wash dishes. I quickly learned that I would rather be out there mowing
the lawn. . . . I remember my dad always saying, 'You are a tomboy. You
should have been a boy.'" Aguilar remembered consciously deciding that

female roles were constraining, so she purposely engaged in behavior that is traditionally considered "male." For example, she always found a way to get out of doing domestic chores by doing the lawn, washing the car, and learning to do small motor repairs, thus endearing herself to her father so that he would teach her and invite her to engage in doing nontraditional work. In this quest, she developed a strategy for doing the things she enjoyed, without feeling constrained by "girl things." She carried out nontraditional tasks without experiencing repercussions. Because of what she called her "tomboy" persona, she was allowed to stretch her parents' expectations. Rejecting gendered expectations gave her the freedom to engage in activities ascribed to both sexes.

Linda Soto, deputy director of a vocational training program of national repute, and Maria Elena Gómez, a cultural worker, leader, and activist, recalled strong male influences in their lives, but they also experienced relationships with strong women that gave them an alternative for understanding themselves. However, the vestiges of gender socialization still minimized their achievements because they interacted in the social expectations of a "girl." Soto recalled: "I remember women, and I was one of them, girls being very strong and in control. I don't remember that there were differences in that women were considered less, or at least not in my little circle – I was always kind of lucky – people kind of followed me and looked up to me. My opinion counted with teachers and with peers. When I grew older, I think I began to realize that at home there was a double standard." Along with the esteem she drew from her peer interactions, Soto learned to perceive herself as a capable person because of her exposure to strong women. Still, being a girl placed constraints on her. Within her family structure, even though she felt supported and encouraged by her family, she experienced limits. She explained: "I don't want to diminish the support that my dad gave me; he always encouraged me. He used to tell me, 'You can do anything. You're so smart. You can lick the world.' Things seemed as if that's the way they were supposed to be; it was not until later that I realized that it wasn't. I never stopped to think that because you're a woman you are treated differently, you are left out. Maybe I was, and I didn't notice it." The encouragement she received about her intellectual abilities guided Soto into thinking she could achieve anything she desired. Achieving an education was her strongest desire. However, in her family's perception, Soto was expected to leave home and get married; for them, her education was not a priority. Gómez similarly recalled the value that her father placed on "his son's education" but not on hers. She elaborated: "[My father] never really encouraged us [girls] to value education . . . he never really sat down and advised, 'ok. *M'ija* (my daughter), how are you going to attend Cornell?' [She has been accepted.] 'How can we help you to go to college?' No. All my education, filling out the application, the plans, it was all up to me, totally. I don't think that he really thought that we would go through with it." Although from a more recent generation (from the seventies rather than the fifties), Gómez internalized the traditional expectations of marriage and a family. These notions emerged from the belief that girls were not worth the investment, as they would soon become someone else's responsibility. In the 1970s, boys were still expected to achieve and pursue a public life, while girls, like their mothers before them, were expected to remain within the bounds of feminine or domestic arenas, unless their role was to support male achievement.

In their analyses of gender relations, Chicanas in Milagro County expressed a complex view of the relations between men and women. Rosal Oser, a nationally recognized educational and diversity consultant who grew up in the fifties, shared a similar recollection of the ongoing discussions among women as they organized fund-raisers and other public events. She remembered that complaints and anger were plentiful. A lot of anger was expressed by women, but they never showed an understanding that they had an option to change their condition. "I remember sitting with the women, as they were making the tamales for the fund-raiser," explained Oser. "They had one big complaining session about the men. They never resisted." Along with these gendered notions, Oser was exposed to the traditional double standard as women discussed their husbands' extramarital affairs. As with the other complaints about their daily life with men, a "let-it-be" attitude became the expected response for women, and male infidelity was constructed as just one more male weakness. In her experience, most women of her childhood failed to resist gendered relations and acted within expected and accepted conventions of the time. Oser explained: "I remember the men screwing around, and having affairs, and drinking, and just assuming '*Así son los hombres.* (That's how men are.)' And, then I remember hearing: 'A man doesn't wander if a woman keeps him happy.' So, no matter what I heard that was wrong with men, it was always the woman's fault. The woman, she must be frigid, she must be this, she must be that, and that was the line – and the women bought it as much as the men – it was always the women's fault, no matter what." Even when men violated the marital agreement, women were not hesitant to blame the female spouses for not knowing how to keep their husbands from straying.

Men's faults were directly assigned to women as something they could change or modify to keep their men happy at home.

When speaking of men and women's relations within the confines of an organization, Gardea recalled the interactions that transpired with other male activists. The first one sheds light on men's misapprehensions about women's organizational abilities: "*¿Sabes que me dijeron a mí?* (You know what they said to me?) *Y me lo dijo* (And, he said it to me) loud and clear – I'll never forget. Jesse Briones told me, '*Sabes porqué* (Do you know why) you are running the organization? *Te voy a decir en un sentido porqué* (Once and for all I'll tell you why). Because when us men figure this tool doesn't work anymore, we throw it out the door, we let the women pick it up. We figure they can't do anything because it's not working anymore anyway. So we figure they can't do nothing with it, and that's why.'" Fully aware that this is a misogynist statement, Gardea used this recollection to challenge the myth of gender powerlessness. To keep Chicanas out of the social justice and social change arena, Latino males with class and gender privilege internally imposed limitations and barriers. For these activists, gender discrimination was a familiar social experience.

Gardea recalled when a Raza organization she worked with hired a secretary. Since men held the leadership positions in the organization, they expected to hire a candidate that would support and protect their interests. However, because the women comprised the majority of the membership, they got the organization to hire their own candidate instead, someone who would give inside information to the female members. For example, the secretary reported about an organization leader, "He gets the men jobs. Any job that comes in goes to him – he's pulling *movidas* (moves)." The women decided to do something about the situation. Gardea recalled: "We go upstairs into the bathroom *estaba allá arriba de* (that was above) Kragens *un cuartito así, y luego la oficina, y acá la secretaria* (it was a little room like that [marking the parameters in the air], and then the office, and the secretary here [pointing to where she sat]). We took turns *con un vaso* (with a glass), put it against the wall. We could hear real loud *lo que estaban hablando allí los hombres* (what the men were saying), and marked down *esto, y esto, y esto* (this, that, and thus). We came out *para que no se dieran cuenta* (so they would not notice), taking turns is how we caught them. *Fíjate!* (Can you imagine!)" A surreptitious game of espionage ensued, wherein the women developed a rotation system to go to the bathroom upstairs to hear how resources were being distributed for the job bank. This took ingenuity and organization, and, to this day, the women who participated in the action get a laugh out of the strategy they devised "to keep the men honest." These types of activities were not limited to their public and activist involvement. In their daily struggles, these activists devised many creative strategies to challenge injustices and unfair treatment of Raza, without failing to claim their rights as women.

RACIALIZED INTERACTIONS: BOUNDARIES, OPPORTUNITIES, AND LIMITATIONS

The subjects of this study have had to negotiate racial structures of inequality in their daily interactions in addition to negotiating relationships among family members and the nuances of gender. Each woman spoke of her awareness of her racial differences and marginalization within the racial dynamics of her community. For example, Aguilar realized the difference in race and how she was perceived because of race relations in her hometown, where the railroad tracks marked the boundary of the segregated town. Both class and racial differences were used against her and her people. Despite the pain she experienced, she acknowledged and accepted her ethnic/racial origins. Aguilar described racial relations in her town: "Only the whites lived in the good part of town. We used to go there at Christmastime. When my sister was real small, my brother and I would drive. We would look at the nice homes because those are the ones that had the lights. Literally, there was that side of the tracks and this side; I was very aware of that." Aguilar and the women in this study realized that their race and ethnicity were factors in how they were perceived and in what they were allowed to achieve. Without exception, women had negative experiences as individuals of color, yet they turned their experience to their advantage. Specifically, Chicanas in this study did not reject who they were within their own culture, nor did they come to "accept" the "white way" or assimilate into the dominant culture. They learned to negotiate the subtleties of racism as competent and capable individuals, framing their experience on a personal and cultural value of worth. Moreover, negative experiences inspired them as they sought to make a difference in their respective communities. For example, the rejection of Spanish by the dominant culture became a site of resistance for many of the subjects. Gardea, Melgoza, and Soto, who were punished for speaking Spanish when they were in school, carry a history of activism and long-term support for bilingual and bicultural education.

Race, while a visible marker and a great source of pain for the women in this study, has fueled their commitment to create an equal society. For example, Gómez remembered racial conflict as a subtle, painful, and indirect experience she witnessed when her "Mexican-looking darker sister" confronted racism. Gómez elaborated: "People didn't say things, but then if things kind of broke up – like the little girls taking sides, *disgustos* (quarrels or disagreements) – racism came up, especially with my sister. She came home crying because somebody called her nigger. I had a kid tell me to 'smile because we can see the white of your teeth, otherwise you're too dark.' It was very stupid stuff, coming from kids, my level, and the overt kind of stuff." Still, racist behavior was not the exclusive domain of youth. The more subtle affronts were experienced at the hands of mainstream educational institutions that marked the respondents because of their Mexican heritage. There were other complications for some. Gómez, who felt herself an outsider because she did not have access to her racial and cultural background as the child of a Mexican father and an Irish mother, was confused about her ethnic heritage. She struggled with the meaning of race in multiple contexts as she attempted to interact in both cultural worlds, the Mexican and the Anglo.

Race is a complex issue for subjects in this study. According to Chaidez Navoni, who was born and raised in Milagro County, she is thankful that Mexican Americans, Chicanos, and Latinos are now perceived as visible groups of people who have political power and the numbers to make a difference. The invisibility these groups experienced in the past along with tolerance for attacks on immigrants and minority bashing, is no longer something Chicanos accept without question.

CLASS RELATIONS: WE WERE ALWAYS DIRTY, NO MATTER HOW CLEAN

In addition to gender and racial discrimination, Chicanas in Milagro County also had to negotiate class dynamics. Yet, having a poor or working-class background was not something that initially generated trauma for the women in this study. Most spoke of not realizing that they were poor until they were able to compare their situation to those who were better situated economically. This did not occur until they ventured into the world of public education. Aguilar, when speaking about her social and economic location, observed that those who were better off lived in "better homes, everything was better." She explained that she "used to fantasize a lot about what I wanted, and I was going to have it." However, some recalled comparing their situations ethnically rather than economically as a child. Ronstedt, for example, remembered that her economic situation was not particularly painful. It was not until she became a leader that she became aware of class because of the unequal, unjust, and unfair treatment of the poor based on their economic class. "*¿Cómo te diría?* (How could I tell you?) *No queríamos cosas o no deseábamos cosas que no podíamos tener – porque no sabías* (We did not desire things nor did we wish to have something we could not have – because we did not know). I don't remember wishing for anything or desiring something we couldn't have. . . . My mother was thrifty. She managed the money we earned working for six months; we lived on it a whole year. She would always buy at the garage sales. She would always buy at the secondhand stores. She would always take care of our clothes. I assume that most of the time we looked decent. I don't know. We don't have a whole lot of pictures to show." Most of the participants' families of origin were good at managing their resources. As Ronstedt noted above, poor families managed resources carefully because they had to make ends meet to live within the fiscal constraints of seasonal or low paying jobs. Ronstedt's experience resonates with that of Ambriz, who remembers poverty not being unique to her childhood experience: "I'm sure it happened to many children all over the Southwest or in areas where there's poverty, but there were clearly the 'haves' and the 'have-nots.' The haves were the ones that we went to, and there were five families that we were sent to at Christmastime, much as we do here in the . . . Halloween tradition. At Christmastime, the only time that we ever got a piece of candy or a piece of fruit was when we went to the superintendent's house or the priest's house or to the teacher's house to get 'May Chreesmas, May Chreesmas,' and we would get a piece of candy." The physical separation imposed by poverty was not something that Ambriz questioned at the time. She grew keenly aware of poverty and disparity over time. She noticed that some of the "haves" did not shop at the company store, as her family did. She also grew aware that families with means went downtown to shop. Unlike Ambriz's family, wealthy families had their own physician and had no need of the company doctor for their medical care. Ambriz did not recall seeing them in the doctor's office, "So it was clear they had their place and we had ours."

Because Ambriz and the activists in this study understood that difference did not mean acceptance of the inequality that came with having fewer economic resources, they noted the separation of those who had means and those who lacked them. Soto, like Ambriz, was keenly aware of the disparity, especially as it related to older people who were the poorest of the poor in their neighborhood. From a very early age, Aguilar was also aware of the economic disparities. As a child she realized that her side of town was not like everyone else's. She recalled always wanting something better for her people and herself and often wondering what that better life would be like for her.

DIVERGENCE IN CHICANA THOUGHT: FEMINIST CHICANAS OR *LAS ADELITAS:* IF THAT'S WHAT IT MEANS, I AM NOT A FEMINIST!

Along with internalizing messages of race, class, and gender, which were informed by cultural markers, the women in this sample learned to examine and reflect upon their experiences as they negotiated the nuances of power from the position of Other within a feminist ideology. Their identity as women, cast within a nationalist Chicano movement and a traditional Mexican culture, provided them with an arena in which to negotiate the intersections of race, class, and gender without having to claim their actions as feminists. Yet, because they became adult when the women's movement was active, some of the women interviewed situated themselves within feminist ideologies and claimed feminist values as the foundation for their activism and leadership.

Four of the thirteen women claimed a feminist identity, but even when they claimed a feminist identity, they diverged in how they positioned themselves: One located herself in the radical camp, which she defined as completely anti-male, women-centered, and revolutionary; three others identified more closely with cultural feminism, that is, with a feminism that promotes the culture of women without excluding men as partners and that leaves patriarchy intact.

Bertha Riley, a longtime political activist and domestic rights worker who identified herself as a radical feminist, clearly based these notions on her belief in women, emphasizing that women are no different from men. "I believe in women," she explained. "I believe we have the same rights as men. We have the same strength and the same abilities and deserve everything equally as men with no exceptions. I am a feminist because I care for women." While she referred to herself as a radical feminist, she assigned a liberal feminist ideology to herself when discussing women's rights. Despite her identification with feminism, Riley experienced contradictions with feminist politics because of her race and class consciousness. In the early years of the second wave of feminism, she clearly assessed the feminist movement as race- and class-biased. Illustrating her position, she recalled an address to a conference on family violence where she chastised activists for what she perceived as lack of support for bilingual services: "I'm never ever going to quit believing the way I do. It's okay with me if you don't want to have bilingual services. . . . Every time there's a grant available on the national level, I'm going for that grant. . . . From the get go, I'll offer more services. You don't see the importance of bilingual services, and that's fine with me. You just keep going on your white middle-class ways." Riley's agenda deviated from that of women of the dominant culture who were middle-class because of her race and class location. She targeted race, class, and language insensitivity as the crux of her difference with other feminists. From her experience working with domestic violence, Riley concluded that feminists can only overlook language if they are unconcerned about reaching the women who are most affected by structural inequalities – immigrants, the poor, and monolingual Spanish speakers.

In contrast, Riley's notions were more radical than those upheld by Ambriz, Mesina, and Oser, who all identified with the culture of women as a site of strength. Ambriz spoke to this in discussing her notion of feminism: "First and foremost, I am a feminist because I'm very, very happy with my femininity; I love being a woman. Feminism, which is kind of the word that has been coined to advocate and crusade for women's issues, is all about justice and equality. It is not inconsistent to be a feminist, if one has been a crusader for justice, for minorities; it just goes hand in glove; there is no separation." Ambriz did not make gendered distinctions regarding justice and equality. For her, social justice includes Chicanas and Chicanos because of their common experiences as minorities. In contrast, Oser claimed a feminist ideology that is a site of angry interactions. She remembered "blaming men for everything." While she still saw "sexism under every rock," when it came to gender interactions, her feminist consciousness had transcended those anti-men days. She now felt "further along, trying to move away from the blame." Her analysis of men and women's relations had moved beyond the personal; she situated the struggle in a social context.

Mesina fit herself within an understanding of cultural feminism, claiming to have been "born a feminist, now that I look back." Like Riley, she acknowledged confronting race and class issues in her leadership interactions with middle-class white feminists. She explained, "They did not want to hear that there was [race and class] oppression and sexism; the reason women are poor is because of that, and they [feminists] couldn't understand that." She criticized what she perceived as their emphasis on the reorganization of language over focusing on "changing the hiring process, so women can get in." She underscored the need for structural change: "If you get women hired, it would be very hard for people to keep saying firemen," Mesina claimed. If society makes spaces for women to have equal access regardless of race and class, the struggle for gender neutral language becomes a moot issue. Her struggle for Chicana feminist rights was different because it was grounded in structure rather than on individual rights to equality, as evidenced by her race and class concerns. Mesina's identification with a cultural feminism position for women has been in conflict with the race and class consciousness that informs her activism, yet it has been useful to her as she sorted out the conflicts she experienced with Chicanos based on gender and cultural tradition.

Differences are also present among Chicana leaders who do not identify with feminism as an ideological reference point. Although these women disclaim ties with feminism or a feminist ideology, a woman-centered or female consciousness emerges in their struggle for social justice and equality by way of contesting the power of patriarchy. For example, as Gardea shared her meaning of feminism, she provided insight into this consciousness: "*Yo creía que una feminista era alguien que está contra los hombres.* (I thought a feminist was someone who was against men.) *Yo no estoy ni en contra ni a mitad, no puedo estar en contra porque estuviera a contra de mi padre, mi esposo, y mis hijos.* (I am not against nor halfway on this – I can't be against because if I were, I'd be against my father, my husband, and my sons.) *Ves, yo no soy feminista, pero a la vez, las ideas que traigo yo y lo que quiero cambiar – si los hombres se oponen porque yo soy mujer* (See, I am not a feminist. But, at the same time, the ideas I hold and changes I want to carry out – if men opposed them because I am a woman) – I wouldn't put up with that." Gardea acknowledged the power differentials found in a sexist society. However, she clearly recognized the limitations imposed on her by race and class location as a Chicana. She acknowledged the barriers set up by male privilege, yet she emphasized that she would not accept unequal treatment from males because she is a woman: "I wouldn't put up with that."

Differences between men and women were irrelevant for Aguilar. In her women-centered understanding of struggle, she incorporated family, ethnicity, and Chicano rights while rejecting feminism, which she perceived as individualistic in its motives. She elaborated: "I think a Chicana will give [a different] definition because we are very family-oriented. I don't come first; it's my family. . . . Also, we have a cause where white women didn't have a cause; they're searching for a cause and we have our cause. We're fighting for our own people; they are fighting for their individual rights." Melgoza situated inequality on multiple fronts, emphasizing that inequality is an issue of justice for both sexes. She saw sexist treatment as a structure of subordination that inflicts equal damage upon men and women, but she nevertheless argued against feminist liberation. She added, "How can I talk about liberation when my husband isn't liberated? He isn't . . . I'm against male chauvinism." For Melgoza, social justice issues are framed within a race and class analysis; sexism, in particular, is a condition that hurts those perpetrating it and those who are the objects of it. Thus, Melgoza concluded, gender subordination cannot be reduced to simplistic oppositions.

Concurring with Melgoza, Renée Armada, executive director of a local training program, maintained that women in dominant culture have pitted their rights against those of minorities when arguing for feminist causes. According to Armada, white feminists focus only on their own issues while minimizing those problems that pertain to women of color, poor women, or minority men. She explained: "When I think of feminist, I think of statistics. They say, 'Well, we have minorities, starting with white women.' It's always seen as more competition for Chicanos in general. To me it's rather negative. I would say I was a Chicana, but not a feminist, unless it's a feminist Chicana." While emphasizing that she believes in people's rights, Armada explained that the arenas of struggle with which she contends embrace more than gender issues, and competition for resources is at the core of these inequalities.

Ronstedt provided a bicultural reflection on feminism in her analysis. From a culturally informed point of departure, Ronstedt called herself a feminist, yet, she emphatically rejected any affiliation with mainstream notions of feminism. She elaborated: "A feminist, in my Mexican culture, is *ser una mujer, una mujer que se comporta con dignidad, una mujer que respeta, y una mujer que sabe su lugar . . . que sabe darse su lugar en público y donde quiera* (being a woman – a woman who carries herself with dignity, a woman who respects, a woman who understands her position . . . who knows how to situate and comport herself in public or wherever). If you define feminist just the way *gabachos* (Anglos) do. No!" In Soto's experience, feminism has been a force that has served to advance the equality of women. She and other participants in this study understood that having negotiated individual or institutional relations with raced, classed, and gendered structures has provided them the ability to assess themselves from an internalized understanding of (in)equality. Because of this, Soto rejected feminism as an organizing concept in her leadership or activism as it would force her to pursue leadership from what she felt was a reductionist perspective.

Chicanas in Milagro County, whether claiming a feminist ideology or not, espoused a female consciousness to gauge an analysis of power from multiple sites. They have had to "make sense" of their gender identity and how it informs their activism, while accounting for their class and race locations. All the while, they have had to carve out and develop an understanding of leadership and activism – with their families and other institutional interactions – that yields an activist approach founded on relational interactions rather than ideologies. For these Chicanas, their negotiated multiple ideologies have served, and continue to serve, as analytical tools in their leadership and activism.

I have argued that Chicanas have engaged the subtleties and complexities of race, class, gender, and culturally nuanced interactions in their struggle for social justice and equality. I argue that these women learned to engage and manage a myriad of power interactions, negotiating a multiplicity of identities in their activist and leadership endeavors because of their awareness of their raced, classed, and gendered social locations. Moreover, these relationships have allowed Chicana leaders and activists to gain and sharpen their understanding of the subtleties of power. While arriving at a Chicana consciousness, these activists and leaders have learned to engage leadership and activist processes anchored in relationships with those who, like them, are interested in pursuing social change regardless of leadership perspective.

I propose that these women, whether identifying with a feminist ideology or not, cast their venues for change on the centrality of their relationships, even as they refute notions of *marianismo* and claim an activist or leadership voice. Moreover, without privileging a Western feminist analysis or invoking it as the catalyst for their activism or leadership, Chicanas in this study have identified a woman-centered ideology. This female consciousness emerges to inform a relational leadership interaction for Chicanas in Milagro County, California.

In general, the Chicanas in this study have demonstrated that the politics of identity are complex. For them, identity shapes and guides their actions within the politics of daily life. Through them we learn that ethnic/race, gender, class, and cultural experience qualify and shape their leadership and activism.

NOTES

1. Edwin P. Hollander and Lynn R. Offermann, "Power and Leadership in Orga- nizations: Relationships in Transition," *American Psychologist* 45:2 (February 1990): 179–89; and Max Weber, *Max Weber: Economy and Society: An Outline of Interpre- tive Sociology,* vol. 1, ed. Geunther Roth and Claus Wittich (Berkeley: University of California Press, 1978), 3–62.

2. Daniel Kats and Robert L. Kahn, *The Social Psychology of Organizations* (New York: Wiley, 1978); and Gary A. Yukl, *Leadership in Organizations* (Englewood Cliffs, N.J.: Prentice-Hall, 1981).

3. See, for example, Rodolfo Acuña, *Occupied America: A History of Chicanos* (New York: Harper and Row, 1988); Albert Camarillo, *Chicanos in California: A History of Mexican Americans in California* (San Francisco: Boyd and Fraser Pub- lishing Company, 1984); Mario T. García, *Mexican Americans: Leadership, Ideology, and Identity, 1930–1960* (New Haven: Yale University Press, 1989); Juan Gómez Quiñones, *Chicano Politics: Reality and Promise, 1940–1990* (Albuquerque: Uni- versity of New Mexico Press, 1990); Carey McWilliams, *North from Mexico: The Spanish-Speaking People of the United States* (New York: Praeger, 1990); and Carlos Muñoz Jr., *Youth, Identity, Power: The Chicano Movement* (London: Verso Press, 1989).

4. García, *Mexican Americans;* see also Quiñones, *Chicano Politics,* 55–74, 115–43.

5. Examples include Charlotte Bunch, "Womenpower: The Courage to Lead, the Strength to Follow, and the Sense to Know the Difference," *Ms.*, July 1980, 44–48, 95–97; and Florence Denmark, "Styles of Leadership," *Personnel Journal* 2:2 (1979): 99–113.

6. Rosabeth Moss Kanter, *Men and Women of the Corporation* (New York: Home- wood: R. D. Irvin, 1977); and Charlotte Bunch and Susan Schwartz, "What Future Leadership?" *Quest* 2 (spring 1976): 2–13.

7. Martha P. Diosa y Hembra Cotera, *The History and Heritage of Chicanas in the U.S.* (Austin, Tex.: Statehouse Printing, 1979); Magdalena Mora and Adelaida R. del Castillo, eds., *Mexican Women in the United States: Struggles Past and Present* (Los Angeles: UCLA Chicano Studies Research Center, 1980), 7–16; Alma García, "The Development of Chicana Feminist Discourse, 1979–1980," *Gender & Society* 3:2 (1989): 217–37; Anna Nieto Gómez, "La Feminista," *Encuentro Feminil* 1:2 (1974): 34–47; Beatríz M. Pesquera and Adela de la Torre, eds., *Building With Our Hands: New Directions in Chicana Studies* (Berkeley: University of California Press, 1993); and Mary Pardo, "Creating Community: Mexican-American Women in Eastside Los Angeles," *AZTLAN: A Journal of Chicano Studies* 20:1/2 (1991): 39–71.

8. Relational leadership strategies are those processes or activities that anchor

relationships with others. That is, regardless of ideology, leadership style, position, or issue, these women accomplish change through or because of their relationships with others, using common ground as the foundation of change.

9. Kanter, *Men and Women of the Corporation;* and Pardo, "Creating Community," 39–71.

10. I am using a fictitious name, Milagro County, to identify the community I studied, a name one of the Chicanos I interviewed used to describe the leadership climate in the community under study. The population of Milagro County is about two million. I make this choice to protect the privacy of those individuals who selected to not be identified by their given names. Although some requested I use their actual name, I am choosing to give them pseudonyms as well. The Chicano/ Latino population is about 36 percent of the general population, with a larger percentage of Chicanos/Latinos residing in the county seat municipality.

11. To identify the ethnic identity of those individuals participating in this study, I use Chicana and Latino when referring to the individual participants. Invariably, women participants opted to use Chicanas as their identity category of choice, while males chose the term Latinos to identify themselves.

12. Acuña, *Occupied America;* and Quiñones, *Chicano Politics.*

13. Margaret Rose, "Traditional and Nontraditional Patterns of Female Activism in the United Farm Workers of America, 1962 to 1980," *Frontiers: A Journal of Women Studies* 11:1 (1990): 26–32.

14. Acuña, *Occupied America;* Alma García, "The Development of Chicana Feminist Discourse"; Mario T. García, *Mexican Americans,* 153–55, 146–50, and 155–57; and Quiñones, *Chicano Politics,* 50–51.

15. Mario T. García, *Mexican Americans;* and Weber, *Max Weber: Economy and Society,* 212–99.

16. John W. Gardner, *Excellence: Can We Be Equal and Excellent Too?* (New York: W. W. Norton and Company, 1984); Hollander and Offermann, "Power and Leadership"; and Joseph C. Rost, *Leadership for the Twenty-first Century* (New York: Prager Publishers, 1991).

17. Carol Hardy-Fanta, *Latina Politics, Latino Politics: Gender, Culture, and Political Participation in Boston* (Philadelphia: Temple University Press, 1993), 15–36.

18. Migdalia Reyes, "Latina Lesbians and Alcohol and Other Drugs: Social Work Implications," in *Alcohol Use/Abuse Among Latinos: Issues and Examples of Culturally Competent Services,* ed. Melvin Delgado (New York: The Haworth Press, 1998), 179–92.

"Checkin' Up on My Guy"

Chicanas, Social Capital, and the Culture of Romance

ANGELA VALENZUELA

The purpose of this paper is to examine the culture of romance among regular-track Chicanas in a large, inner-city, virtually all-Mexican high school in Houston, Texas, fictitiously known as Juan Seguín High.[1] By culture of romance, I refer to a romanticized view of heterosexual relations where love, warmth, and intimacy are dominant emotions. In their classic study of romance among college-going women, Dorothy C. Holland and Margaret A. Eisenhart refer to the culture of romance as one of the main factors explaining why women scale back their own aspirations. That is, to achieve love and attention from males, women often make compromises to the detriment of their careers. An irony of romantic love for these college-going women is that as they become more deeply involved in their relationships and as they envision more traditional roles for themselves as future spouses, women minimize their investment in academics, and their pursuit of careers becomes less important.[2]

Romantic relationships at Seguín clearly involve similar kinds of compromises. However, qualitative evidence gathered from fieldwork lends support to a complementary hypothesis: At least for the more seriously involved, when young women provide support to their male friends, however excessive, they enact or perform a version of femininity that promotes school as a goal. For reasons that are largely related to context, the evidence suggests that a cultural meaning system can develop that runs in the opposite direction of what Holland and Eisenhart would predict. That is, romantic love can evolve into a pro-school ethos. Whether this ethos translates into higher academic achievement, however, depends on the levels of social capital that students possess.

By social capital, I mean the social ties that connect students to each other, as well as the levels of resources (like academic skills and knowledge) that characterize their friendship groups.[3] In contrast to other better known forms of capital, like human and cultural capital,[4] social capital is known by its function. That is, through the interactive web of social relationships, social capital enables the attainment of goals that cannot be accomplished solely by the individual. This collectivist ethos is evident among youth at Seguín when, in the context of their peer group and even their romantic relationships, exchanges involve a marshaling of academically productive social capital.[5]

Holland and Eisenhart maintain that the shape that the culture of romance takes will vary depending on social context. For this reason, I do not see my findings as seriously challenging theirs. The present discussion instead highlights the capacity of social context to engender a pro-school ethos within the boundaries of romance. After describing the larger study and addressing some of its key findings, I turn to the primary sources of data, participant observation and group interviews, that permit me to explore my hypothesis.[6]

THE SEGUÍN HIGH SCHOOL STUDY

This research is part of a larger study that investigates generational differences in achievement and schooling orientations between immigrant and U.S.-born Mexican youth.[7] Data were collected through a survey, participant observation, and open-ended interviews with individuals and groups of students between 1992 and 1995.[8] My study helps explain a widely observed empirical pattern of higher immigrant achievement vis-à-vis their acculturated, U.S.-born counterparts found in both small-scale ethnographies and national-level data.[9] Rather than revealing the upward mobility pattern historically evident among European-origin groups, research on generational attainments points to an "invisible ceiling" of blocked opportunity for Mexican American people.[10]

Although these widely observed differences between early- and later-generation youth are regarded by scholars as reflecting a "decline in achievement,"[11] the framework I elaborate recasts the evidence as reflecting how schooling subtracts resources from youth. Borrowing from Robert D. Putnam, I argue that Mexican immigrant and U.S.-born Mexican youth alike are subjected to forces of "social decapitalization" (or loss of social capital in students' networks) through a process I term "subtractive schooling."[12] This means that the ways that youth are schooled or assimilated translates into the following interrelated outcomes: students' cultural and linguistic divestment, including their de-identification from Mexican culture and the Spanish language; psychic, social, emotional, and cultural distance between immigrant youth and their more culturally assimilated U.S.-born peers; and finally, a limited presence of academically productive social capital in the peer group networks of U.S.-born youth.[13]

As I argue in *Subtractive Schooling*, institutionally mediated social decapitalization is the antithesis of social capital. It not only fails to build on the cultural value that Chicanas and Chicanos attach to the sharing of norms, values, and resources, but also obstructs the transference of human and cultural capital. James C. Coleman forcefully argues that without social capital, human capital, embodied in individuals' levels of training and educational attainment, is negligible for the goal of academic success.[14] In Coleman's view, it is therefore not enough to possess human capital. One must also be enmeshed in exchange networks characterized by bonds of trust that permit an easy flow of resources and support that benefit both the individual and the collective.[15]

I describe the divisions I observed between youth and the paucity of social capital among U.S.-born youth, in particular, as two sides to the same coin. If one assumes as I did that achievement is a social process whereby orientations toward schooling are nurtured in familiar contexts among those with similar dispositions, then divisions between those with more and those with less social capital will be especially consequential to the latter.[16] More directly, the broader Mexican community's collective interest to achieve academically gets compromised by a schooling process that exacerbates differences among youth and makes them inaccessible to each other.

Analyses of gender within peer groups reveal that, were it not for the females in these groups, U.S.-born youth would be virtually devoid of social capital. Both quantitative and qualitative sources of evidence illuminate this finding: Regular-track females in every generational group tend to outperform their male counterparts.[17] However, placement in the honors track appears to erase the differences of both gender and generational status. Taken together, these findings suggest that regular-track placement cannot be overemphasized as an organizational feature of schooling that exacerbates differences between males and females, as well as between immigrant and U.S.-born youth.

Moreover, since never more than 10 percent to 15 percent of Seguín's entire student population is ever located in the honors college-bound track, the academic trajectories of the vast majority are circumscribed by regular-track placement. The salience of tracking is also underscored by Laurie

Olsen who similarly observes how immigrants' placement in the ESL track and U.S.-born youths' placement in the regular track compromises the achievement possibilities of the group as a whole.[18]

The firsthand accounts provided below show that romantic involvement for the females translates into helping boyfriends with their school work, even at their own expense. Females' support ranges from giving advice on courses, translating assignments, offering encouragement to stay in school, and acting as sounding boards for problems, to providing assistance on written assignments and exams. While the discussion that follows suggests that social capital can flow through romantic relationships, a countervailing force that mutes its impact is an uneven system of exchange occurring at young women's expense.

The data further suggest that Chicanas are cognizant of gender inequality in their relations with the young men in their lives. They nevertheless seem willing to persist in such relationships. Irene I. Blea sheds light on this tendency with her suggestion that, in contrast to white women, Chicanas prefer unity over distance with Chicano males.[19] This sense of unity, she argues, is born out of a shared experience of racial subordination that they must collectively confront. Another complicating factor Blea mentions is that Chicanas are socialized to believe that marriage, children, and family are to constitute their highest aspirations. When such cultural issues intersect with institutional barriers like tracking and low expectations, Chicanas might very well be more tolerant of uneven exchange relationships than their more socioeconomically privileged counterparts.

My exploration into youths' culture of romance below begins with a finding from participant observation that simultaneously allows me to address further the conditions of schooling at Seguín that influence the likelihood of a pro-school, romantically involved peer group culture. I then follow with detailed accounts of three couples who belonged to three different groups of students that I interviewed. Though the females in these groups accorded varying degrees of emphasis to family, peers, and school as rationales for both their romantic involvement and personal investments, their references to their social context help explain how their culture of romance translates into its unique, pro-school form.

THE CULTURE OF ROMANCE AND THE CONDITIONS OF SCHOOLING

Several weeks into the fall 1992 semester, while observing scores of students on the school's front steps as they make their way to their third-period class,

I spy a nervous-looking young female who seems to be desperately trying to find someone. Though only a few feet away, she seems not to notice me and continues glancing furtively into the building, across the school lawn, and across the street. With a preoccupied look on her face, she pauses momentarily to smile widely and yell to a group of three young males, presumably friends, cruising by in a white, small-wheeled truck listening to Tex-Mex music blaring through large speakers spread across the truck's bed. "Go to class!" she screams as the driver waves to her. "Ah, they can't hear me," she mumbles to a female friend who chances upon her at that very moment. "They're crazy," she continues. "Those guys are skipping class already and school's barely started!"

"What's happenin'?" her friend asks.

"Checkin' up on my guy," the first girl replies in an anxious tone.

At first, I think she is referring to one of the young men in the truck. I soon realize, however, that she is talking about another male who is her boyfriend. The two friends exchange several concerns they have about their schedules. I overhear them grumbling about courses to which they have been assigned that they already do not like and changes in their lunch schedules that mean that they will not be able to eat lunch together.

"At least I'm still with Andy [for lunch]," the first girl says. "He needs me."

Though I have trouble hearing how her friend is responding, I can tell that she is mainly in a listening mode because the other is dominating the conversation.

I overhear Andy's girlfriend say with concern in her voice, "He's not such a great student, but I promised myself that I would help him out in any way I could this year."

She informs her friend that Andy has gotten off to a bad start. Andy has apparently been moved to several different classes in the past couple of weeks because the counselors keep confusing him with another student with the same name. Though a freshman, Andy keeps getting assigned to junior-level courses. "He still has to go to class, even if it's not the right class!" exclaims his girlfriend excitedly as she begins again to glance nervously about the school's front lawn.

Since the bell is about to ring, only a few remaining students are within sight. As her friend gets drawn into the action, her words become audible: "I can help you find Andy. Maybe he's hiding behind the T-[temporary] buildings. But we have to hurry!"

Showing embarrassment, Andy's girlfriend backtracks and confesses, "Naw, it's a waste of time. He's not the skipping type."

Her friend then waves her arms, palms up, in disbelief. After exhaling loudly, she shouts, "Girl, what are you putting me through? Did you even try to check in his room to see if he was there?"

As Andy's girlfriend doubles over, bursting with laughter, I can only hear her friend's voice, which gets louder with each passing word: "Oh man, I know what this is about. It's like you gonna tell Andy how much you love him, how much you care for him today. It's like you gonna tell him what you did for him today, all lovey-dovey!"

Andy's girlfriend's face turns bright red as tears of laughter stream down her face.

In sheer delight, her friend snaps, "Busted! I got your number, girl!"

The bell rings, and they dart into the building and disappear. As I assemble my thoughts about the significance of this emotional display, the males in the white truck drive by again.

Before addressing my interpretation of this exchange, it is worth elaborating further on the schooling context wherein youths' capacity to prevail is severely put to the test. Since the first few weeks of school in any semester at Seguín are always chaotic, the kind of scenario presented by the students above is hardly unusual. According to school officials, the school was built to hold only 2,600 students. However, the school is typically responsible for enrolling several hundreds more beyond that limit. With no obvious plans for any new construction, classrooms in "temporary buildings" provided by the district have proliferated annually to accommodate the demand for space. Too few counselors to process too many students results in a scheduling nightmare with frequent placement errors. In a "good" year, by the third week of school most students' schedules are "fixed," meaning that students are assigned to the classes they should have been enrolled in from the first day of school.[20]

In the first few weeks, teachers typically face huge classes composed of a random mix of students, only some of whom belong where they are. Even larger than the actual classes are the rosters of students who are supposedly present in their classrooms. Students' displeasure over schooling combines with massively long class rosters, teachers' and students' conflictual relations with counselors, extraordinarily large class sizes, insufficient numbers of desks, books, and teaching materials, and inadequate space to make for a state of high tension and normlessness. Under such circumstances, the administration's attempts to both keep students in class and minimize disorderly conduct are often futile – hence, the three males in the white truck.

With soaring dropout rates, freshmen invariably make up more than half of the school's student population of three thousands. Academic failure is so common that a full quarter of the students have to repeat the ninth grade for at least a second time. In this kind of environment, students tend to gather fairly quickly that they need to look out for themselves and for each other lest they "fall through the cracks." By assuming a special responsibility for her boyfriend, Andy's girlfriend cogently illustrates how caring for one another can become an institutionally driven imperative. That females tend to take care of males also suggests that the ancient, one-way, woman-as-helpmate-to-man role persists.

What remains unanswered in the preceding account, however, is why Andy's girlfriend acted like she was desperately trying to find Andy if she knew all along that he was most likely in his classroom. Either skipping class was within the realm of possibility or something else was operating. While at face value, little more than childish play could have been at hand, the girlfriend's intense embarrassment after having been "busted" by her friend lays bare her hidden desire: to act in a caring way toward her boyfriend so that she could later tell him just how much she cared for him. Though away from him during the day, she nevertheless attended to him in a "caring" way, even if this involved momentarily convincing herself about his chances of skipping class. In a state of romantic love, Andy's girlfriend thus performed a version of femininity that combines several important elements that also appear in the group interviews that follow. That is, romantically involved females not only express their caring by promoting school as a goal, but this caring also gives them a sense of self-worth, connectedness, and status. Such benefits appear to accrue in schooling contexts that are especially difficult, challenging, or alienating.

GROUP INTERVIEWS

Close to half of the twenty-five groups I interviewed contained both females and males, the majority of whom were "just friends," or not romantically involved. I also interviewed gender-mixed groups in each generation (four groups are first-generation, one is mixed-generation, and six are U.S.-born). Across my sample of eleven gender-mixed groups, females exhibit a clear pattern of being the providers of academic-related support.[21]

Although there were numerous instances I came across of females helping out males who were friends, I focus on romantically involved couples because they allow me to address my concern with how the culture of romance translates into the everyday lives of young women and men whose groups are differentially endowed with social capital. These issues are examined through the experiences of three couples presented below in order from lowest to highest level of social capital.

The "Achievement Gang"

These students jokingly refer to themselves as the "Achievement Gang." The females play the role of encouraging and overseeing their male friends in the group. None of these students actually does very well in school, and, as a group, they have only a low level of social capital. They nevertheless see themselves as an "achievement gang" because they combine the elements of a pro-school ethos with gangster-like attire.

Betty, a sophomore, regularly checks up on her friends Jerry, a sophomore, and Benny, a freshman, throughout the day. She monitors whether they come to school, show up at their classes, and turn in their assignments on time. I ask Betty whether she provides other kinds of assistance, like helping her friends with their homework. In a bantering tone, with Jerry and Benny listening and laughing, Betty responds, "Man, I'm the one who needs help! And do I get it? No! From these guys? You know we're in bad shape if I am helping them." She throws some hard punches, but the young men are unfazed.

In a matter-of-fact tone, Jerry states that Betty helps him not to "mess up." This is important because he says he's "very weak" and easily tempted when someone asks him to "skip and go get high." Benny contends that his only weakness is his best friend, Jerry. He appreciates Betty's riding hard on Jerry because he knows that "if Jerry's in line, I won't skip." Jerry and Benny argue over which of them is the worst influence, but they both agree that Betty is a great influence. Jerry mentions that his mother encourages him to hang around with Betty because, in the past, whenever he's gotten into a group with "all guys," he inevitably "take[s] a wrong turn": "She knows I'm in good hands with Betty," he says, confidently. ("From one woman's arms to another," I mutter to myself.)

Jerry's comment about his mother reminds me of a conversation I had with a parent whose son, David, had run into serious trouble with some boys at school who threatened his life. Throughout middle school, this parent had cautioned her son to avoid other children, telling him, "At school, you are to have no friends! After school, you are to come straight home!" In practice, this directive led David to hang out exclusively with girls. This made his mother feel more comfortable, but David told me that having female friends was a mixed blessing, for it made other males extremely jealous. These jealousies followed him into high school and led to death threats. David's reaction was to transfer to another school before the end of his first six weeks.

Jerry's and David's mothers apparently believe that their sons' interests are best served by females who nurture and watch over them. For their part, the young women in the gender-mixed groups seem very comfortable with and uncritical of this role. The only resistance to gender-role expectations that I heard young women at Seguín express was directed at their parents' expectations.

Several weeks after the interview, I see Betty and Jerry holding hands as they walk slowly to class together. Out of curiosity, I ask them if they were already going steady at the time that I had interviewed their group. They reply that they had been going steady but were on shaky ground at that point.

In response to my question about what made the difference, Betty explains that she threatened to leave the group if Jerry and Benny skipped to get high one more time. After a big fight about this, Jerry and Betty again realized just how much they cared for each other. Jerry grits his teeth and admits that Betty has her "act together." Filling me in quickly on a great trip that he took with her family to Mexico one weekend, he also indicates that he likes and admires her family. A pensive Betty suggests that she's really not as together as she appears. "Next time, it's going to be me [messing up] and you'll do the same for me," she says.

Had I not spoken to Betty and Jerry this second time, I would have remained concerned about her relationship to these young men. As a friend, she helped Jerry to assess his academic trajectory and his goals. This process encouraged them to explore their relationship further. They both shared with me that they really want to graduate from high school and go farther than their parents had. It was Jerry who best expressed the relation between romance and achievement: "When you're steady, guys and girls leave you alone. I've seen enough of the 'punk scene.' Now it's time to focus on getting out of here." Hence, Betty and Jerry's relationship enabled them to articulate and act on instrumental goals at the same time that it foreshadowed their impending status as responsible future adults. While the support in this relationship was definitely tilted in Jerry's direction, the growth that he had undergone led Betty to expect that it would eventually tilt in her direction as well.

The Rappers

This group comprised two females and three males. All three males in the group share an interest in rap music. I meet them during the lunch hour in fall 1992 as they are huddled around a TV monitor that has somehow found its way into the school cafeteria. Unabashedly, the three males in the group dance to the beat of the rap tunes being sung by the rap artists on the music video that is being broadcast at the moment. With their baggy Girbaud jeans folded at the cuff, their gold necklaces, and a couple with baseball caps turned sideways, the three dancers come across as rather stylish in their appearance.

As students make their way into the cafeteria, the audience around them grows. After the rap tune ends, their dancing stops, and everyone observing them, including myself, applauds loudly. After their performance, they playfully bow, taking their caps off. With the crowd dispersing, their girl-friends laugh as the two males with the baseball caps fall backward into their arms. In the interview that I conduct with this group, I learn most about Norma and her relationship to her boyfriend, Chach. Norma and I hold the group's place at a nearby table as the rest enter the cafeteria lines to get food. During this several-minute interval, we warm up quickly to each other. After telling her that I'm writing a book and would like to see if she and her friends would like to be in it, Norma expresses immediate interest, "Sure, that sounds great!" Asking her to tell me about the guy who fell into her arms seems a logical place to start.

"So, who is that guy?" I ask.

"Oh, that's Chach!" she says. "He's a nut!"

After telling her that he dances really well, Norma shakes her head in disapproval. I ask her what is wrong. She then explains that, while she likes rap, she doesn't like it "if it gives you an attitude." I quickly confirm that he is her boyfriend and that she is very concerned about his cultural identity and commitment to school. She seems to think he needs her help in all kinds of ways.

Knowing that her group will be joining us shortly, she crams a lot of explanation into a few minutes. She divulges how her relationship to Chach has led her to spend more time on his homework than on her own. Admitting that her school work has begun to suffer, Norma justifies her invest-ment in her boyfriend's school work by saying that if she does not help him, "Chach will definitely drop out of school." She confesses that she is working on both her boyfriend's attitude toward school "and his taste in music."

Norma explains that none of Chach's teachers like him. He got in trouble with the law just once, and it was all downhill after that. "Don't take much to get a bad rep, you know." She claims that "helping Chach helps him to feel good about himself – you know, getting a good grade now and then." After every good grade, Chach takes Norma for a "really nice evening out on the town." She adds that doing Chach's homework teaches her "a lot." "It just doesn't show in my grades," she remarks, smiling.

Since both Norma and Chach are freshmen, I take the liberty of mentioning that they seem rather young to be dating. Norma replies that now that she's had her *quinceañera,* or her sweet fifteen ceremony, her parents feel that she is old enough to date. I ask her if her parents know how much she helps Chach. She says that she would never tell them, partly because they are not "too excited" about him.

"They think he's *agringado* (too white)," she explains.

"What about the time it takes away from your own work?" I probe.

"I make Bs and some Cs. Not bad if you ask me. As long as I'm not failing, they don't notice anything."

With respect to his taste in music, Norma is critical of Chach's interest in gangsta rap, which she believes is too violent and "talks too much about 'bitches and hos.'" She says that he needs to listen to more Mexican and *Tejano* (Texas Mexican) music.

"It's like he doesn't know who he is, like he wants to be black. So I always tell him to take me to *Tejano* clubs when we go out. He's starting to get into Selena, La Mafia, and Emilio Navaira. I feel kinda sorry for him."

Out of curiosity, I ask her if her boyfriend's attitude toward school and his taste in music have anything to do with one another.

"I think so. It's like he's angry and the music's angry. He can't understand why I'm not angry."

"Like with what?" I press her.

"You know, with whites and the system gettin' you down. It's a black thing. What I think is if he's more Mexican or *Tejano,* there's more to live for."

"What do you mean?" I query.

Norma either would not or could not explain.

"I don't know . . . but he's Mexican and I'm helping him to know it and feel good about it."

I am glad to have had these few minutes with Norma because she probably could not have made any of these statements before any of the members of her group. The group interview reveals the students to be friends from both the same neighborhood and the middle school that feeds into Seguín. Despite these similarities, the differences at least between Chach and Norma seem great enough to make me wonder how long they will remain together.

Fortunately, I run into Norma the following semester. Without my even asking, Norma volunteers, in halting speech, that she and Chach are no longer together. Since I can tell that she is hurting, I hug her and tell her that I am sorry.

"So you're no longer with your group either, huh?" I ask.

"No, how could I be? This is all so upsetting to me."

I ask Norma what happened. She replies that "the beginning of the end" happened one night toward the end of the fall semester when she was helping Chach study for an exam. In the middle of their session, he expressed his dismay with the whole "setup." He said that he was tired of school and that all of his teachers were against him. Norma responded by telling him that he was exaggerating. But then when he said that none were "for him," she couldn't disagree. "So I told him, 'I'm for you, Chach.' " "But this didn't work either," Norma continues. "He then got an attitude toward me and told me that he didn't need me either." At this point, Norma stops talking, attempting to remain in control of her emotions.

After a long pause, I tell her I am sorry. I then suggest to her that maybe with more time on her hands, she can dedicate herself more to her own studies.

"It's his self-esteem," she explains. "You can't love anyone if you can't love yourself." "You know," she continues, "I don't want to do this school thing alone. I know I can, but I don't want to," she responds, quietly. She tells me how now that Chach is not part of her life, school is less interesting. Somehow, Chach made her feel like everything was "in its place."

"It's like it made me feel important," she says.

"What did?" I ask.

"To know that I was helping him out," Norma reminisces.

"Even if it meant that your grades went down?" I suggest.

She defends Chach, saying that it wasn't his fault. She then rationalizes that her grades are not any better this semester anyway. With anxiousness in her voice, she says, "I just can't get into school right now. I'm not going to fail, but I'm not going to do too well this year. Maybe next."

This young woman is clearly in need of as much help and support as Chach ever was. Unfortunately, the only sense of direction that she conveys is that provided by her relationship with Chach. We spend a long time talking through her difficulties. Fortunately, as she has many other friends and is not one to withdraw into herself, her school work seems more at issue for me at the moment. She responds well to my suggestion that she try to organize a study group for her more difficult courses. I also suggest that it is not too early for her to be planning for college. She says that no one has ever talked to her about college but that she will definitely consider it.

While I at first thought that her breakup would get her out of an exploitative situation, I realized that matters were not so simple. Except for her grades, most things actually did seem to fall into place while she was with Chach. She went out on dates, was part of an interesting group of friends, and she was also more interested in school. She further derived a strong sense of stability and self-worth from having someone like Chach whom she felt needed her. I was able to glean from this and other discussions I had with students that in a fairly capricious environment, where students drop out in great numbers and where youth have few attachments to adults at school, they place a premium on the stability and continuity that relationships provide.

A number of unique conditions thus combine to form this kind of meaning system that equates romantic love with a pro-school orientation. I am not suggesting that Norma's orientation toward schooling was ever sufficient for her to reap unequivocal success. I merely suggest that within the confines of her social world, where few peer models of achievement exist for reasons that are largely attributable to subtractive schooling, Norma's interest in school – both for herself and her boyfriend – may be appropriately characterized as a pro-school orientation. While Norma understood her disaffection from schooling as related to her loss of connection from Chach, I doubt whether such a responsible and intelligent young woman would have arrived at such a conclusion in an academically rich environment composed of adults interested in her well-being and where numerous peer models for achievement exist.

Current Events/ESL/Students

I labeled this group this way because they most enjoy reading Spanish-language newspapers and watching Spanish-language television news. Graciela, a sophomore immigrant in the group, regularly completes her boyfriend Armando's homework assignments, forging his handwriting. She explains that she does his homework because the long hours he works at a local meat market leave him little time for school work. "*Lo hago porque él trabaja mucho [después de la escuela] y no tiene suficiente tiempo*" ("I do it because he works a lot [after school] and he doesn't have the time"). Graciela does not have a salaried after-school job, but her daily responsibilities at home include housework and taking care of three younger siblings for several hours until her parents return home from work. Given her own time constraints, I cannot help wondering whether what Graciela really means is that Armando's time is more valuable than hers.

I suggest to them that their actions will minimize Armando's learning if he doesn't do the work himself. "*Como quiera aprendo,*" ("I learn no matter what,") he counters. They maintain that he simply skips a step by reading over the work Graciela has already done. This arrangement, which evolved over time, began with Graciela translating the homework assignments Armando received in his regular (non-ESL classes) such as math and social studies, which are taught in English. Graciela fears that without her help, her boyfriend might fail.

"But what good is passing if you don't know the material?" I object.

With no apparent misgivings, both assure me that Armando is indeed learning. What strikes me as I talk with them is how perfectly able Armando appears. When I first joined the group for lunch that day, I interrupted a discussion they were having about the aftermath of the L.A. riots. Mentioning ex–Police Chief Darryl Gates, Peter Ueberroth – the political leader in charge of rebuilding South Central Los Angeles – and the impending trial of the three African American men accused of beating white trucker Reginald Denny during the riot, Armando demonstrated a thorough and up-to-date understanding of the intricacies of L.A. politics. Despite the many hours he may work at his after-school job, he clearly has time and energy available for watching and listening to news media.

The conversation then turns to a discussion about Graciela's parents, who are really strict and do not yet know about their romantic involvement. Since their relationship has gotten pretty serious, Graciela eventually plans to tell them. One of their friends, Jesús, asserts jokingly, "*¡Se quieren casar!*" ("They want to get married!") Perhaps out of nervousness with the subject of marriage, this comment makes us all laugh. Graciela nevertheless holds firm, saying in Spanish that she wouldn't be doing all that she is doing for Armando if they didn't have big plans.

"*¿Cuáles son sus planes?*" ("What are your plans?") I ask. Armando then explains that they would like to get married, go to college, and have children . . . "*algún día*" ("someday").

"*Qué jóvenes están ustedes,*" ("How young you two are,") I note. Graciela responds by saying that her parents were young, too, when they got married, and everything turned out fine. She feels confident that after her parents meet Armando that they, too, will understand why she's in love with him. Armando then interjects that Graciela tells him that he's exactly like her father's side of the family and that he'll fit in perfectly. Graciela then elaborates that her father is a musician who plays many instruments and that Armando plays guitar and sings. Like her father, Armando also loves going to the *pulga* (flea market) on Saturdays "*y tantas otras cosas,*" ("and many other things,") Graciela says, beaming.

"*Tú quieres mucho a tu papá,*" ("You love your father a lot,") I note.

With affection, she responds, "*Ay, sí*" ("Oh, yes").

In Spanish, I ask her how she thinks she'll break the news about their dreams to her parents. Graciela says that she plans to emphasize her college-going plans. When I ask them when they think they might go to college and when they think they'll get married, they are unclear how it will all work out for them. Graciela is especially unclear whether "*manteniendo a una familia*" ("maintaining a family") should occur before or after she goes to college. She phrases this concern in a way that suggests an inevitable sacrifice to her career rather than to Armando's. What is clear, however, is that what would most legitimate their relationship in Graciela's parents' eyes is her continued interest in education.

These rationalizations do not erase the fact that Armando is taking advantage of Graciela's generosity, especially in light of her many household responsibilities. As Graciela is a very bright and articulate student, I question whether she cannot or will not grasp the unfairness of this arrangement. Since her strategy is so deliberate, I am inclined to believe the latter. That Graciela herself dreams of someday "maintaining" her own family suggests how a mix of traditional and liberal gender role expectations forms her own personal ideology.

Olsen's ethnography of immigrant high school youth has direct bearing on Graciela's situation.[22] Olsen finds that when females' behavior is subject to strict parental monitoring, schools – and the relationships that naturally develop within them – become liberating places. At school, immigrant girls can exercise more fully their quest for individuality and independence. However, when this quest lands them into demanding and exploitative relationships, the sense of independent thought and action in a system of patriarchy is mere illusion. Ironically, it may be the girls' lifelong experience with stronger social control mechanisms that results in their ability to provide "safe spaces" for potentially wayward males. Thus, while the culture of romance that Graciela and Armando enact relies on the quest for education as its key source of legitimation, their system of exchange occurs at Graciela's expense – and ultimately at Armando's own, as well.

What I identify as problematic in *Subtractive Schooling* is the lopsidedness of the support system, with males not adequately reciprocating females' support. I interpret this uneven pattern of support as a reflection of females' nurturing role extending into the life of the peer group. While the data continue to suggest this imbalance, a more focused analysis of intimate relationships among youth reveals how the young women in these relationships have practical concerns, either about school or their futures. That is, rather than simply finding ways to express heterosexual love and attention, they also express a level of pragmatism that is more often characteristic of adult relationships. Building social capital and romantic relationships thus work in tandem to help these young women imagine and prepare for their future adult roles in society.

These young women's failure to see their inordinate contributions to their male friends' well-being as exploitative is attributable to a number of factors. While love is blinding, traditional gender role expectations are, too. Indeed, the power of convention helps explain why I never came across a situation in which a male assumed full responsibility for a female's school work. Another blinding factor is their enhanced sense of self-worth that derives from their enactment of stabilizing, adult-like roles. As a result, they neither see their support as a chore nor as the fulfillment of sexist expectations.

Instead, the girls appear to be involved in exchange relationships akin to the culture of romance that Holland and Eisenhart observed in their study of college-going white women. That is, the construction of a female identity in traditional terms invariably translates into compromises women – and, in this case, girls – make to secure the love and affection of a male. As Holland and Eisenhart suggest, young women derive pleasure from the thought that their interventions are crucial to their boyfriends' academic success and/or to their psychological well-being.[23] In contrast to the college-going women in their study, however, a pro-school ethos among the seriously romantic at Seguín is an entirely compatible proposition. Jerry may capture best an internal dynamic that may be operating for many couples: "When you're steady, guys and girls leave you alone." As the words of the young females also tend to convey, romantic relationships provide a secure, loving space that provides some measure of stability and protection in a difficult and capricious environment.

Unfortunately, the school unwittingly promotes a "survivalist" rather than an achievement-oriented mentality. When the hallways themselves are jampacked with anxious students attempting to maneuver their way to the next class within a brief, five-minute time span, it's not hard to feel objectified and preoccupied with one's own survival in this overcrowded, heavily bureaucratized environment. Since so much effort is dedicated to either avoiding or rectifying the kind of bureaucratic harm that often accompanies the processing of huge masses of students, one's placement within the academic hierarchy is scarcely an afterthought for most students within the regular track. Against this backdrop, it comes as no surprise to find a cultural meaning system that equates romance with a pro-school ethos.

The quality of school-related support that females are able to provide, as Betty explicitly notes, is contingent on their own abilities and prior academic training. The more academically adept, like Norma and Graciela, have much more to provide their boyfriends than the more academically challenged Betty. All three nevertheless purvey whatever measure they seem to possess. Since the provision of support appears to be a given, these young women would do well to assess how they provide the support they do provide. This concern especially emerges in the case of Norma and Chach, with Norma perhaps investing too much into Chach and, in so doing, repelling him. In the other cases, imbalances in the provision of support remain a central concern.

As social capital theory predicts, the potential of those enmeshed in exchange relations to achieve success increases, especially if a give-and-take process, like the one Betty expresses, develops. Indeed, within Betty's own group, Benny, her boyfriend's friend, benefits from Betty's concern for both. Taken together, the findings at once reveal how social capital and a culture of romance can work hand in hand. Although more research is needed on the subject, the evidence suggests that, for these young women, a culture of romance can provide both the connective interpersonal tissue that cements students to one another and the justification for social capital investments.

Although young females seem to indeed find academics more meaningful in and through these relationships, the precariousness of their schooling environment also seems to enhance the salience and hence the probability of close-knit relationships of various kinds, including heterosexual unions. It is unfortunate that regular-track females' capacity to give is oftentimes blunted by their weak academic skills even if their average grades are higher than those of their male peers. It is also unfortunate that gender inequality minimizes what would otherwise be a stronger collective impact of social capital. Institutional policies and practices like tracking that subtract resources from youth thus persist as a concern. They neutralize students' social capital and compromise the educational mobility of even the most talented. If Latinas are to emerge as leaders in the coming century, institutional constraints and traditional gender role expectations must be equally challenged.

NOTES

1. All names herein are pseudonyms.

2. Dorothy C. Holland and Margaret A. Eisenhart, *Educated in Romance: Women, Achievement, and College Culture* (Chicago: University of Chicago Press, 1990).

3. For more on social capital, see James S. Coleman, "Social Capital in the Creation of Human Capital," *American Journal of Sociology* 94 (1988): 95–120, and *Foundations of Social Theory* (Cambridge: Belknap Press, 1990); and Angela Valenzuela and Sanford M. Dornbusch, "Familism and Social Capital in the Academic Achievement of Mexican Origin and Anglo Adolescents," *Social Science Quarterly* 75:1 (1994): 18–36.

4. For more on these forms of capital, see Pierre Bourdieu and Jean-Claude Passeron, *Reproduction in Education, Society, and Culture,* trans. Richard Nice (Beverly Hills: Sage, 1977).

5. Ricardo Stanton-Salazar, "A Social Capital Framework for Understanding the Socialization of Racial Minority Children and Youth," *Harvard Educational Review* 67:1 (1997): 1–40.

6. I attended, either as an observer or as a participant, numerous school and community functions. School activities included pep rallies, orientation and registration activities, football games, speaker presentations, and parent and faculty meetings. I deliberately sought out students at times and in places when/where they were likely to congregate. These included the cafeteria area during the lunch hour, the hallways between class sessions, the girls' restrooms during some physical education classes, in front of school buildings before or after school, and under the stairwells and in other out-of-the-way places students favored throughout the day, especially when they were skipping classes.

I also conducted open-ended interviews with twenty-five groups of students from fall 1992 through the spring 1993 semester. I spoke with student groups of between two and eight members during their lunch hour. To qualify, group members had to be either ninth- or tenth-graders and to describe themselves as "close." My questions about their shared interests and factors that made them "close" resulted in the information for the present analysis.

Groups corresponded to the following major categories: immigrant, U.S.-born, and generationally mixed friendship groups composed of both immigrant and nonimmigrant youth. First-generation students were, along with their parents, born in Mexico. Second-generation students were born in the United States but have parents born in Mexico. Students were classified as third-generation if they and their parents were born in the United States. I use the self-referents "Mexican American" and "Chicana/o" and the term "U.S.-born" to refer to nonimmigrant, later-generation youth. Most of the interviews with immigrants were conducted in Spanish, while most of the interviews with U.S.-born and mixed-generation groups were conducted in English or "Spanglish," a combination of English and Spanish.

In addition to differences in generational status, the groups I interviewed also varied in their gender composition, some being mixed and some being single sex. The romantic couples investigated herein belong (or belonged) to gender-mixed friendship groups.

7. Angela Valenzuela, *Subtractive Schooling: U.S. Mexican Youth and the Politics of Caring* (Albany: State University of New York Press, 1999), and "Subtractive Schooling: U.S.-Mexican Youth and the Politics of Caring," in *Reflexiones: New Directions in Mexican American Studies* (Austin: University of Texas Center for Mexican American Studies, 1998).

8. In November 1992, I administered a questionnaire to all three thousand students at Seguín. It included questions about students' family backgrounds, English and Spanish language abilities, generational status, school climate, teacher caring, and academic achievement. With a 75 percent response rate, a sample of 2,281 students for analysis resulted.

9. For an example of a small-scale ethnography, see Mara Eugenia Matute-Bianchi, "Situational Ethnicity and Patterns of School Performance among Immigrant and Nonimmigrant Mexican-descent Students," in *Minority Status and Schooling: A Comparative Study of Immigrant and Involuntary Minorities,* ed. Margaret A. Gibson and John U. Ogbu (New York: Garland Publishing, 1991), 205–47. For examples of national-level data, see Alejandro Portes and Rubén G. Rumbaut, *Immigrant America: A Portrait* (Berkeley: University of California Press, 1990); Alejandro Portes and Min Zhou, "The New Second Generation: Segmented Assimilation and Its Variants," *Annals of the American Academy of Political and Social Sciences* 530 (1993): 74–96; Grace Kao and Marta Tienda, "Optimism and Achievement: The Educational Performance of Immigrant Youth," *Social Science Quarterly* 76:1 (1995): 1–19; and Barbara A. Zsembik and David Llanes, "Generational Differences in Educational Attainment Among Mexican Americans," *Social Science Quarterly* 77:2 (1996): 363–74.

10. Jorge Chapa, "The Question of Mexican American Assimilation: Socioeconomic Parity or Underclass Formation?" *Public Affairs Comment* 35:1 (1988): 1–14,

"The Myth of Hispanic Progress," *Harvard Journal of Hispanic Policy Issues* 4 (1990): 3–17, and "Special Focus: Hispanic Demographic and Educational Trends," in *Ninth Annual Status Report: Minorities in Higher Education* (Washington, D.C.: American Council on Education, Office of Minority Concerns, 1991); Herbert J. Gans, "Second-generation Decline: Scenarios for the Economic and Ethnic Futures of Post-1965 Immigrants," *Ethnic and Racial Studies* 15:2 (1992): 173–92; Frank D. Bean, et al., "Educational and Sociodemographic Incorporation among Hispanic Immigrants to the United States," in *Immigration and Ethnicity: The Integration of America's Newest Arrivals,* ed. Barry Edmonston and Jeffrey S. Passel (Washington, D.C.: Urban Institute Press, 1994), 73–100; and Valenzuela, *Subtractive Schooling.*

11. Alejandro Portes and Min Zhou, "Should Immigrants Assimilate?" *The Public Interest* 116 (1994): 18–33, and "The New Second Generation."

12. Robert D. Putnam, "The Prosperous Community: Social Capital and Public Life," *The American Prospect* 13 (spring 1993): 35–42, and "Bowling Alone: America's Declining Social Capital," *Journal of Democracy* 6:1 (1995): 65–78.

13. A number of assimilationist policies and practices are implicated in the process of subtractive schooling, including the consequences of "cultural tracking" (see Valenzuela, *Subtractive Schooling*). Cultural (nonacademic) tracking refers to the practice of separating Spanish- from English-speaking students through the English as a Second Language (ESL) program. ESL is a stigmatized track within the regular track. Inasmuch as there is any mobility out of the ESL track, it occurs horizontally with students moving into the English-only, regular-track curriculum. Never mind that many immigrant youth I came across entered U.S. schools with well developed cognitive skills about which their ESL teachers frequently boasted. Indeed, many had attended *secundaria* (known more formally as *educación media*) in Mexico.

Since only 16.9 percent of the total middle school-age population in Mexico attends *secundaria,* any *secundaria* experience is exceptional (see Gerald L. Gutek, *American Education in a Global Society: Internationalizing Teacher Education* [White Plains, N.Y.: Longman, 1992]). Though members of an elite group, they are seldom recognized or treated as such by school officials, including counselors who either do not know how to interpret a transcript from Mexico or who are ignorant about the significance of a postprimary educational experience. At least for youth emanating from the urban centers, anecdotal evidence suggests that *secundaria* is more rigorous than postprimary education in the United States. Comparisons are difficult to make, however, since the two systems are quite distinct. In Mexico, occupational and academic tracking occur immediately after *primaria,* depending on whether students are anticipating entering the labor market or university-level schooling, respectively.

14. Coleman, "Social Capital in the Creation of Human Capital," and *Foundations*

of Social Theory. See also, Valenzuela, *Subtractive Schooling;* Annette Lareau, *Home Advantage: Social Class and Parental Intervention in Elementary Education* (New York: The Falmer Press, 1989); and Stanton-Salazar, "A Social Capital Framework."

15. Although Coleman fails to extend this reasoning in his writings to the concept of cultural capital, a parallel logic can be inferred. See also Lareau, *Home Advantage*.

16. In contrast to U.S.-born youth, immigrants were typically found marshaling their resources to promote the academic well-being of their entire group. In accordance with their esprit de corps, pro-schooling ethos, their teachers often affectionately referred to them as "organized cheaters."

17. Although she did not control for track placement, Matute-Bianchi similarly observed this pattern in her study of generational differences in achievement at Field High, a school located in a central coast California agricultural community ("Situational Ethnicity").

18. Laurie Olsen, *Made in America: Immigrant Students in Our Public Schools* (New York: The New Press, 1997). Neither Olsen nor I should be interpreted as suggesting that immigrants should not be accorded their much needed, and oftentimes deficient, language support systems. Instead, we both take issue with how schooling fosters and legitimates divisions among youth, most notably through the stigmatizing ESL curriculum. While youth do enter schools with certain prejudices and attitudes, schooling is shown in both of our works to exacerbate these differences. In *Subtractive Schooling*, I suggest that a more inclusive, culture-affirming pedagogy would help reverse the effects of subtractive schooling, particularly the "loss" of students' language and culture.

19. Irene I. Blea, *La Chicana and the Intersection of Race, Class, and Gender* (New York: Praeger, 1992).

20. With counselors carrying caseloads of over three hundred students each, expediency rules in placement decisions. Because of their status, seniors are always attended to first and are therefore always among those whose schedules are "fixed" first.

21. Valenzuela, *Subtractive Schooling*.

22. Olsen, *Made in America*.

23. Holland and Eisenhart, *Educated in Romance*.

Frontiers 20:1 (1999): 60–79.

Sense and Responsibility

MARIBEL SOSA

We were never taught to believe that horizons were intangible things. The bold black line where the sky and earth met seemed always to exist only several miles away from our home, and, if our mother would only let us, my sister and I were positive that on a Saturday afternoon we could reach that line before it disappeared to the other side of the world. But we were at an age when we could also block out whole cathedrals, mountains, and moons with our right eyes squinting and the left ones shut, our thumbs held out, eclipsing the intended object. Our world seemed, to us, the center of the entire God-fashioned universe. My sister and I would sit on a couple of empty fertilizer pails drinking strawberry Kool Aid, leaning back against the trailer's aluminum walls, our legs dangling and swaying back and forth to an understood rhythm. There we would sit and contemplate the seconds it would take the mountains to engulf the sun, to transform gracefully from an immense royal blue, and to disappear and be replaced by the striking sincerity of the desert night. My parents never invaded or countered our wondrous musings; it was, instead, in town and at school where we learned to deal with perspective.

Both my parents had a very limited knowledge of English. Their English was forced, painful, unmelodious. They knew enough to get by. When we would go to town for visits to the dentist, to the bank, or to shop for groceries, my sister or I would translate for my mother. With age the novelty of it all wore off. It became apparent to us how people treated my mother, how they talked down to her and easily bypassed her. It became apparent how a person without possession of English went easily unnoticed. By fourth grade I refused to translate for my mother. I would, instead, sit off to the side in an uncomfortable, orange chair and watch her wrestle with a language that tore her throat and pained of shattered pride. Shame became synonymous with being Mexican, with speaking Spanish. Shame came when the women laughed, the ones who sat behind counters, who spoke to my mother, shouting like they were housebreaking some stupid, lazy dog. And when the words finally did emerge from my mother's throat, they were dry and gray, a mouthful of ashes that floated meaninglessly to the four blank walls of an air-conditioned office. After a while I even refused to go inside those offices with my parents. I would prefer to sit in the car, in one-hundred-and-ten degree weather, enraged, suffocated, and embarrassed rather than watch those people smile condescendingly at my father, who stumbled over his stubborn, heavy syllables and wrung the obscure vowels into the creases of his sombrero.

At home, though, my mother brought us up on Spanish. She would rub it slowly into our chests until the sore throat was gone, until we could return to school the next day and struggle with the cryptic sounds of instruction. Spanish, then, was the soothing voice of my mother reciting poems and prayers to me before I fell asleep. It was the faint memory of my grandparents singing love songs in the coolness of their adobe kitchen. Spanish was the sound I thought the stars must make. And when I heard love in Spanish it was the angels in church wanting and whispering to each other from across the altar.

English was functional, precise, and calculated. English was also *Sesame Street*, Bugs Bunny, Judy Blume, Laura Ingalls Wilder, Mickey Mouse, Big Macs, and movie stars. But perhaps, most importantly, English was the language of what really appeared to matter. English was the language of instruction, and when I sat in my school chair twisting my fingers into the shape of a cross under my desk, praying ten Ave Marias hard and determined so that the teacher wouldn't call on me, she still would. Even God, His mother, and all the saints, it seemed, would ignore my prayers if I did not recite them in English.

It would be easy to lie, to say that my elementary and middle school education was strenuous, but it really wasn't. It is much easier to learn a language at a young age, to let its grammar seep into one's unconscious. Unconscious, also, was my assimilation. The people I most respected at that time were my teachers – Ms. Reynolds, Ms. Tite, Ms. Fairbanks, Ms. Sexton, Mr. Cox, Mr. Kruse, and Mr. Applegate – and they were all white. I associated my parents with a different kind of knowledge. Theirs was the one of manners, of *Educación;* of "yes, sir," "no, ma'am," "thank you," "may I," and "please." My teachers had the knowledge of books. There were written sources behind their reasons. They were the progeny of Shakespeare, Washington, da Vinci, Lincoln, Kennedy, the Declaration of Independence, Custard, the Alamo. Their ancestors had so valiantly defeated the Indians for us; they had traversed a frozen Delaware for us, sailed the Mayflower, and walked on the moon for us. How in any way could they not be right? And us, the Indians, the Mexicans, the poor, white trash, what did we have? From what glory had we sprung? My pride was in my country, in my founding fathers, in the great nation of English. Mexican, my Spanish accent, was my burden and I was expected to rise above it.

By the time I was in first grade I was reading at or above the level of my English-speaking peers. It tormented me to wonder why my parents couldn't do the same. My mother, especially, caused me some anguish those first years in school. I wanted her to be heard, to act as confidently as she seemed to at home. I needed her to have conversations with my teachers instead of nodding her little, grateful smile to the praise and advice I knew she only half understood. My sister and I were learning English and speaking it more often in the home, and my mother happily encouraged it. She would save what money she could and subscribe to children's magazines and book clubs. Kids from our trailer park would come over to play and would end up, instead, with a book in their hands. She was never jealous or afraid that we would lose our Spanish, that we would someday forget how to speak to her. If she was concerned to even the slightest degree, she must have kept it well concealed in order for my sister and me never to think twice that the acquisition of English could cause some sort of rift between us.

The memories left from those days are slight bruises, small nips of growing pains. Perhaps if I had grown up in a segregated ghetto of East L.A. or in a small barrio of South Tucson instead of the rural farm-working community of Poston, Arizona, things might have been different. Perhaps if I had been born to different parents instead of the ones who drilled it into my child's conscious that we should work our minds hard in school and that the body could only last so long: Work your mind hard now so you can save your body later. An A was rewarded with great praise from my teachers, an ice-cream cone from my mother, and an occasional smile from my father. Bs he considered disastrous and required ample explanation. Bs were followed with loud litanies, what seemed like endless lectures.

"Look at me. Look at me," he said. "Me only go to fourth grade, but you think I be stupid? You think your father stupid? No, I work hard; I have my house, my car, my job. You do better next time."

Sometimes my sister and I would laugh, thinking it all trite exaggeration, but eventually we came to accept the reality of it all, especially after the summers that we would spend in Mexico, or, when we were older, the summers that we would work in the fields. My father wanted us to understand the concept of hard labor, so he arranged with one of his friends to have us work in the fields, cleaning cotton and packing melons. My mother cried and asked him please not to make us go, that maybe we could get a job in town, we knew English, we did well in school. But my father's mind could not be changed. He woke us up one morning at three thirty so we could be at the fields by four.

During those long, summer weeks I learned to appreciate the great dignity in the job of the field-worker. It is immensely physical, the hours demanding, the pay substandard, and the status obsolete. I realized how honorable and necessary those jobs are, but I could also discern how such jobs also act as holding bars, restrictive chains that grip down the hopes of the spirit and encourage quiet acquiescence. Perhaps it is not the jobs themselves that are oppressive; perhaps it is the poverty that they perpetuate that is, in the long run, more destructive. I became aware that it was not pity that I experienced when I saw Mexican and Native American workers out in the fields, rather it was anger. I was angry that a fifty-five-year-old woman was still out there, in the fields, back bent and doubled over her old spade, so disheartened that none of her children had escaped the same fate. I was angry at the wages, the tepid drinking water, the stinking portable toilets. Angry at the ignorant kids who would drive by the fields yelling, "*¡La migra! ¡La migra! ¡Córrenle! ¡Allí vienen!*" ("Immigration! Immigration! Run! They're coming!") And these proud, hardworking people would run for cover into the nearest dried-up irrigation ditch. At times pure instinct would drive me into wanting to run with them, but in the briefest seconds I would recognize that I would never need to share their fears. I was there only to learn a lesson and their fate would not be mine.

The summer I spent at college preparing for my freshman year, my younger sister spent back home working in the packing sheds sorting melons. I realized how different our two worlds had become when I came home from that summer and noticed, when I hugged my sister, how her thick braid smelled of sweat and the trailer of soup and stale lard. For two months my roommates ceaselessly complained that the air conditioner in our dorm room wasn't cool enough, while my mom worked in a windowless factory where the swamp cooler broke down routinely, my sister had only the luxury of a shade over her work, and the only thing that protected my father was his long-sleeved jumper and green John Deere baseball cap. As my roommates constantly protested the lack of space and privacy, I was in complete awe that my dorm room encompassed the same living area that my whole family shared for so many years.

When we reunited at the end of the summer, my sister could sense my discomfort. After she hugged me, all she could say was that if my head were a melon she could fit six to a box. I was treated as a guest by our neighbors. I was the stranger, the one who had changed, become lighter from staying indoors. And I suppose I acted like it. I became something of a tourist, knowing that I didn't have to stay there, that I could observe and relegate the experience to mere memory. I found the manner in which the adults wanted to make me more comfortable, turning the metal electric fan toward only me, so strange. They pointed me out to their children, asked me to talk to them, thought maybe they'd do better in school. I remember those little girls now. Most of them are either married or separated, but they all have children, their men all work in the fields, and they all live in run-down trailers exactly like the one I grew up in.

In a few days none of it was to matter. It was mid-July in rural northwestern Arizona. The melon crop was just about to rot over, and the waves of flies and the stench of cantaloupe skin shriveling up in the dry, desert air extended for many acres. But I don't remember really wanting to leave. My mother, with all her coupons, had stocked me with at least a two-months' supply of shampoo, soap, toothpaste, cleaning supplies, and twelve brand-new pairs of Hanes cotton underwear from Kmart. She had bought me some canned food and was packing it carefully into a large cardboard box. The box was stamped on its sides with "USDA." I could only imagine the complete sets of Hugo Bosca luggage the other girls had, compared to the brown garbage bags where my shorts and jeans and shirts were packed. My mother must have picked up on something and, although she was hurt and saddened, she understood; without a word having been said, she repacked the cans into plain, brown paper bags from Safeway.

The last sleepless night I spent in my twin bed, with my back against the plywood wall of the trailer and my sister's head in my lap, where finally I must have fallen asleep, stroking her long, brown hair with my nervous fingers. The day my family dropped me off at the dorm, my sister had on her favorite pair of purple denim shorts that were barely held together at the seams by shredded thread. She was wearing her favorite T-shirt, an ugly, bleached-out lilac one with holes everywhere. I was embarrassed by my father, the swagger in his walk, the braggart's confidence his Stetson gray felt cowboy hat exuded. It was an attitude that didn't compare, in any way, to the easygoing smiles of the other fathers, the sherbert-colored polo shirts they wore, the tennis shoes, the Dockers slacks and Ralph Lauren shorts. And there was my father in his cowboy boots, his eyes so sad, defensive, and watered-down. My sister left without saying a word. She wanted me to admit that I was embarrassed by her: "You're so stupid. Clothes don't matter. What should you care what I'm wearing? At least I'm clean." And my beautiful mother, full of pride and contentment, put my clean sheets on the bed, folded my few clothes away into the drawers, and held on to me. She didn't have to remind me to be good, to have good manners, to do well in school. She just had to hold me for a while longer, just a little longer she implored my father who was becoming impatient and could only say, "I know you do good *cosita*, you smart girl, you do good." He slipped me two fifty-dollar bills and told me to call whenever I needed more money. The rent that my family paid for the lot in the trailer park was a hundred dollars; my room was at least double that amount.

The room was cool, empty, and, at least until my new roommate was there, it was all mine. There was a tremendous freedom in walking down to the student union and actually buying lunch. Bagels! What a marvelous, beautiful, delicious invention. I couldn't finish my sandwich. Halfway through I wondered when my parents were to eat the white-bread-and-bologna sandwiches they would eat somewhere off the side of the road. It was then that I realized, fully, the expense it was for them to have me at the university.

Once my first fall semester of college began, everywhere I turned it seemed as if waves of lily-white people would come flooding at me. In my smaller classes, by some rare coincidence, I would be the only Chicana student. I kept wondering where the 15 percent minority population the school boasted of was hiding itself. I compensated for my lone ethnicity by trying to prove myself to my classmates and my teachers. I overstudied, overwrote, and overrevised everything. It seemed that the whole school had this marvelous vocabulary of expression and experience, and my inadequate small-town education would never measure up.

I was terrified of not being up to par with the other students. I never said anything in class and would instead sit in the back row, sheltered behind my long hair from making eye contact with my instructor. I remember being especially preoccupied with doing decent work in my freshman composition class. When conference time came around, I was absolutely petrified.

Sitting there in the freshness of my instructor's anticipation, I could only think to push the paper into her hands and search frantically for something to focus my stare on. She was young, optimistic, and kind.

"It's lovely, Maribel, simply lovely," she said.

I mumbled an incredulous "thank you" and stumbled out of her office. From the back of my mind kept pounding the sentiment: "It's Mexican, Maribel, it's Mexican. That's why she likes it. That's why you wrote it. Just remember to throw in a couple tortillas, the color bronze, and scatter a few rosaries about, and you're there."

I felt irresponsible, foolish. As if I were disappointing, mocking someone or something as great as the remembered shadow of my mechanic father who melted under the hoods of cars. My father, who once took me to Mexico and made me listen to his people's stories: "Pay much attention, big birdee, they're verree *importante,* someday you write about them, don't forget." He was there when I wrote, and his presence wouldn't allow me to make a freak show of his pride. I saw my parents everywhere in dark, hurried glimpses around campus. The woman who cleaned the toilets in my dorm was Mexican. The man raking leaves outside was Mexican. The whore on the corner was Mexican. The scoured drunk on the street was Mexican. The most recently captured murderer on the six o'clock news was Mexican. My warm, precious mother was Mexican, and my strong, pensive father was Mexican.

Being Mexican, it seemed, had worked to some advantage. Especially when I wrote. In junior high and high school, English had always been my favorite subject. In my writing (especially the pieces my instructors admired the most) my Mexicanness would almost always come up. I would abuse this topic to the point of absurdity, where it became some blunt edge for the anger I harbored toward my identity. I was using the name again, just to get that A I knew was waiting if I wrote about the splendors of the Sonoran Desert, the Taruhumara Indians my father grew up among, or the fact that my childhood friends had all had *quinceañeras* and never even bothered to send me an invitation because I associated mostly with Caucasian people. My teachers, I believe, would praise my paper for its content. They would overlook my ambitious, adjective-strewn writing and say, "You have an obligation to write about these places, these people; not everyone has the chances that you do." This sentiment was echoed in my father's voice.

I found it easy, then, to vent my frustrations on paper, as if I had been granted permission to write about the fact that my mother had never learned English, that I came to favor the heavy metal urgency of Metallica over the romantic ballads of Agustin Lara, that I sat alone for hours at a Mexican dance while my dark-skinned, younger sister danced endless *corridos* in the arms of a Mexican boy. I always possessed this horrid feeling of inadequacy for not being white, for not being Mexican enough. I had decided, since an early age, that I would "fit in." It was mostly embarrassment that drove me to it.

Last week my father called me. He was drunk; his speech was slurred, he had been crying, and was alone.

– You were happy, right *m'ija?* You never need nothing, *¿verdad?*
– Sure.
– *Dime pues,* what did you need that you didn't have?
– A house.
– You have a house.
– *Pero papi, es una trailer, está vieja, y sucia.* How can you live in that trailer? It's falling apart.
– No, *usted no sabe lo que es sufrir m'ija. Usted tuvo todo.*[1]
My father pauses, takes a drink.
– *¿Qué ha escrito m'ija? Aver cuénteme.*[2]

NOTES

1. You don't know what it is to suffer. You had everything.
2. What have you been writing, Daughter? Tell me.

The Making of a Token

A Case Study of Stereotype Threat, Stigma, Racism, and Tokenism in Academe

YOLANDA FLORES NIEMANN

Ethnic/racial minority faculty continue to be underrepresented in the U.S. professoriate, representing only about 6 percent of all professors in the academy.[1] Obstacles for reaching the academy abound, including institutional racism, socioeconomic barriers, and, for Latinas, traditional gender role expectations.[2] Once Latinas overcome these obstacles and "make it" into the academy, they, like other faculty of color, face yet another set of obstacles, including experiences of racial tokenism, overt and covert racism, and stigmatization. These experiences are generally grounded in the undermining attitudes and behaviors of people within the institution.

Largely as a result of these experiences, faculty of color may also undermine their own competence. That is, they may fall victim to stereotype threat, which is defined as being vulnerable to internalizing the negative stereotypes about one's own group in a given situation, even when one does not endorse these stereotypes.[3] A prevalent stereotype about Latinas/os and African Americans is lack of competence in academic domains, making faculty from these groups particularly vulnerable to the self-undermining effects of stereotype threat.[4] This situation reflects a threat and vulnerability independent of the behavior and attitudes of colleagues. As a result, the obstacles faced by faculty of color involve interactive forces of two types of undermining – that done by others, and the self-undermining of competence.

Such was the case with my first faculty experience. I went from having strong feelings of self-efficacy in the academy to wondering why I had the arrogance to think I could succeed in an academic career. Only distance from that experience has enabled me to analyze the processes that occurred during those first four shaky years as an assistant professor. Based on a daily journal I kept during that time period, the following is an analysis of that situation in which I illustrate how the insidious, psychologically damaging processes of stereotype threat, tokenism, stigma, and related racism may occur. While publishing this personal essay represents a certain amount of personal risk, I believe it is important to openly discuss the effects of what is a reality for many people of color in academia. It is my hope that this article will help illuminate these processes such that others either just entering academia or struggling to survive in the academy may benefit from enhanced awareness of pitfalls associated with being a scholar of color. Awareness can lead to prevention and facilitate coping. Institutions attempting to recruit and retain minority scholars may also gain insight on the undermining processes that might occur for faculty of color at various levels of the institution.

THE RECRUITMENT PROCESS

Until I was offered a tenure-track position, my graduate experience in a rigorous social science program of a large, predominantly white, urban university was relatively uneventful. I was a very successful graduate student, having defended my master's thesis, sailed through most of my course work, completed my doctoral minor, successfully completed my comprehensive exams, and moved my way toward defending my dissertation proposal – all within a three-year period. I had also lobbied for, and been allowed to develop and teach, the first course on ethnic/cultural issues in the department. My advisors referred to me as a "star student" in the program. Then, in my third year of the program, and two weeks before my dissertation pre-orals, the chair of the department (who was also my principal advisor, chair of my dissertation committee, and director of the program) called me into his office, and everything about my experience at the university began to change – from very good to very bad. Yet the day began with seemingly good news for me.

The chair informed me that a junior faculty had just tendered her resignation (she left for a more prestigious university). He further stated that the dean had given the department permission to replace that faculty member, but with the very strong encouragement that the department hire a Mexican American or African American faculty member. At that time there were about thirty tenure-stream faculty in the department – all white, and only a handful of women. The department had been under fire from the faculty-of-color associations on campus for this lack of representation. The chair enthusiastically reported that the faculty wanted me to apply for the tenure-track position and that they believed I could be successful in achieving tenure at the institution. He further elaborated that under no circumstances should I think I was getting the opportunity because I was Mexican American; it was just a coincidence that my ethnicity met with the dean's preference. I asked the chair about the extent of the search, and he replied that they had other applications on file to consider and that they would be working hard to put out feelers for others, but that I was considered the leading candidate.

I was surprised, as the university was not known to hire its own students, and I was quite flattered by what I then interpreted as my faculty's faith in my competence and their eagerness to keep me around. In terms of the ethnicity requirement, I reasoned that because affirmative action was still a viable hiring tool in most universities, my ethnicity would likely have been a factor at any institution. I was then too naive to realize that the dean's ethnicity preference was undermining me before I even interviewed, especially given the anti-affirmative action sentiment in that department.

There is strong documentation for the idea that a stigma of incompetence arises from the affirmative action label,[5] especially when the label carries a negative connotation in the hiring department.[6] Once tagged as an affirmative action hire, colleagues may discount the qualifications of the hiree and assume she was selected primarily because of her minority status, thus leading to the presumption and stigma of incompetence.[7] Beginning with the recruitment and hiring process, academics of color may be vulnerable to stereotype threat and begin consciously or unconsciously to internalize stigmatizing myths and stereotypes relative to academia.[8] In my case, the stigma of incompetence and my tokenization began almost immediately with the dean's strong request that the new faculty be African American or Mexican American. However, I was then unaware of the processes taking place that would undermine my competence and my colleagues' perception of me. Unawareness equaled blindness and exacerbated my vulnerability.

In retrospect, the signs of my harsh future in the department were glaring. For instance, a white, female junior faculty member spent the entire interview time with me relaying how much she was against affirmative action. I dismissed her behavior by convincing myself that if she knew how competent I was, she would not think of me as an affirmative action hire. Another sign of future trouble was that an unusually small number of the faculty showed up for my colloquium. This was particularly unsettling because, in this rigorous research department, the faculty generally wanted to know if potential faculty members could conduct and discuss research. They couldn't evaluate me as a scholar if they were not present to assess my performance in the colloquium.

I learned later that the program's faculty had been "explaining the situation" to faculty in other department programs and lobbying them to vote for me. In essence, then, the decision to hire me was made before my colloquium. Still, I could not bring myself to think that this lack of interest in my research skills meant they didn't see me as a scholar. I convinced myself that many of the department faculty already knew me and respected my ability.

At about that same time the director of an ethnic studies program asked me to apply for his program's postdoctoral fellowship (post doc). We both reasoned that the post doc would allow me a year of distance from my advisors before becoming their colleague. Post doc positions are often coveted by new Ph.D.'s as a way to begin achieving their independence from training professors and to get their research off the ground before becoming fully engaged in a tenure-track position. This turn of events seemed fortuitous. I informed my department chair that I was also applying for the ethnic studies position and, since he was my principal advisor, that I would need a letter of recommendation from him. He said he would do it, but reluctantly, because my program was counting on me.

Shortly after my colloquium I was offered both positions. My department's vote had been unanimous, with one abstention. I was later told by a voting faculty member that someone at that meeting had asked about my possible post doc and that the chair had immediately said the department wasn't interested in that for me, and it was not to be discussed. Still, I convinced myself that the department was just afraid to lose me.

The day after the department's vote, I received anonymous racist hate mail in my department mailbox. I immediately took the letter to the department chair, who stated that he was horrified at the letter's content but took no action on the letter. He advised me to ignore it, saying it could happen anywhere. He said he wanted to keep the letter, and I naively gave it to him. Incredibly, *I felt ashamed* for having received such a letter, a symptom of stereotype threat. I felt somehow responsible for having received hate mail.

I was so embarrassed that I didn't even tell the dean about the hate mail. I did tell him that I wanted the year of post doc, to be followed by the tenure-track position in my department. He told me that such an arrangement was not unusual and that universities often waited for a new faculty member who had a fellowship and/or was on leave. He agreed that the extra year to get my research off the ground would give me an edge, especially since I was completing graduate school so quickly. The dean further said that he could arrange it so that my tenure clock would not begin until after the year of post doc and, that as far as the college was concerned, I would be a department faculty member on a year's leave of absence, so my faculty position would be secure. I was excited; things seemed to be taking a turn for the better.

This excitement was replaced with the foreboding of upcoming trouble when I subsequently met with the department chair. He told me in no uncertain terms that the department's wishes were that I accept only their position. He further stated that I should consider that memories die hard and that the department could hold it against me on my future tenure vote. He explained that I should keep in mind that the current dean might or might not have the power to help me in the future. He also stated that a senior program faculty member, who was quite powerful because he brought in extensive grants (hereafter referred to by my pseudonym for him, Dr. Grant), had lobbied the department heavily for me, and I should be grateful.

My reaction, kept to myself, was that I would have preferred it if the faculty had voted for me because they had been impressed with my colloquium and competence, and not due to political lobbying. I felt stigmatized to learn that someone had to lobby department faculty to vote for me. Was I a charity case? Now my ego was beginning to feel the blow. I slowly began to question my own competence. After all, these were smart people with experience in academia. Did they know something I did not know? Besides affecting me personally, the stigma of incompetence, facilitated by the "lobbying," consciously or unconsciously allowed my future colleagues to begin thinking of me not as a fellow scholar, but as a token minority.

The prospect of staying at that university now seemed unappealing. I dearly wished I had immediately said no to the chair when he first made the offer and that I had never mentioned it to my family or to the ethnic studies director. At the time of the offer, however, the temptation to stay in that department was great for several reasons. For instance, I would not have to endure the stress of going out on the job market the following year, as I had planned. Job hunting is an anxiety-provoking experience for most graduate students, and I was no exception.

However, my most compelling reason to stay was my family. My husband had a well-paying job, and our children, then fourteen and eleven, were happy, settled, and had established long-term friendships. When I told them about the offer to stay in my current department they were thrilled. They would get to stay in school with their friends and continue with their sports teams. They were so relieved not to have to move out of town. My husband had faithfully supported me, economically and emotionally, throughout graduate school. After my announcement of the job opportunity, we started talking about how, with both of us employed, we could finally pay our debts and save some money for our children's college education.

I had dealt with role strain as a graduate student, making sure that I attended all of my children's extracurricular activities. Consistent with Latina/o values, my family had always come first. As I began to see ominous signs of trouble for me in the department, I was put to the test: do what is in my best professional interest, or what seemed to be in my family's interest? From the time I told my family about the job opportunity and felt their reaction, I really did not believe I had the option of applying for a job in another city.

Other role strain affected my decision, especially my role as a student with strong ties to the chair of the department, who had been my principal advisor for three years. Until this situation, he had treated me respectfully and had spoken highly of my course work and research. The ties between graduate students and advisors are strong, but the power is always with the professor. His power in that role was still very evident when he asked me to apply for the job. However, his ability to advise me was now diminished. He was chair of the department and director of the program at the same time, so he acted on behalf of program and department interests. A lesson here to future job candidates is that, when the job offer is in your own department, your advisor may find it difficult to be loyal both to the department and to you.

In terms of deciding which position to accept, the pull involved personal and political loyalty to the ethnic studies program, which had been very generous in supporting me. I wanted the post doc year to get my research started without the ticking of the tenure clock. On the other hand, I still wanted eventually to be successful in the social science tenure-track position. I remembered the chair's threat – what if they made me pay by denying me tenure?

It seemed to be widely known in the department that I was strongly considering the ethnic studies position. A senior faculty member called me into his office and said I needed to answer one question: "What are you, a scholar or a Mexican American?" He said that if I answered Mexican American, I should take the post doc but not follow it with the department position because "the department is only interested in scholars, not Mexican Americans." I replied that I didn't cease to be Mexican American by becoming a scholar any more than he ceased to be a man when he got his Ph.D. He retorted that it wasn't the same thing and that I should give the matter serious thought. He also said that other faculty shared his views.

It had never occurred to me to choose between my ethnicity and my identity as a scholar – it was neither possible nor logical. Before this experience, my holistic identity included being mother, wife, scholar, social scientist, friend, Mexican American, and woman. Separating them would be like expecting my major organs to work independently of each other in my body. I was bewildered.

This struggle to separate aspects of themselves will likely affect other ethnic/racial minorities applying for academic jobs. It is critical for ethnic/racial minorities to understand that the forced duality (scholar or Mexican American) is a facade. For women, in particular, identity includes, at minimum, issues of being a woman in a male-empowered academic workplace, personal role issues (e.g., mother and wife), professional roles, as well as ethnicity. Nevertheless, the forced duality reinforced the feelings of tokenism and, by extension, of stigmatization and stereotype threat. The professor had made it seem like being Mexican American was a disease.

The duality was further played out in the tug-of-war for me between the social science department and ethnic studies program. The pull was so great that the department chair asked a respected Mexican American tenured professor to "arbitrate" between the department and the ethnic studies program and convince the program director to persuade me to accept only the department position. I now felt guilty because there was disagreement among campus Mexican American faculty about what should be occurring with my situation. I felt as if everyone was talking about me. This sense of extreme visibility is consistent with the experience of tokenism.[9] My identity as Mexican American was more salient to me than ever before in my life, and my holistic sense of self was being shattered.

I began to have trouble sleeping and focusing on my classes (I was still a third-year graduate student). My close friends, most of whom were also students in the department, were greatly concerned about me. The stress showed so much that the professor of the department's ethics course, the only female full professor in the department, approached me to discuss my options. She was quite fair and said she believed the post doc would give me the needed distance from my advisors before becoming a member of the department faculty. She also thought the year would give me more respectability (someone else valued my work) and diffuse the perception that the department was strong-armed into hiring me without a search. I had not yet even been hired, and already I was stigmatized and tokenized by the perception that the department was forced to hire me. The reality was that the department faculty did not take the time and effort to widely solicit other candidates for the position. I was the one paying the price for their reliance on convenience.

The ethics professor was so concerned about the political ramifications of my accepting the post doc that she made arrangements to become my dissertation chair (replace my current chair) if I should accept the post doc. That way, reprisals from the faculty might be minimized. She had reason to be concerned about my future as a student. I had rapidly gone from being a "star student" in my program to being thought of as a potential problem. She explained that the department faculty felt a sense of benevolence for having offered me the tenure-track position. I was told that they were incredulous that I would consider postponing working with them to work with the ethnic studies program for one year.

MY EXPERIENCE AS A FACULTY MEMBER

I accepted the social science department position and turned down the post doc. I convinced myself I could make this situation work, in spite of my newfound awareness of the racism of some members of the department. As a Mexican American woman raised in economic poverty and the daughter of two people with third- and seventh-grade formal educations, I had overcome obstacles before. Although my identity was in turmoil, and I felt stigmatized by the hiring process, I had retained substantial confidence in my ability to achieve tenure and believed things would be different after I was "one of them." It didn't occur to me that I would never feel like I belonged there. My competence had not yet been completely undermined. I defended my dissertation in July (having collected all the data, analyzed it, and written the results and discussion since my pre-orals in April). One month later, after only three years as a social science graduate student, the tenure clock started ticking, and my life in the department went from a bad hiring experience to an even worse faculty experience. I was about to feel the interactive, psychologically damaging effects of others' racism and my internalized racism.

Stigmatization

The social science department's failure to conduct a national search for my position had created legal problems for the university administration, which had received complaints about my hiring process. One of the Mexican American faculty from the law school had to present legal precedents to the administration for my hiring to be approved. It seemed that the circumstances surrounding my hire had become common knowledge in the university. I felt that when people saw me they believed, "She's the one the dean forced the social science department to hire." I felt lonely and stigmatized.

I believed I had alienated the ethnic studies faculty who might now see me as a traitor for not taking their post doc. In the social science department, except for some polite greetings, I had little or no conversation with colleagues. The faculty distanced themselves from me and made no attempts to mentor me or facilitate my road toward tenure. As for the ethics professor, I was not sure whether she had the interests of the department, rather than mine, foremost in her mind, so I did not trust her. I did not trust the department. I did not know whom to trust!

This lack of trust is debilitating for junior faculty who are still in the early stages of their professional development. Generally, feedback allows us to improve, but in situations where colleagues may be two-faced and/or racist, feedback becomes meaningless. Improvement thus happens much more slowly because we have less feedback to work with. This situation is exacerbated for faculty of color and can permeate all professional interactions, in and out of the institution. Research indicates that due largely to the societal prevalence of racism in society, people of color often make attributions about race when considering feedback or reactions of others to them, *whether the feedback is positive or negative.*[10] Once the boundary of distrust is crossed, we cannot will ourselves into trusting again in that environment. The cycle of not trusting any feedback continues, even when it is self-defeating.

For instance, I received fairly positive reviews with a request for a revision on a paper I submitted to one of the top journals in my field of social science. However, that feedback was inconsistent with the racism and stigmatization I felt from the department. The positive feedback was therefore disorienting. I did not know what to believe. I had begun undermining my competence and did not have the confidence to submit a revision. I later learned that the editor had put that paper in a file indicting the revision would have a 70 percent chance of acceptance, but he never got my revision, an example of self-undermining behavior.

Tokenism and Covert Racism

During my first year I was the only faculty of color in the entire department. My colleagues seemed content with that situation and oblivious to its effects on me. I was told, "Now that we have you, we don't need to worry about hiring another minority." This sentiment is an example of covert racism in academia, which includes the "one-minority-per-pot syndrome."[11] This tokenism also occurred with social science graduate students. For instance, in my first year as faculty, I argued to bring in two Latina graduate students with excellent credentials, though other program faculty disagreed with me. After I persuaded faculty to conduct a person-to-person interview with these women, both were found acceptable, but I recall Dr. Grant arguing that "one minority is enough." I accused him of tokenism and insisted that both women get into the program. The faculty reluctantly agreed.

One of the effects of tokenism is what is known as the pressure of a double-edged sword: "simultaneously, a perverse visibility and a convenient invisibility."[12] That is, I was inordinately visible as a minority female in a predominantly white, male department. I was also visible when it was in the department's best interest to have an "ethnic scholar," such that my name, teaching, and research were brought up during site visits of the national program accrediting association and during visits of international scholars and elected officials of color. Even some of the well-meaning faculty seemed oblivious to this tokenism. For instance, after one of these visits, one of my senior colleagues pulled me aside and excitedly said, "We told them all about your class and your research! They were really impressed with our diversity." I believed this colleague was well-intentioned and that his comment was meant to be encouraging and supportive. However, the effect of the statement was one of feeling tokenized and devalued as a scholar. I felt representative of all ethnic/racial minorities and believed that the department cared only about the *appearance* of diversity without actually valuing diversity. In such a manner, people who are well-meaning and unaware of their own racism contribute to a racist climate.

In my second year as faculty, an African American woman was hired in another department program. Her presence helped diffuse some of the attention from me. However, her research and teaching were considered mainstream while I was considered the "ethnic" researcher. This label also meant that my research was undervalued and not considered scholarly, an experience consistent with that of other faculty of color who believe that they, and their research, are underrated and seen primarily as affirmative action cases and only secondarily as scholars in their own right.[13]

My increasingly salient ethnic identity continued to play a role in relations with colleagues. In program faculty meetings, I was the only person who openly argued in favor of admitting minority graduate students. The other faculty wanted to "be objective" and "color-blind." One of the biggest ironies of this whole situation was that the department "party line" was that they were color-blind and only saw people. This attitude, in conjunction with racist behaviors, is consistent with what has been labeled "aversive racism." Aversive racists are people who outwardly proclaim egalitarian values but who express racism in subtle, rationalizable ways, such as unfair hiring procedures with respect to nonwhite group members.[14] It was hypocritical, then, that the department paid attention to race/ethnicity when it was in their interest.

For instance, one of the Latinas whom I was successful in getting admitted into the program had worked with me as an undergraduate and wanted to be assigned as my advisee. However, Dr. Grant argued that he needed minorities on his team for the sake of getting grants and had her assigned to him. In a related occurrence, I learned that Dr. Grant had listed me as an unpaid consultant for a grant in which the granting agency required ethnic/racial expertise – without ever asking my permission or discussing this grant with me.

I was told that Dr. Grant routinely made negative, cutting remarks about me personally, about my teaching, and about my research. I learned about many of these remarks from the people who worked for him, as he did not seem to have any qualms about openly disparaging me. As one of my colleagues told me, "Dr. Grant is not your friend. Watch your back." When I discussed Dr. Grant's behavior toward me with the department chair, he advised me just to dismiss the remarks and not to take him seriously. He argued that, after all, no one would really listen to such comments from Dr. Grant. He was wrong, as was evident later in my "third-year review."

I was furious with the chair's response but did nothing. I didn't have the courage or know-how to file a claim with the university center for human rights. This lack of action went against my sense of personal integrity, and, consequently, my self-esteem further plummeted. I "contained" my anger and gained forty pounds, most of it within my first year as an assistant professor. I began to question why I ever thought I would do well in academia. If I was struggling, I reasoned, it must be due to my lack of competence. Of course, I also blamed the program faculty for not supporting me. However, I reasoned that *if I were really good enough*, I wouldn't need their support. In the midst of this experience, I could not see what external forces in my situation were doing to me even though my academic training had prepared me to do so.

This lack of awareness is particularly ironic because the hallmark credo of my field of study is that behavior is a function of the *person and the environment,* that, when it comes to explaining behavior and attitudes, *the situation matters.* Still, the effects of stereotype threat, stigmatization, tokenism, and racism are so insidious that I couldn't see them relative to myself at that time. That I undermined my sense of competence is particularly indicative of the power of the situation because by then I had begun studying the psychological effects of tokenism. Though I was well versed in the scientific literature in the area I was nevertheless too immersed in the situation to apply the knowledge to myself.

EVIDENCE OF TOKENISM AND RACISM — UNDERMINING BY WORKLOAD

My teaching and advising load was unprecedented for recently hired junior members of the department. In the four years I was a member of that department, I taught four different graduate seminars and three different undergraduate courses. From my discussions with colleagues I learned that most new professors in the department taught only one or two graduate seminars in their area of specialty, which they continued teaching for the first few years before they added others. Included in my teaching load were both core graduate courses in the field. My experience was consistent with documented disparities in the teaching load assigned to women relative to men.[15] These disparities, evidence that one's scholarship is not valued, are exacerbated for women of color.

I was also the principal advisor for eight graduate students as well as chair of their thesis and/or dissertation committees. Two of the students assigned to me had been considered "problem students" previous to my becoming faculty. Two of the other program faculty, both full professors, had only two graduate students each, and one of those students later transferred to me. I also supervised and advised approximately fifteen undergraduate students as members of my research team.

This workload may be contrasted with that of the faculty member I replaced. She was white, a graduate of an elite university who was hired after an extensive national search, and the department had high expectations of her. Although she taught two critical graduate courses, she had been sheltered from extensive advising responsibilities. After three years in the department, she was formally advising only one student, an advising load consistent with department standards for junior professors. The difference in the department's perception of us was evident by the disparities in our workloads.

I was assigned complex and time-consuming administrative tasks necessary for the program. What this workload meant was that there was little time for research. I was working every day and late hours at home every night to try to complete manuscripts, prepare classes, grade papers, and do program administrative work. I wanted so very badly to succeed. The more overwhelmed I became with nonresearch responsibilities, the more incompetent I felt.

The assigned teaching and administrative load was made significantly heavier by *unassigned* responsibilities and obligations. As a woman of color, I felt duty-bound to respond to students who felt marginalized in the institution, especially ethnic/racial minorities. These students often sought me out to advise their student organizations and to listen to their experiences of racism, sexism, or homophobia in the university. Sometimes they asked me to help them take action on their discriminatory experiences. For instance, I assisted a white, female student who was being sexually harassed by a professor. Several Latina/o students sought guidance as they experienced conflict between their own academic goals and their family's financial needs. Of course, at one level, I did have the choice of turning these students away. Emotionally, however, I felt pulled to respond to them. I believed that if I did not, no one else would be receptive to their issues. Furthermore, I would not have been able to face myself if I had turned away these students, especially knowing about the difficulties for students of color in predominantly white institutions. This work was necessary and important, and even fulfilling, as I knew my response to them, at the very least, validated their needs and concerns. Nevertheless, it was emotionally draining to constantly hear about students' experiences with discrimination, especially as I was experiencing the effects of racism myself.

When I discussed the overwhelming teaching/advising/administrative load with the chair, he explained that the social science faculty were very busy with administrative duties, so I had to carry the load. He said he wanted me to know that the faculty appreciated my service to the department. I knew that between my assigned duties and unassigned obligations as a woman of color my time and energy were being drained. It was a situation I felt powerless to change, and I was feeling increasingly incompetent as a faculty member.

Overt Racism and Isolation

I endured overtly racist comments from a few department faculty. For instance, one senior faculty member stopped me in the hall one day and asked, regarding a graduate student fellowship being offered by the ethnic studies program, "If one of our students accepts that fellowship, will they have to do Mexican shit or can they do real research?" I replied that research on Mexican Americans was real research – period! Then I simply turned and walked away. These types of incidents happened to me regularly. I wished I had had the courage to say more. What had become of the feisty and confident person I had been only recently? I would often sit in my office and think about things I could have, and wished I had, said in response to racist statements. Of course, I knew this was not productive use of time. The more I ruminated about racist comments, the more incompetent I felt.

Another example of departmental racism occurred when I was serving on a thesis committee for a student working on depression. During his defense, I pointed out that he had not conducted any analyses by gender or race/ethnicity. Although it was typically considered disrespectful to contradict other faculty during student defenses, one of the other committee members replied, "*Why in the world would gender or race make any difference? A brain is a brain!*" This devaluing of the central role of ethnicity in the human psyche, a role now recognized by the American Psychological Association, appeared to me to be another example of aversive racism in the department, a racism disguised as "color blindness."

In my third year, I applied for and received a one-semester fellowship from the university ethnic studies program. As protocol required, I asked the department chair's permission to go on one-semester leave. He replied that I was "valuable" to the department, and he would approve the leave as long as I continued to advise my many students during the semester. He also said that, unlike other fellowships, this one would not be considered prestigious for me because it would be assumed I attained it only by being Mexican American and not due to my accomplishments. What an ironic twist. I believed he had hired me, in part, because I was Mexican American. Now he seemed to be telling me that an otherwise prestigious fellowship could mean nothing for my evaluation because it was intended for Mexican Americans. Nevertheless, I took the leave and continued to meet with my graduate and undergraduate students throughout that semester. I did not know that it was not necessary, nor was it the norm, for faculty to continue meeting with and advising students while on leave.

I must point out here that the overt racism I experienced came from a relatively small portion of the department members, a few powerful full professors who created a hostile department climate for minorities. While the more junior faculty did not seem to agree with these attitudes, they were not in positions of power to confront the full professors. It did not seem to me that the fair-minded, nonracist full professors in the department attempted to keep their racist colleagues in check, nor did they create a support system for those affected by the hostile climate. It seemed impossible to me that they could be unaware, as some racist statements were made during faculty meetings. Thus, racists and nonracists contributed directly and/or indirectly to the negative department climate.

Some Companionship and Support

I eventually sought out and found companionship and mentoring among the Mexican American, African American, and Puerto Rican campus faculty. Whatever feelings there may have been among the ethnic studies faculty because I had not accepted the post doc were now replaced with expressed desire for me to succeed. These groups of faculty supported me emotionally and with professional opportunities, such as speaking engagements, collaborative research, small grants, and a fellowship. Within my social science department, one white, male full professor befriended me and seemed to have my interest rather than the department's interest at heart. He listened and offered to pre-review my manuscripts, which I did not give him. I still could not bring myself to trust anyone on the department faculty. Fortunately, I did rely on my close friends from graduate school. Having trusted friends listen and validate my reality helped me maintain a sense of sanity.

Stereotype Threat

In spite of this support, I quickly became resistant to positive feedback as my negative self-perception increased. For instance, over the course of my four years at this institution I became well acquainted with three highly esteemed, internationally known and respected, widely published scholars in my discipline, each of whom worked at different institutions. Each of them gave me positive feedback regarding my research ideas, writing, and potential. I even began publishing with two of them and planned collaborative research with the third. Each of these professors was more highly esteemed in the discipline than any of my faculty colleagues. Even so, when they praised my work I reasoned that they were good, generous men who just felt sorry for me but didn't really believe I was competent. This is another example of the disorienting effects of feedback when one does not know whom to trust. An esteemed woman faculty member in a closely related field from another university also stayed in contact with me and practically pleaded with me to leave my university. She argued that I could not possibly flourish under those conditions. I reasoned that she liked me enough not to care whether or not I was competent. By discounting this feedback from people who were trying to help me, I undermined myself in several ways. Most especially, I slowed my professional development by not trusting their input.

In retrospect, my discounting of the input these esteemed, decent scholars gave me relative to my work and potential was one of the most obvious symptoms that my self-esteem and sense of self-efficacy in the academy had suffered great harm. I no longer recognized the person in the mirror. The energetic, healthy, enthusiastic person I had been up until the time I became a faculty member seemed to have disappeared. I wondered what *I* had done to destroy her. This self-blaming is a mark of the effects of stereotype threat, stigmatization, racism, and tokenism. Yet, at the time, even with my social science professional training, I could not account for what was happening to me.

Third-Year Review – Oops! We Forgot!

The worst of my experiences, but the one that finally sent me on the road to physical and psychological health, centered around my third-year review. My department "forgot" to administer the review, an unprecedented occurrence in the department. That my review was "forgotten" was indicative that my identity as a scholar was never acknowledged by the department. The third-year review was a university requirement designed to facilitate faculty's successful road toward tenure. It was explained to me that this forgetfulness had occurred because of transitions in the department. By the end of my third year the dean who had insisted on my hiring had been fired as dean and transferred (I don't know if there was a connection between my hiring and his dismissal), and the department chair, my former advisor, was named dean. In my *fourth year,* then, my "third-year" review was administered.

From all accounts by other department faculty, my review was conducted like none other in the department. The established general procedure was for the review committee to meet individually with faculty in the reviewee's program and then determine where there was consensus. The committee was also to read the reviewee's published work, third-year review statement, and teaching evaluations, and ascertain the probability of the reviewee's success should he or she continue on their current track. It was generally considered a helpful, though stressful, process, expected to guide the reviewee toward tenure. In my case, however, the committee met with the entire department faculty at one time, including the very powerful, very vocal Dr. Grant, who was known to have made disparaging remarks about me since I had been hired. Immediately after the review committee met with my program faculty, it was my turn to meet with the committee.

The first question they asked me was, "What do you have to say about your poor teaching evaluations?" I was astounded. I knew from the department data that my teaching evaluations were not only outstanding, they were among the highest in the department. I had also been nominated as outstanding teaching fellow for the university. My teaching evaluations had been so high that the previous fall they had been found to be *more than one standard deviation above the department norm* and had thus netted me a raise in salary. I asked if the committee had read my teaching evaluations. The committee chair, the same person who had earlier said "a brain is a brain," pulled out what may have been the only two negative evaluations in the stack (I had taught hundreds of undergraduate students and about forty graduate students). As I made this known to the committee, the committee chair stated that my faculty had indicated that people complained about my teaching. I was later told that Dr. Grant had made a negative statement about my teaching of the only course on ethnicity and race taught by tenure-stream department faculty; my more mainstream courses were not mentioned. In terms of research, although I had a couple of publications in top refereed disciplinary journals, a chapter in press, and several other manuscripts under review (all in "mainstream" peer-reviewed journals), I was told that my faculty colleagues questioned the quantity and quality of my research.

Later that evening, two of the persons present at the meeting told me that most of the talking had been done by one person, Dr. Grant, and I learned most of what he had said. I was told that he said, "She'll never be a superstar. She doesn't fit in this department." Let me point out that in this department, as in most others in public universities, the majority of the faculty were not "superstars." So I was being judged by unique and stringent standards. I was also told that because of political ramifications, with the exception of one retired professor, the other full professors, who were my former advisors, did not speak up to contradict Dr. Grant or defend me.

The day after my meeting with the review committee I placed a call to the chair of the committee and told her that it had seemed to me that the review was extremely negatively biased. She agreed and told me that in her opinion I would never be able to shake the circumstances surrounding my hire and that the department resentment was still deep. She stated that Dr. Grant would never evaluate me fairly and that the committee had no choice but to listen to his opinion as he was now director of the program. She further stated that my case would be better if I agreed to disassociate myself from any ethnic/cultural related research and teaching.

I needed help. Still in shock from the unfair review, that weekend I met with my former advisor, then dean of the college, who was among the faculty the committee had met with. I told him that I had heard about what had transpired in the meeting and that I was not receiving a fair evaluation. I also told him I had been extremely disappointed and hurt to learn that he had not spoken up on my behalf and against Dr. Grant. He replied that he was embarrassed to hear Dr. Grant go on but that when Grant was in the room, it was pointless to try to get a word in. He explained that the committee had made a big mistake by meeting with all the faculty at one time. However, he also stated that the review committee had the final word, and he really had no say in their conclusions. He had no response to my argument that the committee's conclusions had to be biased by what had been said, and *not* said, by my colleagues during the review meeting.

The following week I met with the new department chair and told him what had transpired in the review and of my other negative department experiences, including the hiring process. The new chair seemed genuinely surprised and unaware of my situation and expressed anger over the way the review was handled. He, too, stated that the faculty should have been interviewed separately. For political reasons, faculty often do not contradict each other in meetings of this nature. However, to my knowledge, there was no subsequent attempt to re-interview faculty individually.

In retrospect, the evaluation of my work is consistent with literature that indicates that stigmatization results in negative expectations. Madeline E. Heilman, Caryn J. Block, and Jonathan A. Lucas, for example, state, "Negative expectations of these individuals that would be spawned by a stigma of incompetence could cause distorted perceptions of their behavior and work performance."[16] This situation demonstrates one of the perils of being a Latina faculty member, 80 percent of whom teach courses and conduct research related to their own specific ethnic group.[17] Although 90 percent of Latino scholars consider themselves intellectuals, and 85 percent are committed to the rules and standards for scientific pursuits, most also believe that their research is seen as academically inferior and illegitimate.[18] They cite the taboo of "brown-on-brown" research as one of the top reasons why they are denied tenure.[19]

Also, in retrospect, for my colleagues to have spoken up about my extensive advising and service would have been an admission of how they were using me to take care of program needs while pursuing their own agendas. It would also have meant defending me before faculty who knew they had pushed for my hire, in spite of department resentment. I came to believe that *my faculty colleagues could only have felt redeemed in the eyes of the department if I had achieved superstar status in only three years.*

MY DECISION TO LEAVE AND RETURN TO IDENTITY INTEGRATION

I was devastated by the events of the "third-year review." Throughout my tenure there, I had increasingly lost self-confidence, as my research was constantly referred to as "ethnic stuff" and not "real" science. Again, the publication of my work in prestigious journals indicated that several reviewers and editors did consider my work good. However, I did not think about that positive feedback. I had begun to have difficulty focusing on my writing, something that had previously come easily to me. Once again, my lack of confidence had become such a problem that, in a couple of cases in which editors recommended that I revise and resubmit a manuscript, I convinced myself that the quality of my work was not good enough to revise. All of this was symptomatic of the effects of tokenism, stigmatization, racism, and stereotype threat. It was also an example of how attributed ambiguity made me question whether I ever deserved to be hired or published.[20] Thus, my state of mind resulted from the negative attitudes and beliefs I had internalized as well as the behavior and attitudes of others.

After the review I came to the belief that the department had used me with no intention of keeping me on as a tenured faculty member. I conferred with friends and scholars from other universities who had become aware of and come to be concerned about my life in that department. They all agreed that, because of how it had been handled, the review could not be considered valid. However, there was also consensus that the "third-year" review was evidence of my department's perception of me – that in that department I would always be perceived, not as a scholar, but as the token minority the department had to hire. I came to understand that in this department I would likely continue to be overwhelmed with advising responsibilities and trivial, nonprestigious administrative duties, leaving little time for my own research. I came to the difficult and painful conclusion that I had to leave to regain my holistic identity. That week I sent out job applications.

Transition from Mexican American to Chicana

The Mexican American faculty reacted negatively to my intention to leave the university. They wanted me to stay and legally fight what seemed an inevitable negative tenure decision in a couple of years. Their contention was that if I left, the department would win. The department would have used me to appease temporarily those who had demanded racial/ethnic representation, and then discarded me. The department would claim that they had hired a Mexican American, and it had been *her choice* to leave. Better to stay, some Mexican American faculty argued, and make the department own up to its members' behavior toward me, especially since I had documented their treatment of me in my journal. The ethnic studies program was even supportive to the extent of offering me another fully funded, one-year fellowship. The director of that program argued that with the year of fellowship I could get more publications in press, and he would fight to keep that year off the tenure clock thus buying me one additional year of time before my final tenure review.

His argument strongly appealed to my political identity. After the "third-year" review, I had made the transition in identity from Mexican American to Chicana, the self-identifier used by politically conscious Mexican Americans. My university experiences had changed me from a naive, politically insulated and unaware Mexican American to a person whose consciousness about racism and its effects were raised to heights I had not previously imagined.

I met with the university provost, who had already heard about my situation from campus Mexican American faculty. She seemed embarrassed about and apologized for the delay in my "third-year review." She offered to extend my tenure clock by one year to make up for that "mistake." However, she did not agree to stop the tenure clock for the one-year fellowship from ethnic studies. Additionally, when I told her about Dr. Grant's role in my experience, she avoided the subject by discussing how important grants were to the university.

More than ever, I was now convinced that if I stayed my shattered sense of competence and identity might not recover. I believed that it was in my best personal and professional interest – and, by extension, my family's interest – for me to leave. At the time, I needed badly to win for myself; then later, through my future success, I could make contributions to my ethnic community. I no longer wanted to just survive; *I wanted to thrive* – a sign that I was recovering.

That spring I made the short list for positions at two university social science departments and one ethnic studies department. I accepted the latter. My writing is once again focused and consistent. I have published about a dozen articles, most all of them in mainstream refereed journals, and have obtained roughly $75,000 in grants in the two years since I left the first institution. I feel respected and valued. I am productive and once again ambitious and motivated. I've lost most of the weight I gained in those first four years. My identity feels integrated. I once again recognize and like the person I see in the mirror. I feel personal peace.

RECOMMENDATIONS

Several recommendations for faculty of color and for institutions hiring them are already evident in this article. In addition, I offer the following:

Faculty of color must be aware of the consequences of putting themselves in a situation whereby they are vulnerable to effects of tokenism, racism, stigmatization, and stereotype threat – all related concepts. These effects can be psychologically, physically, and professionally damaging. If you do want to continue working where you were trained, I recommend insisting on two things. First, temporarily leave your training institution for at least a one-year post doc in order to gain distance from your advisors. Leaving for a period of time also lets your faculty know that your work is valued elsewhere. Second, to help keep from having your sense of competence undermined, insist on an extensive, national search. When you come out on top, your own sense of competence will be heightened, as will your colleagues' perception of you. Contentment as an academician does not depend upon your working in an ethnic studies department. It depends on working in an accepting and validating climate.

I recommend accepting a position in a department in which you are not the only minority and not the only faculty conducting research and/or teaching on ethnic/racial issues. My own research on tokenism indicates that solo minorities are less satisfied with their jobs than those who have minority colleagues.[21] People who feel like tokens tend to believe they are always representative of their ethnic groups, constantly in the spotlight and living in a "glass house," and they often have reason to believe that their white colleagues are threatened by their accomplishments.[22]

It is also important to look for signs of overt, covert, and unconscious racism among potential colleagues; racists cannot evaluate ethnic/racial minorities fairly. For instance, do comments indicate an assumption that minorities are not as qualified as whites? Does the department undervalue publications in ethnic studies journals? Is the department under pressure to hire a minority? Does the department "showcase" its only minority? These are signs you may become a department token, with detrimental psychological consequences. Inquire as to the reactions of faculty when a colleague makes a racist or sexist statement. Do others just stand by and say and do nothing, or do they take action. Remember that those who just stand by help maintain a negative climate.

For institutions, one interpretation of this article could be that affirmative action policies are inherently detrimental. I do not believe that is the case. Research indicates that when affirmative action policies are framed in a positive manner (e.g., increasing our diversity will contribute different, valued perspectives to the discipline), the potentially stigmatizing effects of the policies may be avoided.[23] Additionally, because departments often do contain racist members, "good intentions are not sufficient to guarantee that equal opportunity will insure equal treatment,"[24] thus rendering affirmative action policies necessary at this time. Departments must therefore be encouraged by the administration to frame affirmative action hiring in a positive, nondetrimental fashion.

It is important for nonracist members of departments, especially the more senior, powerful members, to be aware of the pitfalls faced by faculty of color and to insure support and mentorship for these faculty. It is not enough to rationalize that if one is not being personally racist or unfair that the behavior of others is not one's business. It is incumbent on the powerful members of departments to use their power to develop a positive working climate for faculty of color and, by extension, for all faculty.

It is also important to recognize the detrimental effects of covert racism, such as tokenism, which often occurs concurrently with denial of the importance of race/ethnicity (for example, "color blindness"). To deny the role of race/ethnicity of members of societally oppressed groups is to deny their realities. This denial may be especially harmful for Latinas/os and African Americans, who are particularly stigmatized in the realm of academia.

It is critical for administrators and colleagues to understand that faculty of color have responsibilities and obligations to respond to students who seek them out precisely because they are faculty of color. This situation is exacerbated for women of color, who are also sought out by white women in predominantly male departments. Due to gender role expectations, women often do not feel the freedom to maintain distance from students. Latinas, in particular, often feel that to be successful they may have to behave in a manner contradictory to their cultural values for women. As Ana M. Martinez Alemán states about Latinas, "To be womanly is to be unprofessorial. . . . Women professors must conform to, and accommodate, cultural values outside of her gender role."[25]

Keeping in mind these added obligations, easing the assigned load for these faculty is not a sign of favoritism or lowered expectations. It is a sign of recognition of their additional responsibilities, especially to communities of color. It is also critical, at times of evaluation, to value how these interactions serve to enhance the reputation of the department. Additionally, administrators and faculty must understand that *department and institutional climate can affect individual performance.*

Finally, it is absolutely critical for faculty of color to understand their own role in undermining their competence. This self-undermining often happens as a result of others' racism or at least interacts with the behavior and attitudes of others. However, awareness of one's own attitudes and behaviors in these situations can be empowering in diffusing self-undermining behavior.

In my view, no one was blameless for the negative department climate and my resulting harsh experience, including myself. Five interactive forces contributed to the sustenance and maintenance of racism, stigmatization, tokenization, and stereotype threat: (1) the negative framing of hiring associated with affirmative action policy that set the stage for tokenization and stigmatization; (2) the overtly biased persons who produced direct, adverse effects; (3) those persons who didn't recognize their negative biases and whose manner of encouragement was in itself indicative of racism and was thus undermining; (4) those persons who were not biased, but stood by and let racist behavior occur without attempts to intervene; (5) my own undermining of my competence. My credentials as a scholar cognizant of these effects did not prevent my susceptibility to the effects of stereotype threat. Being vigilant of these effects on the self in these situations and adhering to one's sense of competence are necessary to overcome these potentially psychologically damaging situations.

In conclusion, people of color who pursue an academic career and conduct ethical research contribute admirably to their ethnic communities and universities in many ways. They are role models and mentors for other students, faculty, and community members. Through their research they can facilitate understanding of and improvements in their communities and more trust in academic institutions, which are often perceived as "ivory towers" with no relation or applicability to surrounding communities. The case study in this article is not intended to scare Latinas or other people of color away from academia. Quite the contrary, if we are aware of the processes that might undermine our competence and physical and psychological health, we can co-opt those oppressive processes in our own interest and in the interest of our communities. As Paulo Freire states regarding the oppressed, "Their perception of themselves as oppressed is impaired by their submersion in the reality of oppression."[26] With awareness comes power. I hope this case study description and analysis has been helpful in that regard. Equally, I hope that this narrative facilitates better mentorship of and appreciation for the needs and realities of faculty of color from their faculty colleagues and administrators.

NOTES

I wish to thank the persons who provided guidance and comments on previous drafts of this paper, especially John Dovidio, Pamela Cole, Kelly Ervin, and Tatcho Mindiola.

1. Hisauro Garza, "Academic Power, Discourse, and Legitimacy: Minority Scholars in U.S. Universities," in *Community Empowerment and Chicano Scholarship: Selected Proceedings,* ed. Mary Romero and Cordelia Candelaria (Los Angeles: National Association for Chicano Studies, 1992).

2. Ana M. Martinez Alemán, "Actuando," in *The Leaning Ivory Tower: Latino Professors in American Universities,* ed. Raymond V. Padilla and Rudolfo C. Chávez (Albany: State University of New York Press, 1995); Patricia C. Gándara, *Over the Ivy Walls: The Educational Mobility of Low-Income Chicanos* (Albany: State University of New York Press, 1995); and Yolanda Flores Niemann, Andrea Romero, and Consuelo Arbona, "The Effect of Cultural Orientation on the Double Bind for Chicanas and Chicanos" (unpublished manuscript, 1998).

3. Claude M. Steele, "A Threat in the Air: How Stereotypes Shape Intellectual Identity and Performance," *The American Psychologist* 52:6 (1997): 613–29.

4. Yolanda Flores Niemann et al., "Use of Free Response and Cluster Analysis to Determine Stereotypes of Eight Groups," *Personality and Social Psychology Bulletin* 20:4 (1994): 379–90.

5. Madeline E. Heilman, Caryn J. Block, and Jonathan A. Lucas, "Presumed Incompetent? Stigmatization and Affirmation Action Efforts," *Journal of Applied Psychology* 77:4 (1992): 536–44.

6. John F. Dovidio and Samuel L. Gaertner, "Affirmative Action, Unintentional Racial Biases, and Intergroup Relations," *Journal of Social Issues* 52:4 (1996): 51–76.

7. Heilman, Block, and Lucas, "Presumed Incompetent?"; and Dovidio and Gaertner, "Affirmative Action."

8. Anthony R. Pratkanis and Marlene E. Turner, "The Proactive Removal of Discriminatory Barriers: Affirmative Action as Effective Help," *Journal of Social Issues* 52:4 (1996): 111–32.

9. Rosabeth M. Kanter, *Men and Women of the Corporation* (New York: Basic Books, 1988); Yolanda Flores Niemann and John F. Dovidio, "Relationship of Solo Status, Academic Rank, and Perceived Distinctiveness to Job Satisfaction of Racial/Ethnic Minorities," *Journal of Applied Psychology* 83:1 (1998): 55–71; Kathryn Pollak and Yolanda Flores Niemann, "Black and White Tokens in Academia: A Difference of Chronic versus Acute Distinctiveness," *Journal of Applied Social Psychology* 28:11 (1998): 954–72.

10. Jennifer Crocker et al., "Social Stigma: The Affective Consequences of Attributional Ambiguity," *Journal of Personality and Social Psychology* 60:2 (1991): 218–28.

11. Maria de la Luz Reyes and John J. Halcón, "Racism in Academia: The Old Wolf Revisited," in *Latinos and Education: A Critical Reader*, ed. Antonia Darder, Roldolfo D. Torres, and Henry Gutíerrez (New York: Routledge, 1997), 429.

12. William G. Tierney and Robert A. Rhoades, *Enhancing Promotion, Tenure, and Beyond: Faculty Socialization as a Cultural Process*, ERIC Clearinghouse on Higher Education Report No. 6 (Washington, D.C.: School of Education and Human Development, George Washington University, 1993), 69.

13. Garza, "Academic Power, Discourse, and Legitimacy."

14. Dovidio and Gaertner, "Affirmative Action."

15. Linda K. Johnsrud, "Women and Minority Faculty Experiences: Defining and Responding to Diverse Realities," in *Building a Diverse Faculty*, ed. Joanne Gainen and Robert Boice (San Francisco: Jossey-Bass, 1993): 3–16.

16. Heilman, Block, and Lucas, "Presumed Incompetent?" 544.

17. Garza, "Academic Power, Discourse, and Legitimacy."

18. Garza, "Academic Power, Discourse, and Legitimacy."

19. Hisauro Garza, "Second-class Academics: Chicano/Latino Faculty in U.S. Universities," in Gainen and Boice, *Building a Diverse Faculty,* 33–42; Johnsrud, "Women and Minority Faculty Experiences"; and Reyes and Halcón, "Racism in Academia."

20. Brenda Major, Jeffrey Feinstein, and Jennifer Crocker, "Attributional Ambiguity of Affirmative Action," *Basic and Applied Social Psychology* 15:1/2 (1994): 113–41.

21. Niemann and Dovidio, "Relationship of Solo Status."

22. Kanter, *Men and Women of the Corporation.*

23. Dovidio and Gaertner, "Affirmative Action."

24. Dovidio and Gaertner, "Affirmative Action."

25. Alemán, "Actuando," 74.

26. Paulo Freire, *Pedagogy of the Oppressed,* trans. Myra Bergman Ramos (New York: Herder and Herder, 1970), 26.

Frontiers 20:1 (1999): 111–34.

Contributors

CORDELIA CANDELARIA has been a professor of American literature and Mexican American cultural studies in the English Department at Arizona State University since 1991. She began her tenure as chair of the Department of Chicana and Chicano Studies in 2001. She was named 2001 NACCS Scholar by the National Association for Chicana and Chicano Studies. Candelaria's recent books include *Seeking the Perfect Game: Baseball in American Literature, Chicano Poetry: A Critical Introduction: Arroyos to the Heart,* and *Ojo de la Cueva/Cave Springs.*

MARGARITA COTA-CÁRDENAS was born in 1941 in the rural town of Heber, California, just eight miles north of the Mexico-U.S. border. Margarita graduated from college in Turlock, California, and earned a master's degree from the University of California–Davis in 1968. After returning to teach two years at her alma mater in Turlock, she came to the University of Arizona to pursue her doctoral degree, which she received in 1980. She raised three children during these years. At Arizona State University since 1981, she has taught bilingual Spanish, Chicano/Chicana literature, and Mexican literature courses.

ANTONIA I. CASTAÑEDA was born in Texas and raised at the Golding Hop Farm, Toppenish, Washington. She teaches at St. Mary's University in San Antonio. El ensayo se dedica a las mujeres que trabajaron en los files del valle de Yakima. Ellas me lo elaboraron con su sudor, sus lagrimas, y su risa.

SARAH DEUTSCH is professor of history at the University of Arizona. She is the author of two books and several articles. She is currently working on a history of the American West from 1898 to 1942.

ROBERTA FERNANDEZ earned a Ph.D. in Romance languages and literatures from the University of California–Berkeley. She taught in the Department of Modern and Classical Languages at the University of Houston and served as an editor at Arte Público Press. Fernandez's work includes a critical study of contemporary fiction by Latina writers of the United States; an edited anthology, *In Other Words: Literature by Latino/as of the United States*; and *Intaglio: A Novel in Six Stories*, which was selected as Best Fiction in 1991 by the Multicultural Publishers Exchange.

YOLANDA BROYLES-GONZÁLEZ is professor of Chicano studies and German studies at the University of California–Santa Barbara. She studied at four German universities and was among the first women of color to receive a doctorate degree from Stanford University. She is a native of the Arizona/Sonora desert and is rooted in the Yaqui-Mexican culture. The main focuses of her research and teaching in Chicano studies are popular culture, gender, oral tradition, and the popular performance genres of the U.S.-Mexico borderlands, of which she is a native. Among her most recent publications is the first study of the legendary singer and National Medal of Arts recipient Lydia Mendoza, entitled *Lydia Mendoza's Life in Music/La Historia de Lydia Mendoza: Norteño Tejano Legacies*. Broyles-González is married to Mexican harp player Francisco González, and they have two children, Esmeralda Guadalupe Broyles-González and Francisco Broyles-González.

ANNLOUISE KEATING is an associate professor of women's studies at Texas Woman's University. Keating is author of *Women Reading Women Writing: Self-Invention in Paula Gunn Allen, Gloria Anzaldúa, and Audre Lorde*; editor of Gloria E. Anzaldúa's *Interviews/Entrevistas*; and coeditor (with Anzaldúa) of *This Bridge We Call Home: Radical Visions for Transformation*. She is working on two other projects: a multigenre anthology, *Entremundos: Creative and Critical Perspectives on Gloria E. Anzaldúa*; and a collection of essays drawing on her personal experiences as a bisexual, light-skinned, mixed-"race" queer that explore pedagogy, transformation, "whiteness," and "race."

JOSEPHINE MENDEZ-NEGRETE received her Ph.D. in sociology at the University of California–Santa Cruz. Having worked at both private and public universities in Texas and California, she is currently an assistant professor of Mexican American studies at the Division of Bicultural-Bilingual Studies, University of Texas–San Antonio. Her areas of research and interest are Chicana/Latino activism and leadership, Chicana/o studies, sociology of the family, and feminist research. Mendez-Negrete is finishing a book titled *Las hijas de Juan: Daughters of Betrayal.*

YOLANDA FLORES NIEMANN is an associate professor of comparative American cultures and director of Latina/o Outreach for Washington State University, an affiliate faculty member of women's studies, and a graduate faculty member in American studies. Niemann also serves on the governor's Commission on Hispanic Affairs. Niemann's training is in general psychology with an emphasis on social psychology and management. Her research interests include effects of stereotypes across various domains, including identity and risky behavior, the psychological effects of tokenism, overcoming obstacles to Latina/o higher education, identity issues from Mexican to Mexican American, and the use of stereotypes as justification for discrimination. Her book *Black/Brown Relations and Stereotypes* is forthcoming from the University of Texas Press in 2002. Niemann also has over twenty publications in refereed journals and edited books, including *Journal of Applied Psychology, Personality and Social Psychology Bulletin, Sociological Perspectives, Hispanic Journal of Behavioral Sciences, Journal for the Theory of Social Behavior, The Western Journal of Black Studies,* and *Frontiers: A Journal of Women Studies.*

MARY PARDO teaches in the Department of Chicana/o Studies at California State University–Northridge. Her teaching areas include courses focused on gender, Third World women and the Chicana, contemporary issues of the Chicana, written communication skills, and qualitative research methods. She is the author of articles and a book on Mexican American women and grassroots activism in East Los Angeles. Her book, *Mexican American Women Activists: Identity and Resistance in Two Los Angeles Communities,* received the American Sociological Association Latino Section Award for Outstanding Scholarly Contribution and an honorable mention from the Gustavus Myers Program for the Study of Bigotry and Human Rights in North America. She continues to study women and political activism. She is an executive board member of For Chicana/o Studies, a nonprofit advocacy group providing support for cases of employment discrimination in institutions of higher learning. She is also an executive board member for the Institute for Leadership Development and Education, a new nonprofit organization focused on providing services and leadership training for families in Los Angeles.

MARGARET ROSE earned her Ph.D. at the University of California–Los Angeles, with her dissertation, "Women in the United Farm Workers: A Study of Chicana and Mexicana Participation in a Labor Union." She has been a Rockefeller Foundation Resident at the Walter P. Reuther Library, Archives of Labor and Urban Affairs, Wayne State University.

MARIBEL SOSA was born in Tucson, Arizona, and has been a James A. Michener Fellow at the Texas Center for Writers, University of Texas–Austin. Her work appears in *Saguaro Review* and the *Blue Mesa Review*.

ANGELA VALENZUELA is an associate professor in the Department of Curriculum and Instruction and the Center for Mexican American Studies at the University of Texas–Austin. She is also the author of *Subtractive Schooling: U.S. Mexican Youth and the Politics of Caring*, winner in 2000 of both the American Educational Research Association Outstanding Book Award and the 2001 American Educational Studies Association AESA Critics' Choice Award.

PATRICIA ZAVELLA is a professor of anthropology, specializing in Latin American and Latino studies, and director of the Chicano/Latino Research Center at the University of California–Santa Cruz. Her research interests include feminist theory, the relationship between women's wage labor and family life, sexuality, poverty, and transnational migration of Mexicana/o workers to the United States and U.S. capital to Mexico. Her most recent publication is *Telling to Live: Latina Feminist Testimonios*, coauthored with members of the Latina Feminist Group.

MAXINE BACA ZINN earned her Ph.D. in sociology at the University of Oregon and teaches sociology at Michigan State University. Zinn specializes in race relations, gender, and the sociology of the family with a special emphasis on work and gender in racial ethnic families. Her research includes projects in racial identity and gender inequality, women of color in the social sciences, and home-school linkages in Mexican-origin communities. She is especially interested in how gendered coping strategies in racial ethnic families mediate the impact of broad structural factors and contribute to family diversity.

Index